DAUGHTERS
of the
WINTER
QUEEN

By Nancy Goldstone

The Rival Queens: Catherine de' Medici, Her Daughter Marguerite de Valois, and the Betrayal That Ignited a Kingdom

The Lady Queen: The Notorious Reign of Joanna I, Queen of Naples, Jerusalem, and Sicily

The Maid and the Queen: The Secret History of Joan of Arc

Four Queens: The Provençal Sisters Who Ruled Europe

Trading Up: Surviving Success as a Woman Trader on Wall Street

By Nancy Goldstone and Lawrence Goldstone

The Friar and the Cipher: Roger Bacon and the Unsolved Mystery of the Most Unusual Manuscript in the World

Out of the Flames: The Remarkable Story of a Fearless Scholar, a Fatal Heresy, and One of the Rarest Books in the World

Warmly Inscribed: The New England Forger and Other Book Tales

Slightly Chipped: Footnotes in Booklore

Used and Rare: Travels in the Book World

Deconstructing Penguins: Parents, Kids, and the Bond of Reading

DAUGHTERS

of the

WINTER QUEEN

Four Remarkable Sisters, the Crown
of Bohemia, and the Enduring
Legacy of Mary, Queen of Scots

NANCY GOLDSTONE

Little, Brown and Company
New York • Boston • London

Little, Brown and Company
Hachette Book Group
1290 Avenue of the Americas, New York, NY 10104
littlebrown.com

First Edition: April 2018

Little, Brown and Company is a division of Hachette Book Group, Inc. The Little, Brown name and logo are trademarks of Hachette Book Group, Inc.

The publisher is not responsible for websites (or their content) that are not owned by the publisher.

The Hachette Speakers Bureau provides a wide range of authors for speaking events. To find out more, go to hachettespeakersbureau.com or call (866) 376-6591.

Map by Jeffrey L. Ward

ISBN 978-0-316-38791-0
LCCN 2017942373

10 9 8 7 6 5 4 3 2 1

LSC-C

Printed in the United States of America

To Lee and Larry, with all my love

Contents

Contents

PART III
The Legacy of Mary, Queen of Scots

Nor shall less joy your regal hopes pursue
In that most princely maid, whose form might call
The world to war, and make it hazard all
Its valor for her beauty; she shall be
Mother of nations, and her princes see
Rivals almost to these.

—A prescient description of fourteen-year-old
Elizabeth Stuart, the future Winter Queen,
in a poem by Ben Jonson, June 1610

She has bin long admir'd by all the Learned World
as a Woman of incomparable Knowledge in Divinity,
Philosophy, History, and the Subjects of all sorts of
Books, of which she has read a prodigious quantity.
She speaks five Languages so well, that by her Accent
it might be a Dispute which of 'em was her first.

—John Toland, secretary to the English embassy
to Hanover, reporting on the character of
Sophia, youngest daughter of the Winter Queen,
September 1701

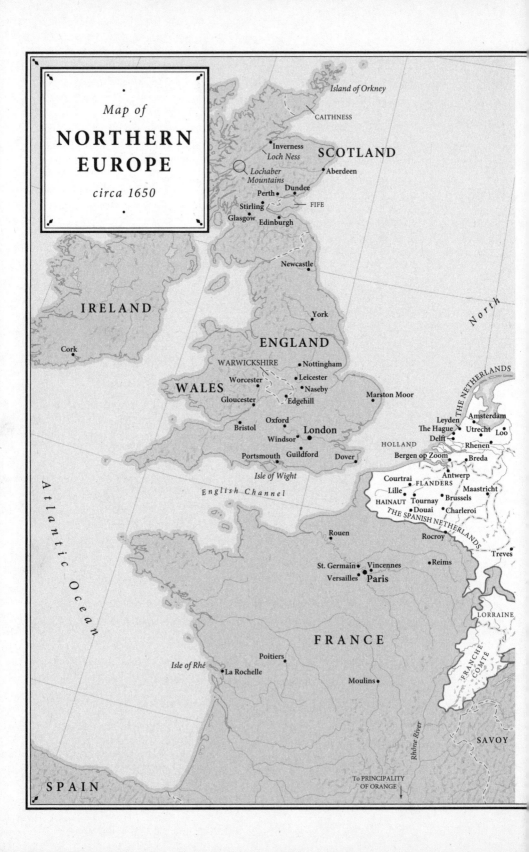

Map of

NORTHERN EUROPE

circa 1650

Island of Orkney

CAITHNESS

Inverness
Loch Ness

SCOTLAND

Aberdeen

*Lochaber
Mountains*

Dundee

Perth

Stirling

FIFE

Glasgow

Edinburgh

Newcastle

IRELAND

North

York

Cork

ENGLAND

WARWICKSHIRE

Nottingham

Worcester

Leicester

WALES

Naseby

Gloucester

Edgehill

Marston Moor

THE NETHERLANDS

Oxford

Leyden

Amsterdam

Bristol

The Hague

Utrecht

Loo

Windsor

London

Delft

Rhenen

HOLLAND

Portsmouth

Guildford

Dover

Bergen op Zoom

Breda

Antwerp

Isle of Wight

Courtrai

FLANDERS

English Channel

Lille

Maastricht

HAINAUT

Tournay

Brussels

Douai

Charleroi

THE SPANISH NETHERLANDS

Rouen

Rocroy

Treves

Atlantic Ocean

St. Germain

Vincennes

Reims

Versailles

Paris

LORRAINE

FRANCE

FRANCHE-COMTÉ

Poitiers

Isle of Rhé

La Rochelle

Moulins

Rhône River

SAVOY

SPAIN

To PRINCIPALITY
OF ORANGE

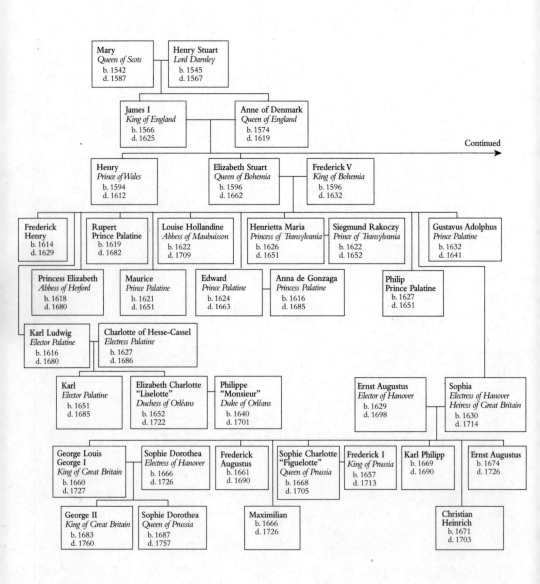

Mary
Queen of Scots
b. 1542
d. 1587

Henry Stuart
Lord Darnley
b. 1545
d. 1567

James I
King of England
b. 1566
d. 1625

Anne of Denmark
Queen of England
b. 1574
d. 1619

Continued →

Henry
Prince of Wales
b. 1594
d. 1612

Elizabeth Stuart
Queen of Bohemia
b. 1596
d. 1662

Frederick V
King of Bohemia
b. 1596
d. 1632

Frederick Henry
b. 1614
d. 1629

Rupert
Prince Palatine
b. 1619
d. 1682

Louise Hollandine
Abbess of Maubuisson
b. 1622
d. 1709

Henrietta Maria
Princess of Transylvania
b. 1626
d. 1651

Siegmund Rakoczy
Prince of Transylvania
b. 1622
d. 1652

Gustavus Adolphus
Prince Palatine
b. 1632
d. 1641

Princess Elizabeth
Abbess of Herford
b. 1618
d. 1680

Maurice
Prince Palatine
b. 1621
d. 1651

Edward
Prince Palatine
b. 1624
d. 1663

Anna de Gonzaga
Princess Palatine
b. 1616
d. 1685

Philip
Prince Palatine
b. 1627
d. 1651

Karl Ludwig
Elector Palatine
b. 1616
d. 1680

Charlotte of Hesse-Cassel
Electress Palatine
b. 1627
d. 1686

Karl
Elector Palatine
b. 1651
d. 1685

Elizabeth Charlotte
"Liselotte"
Duchess of Orléans
b. 1652
d. 1722

Philippe
"Monsieur"
Duke of Orléans
b. 1640
d. 1701

Ernst Augustus
Elector of Hanover
b. 1629
d. 1698

Sophia
Electress of Hanover
Heiress of Great Britain
b. 1630
d. 1714

George Louis
George I
King of Great Britain
b. 1660
d. 1727

Sophie Dorothea
Electress of Hanover
b. 1666
d. 1726

Frederick Augustus
b. 1661
d. 1690

Sophie Charlotte
"Figuelotte"
Queen of Prussia
b. 1668
d. 1705

Frederick I
King of Prussia
b. 1657
d. 1713

Karl Philipp
b. 1669
d. 1690

Ernst Augustus
b. 1674
d. 1726

George II
King of Great Britain
b. 1683
d. 1760

Sophie Dorothea
Queen of Prussia
b. 1687
d. 1757

Maximilian
b. 1666
d. 1726

Christian Heinrich
b. 1671
d. 1703

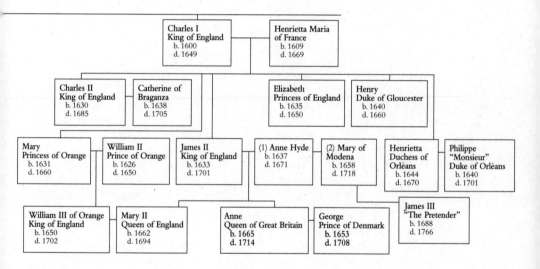

DAUGHTERS
of the
WINTER
QUEEN

Introduction

The castle at Fotheringhay, about sixty miles northwest of London, Wednesday, February 8, 1587

THE DAY HAD DAWNED INCONGRUOUSLY fair, the soft rays of the winter sun gradually diffusing the darkness to illuminate the forbidding aspect of the vast medieval fortress, nearly five centuries old, that dominated the surrounding landscape. But the warming light did nothing to lift the spirits of those sequestered behind the citadel's impregnable walls, for on this morning, Mary Stuart, queen of Scotland, was to be executed.

She had been convicted four months earlier of treason against her cousin the English queen Elizabeth I. At a trial eerily reminiscent of the inquisition of Joan of Arc, against all protocol, Mary had been denied counsel and forced to face her accusers alone. Her crime lay not so much in the details of the charges against her but in the unshakable constancy of her faith. In an effort to intimidate her, her interrogators, all men well versed in the complexities of English law, thundered their impatient questions at her so rowdily that it was impossible for her to answer them all. It was critical that Mary acknowledge her guilt, but her bold responses and repeated protestations of innocence denied her judges the confession they sought. In length alone did the queen's ordeal differ materially from the saint's. It had taken the inquisition months to condemn Joan, a simple peasant girl, to the stake. Mary, once queen of France as well as Scotland, was convicted and sentenced to beheading in just ten days.

The delay between verdict and punishment was attributable to

Elizabeth I's obvious reluctance to sign her cousin's death warrant. It was not simply a matter of weighing the probable consequences of the act on the kingdom's foreign policy. Elizabeth's ambassadors had already sounded out Mary's only child, James, king of Scotland, and confirmed that, provided his mother's execution in no way adversely influenced his own prospects of succeeding to the English throne, James would undertake no reprisals should Elizabeth decide on this final, irrevocable step. And although the Catholic kings of France and Spain protested vociferously through envoys against the brutality of the sentence, Elizabeth's ministers had concluded that their opposition did not extend to the point of armed intervention in Mary's favor. But still, Elizabeth, the Virgin Queen, wavered. It was a grave matter to behead a fellow monarch. It set a sinister precedent. Mary herself recognized this. "Please do not accuse me of presumption if, about to abandon this world and preparing for a better one, I bring up to you that one day you will have to answer for your charge," she wrote keenly to Elizabeth from her cell at Fotheringhay.

But by degrees, the queen of England had allowed herself to be convinced of the necessity for ruthlessness by her Protestant councillors, and on February 1, 1587, she added the authority of the Crown to the judgment against Mary by signing the death warrant. Four days later, on February 5, this document was secretly dispatched to Fotheringhay by courier, and on the evening of February 7, as she prepared for bed, Mary was brusquely informed that she would meet her death the following morning at eight o'clock.

The Queen of Scots' reaction to the news of her imminent execution was tempered not only by the extreme duration of her captivity—she had been confined under house arrest for more than eighteen years—but by her profound belief that her martyrdom at Elizabeth's hands would benefit the Catholic cause in Europe. Consequently, she made no scene, not even when she was refused the services of a priest and the solace of last rites. Rather, she was tranquil and dignified throughout. She spent her last hours composing her will, making bequests, and comforting her servants. She dispensed the few personal items that remained of her once magnificent equipage. She knelt in prayer. All the while, she and her attendants could hear the sound of the wooden platform that would hold the block on which she would lay her head in preparation for decapitation being noisily constructed in the castle's great hall.

She was summoned to her ordeal at a little after eight in the morning. She appeared in full court dress, accompanied by her small household, one of her manservants holding a crucifix aloft before her. Her flowing gown was of black satin and velvet, highlighted by hints of purple, symbol of royalty. Her trademark red-brown curls — a wig now, as the forty-four-year-old queen's real hair was gray — were draped by a floor-length white lace veil, signifying purity. A throng of people, both officials of the royal court and local gentry, crowded the hall, having been invited to witness the spectacle of the queen's beheading. They took their places around the raised dais as Mary, with quiet majesty, mounted the steps to her fate. A heavy stone ax, instrument of her death, "like those with which they cut wood," an eyewitness later reported, was displayed prominently on the stage.

The ceremony of state execution began. A Protestant clergyman who had been engaged to sermonize the queen began a lengthy discourse. Mary countered by praying aloud, first in Latin and then in English, for the protection and advancement of the Catholic Church. The competing religious devotions having concluded, the queen of Scotland was then divested of her veil and outer gown, as was customary. Her underskirt and bodice were of russet burgundy, another deliberate choice, representing the blood of martyrs. In this costume, she was led to the block and there knelt upon the pillows placed in front of it for that purpose. Weeping softly, her oldest and most loyal maidservant gently bound her mistress's eyes in white silk and arranged her hair so as to leave her neck bare. Then Mary laid her head upon the block.

Although horrifyingly gruesome by modern standards, decapitation was actually the elite method of execution in the sixteenth century. Because it was over in one quick stroke, suffering was assumed to be minimal, so only those of very high rank were granted the privilege of dying in this manner. Criminals and commoners, by contrast, were almost always hanged, which took much longer. If the offense committed was of sufficient gravity, a culprit might be subjected to the torture of being drawn and quartered. The most excruciating punishment—burning at the stake—was reserved for cases of witchcraft or heresy, as an effective means of discouraging others who might be tempted to follow the profane teachings of the condemned.

But however humanely intended, any diminution of pain was of course entirely dependent on the dexterity of the person wielding the ax, and Mary was not fortunate in her practitioner. The first stroke missed her neck completely and landed on the back of her head. Despite the presence of the blindfold, those spectators close to the stage could see the queen's expression change and her mouth open and close in shock, reportedly forming the words "Lord Jesus, receive my soul." The executioner was forced to extract his bloody instrument and raised his arms to try again. The second blow fell with more success—he hit her neck—but failed to cleave all the way through. Rather than lift the weapon a third time and admit his ineptitude, her killer simply hacked at the remaining tissue until at last the queen's head tumbled from her body. Her lips were still moving when he raised his ghastly prize high for all to see, and continued to move, as though struggling to speak, for ten minutes more, before finally coming to rest.

"Such be the end of all the Queen's, and all the Gospel's enemies" was the final verdict solemnly intoned by the presiding magistrate, and with that concluded the formal ritual of death. No witness present in the great hall of Fotheringhay that February morning doubted that Elizabeth had utterly vanquished her rival and that the name Mary Stuart would from that day forth pass into infamy.

But history has a way of confounding even the most seemingly infallible expectations. For it would not be the descendants of the renowned queen Elizabeth I who survived to rule England. Rather, through a series of astonishing twists and turns of fate, through danger, adventure, courage, heartbreak, and, ultimately, triumph, it was Mary's legacy that prevailed through the fearless person of her granddaughter Elizabeth Stuart, the Winter Queen, and her four daughters, Princess Elizabeth, Louise Hollandine, Henrietta Maria, and Sophia. It is from the female line of this family that *every* English monarch beginning with George I, including the memorable Victoria and the indomitable Elizabeth II, all the way down to the wildly popular children born to the present-day duke and duchess of Cambridge, Prince William and Kate Middleton, has sprung in an unbroken line.

But theirs is so much more than the legacy of a single realm. Together, these women formed the loom upon which the great tapestry of Europe was woven. The lives of Elizabeth Stuart and her daughters were intricately entwined with all the major events of their day, not only political contests, but also the religious, artistic, and philosophic movements that would dominate the period and set the stage for the Enlightenment to come. It is simply not possible to fully understand the seventeenth century in all of its exuberant, glorious complexity without this family.

This is their story.

PART I

Elizabeth Stuart,
the Winter Queen

Granddaughter of Mary, Queen of Scots

Elizabeth Stuart   Mary, queen of Scots

1

A King's Daughter

That princess rare, that like a rose doth flourish.
—James Maxwell, *The Life and Death of*
Prince Henry, 1612

ELIZABETH STUART WAS BORN ON August 19, 1596, at Dunfermline Palace, her mother's preferred summer residence, in Fife, just across the bay from Edinburgh. Her father was James VI, only offspring and heir of Mary, queen of Scots; her mother was Queen Anne, daughter of the king of Denmark. Elizabeth was her parents' second child. An older brother, christened Frederick Henry but known simply as Henry, had been born two years earlier.

Unlike the wild, spontaneous public celebrations that had greeted her brother's arrival—"moving them to great triumph...for bonfires were set, and dancing and playing seen in all parts, as if the people had been daft for mirth," as one eyewitness noted—the news that Queen Anne, suspected of Catholic leanings, had been successfully delivered of a daughter was received with stony indifference by the unruly Protestant population. The Presbyterian ministers of nearby Edinburgh, the most outspoken and radical element of Scottish society, incensed by James's recent decision to allow two formerly exiled Catholic earls to return to the realm, sent an emissary, not to congratulate the new father but to bait him, insultingly calling James "God's silly vassal," among other choice put-downs, to his face.

There were not too many kingdoms in Europe where a subject could address his sovereign lord in this fashion without risking imprisonment or execution, but fiercely implacable, wayward Scotland was one of them. The Scottish aristocracy was hopelessly, almost comically fractured by geography, ancestry, religion, and politics. Jealous of one another's privileges, constantly engaging in conspiracies and treachery or jostling for advantage, about the only quality the various clans had in common was a tendency to take offense at the slightest provocation, a predilection that more often than not quickly escalated to violent civil unrest. To be king of Scotland at the turn of the seventeenth century was not an especially enviable employment. "Alas, it is a far more barbarous and stiff necked people that I rule over," James observed morosely.

Exacerbating the country's political woes was its extreme poverty. Trained almost from birth in the habits of frugality, James had become adept at sidestepping unnecessary expenses. To reduce costs, Elizabeth's christening was held on November 28, when bitter cold and inclement weather would ensure that attendance at the ceremony was kept to a minimum. Those guests who did accept the royal invitation were instructed to bring their own dinners. Ever on the lookout for ways to squeeze a profit from events, to ingratiate himself with his far more affluent neighbor to the south, James fawningly named his daughter for the venerable queen of England. He further nominated Elizabeth I as godmother to the child, as he had done for his son two years earlier, expecting by this means to receive a handsome present. But although the English queen had acknowledged the birth of James's son with "a cupboard of silver overgilt, cunningly wrought," as well as a set of magnificent golden goblets, this time no similarly expensive gift—in fact, no gift at all—arrived to commemorate his daughter's christening. The notoriously stingy Elizabeth I knew a thing or two about thrift herself.

Even before the ceremony, the infant Elizabeth had been removed from her mother's care and sent to Linlithgow Palace, about fifteen miles west of Edinburgh, to be raised by guardians. Queen Anne, who did not wish to be separated from her daughter, had objected vehemently to this arrangement, as she had two years previously when her firstborn, Henry, had been unceremoniously wrenched from her in similar fashion, but James, citing Scottish custom, had insisted. The king, who had himself been brought up by custodians when political upheaval forced Mary Stuart to abdicate, evidently did not consider a mother to be a necessary or even particularly helpful component in child rearing.*

So Elizabeth spent her early youth in the care of her guardians, Lord and Lady Livingston, who in effect became her surrogate parents. The royal establishment was small—Elizabeth had a wet nurse and a governess, and two of Lady Livingston's female relations were marshaled to help look after the little princess and assist with the household accounts. In 1598, when Elizabeth was a toddler, her mother gave birth to another daughter, Margaret, who was again taken from the queen against her wishes and also sent to live with Lord and Lady Livingston. Elizabeth would hardly have remembered her younger sister, as Margaret lived only two years, making the separation even more heartbreaking for her mother. A second son, Charles, was born on November 19, 1600. Although the baby was so sickly that he was not expected to live—he was baptized that same day—Charles managed to rally and so he, too, was removed from his mother's care.†

Lacking ready cash, James paid for his daughter's upbringing with gifts of land and titles. Little Elizabeth's expenses included satin and velvet from which to make her two best gowns, ribbon to trim her nightdress, and four dolls (charmingly, they were referred to as "babies") "to play her with"—an indication of a comfortable if not

---

* In fact, it was not traditional for daughters to be taken from their mothers. Mary Stuart had lived with her mother, Mary of Guise, until she was engaged to the dauphin and sent to France to learn the customs of the kingdom it was expected she would rule.

† Queen Anne would give birth to another son and two daughters over the course of her marriage but none of these children survived longer than two years.

particularly opulent environment. Far more important, her guardians must have treated their small charge with kindness and affection, as Elizabeth retained fond memories of her childhood at Linlithgow Palace and remained close to her wet nurse and adopted family well into adulthood.

This was Elizabeth Stuart's life—sheltered, quiet, unremarkable—until she was six years old. And then there occurred an event that had a defining effect on her fate. For on March 24, 1603, her godmother, Elizabeth I, storied daughter of Henry VIII by Anne Boleyn, vanquisher of the fearful Spanish Armada, royal patron of William Shakespeare and Sir Francis Drake, the resolutely determined woman who had ruled England for an astonishing forty-five years, died at the age of sixty-nine. And Elizabeth Stuart's father, the cerebral but ultimately timorous king of Scotland, ascended to the English throne as James I.

No one in Elizabeth Stuart's long, full life would have more influence over her than her father. The singularity of his character is absolutely critical to understanding what was to come. And the key to fathoming James's depths lay not within the confines of mutinous Scotland but in the far gentler, glorious realm to the south. For no ambition held greater sway over the king of Scots' soul than to rule moneyed England after Elizabeth I. His entire career was spent chasing the rainbow of this one shining promise.

This aspiration may be traced to the hardships of his early existence. Poor James's troubles had begun while he was still in the womb. When she was six months pregnant with him, his mother had been held at gunpoint while a gang of discontented noblemen led by her husband, Lord Darnley, dragged her favorite courtier, her Italian secretary David Riccio, screaming from her presence and then savagely murdered him. To the end of her days, Mary was convinced that she and her unborn child had been the true targets of the assassins' wrath—that the shock from the attack had been intended to provoke a late-stage miscarriage. "What if Fawdonside's pistol had shot, what would have become of him [her baby] and me both?" she demanded of her husband in the aftermath of the slaying.

Not unreasonably, this episode had a deleterious effect on Mary's affection for her husband. In fact, she couldn't stand him. When James was born three months later, on June 19, 1566, Mary, forced by the assassination of Riccio to negate rumors of the boy's illegitimacy, summoned Darnley to an audience at court. "My Lord, God has given you and me a son, begotten by none but you," she proclaimed, holding the baby aloft for all to see. "I am desirous that all here, with ladies and others bear witness." She knew what she was doing; the infant's resemblance to Darnley was unmistakable. "For he is so much your own son, that I fear it will be the worse for him hereafter," she concluded bitterly.

James's birth did not have a placating effect on his parents' relationship. The expedient of divorce or annulment was raised as a serious possibility, but this turned out to be unnecessary when Darnley was conveniently murdered the following February by a group of his wife's supporters, led by the earl of Bothwell. A mere three months later, in May 1567, Mary scandalously wedded her former husband's killer, a union that obviously did nothing to dampen suspicions of her own involvement in Darnley's death. In the event, it turned out to be an extremely short marriage. By June, Bothwell's enemies, of which there were many, had gathered an armed force together to confront the earl. Mary's second husband managed to elude capture but the Queen of Scots was not so lucky. Mary was arrested and confined to the remote island castle of Lochleven. On July 24, 1567, she was forced to abdicate in favor of her son, James. Ten months later, she slipped away from her prison disguised as a maidservant and fled to the dubious hospitality of her cousin Elizabeth I, who would hold her under house arrest for the next eighteen years before finally executing her outright.

James was crowned king of Scotland on July 29, 1567, just five days after his mother's abdication. He was unable to swear the customary oath of office, being only thirteen months old and not yet capable of forming words, so two of his subjects, the earls of Morton and Home, pledged in his name to defend the kingdom and the Protestant faith. Afterward, to mark this solemn occasion, his government granted its new sovereign four servant girls, to serve as "rockers," and a new wet nurse.

The young king of Scots was raised at Stirling Castle, northeast of Glasgow, by his guardians, the earl of Mar and his wife. Conscious of the heavy responsibility entrusted to them, the pair—particularly the countess—kept a stern eye on their charge. It appears that James spent much of his youth in acute fear of his foster mother; by his own account he trembled at her approach. "My Lady Mar was wise and sharp and held the King in great awe," a Scottish courtier concurred. The royal education, which began when James was four years old, was overseen by George Buchanan, Scotland's most renowned poet and philosopher. Buchanan, a fire-and-brimstone Presbyterian, was already in his sixties, brilliant, crusty, and impatient, when he undertook to tutor the child king. It was rather like having Ebenezer Scrooge as a schoolmaster. Buchanan had him reading Greek before breakfast, followed by a full morning of history heavy on treatises by authors like Livy and Cicero. After lunch, he struggled with composition, mathematics, and geography until dark. "They made me speak Latin before I could speak Scottish," James scrawled mournfully in one of his exercise books when he was old enough to write. Unfortunately, warmth and affection, the customs of polite society, and fun—Presbyterians did not much approve of fun—were not incorporated into James's curriculum.

The result of all of this gloomy, concentrated instruction was that James grew up to be perhaps the best-educated monarch in Europe—and one of the loneliest. When he was only eight years old, "I heard him discourse, walking up and down in [holding] the old Lady Mar's hand, of knowledge and ignorance, to my great marvel and astonishment," a visitor to the court reported. By the time he was eighteen, it was judged by an envoy that "he dislikes dancing and

James as a boy
...and his crusty tutor, George Buchanan

music...His manners are crude and uncivil and display a lack of proper instruction...His voice is loud and his words grave and sententious...His body is feeble and yet he is not delicate. In a word, he is an old young man."

Like others of his faith, his tutor Buchanan had a poor opinion of women in general and of his former queen, the Catholic Mary Stuart, in particular. So from a very early age, along with his Latin, James learned that his mother was a whore and a murderess who had engaged in such "malicious actions...as cannot be believed could come from the wickedest woman in the world," a witness to his educator's methods reported. Buchanan's diatribes in combination with James's own experience of the fearsome Lady Mar may have colored the king of Scots' views of the fairer sex.* He had his first

---

* In later life, he developed a great dread of witches and pursued them obsessively. From this aversion sprang the inspiration for Shakespeare's *Macbeth*.

17

homosexual affair when he was thirteen, with his thirty-year-old cousin Esmé Stuart, Seigneur d'Aubigny, recently arrived from the court of Henri III, king of France (also homosexual), and his intimacy with handsome young men persisted into adulthood, despite his marriage to Anne.

In retrospect, it is easy to see the Seigneur d'Aubigny's appeal. "That year [1579] arrived Monsieur d'Aubigny from France, with instructions and devices from the House of Guise [Mary Stuart's relations], and with many French fashions and toys," reported James Melville, one of the Presbyterian ministers, glumly. The young king of Scotland was fascinated by this engaging French relation who treated him like an adult rather than a sheltered schoolboy and who taught him the sort of colorful swear words beloved by adolescent males throughout the centuries. It was d'Aubigny's task to insinuate himself into James's life and favor and he succeeded admirably with the socially awkward teenager. "At this time his Majesty, having conceived an inward affection to the said lord Aubigny, entered into great familiarity and quiet purposes with him, which being understood to the ministers of Edinburgh, they cried out continually against...saying it would turn his Majesty to ruin," observed one of James's secretaries.

But more troublesome than the profane language and bawdy jokes, the fast horses, the open caresses, the afternoons spent in racing and hunting, and the other delightful activities that stretched long into the night was a more subtle form of seduction that d'Aubigny also brought with him from France: an idea. Specifically, the notion of the divine right of kings, which stated that as the person chosen by God to rule over an earthly kingdom, a monarch had absolute authority over his subjects—*all* of his subjects, including the ministers of the church.

This was not at all what the browbeaten James, until only recently chained to his lesson book by Buchanan, had been taught. The Presbyterians, particularly the outspoken ministers of Edinburgh, very conveniently believed that (having been preordained by God as saved) *they* wielded ultimate authority over temporal affairs, which included telling the king what he could and could not do.

D'Aubigny could not have recruited a candidate more receptive to the autocratic French philosophy than the adolescent king of Scotland. Raging hormones combined with a strong intellect and the euphoria of first love soon gave way to open rebellion as James, accustomed to reasoning through long, obscure passages from Greek and Roman scholars, intuitively grasped that in this doctrine lay the instrument of his emancipation. Nor could his ministers argue their former protégé out of his epiphany. So well educated had James become that he could rebuff every objection and answer every remonstrance—and he could do it in Latin.

By the end of d'Aubigny's first year in Scotland, James had raised him to duke of Lennox and showered him with gifts of land and castles. The next year, d'Aubigny, with James's tacit support, engineered the downfall of the once all-powerful earl of Morton.* Morton, who had run the kingdom for a decade, was subsequently accused of treason and executed, with d'Aubigny promoted in his place. The church elders in Edinburgh, used to a docile sovereign, were stunned to find a French Catholic and partisan of the reviled Mary Stuart suddenly the reigning influence behind James's government. (D'Aubigny, attuned to the politics of his adopted realm, made a point of converting to Protestantism, but this fooled no one.) "At that time it was a pity to see so well brought up a Prince...be so miserably corrupted," lamented Melville.

But as the king very quickly discovered, theories about who had a right to command were often challenged by those with perhaps a smaller claim to legitimacy but the advantage in ferocity, numbers, and weapons. Less than a year after d'Aubigny's ascension to power, in August 1582, James was out on a hunting trip when he was invited to visit Ruthven Castle, a fortress owned by a Protestant

---

* Morton was one of the two high noblemen at James's inaugural who had taken the oath of office in the king's stead when he was too young to form the words himself.

nobleman. Unbeknownst to the king, his host, jealous of d'Aubigny's rise, had banded together with a number of like-minded gentlemen (including the Edinburgh ministers) to overthrow the favorite. Separating James from his French courtier and holding him hostage against their demands represented the first step in this revolt. Informed the next morning when he tried to leave that he was not a guest but a prisoner, sixteen-year-old James burst into tears.

And in this reaction lay the crux of the dilemma facing the young sovereign. As a scholar, James was fearless and would remain so throughout his life.* But as a soldier, he was hopeless. Although frequently obliged to raise troops to defend himself over the course of his reign, James rarely rode with his forces. More often than not, when threatened, he would take the expedient of hiding in a tower or behind a locked door. On those few occasions when he did sally forth with his men, he tended to sally back to safety very quickly. "The king came riding into Edinburgh at the full gallop, with little honor," sneered a contemporary after witnessing his sovereign turn tail and flee pell-mell from his enemies after one such skirmish. It was to be James's curse that he had no taste for battle, and inevitably shied away from violence, because he lived in a kingdom wedded to violence.

His subjects were quick to capitalize on their sovereign's weakness. The proprietor of Ruthven Castle and his cohorts held James against his will for nearly a year, during which time he was forced to accede to all the Presbyterian opposition's demands. Although the king eventually escaped in June 1583 with the help of his French relatives and the Catholic clans, it was too late to save d'Aubigny, who had long since fled the kingdom. Nor, once free, could James recall his favorite. Heartbreakingly for the seventeen-year-old king, his cherished companion died in Paris that same June. "And so the King and the Duke [d'Aubigny] were dissevered, and never saw the other again," reported Melville with satisfaction.

---

* He would later commission and personally oversee the production of the King James Bible, a signal achievement.

Sadly, this pattern of aggression was to be repeated many times during James's reign. Because Scotland was so divided, no matter what stance the king took, he inevitably provoked opposition from one faction or another. The disgruntled party knew that the surest way to seek remedy was not to outmaneuver James politically but simply to seize the king bodily and force him to back down. In November 1585, James was again accosted and held hostage by the Presbyterians (whom he never forgave for the loss of d'Aubigny), this time, humiliatingly, in his own castle in Stirling. As late as 1600, when he was in his midthirties and had been married for over a decade, the king, out on a hunt, was lured to a house in Perth by an attractive young man who subsequently threatened his sovereign with a dagger. James only escaped by bawling, "I am murdered. Treason!...help, help!" out the window.

Small wonder, then, that from a very early age, James looked longingly to England, where Elizabeth I, ferociously protected by her inner circle and having earned the respect and love of the majority of her people, ruled for decade after decade in comparative peace and wealth. The queen had enemies, it was true, but for the most part, they came from abroad, the Spanish Armada being the prime example. Nobody tried to take *her* captive while she was out hunting.

James eventually settled on a two-pronged approach in his effort to succeed Elizabeth. First, he actively cultivated her friendship with a view to maintaining amicable relations with England no matter what the provocation. This expedient was somewhat put to the test in the aftermath of his mother's beheading, but the king of Scotland, ever the intellectual, found a way to rationalize his passivity: "If war should ensue, the old quarrels and animosity would be revived to that degree that the English would never accept him [James] for their Prince," the Scottish ambassador to England explained. "But she [Mary] being now executed for such good and necessary causes, it will be more for his honor to see how he can moderate his passion by reason."

Second, and just as important, it was necessary for James to survive his dangerously cantankerous Scottish subjects long enough to inherit Elizabeth's placidly wealthy ones. This feat he achieved primarily by eschewing extremism in any form and by mastering the useful art of dissembling. The king "made many fair promises unto them, and never keeped a word," the Edinburgh ministers complained bitterly at one public audience.

As the years rolled by and James reached adulthood, married, and had children of his own, he must often have wondered whether the queen of England was *ever* going to die. But mortality darkens the bedchamber of even a sovereign as indomitable as Elizabeth I and at long last, in 1603, when he was thirty-seven years old, James succeeded to the prize he had worked so hard to achieve. By the time he left Scotland for England to claim his throne, he had become a man who habitually said "Yes" but almost always meant "No." This was a technicality that his daughter, who was too young to have known her father during his perilous past, perhaps never fully appreciated.

THE ALACRITY WITH WHICH James possessed himself of his new kingdom—he dashed off to England on April 3, a mere ten days after Elizabeth I's death, with instructions for the rest of the family to follow at the earliest opportunity—set off a domestic upheaval that must have been bewildering to his six-year-old daughter. Within two months, Elizabeth Stuart's small store of possessions was packed up and she was whisked away by her mother and elder brother, Henry (her younger brother, Charles, being deemed too sickly to travel), from her modest household at the castle of Linlithgow to begin the journey south.★

★ Henry was initially expected to stay in Scotland, but no sooner had James left for England than Anne defied her husband and went to take possession of her eldest son from his guardian, the earl of Mar, whom she detested for depriving her of her child. James chastised her by letter, observing that it was primarily due to the earl's negotiations on his behalf that they owed their new positions as king and queen of England, to which his wife retorted "that she could rather have wished never to see

The royal family's procession to England, which left on June 1, 1603, was as stately as could be mustered on such short notice. From a way station in Yorkshire (a little less than halfway between Edinburgh and London), James ordered "the sending...of such Jewels and other furniture which did appertain to the late Queen [Elizabeth I]...and also coaches, horses, litters, and whatever else you shall think meet" for his wife's use. A posse of aristocratic ladies, both English and Scottish, swarmed to Anne's side to keep her company on the sojourn, look after her needs, and enjoy the general revelry. Elizabeth was awarded a new, very grand English chaperone, Lady Kildare, who was responsible for riding with her small charge and seeing to the princess's welfare along the way. Often the queen's party outdistanced her daughter's, as, being a child, Elizabeth was easily tired. On these occasions, Anne would arrange to wait for her at a spot farther ahead so that Elizabeth could travel at a more moderate pace.

Although there is no record of the princess's impressions of this journey, the concessions Anne made to her daughter would indicate that perhaps Elizabeth was feeling a little overwhelmed. It took a month to rendezvous with the king—a month that consisted every day of new places and new people, of feasts and long-drawn-out public ceremonies, of rush, rush, rush and ride, ride, ride. On June 15th, the procession alighted in York, where the new queen and her children were treated to a "Royal Entertainment" at which Elizabeth received "a purse of twenty angells [*sic*] of gold"; from there, they passed to Grimson and Newark before straggling into Nottingham on the 21st. At this point any ordinary six-year-old would have tried the patience of even the fondest parent, and this seems to have been the case, as Elizabeth and Lady Kildare broke off from the rest of the procession for a few days. But the respite was brief, as the family was due in Windsor by the first of July, where James had arranged to dub

---

England, than to be obliged for it to the Earl." She chose her moment well. Reluctant to engage in a controversy that might delay his coronation, James relented and allowed Henry to accompany Anne and Elizabeth to England.

his eldest son a knight. The ceremony called for much pomp and splendor; even Elizabeth's small suite was required to make a regal entrance. "The young princess came [into Windsor], accompanied with her governess, the Lady Kildare, in a litter with her, and attended with thirty horse," admired a member of the court. "She had her trumpets and other formalities as well as the best."

The knighting ceremony was the first time since coming to England that the family (with the exception of Charles) was together at a state event, and as such served as a formal introduction to the kingdom. Elizabeth did not have a significant role in the proceedings but was permitted to stand in the great hall and peek at the brilliant, bejeweled company as they sat down to feast. The riches on display were quite outside the experience of its royal participants; to host a gala of this magnificence simply would not have been possible in Scotland, not even if every clansman had brought his own dinner. "There was such an infinite company of Lords and Ladies and so great a Court as I think I shall never see the like," exclaimed one of the guests. Henry acquitted himself well and it was clear that the kingdom was relieved to have acquired so attractive a crown prince after decades of uncertainty over the succession. "I heard the Earls of Nottingham and Northampton highly commend him [Henry] for his quick witty answers, princely carriage and reverence performing obeisance at the altar: all which seemed very strange unto them and the rest of the beholders, considering his tender age," avowed another of the company. James could congratulate himself that the long years of privation and fear, not to mention groveling to Elizabeth I, had been worth it.

The contrast between the royal family's new economic standing and their previous fortunes was so pronounced that it seems to have taken some getting used to. When plague struck London and it was judged best to send Elizabeth and Henry away to a castle in the countryside as an interim precaution, James initially provided his children with a staff of 70 domestics—22 upstairs, 48 downstairs— to meet their needs, far more than had waited on them in the past.

But this was evidently considered inadequate by English standards, for within a week he was persuaded to increase the number of their servants to 104, and by October the children's domestic staff had reached 141. The king seems to have had a similar difficulty reconciling his long-term training in austerity with the riches and dainties now available to him. "Whereas ourself and our dear Wife the Queen's Majesty, have been every day served with 30 dishes of meat; now hereafter...our will is to be served but with 24 dishes every meal, unless when any of us sit abroad in State, then to be served with 30 dishes or as any more as we may command," he decreed in one of the first ordinances he issued in England. Old habits die hard.

But for Elizabeth, who was too young to have been trained in the ways of penury, the transition to luxury was much easier. She had always lived with guardians, and this was the case also in England. By October 1603 a suitable pair had been found: Lord and Lady Harrington, great favorites of James and Anne's. (Unfortunately, Lady Kildare's husband had been accused of plotting against the government, so she was let go.) Lady Harrington had a lovely twelfth-century manor house called Coombe Abbey, formerly a monastery, in Warwickshire, about 100 miles northwest of London. Possessed of its own bell tower and moat and nestled on some 500 private acres that included formal gardens, an orchard, and a substantial lake, all surrounded by pristine English woodlands perfect for hunting, this imposing estate became Elizabeth's new home.

Of course, the care and education of a princess of England in such a fine old abode required the procurement of a commensurately impressive household, and James did not stint on his daughter's behalf. Elizabeth was allotted £1500 a year just for her meals. She was given twenty horses for her stable, so she would have something to ride, and a small army of groomsmen to care for them. She had her own doctor, three ladies-in-waiting, two footmen, a personal French maid, a seamstress, a dancing instructor, tutors in French and Italian, and a host of pastry chefs, cooks, and servers. Her music teacher, Dr. John Bull, whom she shared with Henry, was paid forty pounds a year to train his small pupil. He must have found his duties light, as there is evidence that he had the leisure to compose an early version of "God Save the King," the English national anthem, in his spare time.

It wasn't simply the affluence of her immediate surroundings but the manner in which she was treated that most bespoke the difference between Elizabeth's childhood in Scotland and her life in England. On April 3, 1604, the seven-year-old made her first official visit to the neighboring town of Coventry. Her reception there is illustrative of the vast improvement in her circumstances. "The Mayor and Aldermen with the rest of the Livery rode out of the town in their scarlet gowns," the official report of this interesting event recounted. "The Mayor alighted from his horse, kissed her hand, and then rode before into the City...a chair of state was placed at the upper end of the room, in which her Highness dined; from whence, having finished her repast, she adjourned to the Mayoress's parlor, which was fitted up in a most sumptuous manner for her reception."

It was an existence of the type portrayed in a fairy tale or novel—Sara Crewe from *A Little Princess,* only without Miss Minchin, as Elizabeth's guardians were solicitous and responsible.* She had other children to play with, saw her brothers (Charles arrived in October 1604) and parents regularly at holidays, and received letters and gifts from them. She was a pretty, bright little girl who felt loved and valued and consequently reciprocated the affection bestowed on her. "With God's assistance, we hope to do our Lady Elizabeth such service as is due to her princely endowments and natural abilities; both of which appear the sweet dawning of future comfort to her Royal Father," her guardian Lord Harrington wrote to one of his cousins.

The only shadow to fall on the royal family's otherwise bright prospects occurred in November 1605, when Elizabeth was nine

---

* Elizabeth Stuart's experience replicated that of her grandmother Mary Stuart to a startling degree: born in Scotland, Mary also lived frugally until her engagement at the age of five to Francis, eldest son of Henry II and Catherine de' Medici, whereupon she was sent to France and grew up in splendor at the royal court.

years old. A small group of radical Catholic gentlemen, upset by James's rejection of a petition for "Liberty of Conscience"—the right to practice their religion openly—resolved to avenge themselves by a chilling act of terrorism. Led by Guy Fawkes, a Flemish former soldier specifically imported for the job, they decided to assassinate the king, his young sons, and other representatives of the government by blowing up Westminster Castle on the first day of Parliament. According to the official report of this plot by a member of the French royal council, the conspirators reasoned that "the King himself might by many ways be taken away [murdered], but this would be nothing as long as the Prince [Henry] and the Duke of York [Charles] were alive: again, if they were removed, yet this would advantage nothing so long as there remained a Parliament." To effect this feat of political mass murder, the group planned to place barrels of gunpowder underneath Westminster and then set them on fire during the opening session, from which frightening premise the intrigue was ultimately dubbed the Gunpowder Treason.

The radicals had first intended to position the explosives by tunneling under their target, but the thick walls of the palace proved difficult to penetrate. Instead, by happy chance (for them), in March 1605, they found that a neighboring house had a cellar ideal for their purposes. "Such was the opportuness of the place (for it was almost directly under the Royal Throne) that so seasonable an accident did make them persuade themselves, that God did by a secret Conduct favor their attempt," the French report continued. As the first session of Parliament had been put off until November 5, this gave Guy Fawkes and his men nearly eight months to accumulate the necessary firepower.

During those eight months, it occurred to the group that it behooved them to have a plan in place to seize control of the kingdom after the ruling party had been annihilated. Recognizing that they would need some form of political legitimacy, they determined to make use of Elizabeth, who they concluded would be easy to capture and intimidate since she was young and female. "Therefore the Conspirators did again repeat their consultation, and some were appointed who, on the same day that the Enterprise was to be Executed, should seize upon the Lady Elizabeth...under pretence of a hunting match...Her they decreed publickly to proclaim Queen."

The plot was so horrifically audacious that it very nearly succeeded. The cabal was betrayed by an anonymous letter delivered to a member of Parliament, who turned it over to the Privy Council less than two weeks before the opening session.* But so cryptically was the warning worded that James's ministers could hardly credit it. "For although no signs of troubles do appear, yet I admonish you that the meeting [of Parliament] shall receive a terrible blow, and shall not see who smiteth them," the epistle darkly but inscrutably threatened. Uncertain what to do, the Privy Council waited until the king, who was away on a hunting trip, returned to London on November 1, a mere four days before the session was called, to show him this curious missive.

But James, whose Scottish experience of intrigues dwarfed those of his councillors, and who moreover delighted in tricky literary conundrums, took the warning very seriously. He puzzled over it for an evening and then ordered "that the Palace with the places near adjoining, should be diligently searched." His investigators very quickly found the cellar the conspirators had appropriated, along with thirty-six barrels of gunpowder (hidden under stacks of wood and coal), and Guy Fawkes himself, with matches in his pocket.

The plot having been uncovered in time, a general warning went out and the rest of the band were soon discovered, rounded up, found guilty, and executed. News of his innocent ward's proposed role in these proceedings gave Lord Harrington quite a shock. One "hath confessed their design to surprise the Princess in my house, if their wickedness had taken place in London," he wrote to his cousin,

---

* The informer was concerned that the more moderate Catholic lords (one of whom was his brother-in-law), who were not in on the conspiracy, would be blown to bits along with their Protestant counterparts. The letter urged the Catholic peers to come up with a pretext for avoiding the session.

James I, king of England

obviously appalled. "Some of them say, she would have been proclaimed Queen." As for Elizabeth, "this poor Lady hath not yet
recovered the surprise, and is very ill and troubled," her guardian
continued. "What a Queen should I have been by this means?" the
princess reportedly exclaimed in dismay. "I had rather have been
with my Royal Father in the Parliament-house than wear his Crown
on such condition."

By degrees the furor died down, and royal life returned to its
previous peaceful, prosperous routine. But despite his having triumphantly foiled the plot, and the gratifying way in which the government subsequently rallied around him, it might well have occurred
to James that perhaps being king of England wasn't *quite* as inviolable
as he had always supposed it would be.

2

(An Almost) Royal Wedding

Except for excursions to court for holidays or special occasions, as when her mother's brother Christian IV, king of Denmark, arrived in July 1606 for an official state visit, Elizabeth spent the next few years after the Gunpowder Treason at Coombe Abbey. Her guardian Lord Harrington was responsible for her education and was personally involved in her schooling. Although James demanded that his sons master Latin as part of their curriculum and monitored their progress through letters, Elizabeth was spared this ordeal on the grounds that, as a woman (and therefore inferior, in her father's opinion), it was unnecessary. She did, however, study French and Italian in addition to music and dancing. The French ambassador noted approvingly when she was twelve that Elizabeth "speaks French very well, much better than her brother."

It is possible, though, that the princess's education went further than the traditional finishing school's preparation in pretty manners and the decorative arts. Lord Harrington, cultivated and erudite, with a gentleman's passion for the natural sciences, took his duties seriously. Elizabeth likely was introduced on at least a cursory level to history, geography, and botany. This would have been entirely in keeping with the general intellectual climate of the period and especially the keen interest in these subjects at the beginning of the seventeenth century.★

Whatever the extent of her studies, the time Elizabeth spent at Coombe Abbey was a happy period in her life. She loved animals, and her guardians indulged her passion for exotic pets. Lord Harrington's accounts for his young charge cited expenses for monkey-beds and parrot cages. Religion was clearly emphasized in the household—at thirteen, Elizabeth penned some truly awful verses extolling God and spiritual rewards over worldly delights†—but her guardians' piety in no way inhibited the princess's high spirits or the pleasure she took in music, dancing, beautiful clothes, jewels, and other court entertainments. She was healthy and athletic and enjoyed riding and hunting, and like any girl her age, she gobbled up sweets whenever she had the chance. Lord and Lady Harrington, mindful that they were responsible for their ward's deportment as well as her physical needs, made a point of stressing charity and liberality, so although showered with gifts, Elizabeth never displayed symptoms of selfishness. On the contrary, she was known throughout her life for her generosity.

The result of all this tender, enlightened child rearing was that by adolescence, Elizabeth had developed into a lively, poised, and exceedingly charming young woman. When she was eleven, the French ambassador noted that "she is handsome, graceful, [and] well nourished... I assure you it will not be her fault if she is not dauphiness," while a Scottish diplomat described her as "a princess of lovely beauty... her manners are most gentle, and she shows no common skill in those liberal exercises of mind and body which become a royal maiden."

★ There is also the evidence that Elizabeth's daughters were educated along these lines, and in my experience, parents tend to replicate their own schooling in their children; witness James's insistence that his sons learn Latin.

† "This is only my desire/This doth set my heart on fire/That I might receive my lyre/With the saints' and angels' quire [choir]," Elizabeth rhapsodized. Let's hope she did better with botany.

As was customary, by the age of thirteen, Elizabeth was spending more and more of her time with the rest of her family at court. This was no hardship for her. She was allowed to stay up late for banquets and masques and to help hand out the prizes at the royal tournaments. But best of all, the princess had the opportunity to see more of her older brother, Henry, whom she adored and idolized.

She was not alone in these sentiments. Henry was growing into a prince of great promise. He was glowingly described by his treasurer as "of a comely, tall, middle Stature, about five Feet and eight Inches high, of a strong, straight, well-made Body (as if Nature in him had showed all her Cunning) with somewhat broad Shoulders, and a small Waist, of an amiable, majestic Countenance, his Hair of an auburn Color, long faced, and broad Forehead, a piercing grave Eye, a most gracious Smile...courteous, loving, and affable." He was strong-willed, healthy, and extremely athletic, and demonstrated an early interest in leadership and government. "He studies two hours a day, and employs the rest of his time in tossing the pike, or leaping, or shooting with the bow, or throwing the bar, or vaulting, or some other exercise of that kind, and he is never idle," the French ambassador reported of Henry in 1606, when the prince was twelve. "He shows himself likewise very good natured to his dependents, and supports their interests against any persons whatever; and pushes what he undertakes for them or others, with such zeal as gives success to it."

Henry's and Elizabeth's handsome looks and robust good health stood in stark contrast to their younger brother Charles's physical condition. Sickly from birth, Charles remained feeble throughout childhood, so much so that his parents had trouble recruiting a guardian willing to take on the nurturing of a boy who so plainly was going to die. Charles's tutor described *him* at the age of four as "not able to go, nor scant stand alone, he was so weak in his joints, and especially his ankles, insomuch as many feared they were out of joint." Charles's ankles weren't his only problem; in addition to being unable to walk, he hadn't learned to talk yet either. His young-

Elizabeth's older brother, Henry

est son's painfully slow development prompted James, ever the authority, to suggest a number of helpful remedies, which, fortunately for Charles, his guardians were able to resist. "The King was desirous that the string under his [Charles's] tongue should be cut, for he was so long beginning to speak as he thought he would never have spoke. Then he would have him [Charles] put in iron boots, to strengthen his sinews and joints; but my wife protested so much against them both, as she got the victory," his guardian reported. Charles would eventually learn to walk and talk and, as a teenager, even to ride, but he never matched his older siblings' easy vitality, their radiant charisma, or their tremendous popularity. Henry and Elizabeth were a golden pair. Charles was the odd child out, in their shadow.

If English citizens were proud to have two such exemplary siblings as Henry and Elizabeth in line to inherit the throne, they were rather less enamored of the current occupant of that position. It took James's subjects only a few years to become deeply discontented with their new sovereign. James bears the brunt of the responsibility for the general disillusionment. After so many years of hoping and waiting for the crown of England, once he got it, he felt he had done enough and behaved like a man on holiday or in the mellow years of his retirement. "As the King is by nature of a mild disposition and has never really been happy in Scotland, he wishes now to enjoy the Papacy, as we say [that is, to live the good life] and so desires to have no bother with other people's affairs and little with his own," the Venetian ambassador observed delicately.

James devoted himself, not to his government in London, but to his hunting in the countryside. Rather like a modern-day recreational golfer's, his spirits rose and fell with the sport. If his hounds brought down a stag and he was able to plunge his hands into its entrails and anoint the foreheads of his hunting companions with the animal's blood (a gory tradition that repelled more than a few of his compatriots), he was elated. If the prey managed to escape, he swore and muttered and, on occasion, sullenly refused to consider the government decrees awaiting his signature. He spent so much time tracking game that the rural population, forced to supply the royal party, became rather desperate and took the expedient of kidnapping one of his hunting dogs, Jowler, returning the animal the next day with a sign tied around its neck. "Good Mr. Jowler," the note read. "We pray you speak to the King (for he hears you everyday and so doth he not us) that it will please his Majesty to go back to London, for else the country will be undone; all our provision is spent already and we are unable to entertain him longer." That James refused to take the hint and stayed an extra two weeks did nothing to improve his reputation.

But even more than his dedication to hunting and his commensurate disinterest in ruling, it was the king's manners, or, rather, the lack thereof, that really offended the citizenry. James had never gotten over his adolescent fondness for colorful swearwords. His Majesty's enthusiastic use of expletives and the general coarseness of his language was felt by many to demean the government. This bias in favor of vulgarity unfortunately extended to the royal household and went far beyond mere verbal expression. Drunkenness prevailed at court; Anne's ladies-in-waiting could regularly be found getting sick in the corridors of Windsor Castle after participating in one of the queen's famous pageants. Nor did James's subjects think much of the king's habit of bestowing big bear hugs and long wet kisses on his attractive male courtiers after he'd had one too many cups of wine. And he did not, it seems, believe in bathing or encourage it for others. "We all saw a great change between the fashion of the court as it is now and of that in the Queen's [Elizabeth I's] time," lamented a lady familiar with both administrations. "For we were all lousy by sitting in the chamber of Sir Thomas Erskine [a high-ranking member of James's household]."

Small wonder, then, that the population much preferred the eldest son to the father, a situation that inevitably caused friction. As Henry matured, his youthful interest in sports developed into a distinct prowess in the martial arts. "I perceive, my cousin...that, during your stay in England, you discovered my humor; since you have sent me a present of the two things which I most delight in, arms and horses," Henry wrote merrily to a French relative when he was thirteen. The prince's warlike bent, and particularly his love of ships and desire to augment the navy, made a refreshing change from James's unmanly pacifism and bookish temperament, and caused many of the king's own officials to vie among themselves for his son's friendship. "Will he bury me alive?" his father fretted when he saw the number of visitors to Henry's residence. Nor could the king control his eldest son's behavior as much as he would have liked. When James expressed disappointment with the progress of

Henry's studies and threatened to disinherit him in favor of his younger brother, who was a much better student, if he did not devote more time to his books, Henry merely queried his tutor if Charles was really such a fine scholar. Upon receiving the assurance that this was in fact the case, Henry replied coolly, "Then will I make him Archbishop of Canterbury."

But between Henry and Elizabeth there was no discord, only delight in each other's company and a steadfast devotion. Elizabeth's first letter, written when she was seven years old, was to Henry. "My dear and worthy brother," she inked, being careful to form her letters between the narrow red lines that her writing master had added for that purpose. "I most kindly salute you, desiring to hear of your health, from whom though I am now removed far away, none shall ever be nearer in affection than Your most loving sister, Elizabeth." As they grew older, they exchanged gifts and horses, and Henry interrupted Elizabeth's studies with invitations to ride with him so often that her guardian complained. When her brother hosted a grand feast in January 1610, thirteen-year-old Elizabeth occupied the seat of honor across from him. Afterward, the pair stayed up until three o'clock in the morning to watch a play and then returned with the assembled company to the prince's rooms at St. James's Palace, where Henry, knowing his sister's fondness for sweets, had arranged for a huge table, a third the size of a football field, to be laden with elaborate confections in the form of flowers, windmills, toy soldiers, and even the sun and planets, with sugared rose water spouting from crystal fountains.

But of course, being allowed to stay up late for parties and make more frequent appearances at court indicated that Elizabeth was growing up, and that meant marriage. Naturally, ambitions ran high for so desirable a princess. Recognizing that the competition might be extensive, the king of Sweden got his bid in early. He officially offered his eldest son and heir, Prince Gustavus Adolphus, for Elizabeth's hand in September 1610, when she had just turned fourteen.

This would have been a very good match for the princess—and for England. At almost sixteen, Gustavus Adolphus was just the right age and rank. Intelligent and energetic, he was also an outstanding soldier and, most important, a Protestant. Unfortunately, he was also Swedish, and Sweden was the sworn enemy of Denmark, of which Elizabeth's uncle Christian, her mother's brother, was king. Yielding to his wife's feelings, James said no.

There followed a series of suitors—minor Dutch princes of various shapes and sizes (Maurice of Nassau was corpulent, middle-aged, and balding; Elizabeth was surely glad to see him go) and the son of the Catholic duke of Savoy—all of whom were rejected by the Crown. The prospect of a double marriage with France, Elizabeth to the dauphin, Henry to the eldest French princess, had been hinted at for years, but the likelihood of James achieving this ambitious agenda was seriously called into question when Henry IV, the once Protestant king of France, was assassinated on May 14, 1610, and his Catholic queen, Marie de' Medici, assumed the regency.

Elizabeth's mother, on the other hand, made no secret of her desire for a union between her eldest children and the Spanish royal family, an aspiration that was given a strong boost when the king of Spain's wife died unexpectedly in 1611. Anne, long denied a say in the government by her husband, had compensated by throwing her energies into the theater, where she patronized artists like Ben Jonson and Inigo Jones, the period's leading dramatist and foremost set designer, respectively. But on the subject of her children's marriages, the queen acted with alacrity. She entered into quiet negotiations with the Spanish ambassador to England, intimating that, should the widowed Philip III agree to espouse her daughter, Elizabeth would convert to Catholicism, an inducement that caused quite an uproar when these clandestine conversations inevitably became public. The English ambassador to Spain, appalled that he had not been consulted before this offer was made, complained indignantly to James that members of the Spanish court "have proceeded so far with me, as to tell me they here had already received assurance that, to match with the King of Spain, the princess of England would become a Catholic; which opinion is here so spread, and every man seemeth to speak it so knowingly, that I have been forced, for the king's honor, to use so plain and direct speech as I should otherwise have thought more fit to be omitted."

Queen Anne's indiscretion caused a serious rift between mother and daughter. Elizabeth had no desire to convert to Catholicism, and her beloved Henry supported her in this decision. "The prince hath publicly said that whosoever should counsel his father to marry his sister to a Catholic prince, were a traitor," the Spanish ambassador to England entrusted with these negotiations wrote home in despair. "He is a great heretic!" he added for emphasis.★

When the possibility of a French marriage also fell through — Marie de' Medici snubbed England and instead scored a coup by arranging for her son to marry Philip III's elder daughter, who was supposed to have gone to Henry — James was forced to widen the field of potential suitors. His wife's fruitless effort to wed Elizabeth to the Spanish king had highlighted the antipathy of the populace to a Catholic union, so her father looked around for a Protestant bridegroom. There being a limited number of candidates of the right age and regional affiliation, it didn't take long to find him.

His name was Frederick Henry, and his official title was Frederick V, count of the Palatinate (although he was also sometimes known, for maximum confusion, as the Elector Palatine, Count Palatine of the Rhine, or sometimes simply the Palatine or the Palsgrave). If his

---

★ Although publicly James blustered that he would never allow his daughter to become a Catholic, evidence indicates that he was in fact considering marrying her to Philip III and probably would have accepted this condition provided the conversion ceremony occurred in Spain and not England. But Elizabeth remained ignorant of this, as the Spanish ambassador never made a formal offer of marriage, thus relieving the king of the responsibility for broadcasting his views, and allowing all the blame to fall on the queen.

title was impressive, Frederick's holdings were rather less so. The Palatinate was composed of two separate counties in Germany, the Upper and Lower Palatinates. The Upper Palatinate, near the border with Bohemia, consisted of the provincial towns of Sulzbach and Amberg and the farmland surrounding them. The Lower Palatinate boasted the more affluent (but hardly cosmopolitan) municipalities of Mannheim and Heidelberg and not much else. Frederick was to Elizabeth's former suitors—the kings of Sweden, France, and Spain, even the son of the duke of Savoy—as the local coffee shop is to Starbucks.

Frederick's family was distantly related to Elizabeth's, and James had earlier been in contact with his father concerning a diplomatic initiative known as the Defensive Union. Germany was not a unified kingdom like England but was instead divided into numerous small duchies (like the Palatinate), each presided over by a petty baron (like Frederick). Most of these barons were basically glorified landowners. Each owed allegiance to the Holy Roman emperor, a position held for centuries by one member or another of the Habsburg family. The number of Protestants and Catholics living in Germany being roughly equal (although, as might be expected, the Lutherans vastly outnumbered the Calvinists), these proportions were also reflected in its ruling class, with the result that the subjects of each little fiefdom were either predominantly Catholic or predominantly Protestant, depending on the faith espoused by the local baron.

With so many counts and dukes squeezed so closely together, there was unfortunately always a great deal of trouble about inheritance. This was especially true whenever one of these minor magnates died childless, as those barons living in the immediate vicinity, in the spirit of neighborliness, would thoughtfully move in and try to appropriate the dead man's property. To prevent this from happening (and, what would be more alarming, to prevent a serious power like Spain from taking advantage of such regional squabbles and invading), the Protestant lords of Germany, calling themselves the Princes of the Union, had decided to band together with the sovereigns of other Protestant countries. The alliance they formed very specifically stated that, should any member of the league be attacked, the other members would automatically come to his aid.

James had originally been approached to join by Frederick's father and the French king Henry IV (sympathetic to the Protestants, having been one himself before assuming the throne of France), and it had seemed a good idea and relatively risk-free. Henry IV loved soldiering as much as James detested it, so it was more or less understood that France would do most of the fighting, should it come to that, and James could supplement his efforts if necessary. Even after Henry IV was assassinated, in the spring of 1610, and his death was followed closely by that of Frederick's father in the fall of the same year, James continued to support the initiative, as he believed the mere threat that the Protestant nations would act in concert would be enough to prevent Catholic aggression. "His Majesty is well pleased to enter into a League defensive...as holding it the only means both to preserve the Peace and Tranquility of the Empire and the Countries adjoining thereunto, and to prevent any future Attempt which...some Maligners thereof would set on foot, under one Pretext or other; for that nothing will deter them more, than to see so firm an Association established among so many and so potent Princes and States," wrote the members of James's council on September 28, 1610, to the English envoy in charge of these negotiations. James even provided specific language to be used in the treaty: he bound himself to send material aid "if the Princes be assailed beyond the Course of Justice and Contrary to the Constitutions of the Empire."

When Frederick succeeded to the Palatinate upon his father's death, his worldly uncle the duke of Bouillon, a highly placed member of the French court, sensed opportunity. Frederick was just the right age (fourteen in 1610) and religion (Calvinist) for the English princess. True, he was not of royal birth, but he had inherited an income sufficient to provide Elizabeth, not with what she was used to, of course, but at least with a large, comfortable château and a well-stocked larder. And as an elector, Frederick was on course to become a force in imperial politics.★ The recently signed Defensive Union gave England a stake in German politics; a wedding with one of the principals of that treaty would serve to cement the alliance. It was a long shot but worth the chance. The duke of Bouillon put Frederick forward as a suitor for Elizabeth's hand.

The timing could not have been more perfect. Both the Spanish and French marriages had fallen through, and the son of the duke of Savoy, although still available, was a Catholic. With Frederick, Elizabeth could stay a Protestant and, even better, would not need a significant dowry. James would never have entertained the possibility of such an inferior match for one of his sons; only princesses were considered suitable for Henry and Charles. But Elizabeth was a female, and females didn't really count in the king's opinion, so James had documents drawn up and invited his young cousin to come to England to pursue the engagement.

Anne, who had envisioned her daughter as an important queen, was appalled at the idea of Elizabeth's marrying someone so far beneath her rank, and she publicly opposed the alliance. But Henry, who had been vocal in his disapproval of the Spanish match, embraced Frederick's cause enthusiastically. His reasoning had less to do with Elizabeth's happiness, however, than with his own eagerness for battle. "Prince Henry gave the first encouragement to the Prince Elector to attempt his Sister; desiring more to head an Army in Germany than he durst make Show of," his treasurer revealed.

★ In cases where the office for emperor fell vacant or was in dispute, the matter was settled by election. Out of all the barons in Germany, only seven were allowed to cast votes; hence the term *elector*. Frederick was one of the seven.

In this ambition, Henry would prove far more astute than his father. For where James the scholar had signed the Defensive Union believing that it would secure peace, his son the soldier understood implicitly that, on the contrary, it would inevitably lead to war.

FREDERICK WAS SIXTEEN YEARS old, just Elizabeth's age—in fact, she was exactly one week older—when he arrived in England on October 16, 1612. The hopeful bridegroom turned out to be slender and undeniably attractive; an English courtier described him as "straight and well-shaped for his growing years... with a Countenance pleasing." The Venetian ambassador concurred: "He is very handsome, of pleasant speech, with a French accent," he wrote home in an official state report. Still, Frederick must have been nervous. It had clearly been drummed into him before he left home that this was his big chance and he'd better do everything possible to win over so desirable a wife.

Luckily for Frederick—or the Palatine, as he was called in England—he had some potent weapons in his wooing arsenal. Although his property was in Germany, he had been educated in France by his suave uncle the duke of Bouillon. The duke could not have provided a more thorough or excellent preparation for royal lovemaking. Whatever else the results of Frederick's studies, his uncle had made sure that he knew how to dress, that his manners were charming, that he spoke French to perfection, and, most important, that he was well versed in the art of romance.

Judging by the recollections of an observer who chronicled the Palatine's visit to England, Frederick's first performance at court was nothing short of masterful. He flattered James: "Bending himself with a due Reverence before the King, he told him among other Compliments, that in his Sight and Preference he enjoyed a great part... of the Happiness of his Journey"; conciliated Anne: "She entertained him with a fixed Countenance; and though her Posture might have seemed (as it was judged) to Promise him the Honor of a Kiss for his Welcome, his Humility carried him no higher than her hand"; joked with Henry: "After some few words of compliment… exchanging with him after a more familiar strain certain Passages of Courtesy"; and then knocked it completely out of the park with Elizabeth: "Stooping low to take up the lowest part of her Garment to kiss it, she most gracefully courtseying lower than accustomed, and with her Hand staying him from that humblest Reverence, gave him at his rising a fair Advantage (which he took) of kissing her."

Nor did the lover's attentiveness flag in the probationary interval that followed. All that first week and long into his visit, Frederick remained Elizabeth's devoted servant. "He plies his Mistress so hard, and takes no delight in running at ring nor tennis, nor riding with the Prince…as others of his company do, but only in her conversation," a member of the court snickered. But Frederick's passion for his future bride was genuine. She had been portrayed to him as a beautiful princess, sweet-natured and kind, and so she turned out to be. He must have felt a little like he had somehow fallen into a fairy tale.

Elizabeth would have had to be hard-hearted indeed not to respond to such an outpouring of adoration and from such an appealing source. It wasn't long before she began to reciprocate her handsome swain's affections. "The Princess, who maybe begins to feel the warmth of the approaching nuptials, adorns her great natural beauty by dress and embellishments," the Venetian ambassador noticed. Elizabeth's growing attachment to Frederick did not go unobserved by her mother, who, determined to break the couple up, aimed a dart where she knew it would hurt most. "And 'tis certain (for I had it from good Authority) that Queen Ann was averse to it [the marriage]; and to put the Princess out of conceit of it, would usually call her Daughter 'Goodwife Palsgrave,'" a historian of the period reported. Although Elizabeth bravely shot back that "she would rather be the Palsgrave's Wife, than the greatest Papist Queen in Christendom," it is clear that the barb hit home.

Elizabeth's mother, Anne of Denmark

Her mother's criticisms aside, these first two weeks of courtship were everything a romance should be. There were many banquets and festivities in honor of the young couple, and all the talk at court was of their coming marriage and its preparation. "The Palatine has surpassed expectation, which, on the King's part, was not great," the Venetian envoy observed drily.

The only small impediment to the general merrymaking was a slight indisposition of Henry's, a nagging headache and low-grade fever that he couldn't quite shake through the month of September and on into October. But it wasn't enough for real worry, and anyway, Henry was determined not to allow a tiresome fatigue to ruin his sister's fun or even to change his athletic routine. Tennis being one of his passions, he arranged to play a week after Frederick's arrival with a member of his future brother-in-law's suite, who promised to give him a good game. "Above all the rest, one great Match they had at Tennis, on Saturday the 24th of October," recalled Henry's treasurer, "where his [Henry's] undaunted Courage, negligently, carelessly, and willfully (neither considering the former weak

State of his Body, Danger, nor Coldness of the Season) as though his Body had been of Brass, did play in his shirt, as if it had been in the Heat of Summer; during which Time, he looked so wonderful ill and pale, that all the Beholders took Notice thereof, muttering to one another what they feared." But the prince rallied and made light of his weakness to reassure the bystanders. "He (the Match being ended) carried himself so well, as if there were no such Matter, having all this while a reasonable good stomach to meat, yet this Night, at his going to Bed, complaining more than usual of his Laziness and Headache," his treasurer continued, worried.

The next day, Sunday, Henry rose and heard a sermon, but later that afternoon he was gripped by chills and a high fever and was forced to retreat to his bed. And even though his symptoms abated enough the next morning for him to dress and play cards with his brother Charles for an hour, by evening the headache and fever, now accompanied by a "great thirst," had returned, and it was clear that the heir to the throne of England was seriously ill.

Doctors crowded around, offering the usual seventeenth-century remedies. They debated bleeding him, forced nasty purgatives on him to make him vomit, and, to relieve the headache, shaved his head and had "Pigeons and Cupping-Glasses applied to lessen and draw away the Humor." Alas, none of these cures, helpful though they might have been in other circumstances, were of any use to poor Henry, who most likely had contracted typhoid fever. Delirium seized him; convulsions racked his body; his tongue turned black.

In the beginning his family had been allowed to visit him, but by the third of November, a mere ten days after that fateful tennis match, even the king was turned away. On the fifth of November, James was informed that his son was without hope. He begged the lead doctor to chance whatever he could to keep Henry alive, no matter how dangerous the treatment, but the doctor, knowing that nothing could be done and fearing to take the blame, refused, "saying that it should never be said in after Ages, that he had killed the King's eldest Son." And so, strong, handsome Henry, budding warrior and statesman, the pride and promise of the realm, died in agony in the cold blackness of the early morning hours of November 6, 1612. He was just eighteen years old.

The kingdom's grief was very great. "Our Rising Sun is set ere scarce he had shone," lamented a member of the highest nobility. The mourning spread to the prince's birthplace. "When the women in Scotland, even unto this day, do lament the death of their dearest children, to comfort them it is ordinarily said, and is passed into a proverb, 'Did not good Prince Henry die?'" wrote a later historian. James and Anne were devastated. Whatever friction had developed between Henry and his father was buried with the tragedy. "The King is doing all he can to forget his grief, but it is not sufficient," reported the Venetian ambassador. "For many a time it will come over him suddenly and even in the midst of the most important discussions he will burst out with: 'Henry is dead, Henry is dead.'"

But no one suffered more than Elizabeth. "The Princess has gone two days without food and cries incessantly," reported the Venetian. Elizabeth had tried several times to get in to see Henry during the throes of the disease, even masking herself in an attempt to disguise her identity, but had been denied admittance by the doctors. She never had a chance to soothe him or to say good-bye. Worse, she knew that Henry had wanted her with him, had asked for her, and she couldn't get to him! "The Lady Elizabeth is much afflicted with this loss, and not without good cause," observed a member of James's government. "For he did extraordinarily affect her, and the last words he spoke in good sense, they say, were 'Where is my dear Sister?'"

"The Succession to this Crown," the Venetian ambassador gravely informed his master, the doge, "now rests on one single child of ten years, the Duke of York [Charles], though it is true the law does not exclude the Princess."*

---

* Charles was actually twelve years old when Henry died, but he was so slight and physically immature that the Venetian ambassador may perhaps be excused for thinking him younger than he was.

★   ★   ★

POOR FREDERICK FOUND HIMSELF in a very awkward position. It was obviously not the best time to press for a wedding, what with his intended and all of her family, friends, and subjects prostrate with grief. Yet if he did not act soon, he stood in danger of losing Elizabeth altogether. Already there were murmurings at court that the princess should not leave England as it was likely that she would inherit the Crown. True, her younger brother Charles was next in line, but Charles's prospects were questionable. If Henry, who had been so strong and fit, could be taken so suddenly, what chance did Charles, sick and stunted from birth, have of surviving to adulthood, let alone of succeeding to the throne?

But Frederick had a strong ally in James, who, deprived of his eldest child, kept this endearing future son-in-law near him during the dark days after Henry's death as something of a salve against the pain. He was such a nice boy, and Elizabeth clearly loved him. After an appropriate period of mourning, plans for the wedding went ahead.

In addition to James's fondness for the Palatine, there seems to have been more to this alliance than appeared on its face — a sort of concealed agenda that came out slowly in the wake of Henry's demise. "He [Henry] meant to have conducted her [Elizabeth] on her way into Germany, to the uttermost bounds of the States dominions, which purpose he kept very secret; and it came abroad but since his death," a courtier informed an English ambassador on November 12. Soon, more details of the plan leaked out. Henry and his forces, it seemed, were to have helped Frederick assume a throne. But which throne? "On Tuesday I took occasion to go to court because I had never seen the Palsgrave, nor the Lady Elizabeth near hand for a long time," wrote the same nobleman. "I had the full view of them both, but will not tell you all I think but only this, that he owes his Mistress nothing if he were a King's son, as she is a King's Daughter. The worst is, methinks he is much too young and small-timbered to undertake such a task," he warned. Whatever this task was, it involved soldiering and not romance, for certainly Frederick was capable of performing his marital duties.

Christmas came gloomily, with the court still in mourning. To brighten the holiday, gifts were exchanged—Frederick's to Elizabeth included a necklace, tiara, and drop earrings all glittering with diamonds, plus two magnificent pearls "for bigness, fashion, and beauty, esteemed the rarest that are to be found in Christendom"— and a ceremony was held to celebrate the couple's official engagement. Anne, still not reconciled to the match, refused to make an appearance. "The Affiancy of the Palsgrave and the Lady Elizabeth was solemnized in the great Banqueting-room on Sunday (the 27th) before dinner, in the presence of the King and a great store of Nobility, but the Queen was absent, being troubled, as they say, with the gout," the same courtier reported.★

It was this obstinacy of the bride's mother that brought the clandestine scheme out into the open at last. Piqued by what he perceived to be Anne's slighting of her future son-in-law, the count of Shomberg, Frederick's close friend and top administrator who had come over from Germany with him to take charge of his retinue, disclosed the truth. "The Queen is noted to have given no great grace nor favor to this match, and there is no doubt will do less hereafter, for that upon these things Shomberg (that is chief about him) is said to have given out, that his master is a better man than the King of Denmark, and that he is to take place of him in the Empire, at leastwise of a greater King than he, the King of Bohemia."

The kingship of Bohemia was ostensibly an elected position but

---

★ This was an important ceremony. James sat in state; Elizabeth's remaining brother, Charles, escorted Frederick to his place in front of the king's great throne, where a large Turkish carpet had been specially spread for the occasion. All the government ministers, royal courtiers, and the princess's ladies-in-waiting were in attendance. Frederick wore "a black velvet cloake caped with gold lace"; Elizabeth was also in black velvet, her gown richly embroidered in silver. Gout or no gout, it is difficult to believe that Anne would have missed such a critical day in her only daughter's life if the queen were not intent on publicly signaling her opposition to the marriage.

in reality had been held by the Holy Roman emperor for centuries. This, then, seems to have been what Henry intended by accompanying Elizabeth back to Germany: he meant to help place Frederick on that throne and raise him to her rank, thereby expanding Protestant influence in the empire and securing England's interests in the region. Nor did this ambition die with Henry. To take over Bohemia, which bordered the Upper Palatinate—this perhaps was the task the courtier worried that Frederick was too young and small to undertake.

From a closely guarded secret known to only a small group of intimates surrounding Henry, Frederick, and, it appears, James, the pursuit of Bohemia now became so public that even the Spanish ambassador, whose master was allied with the emperor, picked up on it. After noting that whenever the king of England was questioned about the disparity in rank between Elizabeth and Frederick, he would invariably reply "that he doubted not but that his son-in-law should have the title of a King within a few years," the Spaniard launched an investigation whereby he "procured to learn, whereupon this speech might be grounded, and findeth it to be in respect of the crown of Bohemia, because they pretend it to be elective, and the Palatine hath great intelligence there...and he heareth that France secretly furthereth and helpeth that negotiation."*

Whether James fully understood the implications of his tacit approval for this project is not clear. It's quite possible that the king thought it a nice idea in general that Frederick should become sovereign of Bohemia and humored him in the ambition, believing that to have such a goal was an indication of spirit that could do no harm, and that perhaps his son-in-law might after all achieve the realm one day. But it is unlikely that Frederick—or later Elizabeth, as her husband confided in her completely after their marriage—grasped that nuance. There is little doubt that the couple believed

---

* Certainly Frederick had a conduit to the French government in the person of his uncle, the duke of Bouillon, one of the highest-ranking Huguenots in France.

they had her father's full support and the enthusiasm of the Protestant majority for this quest. And behind the king and this majority stood the formidable financial resources and military might of England itself.

And so the princess and the Palatine were married. The wedding, which was preceded by three days of festivities that included a stunning fireworks display, took place, appropriately enough, on Valentine's Day, 1613. There was great rejoicing. Even Anne, bowing to circumstances beyond her control, relented and took part in the celebrations, oohing and aahing at the brilliance of the fireworks from the balcony with the rest of the royal family and attending the nuptials with good humor. The ceremony was as opulently staged and its participants as richly clothed as would have occurred had the bride been pledged to the most important sovereign in Europe. Elizabeth was resplendent in "a gowne of white satin, richly embroidered...upon her head a crown of refined gold, made Imperial by the pearls and diamonds thereupon placed, which were so thick beset that they stood like shining pinnacles upon her amber-coloured haire." The princess's red-gold curls, always a source of admiration, were mentioned on this occasion as being particularly magnificent. Piled atop her head, individual strands had been painstakingly woven with "gold-spangles, pearls, rich stones, and diamonds; and withal, many diamonds of inestimable value, embroidered upon her sleeves, which even dazzled and amazed the eyes of the beholders." Behind her swept a train supported by a bevy of ladies, some fifteen in all, also wearing white satin "adorned with many rich jewells."

The archbishop of Canterbury solemnly officiated, the king gave his daughter away, and the choir sang a benediction set to the strains of a melody composed specially for the bride by John Bull. Afterward, the entire company repaired to the Banqueting House to prepare for the wedding feast. After so much sorrow, so much heartbreak, there was no mistaking the popularity of this union. As the newlyweds made their first entrance into society as a married couple,

Elizabeth in her wedding dress
(*Princess Elizabeth, Later Queen of Bohemia* by Robert Peake
the Elder: Metropolitan Museum of Art in New York,
Gift of Kate T. Davison, in memory of her husband,
Henry Pomeroy Davison, 1951)

the hundreds of assembled guests rose to their feet as one and a great cry rang out: "God give them joy, God give them joy!"

A little more than two months later, on April 25, 1613, sixteen-year-old Elizabeth found herself on board a ship, her husband by her side, bound first for the Netherlands and from there to her new home in faraway Germany.

3

Goodwife Palsgrave

I T TOOK MORE THAN A month for Elizabeth to reach Heidelberg, site of her husband's primary residence. The slowness of her progress was by design; the trip was as much a goodwill initiative as a honeymoon journey. To ensure that his daughter was treated with the respect she merited as a member of the English royal family, James had attached a party of senior government officials to the bride's entourage. "The commissioners that accompany her have the titles of ambassadors, to give them preceding…in any encounters with Almaigne [German] princes," explained one of James's ministers in a letter to a friend.

Consequently, everywhere she went, Elizabeth was feted by the local nobility and treated, not as the spouse of the Count Palatine, but as a royal representative of the king of England. To announce her arrival at the port of Flushing (present-day Vlissingen), her first stop after leaving the English coast, the lord admiral of the navy, who had personal command of the ships that bore the couple across the North Sea to Holland, set off a deafening barrage of 400 can-nons "to make Heaven and Earth echo forth from the report," a flourish that was answered by a suitably impressive volley of 200 guns from the shore. At Flushing there were fireworks; at Rotter-dam, feasts and plays; at The Hague, hunting and "costly shows." Elizabeth was showered with wedding presents: a coronet sparkling with thirty diamonds, a pearl pendant and necklace, a diamond hairpin, tapestries, fine table linens, furniture, dishes—everything a discriminating young housewife could possibly need to get started in life. A contemporary pamphleteer conservatively estimated the value of this haul at £10,000.

Nor was the bride's cultural education neglected. As she made her way south from Amsterdam to Utrecht and from there into Germany, every municipality, eager to meet so exalted a visitor, made sure to point out areas of interest to help familiarize the English princess with her new surroundings. In the small village of Overwinter, for example, Elizabeth learned of a tower where "the people of the country report that the devil walks, and holds his infernal revels!" In Brobgech she passed "that Castle in which by report a German Bishop was eaten up by the rats."

Finally, on June 10, 1613, Elizabeth reached the outskirts of Heidelberg. Frederick had gone ahead to ensure that all was in readiness for her arrival and to organize an appropriately magnificent reception. Significantly, he chose to welcome his English wife to her new home with a display of the region's martial capabilities. Twenty-five cannons, the sum total of the Palatinate's artillery, were rolled out and fired in her honor. The couple were reunited in the presence of a thousand knights on horseback, "all Gentlemen of the country, very richly attired and bravely furnished with armor, and other warlike habiliments," supplemented by sixteen companies of foot soldiers drawn from the lower classes. Together this force assumed military formation and paraded Elizabeth home to Frederick's château in Heidelberg, where his mother, surrounded by all the principal ladies of the neighborhood, was waiting to greet her. There followed three days of jousting, feasting, hunting, spectacles, and comic performances, much to the delight of the local burghers and their families.

And then, on the fourth day, those who remained of Elizabeth's personal entourage (with the exception of Lord and Lady Harrington, who had accompanied their ward at their own expense, and her maid of honor) said a tearful good-bye and departed for England, and she was left alone with her husband and mother-in-law to begin her new life.

★   ★   ★

BY ALL ACCOUNTS, the castle of Heidelberg was absolutely charming. It was built of stone and stood high on a hill surrounded by gardens. Frederick did everything he could to please Elizabeth, designing rooms and terraced plantings in the English style for her so she would feel at home. Elizabeth, in turn, did her best to accommodate herself to the customs and expectations of her husband and his family and friends.

But there were inevitable frictions caused by her elevated rank. Before she left for Germany, James had insisted that Elizabeth be recognized, not as the Electress Palatine, but as a princess of England. This meant that, like James's ambassadors, she would take precedence over every baron in Germany, no matter how wealthy or influential, including her husband. As there was no pressing political need for this, it was likely that the king was simply attempting to justify his decision to marry his daughter to someone of lower rank by pretending that it had no effect on her social standing. To have one's wife so publicly occupy a position of superiority over oneself was hardly a prescription for a happy marriage. Nonetheless, Frederick, supported in this decision by his principal administrator, the count of Shomberg, who was relying heavily on the alliance with England, felt he had no choice but to adhere to this condition.

Unfortunately, with so many noblemen (not to mention their wives and daughters) squabbling for dominance, the rituals of protocol were jealously guarded in Germany. Who sat at whose table, whose derriere merited the comfort of a prestigious armchair rather than the cushion of a lowly stool, which gentleman or lady should be allowed to pass Elizabeth her cup or serve her a slice of meat but could not do the same for a German of the same rank as the Elector Palatine—these details caused endless difficulties.★ It was particu-

---

★ Lord and Lady Harrington were ensnared in one of these clashes of etiquette and departed in July 1613, a mere six weeks after their arrival in Heidelberg. To Eliza-

larly galling to Frederick's mother to always have to cede to her daughter-in-law the place of honor at social gatherings, and of course she complained to her son.

Sir Henry Wotton, an English ambassador visiting Heidelberg, reported to James that when he had praised Frederick for yielding to his wife's rank at a recent dinner party, the elector suddenly broke out and "fell plainly to tell me that though indeed he had done it... yet he could do it no more; that it was against the custom of the whole country; that all the Electors and Princes found it strange... that King's daughters had been matched before in his race, and with other German princes, but still placed under their husbands in public feasts." To which the ambassador replied sternly "that my Lady [Elizabeth] was not to be considered only as the daughter of a King, like the daughters of France, but did carry in her person the possibility of succession to three Crowns."* The issue was eventually resolved by Frederick's mother staying home whenever she and her daughter-in-law were invited anywhere together or by Elizabeth's absenting herself from any social function where she would not be granted preferred standing.

It is testament to the genuine affection between Elizabeth and Frederick that they did not turn against each other as a result of this destructive requirement. If it had been anyone but James who had commanded her to keep up a royal appearance, Elizabeth would have rejected the idea and accepted her husband's rank. The count of Shomberg, in his letters, described her as being unhappy with the controversy she caused and wishing she could be more amenable to local custom. But Elizabeth yearned for her father's love and approval and sought only to please him. In letter after letter home to him she reiterated her devotion, as in this short note, typical of her style and intensity: "Being desirous by all means I can to keep

---

beth's great grief, Lord Harrington died of fever on the journey back to England. Her maid of honor stayed and married the count of Shomberg.

* The three Crowns were the kingdoms of England, Scotland, and Ireland.

my self still in your M. [Majesty's] remembrance, I would not let pass so good an occasion as this bearer returning to England to present my most humble duty and service to your M. by these, beseeching your M. to continue me still in your gracious favor it being the greatest comfort I have to think that your M. doth vouchsafe to love and favor me, which I shall ever strive to deserve, in obeying with all humbleness whatsoever your M. is pleased to command her who shall ever pray to God with all her heart for your happiness and that she may ever be worthy of the title of Your Most humble and obedient daughter and servant, Elizabeth," she implored. It is clear from her writing that Elizabeth took her father's authority as the law.

And yet, despite the obstacle of her rank, Elizabeth's life with Frederick at Heidelberg was a comfortable and quiet one. To the great joy of both England and the Palatinate, on January 2, 1614, less than a year into the marriage, she fulfilled the primary duty of wedlock and delivered a son, whom the couple named Frederick Henry, after both his father and the memory of Elizabeth's cherished brother. This child was followed closely by another son, Karl Ludwig,* on December 24, 1616. The dynasty had been established, the ties between husband and wife were strong, and the gardens, now filled with English musk roses, flourished. Elizabeth found herself pregnant yet again. The days passed gently in prosperous contentment.

And then, in the spring of 1618, an uprising broke out in Bohemia.

INSURRECTION WAS HARDLY AN uncommon event in Bohemia. It would not be misleading to characterize the history of the region as a state of permanent public disorder punctuated by brief periods of

---

* In English, Charles Louis, but Charles was such a popular name in the Stuart family that rather than always have to identify which Charles I am talking about, I have decided to use the German spelling.

sullen wariness. Yet even by this admittedly cynical status quo, the revolt of 1618 stood out.

The genesis of the upheaval had its roots in the reign of the previous Holy Roman emperor, Rudolf II. Like his predecessors, Rudolf was a scion of the Habsburg dynasty. The Habsburgs were the undisputed moguls of Europe. In addition to truculent Bohemia, one family member or another ruled Spain, Portugal, Germany, Austria, Hungary, the Spanish Netherlands (present-day Flanders and Belgium), and large portions of Italy, including Milan, Naples, and Sicily, not to mention the extremely lucrative holdings of Mexico and South America in the New World. There were in fact so many Habsburgs stretched so broadly with so much property to protect that often the only suitable candidate for marriage to a Habsburg was another Habsburg. While these unions did result in more Habsburgs, sadly, they were not always of the finest quality.

Rudolf II, for example, manifested the sort of eccentric personality not commonly associated with functioning, well-adjusted adults. He was a recluse in whom the traits of the quack, the voyeur, and the paranoid were put to combined use in a quest for quasi-scientific advancement, lechery, and the hoarding of questionable art. For more than thirty years, from 1576 until 1608, he was not only emperor but also king of Hungary, Bohemia, and Austria, which technically made him one of the most powerful rulers on earth. However, as he never left his gloomy castle in Prague, his impressive domain seems to have been of doubtful use to him. He was afraid to sire a legitimate heir for fear that his son would grow up and murder him for his empire, so he never married and instead consorted with local prostitutes and lowborn women. What Rudolf was really interested in was turning iron into gold and accumulating a prodigious art collection devoted mostly to etchings depicting satyrs and large, bare-breasted dominatrices. In the handful of religious paintings created expressly for the emperor by his personal court artist, even the Baby Jesus leered.

Rudolf II

If he had contented himself with squandering the imperial treasury on his erotica and the occult, as well as the junk heap of petrified ostrich eggs, stuffed birds, porcelain knickknacks, and other rare curiosities enthusiastically hawked to him by every flimflam dealer in Europe, it's possible that Rudolf would have lived out his days in relative peace and prosperity. But Rudolf, who had been raised by Jesuits, was also a devout and intolerant Catholic who outlawed Protestantism in Austria, Hungary, and Bohemia, even though Lutherans, Calvinists, and other Protestant sects made up a two-thirds majority of the population in those kingdoms. To add insult to injury, he then appropriated the churches formerly owned by the Protestants and gave them to the Catholic minority.

The outcry over this policy was sufficient to attract the attention of the other Habsburgs, who were already concerned about Rudolf's peculiar governing style, and gave them the excuse they needed to get rid of him. A family meeting was hastily called at which it was decided to depose Rudolf in favor of his much more competent younger brother, Matthias. Accordingly, in 1608, Matthias raised an army of some 10,000 men and invaded Bohemia. He no sooner appeared at the border than an additional battalion of 25,000 disgruntled Protestant Bohemians joined him, and together this force marched on Prague and succeeded in capturing Rudolf in his castle. Having no choice, Rudolf ceded the kingdoms of Hungary and Austria to his brother. It took a little more persuasion and another army, but Bohemia and the imperial crown also went to Matthias, in 1610. Rudolf, who in his fury crushed under his heel the pen he had used to sign the abdication decree forced upon him by his brother, died the following year denouncing his subjects. "Prague, unthankful Prague, who hast been so highly elevated by me, now thou spurnest thy benefactor!" he raged. "May the curse and vengeance of God fall on thee and on all Bohemia!"

Matthias, although a Catholic like the rest of the family, understood that he could not govern if the majority of the population was against him, so he was much more tolerant than his brother had been. Under his rule, the religious liberties that had been taken away during Rudolf's reign were restored in a decree known as the Letter of Majesty. By this charter, the Protestants were again allowed to hold official administrative positions and to practice their beliefs openly. Their churches were returned to them and they were even granted the right to erect new ones.

But Matthias was already fifty-three years old and childless when he took over the empire. As he neared his sixtieth birthday, it became clear that, to facilitate an orderly transition after his death, he would have to name a successor while he was still alive. In 1616, after some wrangling, Matthias nominated his cousin Ferdinand of Styria as king of Bohemia and the future Holy Roman emperor.* The

---

* Philip III, king of Spain, the dominant relation within the Habsburg dynasty, pressured Matthias to name one of his sons (the oldest was eleven) as king of Bohemia. Ferdinand, who was thirty-eight and had at least traveled in Germany and visited Prague, was considered the lesser evil by Matthias and his counselors. No one wanted the Spanish to have an excuse to invade the empire.

Bohemians, overwhelmingly Protestant, were appalled. Ferdinand, raised by Jesuits, was yet another intolerant, fervent Catholic—in some ways, even worse than Rudolf. Ferdinand had not only outlawed Protestantism in Styria, he'd expelled anyone who insisted on practicing the religion, and taken the expedient of importing Catholics from the surrounding duchies to fill their place. He used dogs to hunt down those Protestants who violated his order, chasing his victims into Catholic churches, where they were then forced to convert.

But Matthias insisted, and a diet was held in Prague in June 1617 to proclaim Ferdinand king of Bohemia, as a first step toward his eventually succeeding to the empire. Many of the local Protestant noblemen had been advised in advance of this assembly that if they opposed the emperor's candidate, "it would be well for them to have each two heads." Somewhat cowed by this threat, the delegates decided that they would accept Matthias's choice but only if Ferdinand formally agreed to abide by the religious freedoms promised in the Letter of Majesty. Ferdinand, who considered all Protestants heretics and therefore not people with whom it was necessary to be absolutely truthful, had no trouble agreeing to this condition. Still wary but believing they had secured their liberty of conscience, the Protestant delegates dropped their opposition to Ferdinand, and he was crowned king of Bohemia in grand ceremony at the castle of Prague on June 19, 1617.

Of course, no sooner had Ferdinand secured his throne than he reneged on his promise. Ominously, when both he and Matthias departed Prague for Vienna soon after the coronation, three Catholic ministers were left in power as regents. In November, new orders came through appointing judges to investigate whether the charters of the Protestant churches were in order. Within a month, two newly constructed houses of worship had been identified as being in violation of imperial law and the buildings were confiscated. One was given to Catholic parishioners; the other was demolished.

Infuriated, the Protestants sent a list of their grievances to Matthias, and when the emperor refused to concede to their demands, called for a second diet, to be held in Prague in May 1618. Emboldened by their experience with Rudolf, the delegates arrived in a feisty mood. Many of them were armed. The most perspicacious of the three Catholic ministers left in charge by Ferdinand took one look and fled the city. The other two, whose names were Slawata and Martinetz, as well as their secretary, remained to try to instill order. Sometime between nine and ten o'clock in the morning of May 23, a mob of Protestant delegates swarmed into the castle to confront the imperial regents and determine the fate of the kingdom. After a short conference, it was resolved that Slawata and Martinetz had conspired with Ferdinand and Matthias to subvert the Letter of Majesty.

There remained then only the problem of how to deal with the culprits. The assembly decided to abide by a long-standing tradition known as defenestration or, in more accessible language, "Let us follow the ancient custom of Bohemia and hurl them from the window," one of the delegates suggested. This solution was warmly embraced, and immediately out went Martinetz. "Noble lords, another awaits your vengeance," came the next call. "Jesus! Mary!" cried the hapless Slawata. "Let us see whether his Mary will help him," the delegates jeered, then dragged the struggling Slawata to the nearest casement and also threw him out the window, followed by his secretary, for good measure.

It was a frightening eighty-foot drop to the ditch below, but luckily for the three victims, the castle of Prague was not very hygienic. In fact, the whole place was surrounded by a mountainous sewage dump. Cushioned by this dung heap, all three men survived the fall and scrambled to safety. "Behold, his Mary has helped him!" one of the perpetrators of the act, leaning out the window from above, exclaimed in astonishment.

Having signaled their dissatisfaction with their new king's policies

The defenestration of Prague

by this quaint but nonetheless effective method, the Protestant delegates installed an interim government of their own choosing and prepared for war.

FERDINAND WAS IN HUNGARY making the usual empty promises about religious freedom to the Protestant population in order to secure the throne when he got the news that his Bohemian subjects had revolted. Although Matthias counseled concessions to restore peace, Ferdinand insisted instead on fielding an army to bring his unruly kingdom to heel. The problem was, he was a little slow about it, and the Bohemians beat him to it. With help from their Protestant neighbors Silesia and Moravia, they managed to pull together a respectable battalion of some 15,000 men. Ferdinand, by contrast, was able to marshal only about 12,000 soldiers, as the Protestant populations of Austria and Hungary, who were in sympathy with the Bohemians, refused to contribute to the effort.

On November 9, 1618, these two forces met at the tiny village of

Lomnice, in southeast Bohemia, about seventeen miles outside the regional city of Brno. There, in a battle notable for the lack of artillery on either side, the Bohemians thoroughly trounced their opponents. They then followed up on this remarkable achievement by invading Austria with the intent of marching on Vienna, a Catholic city, to try to force Matthias, who as emperor had the authority to overrule Ferdinand, to restore the religious liberties promised under the Letter of Majesty.

This valiant attempt was ultimately suppressed, not by Ferdinand or Matthias, but by the brutality of winter. The Bohemians lost eight thousand men to terrible privations and illness and were forced to retreat. But the political victory was theirs. The initiative sparked a crisis that threatened the empire to its core. The regional Protestant majorities sensed that their moment had come, that the time was finally right to rise up and shake off the tyranny of tradition as represented by the Catholic Habsburgs. Suddenly, Ferdinand faced revolts in Austria and Hungary as well as Silesia and Moravia. He found himself lectured on freedom of religion in his own halls by the very subjects he had duped by false promises into crowning him king. The threat was so great, he was forced to summon a contingent of imperial archers as protection against a personal assault.

And then, on March 20, 1619, just when it seemed the situation could not become more complicated or critical, a broken and ill Matthias breathed his last, leaving vacant the all-important position of Holy Roman emperor.

THE EFFECT OF THESE events on Frederick and Elizabeth, sitting in their charming château in Heidelberg (now the parents of a third child, a daughter, Princess Elizabeth, born November 27, 1618), is well documented. Their warm interest in the affairs of Bohemia was palpable; this was the opportunity they had been waiting for, what their marriage had been arranged to accomplish! Frederick immediately offered aid and encouragement to the Bohemians and sent a private messenger to Prague to evaluate the situation firsthand. He tried to secure money and supplies from Savoy and England on behalf of the kingdom, but disappointingly, James disregarded his entreaties, preferring a negotiated settlement or at least to delay until the question of who would succeed Matthias was settled. Elizabeth and Frederick consoled themselves with the thought that they would not have long to wait. In accordance with imperial tradition and law, a meeting of the seven electors (of whom Frederick was one) responsible for choosing the next Holy Roman emperor would begin in Frankfurt on July 20.

Frederick did not attend the electoral diet personally, but sent proxies with instructions on how to cast the vote for the Palatinate. Instead, Frederick went to stay in the town of Amberg, in his own territory near the border with Bohemia, so he could get news from his agent in Prague as quickly as possible. The Protestant majority in Bohemia had called an emergency session with the intent to depose Ferdinand and substitute a new sovereign in his place. It was critical that this be done quickly, as the king of Bohemia was also one of the seven electors responsible for choosing the new emperor. Of the remaining six, three were confirmed Catholics and three were Protestants.* It was possible, then, that whoever legitimately ruled Bohemia at the time of the election would cast the deciding vote.

Ferdinand, as Matthias's acknowledged successor, made a point of arriving early in Frankfurt to ease the process of his own election. The Bohemians sent a delegation to try to prevent him from casting a vote, arguing that he had violated his vows and should therefore not be considered as representing the kingdom in the election, but Ferdinand managed to have them excluded from the deliberations. These turned out to be extensive, however, and the diet dragged on into late August as the electors squabbled among themselves about whether it would be better to resolve the question of who ruled Bohemia *before* they chose the emperor, or after. Any delay worked in the Protestants' favor, and Frederick, receiving updates on the

---

* The three Catholics were the electors of Mainz, Cologne, and Treves; the Protestants were Frederick (Elector Palatine) and the electors of Saxony and Brandenburg.

ongoing negotiations from his agents in both Frankfurt and Prague, felt himself on the verge of triumph. "I have heard nothing from Bohemia this week, but it seems likely that, instead of gaining a crown at Frankfurt, Ferdinand may chance to lose two," he observed to Elizabeth from his perch in Amberg on August 13, 1619. "God grant him that grace! What a happy prince is he, to be hated by everybody."

But Frederick had not reckoned with the persuasive pull of the status quo. Toward the end of August, Ferdinand, tired of waiting, made the usual sham concessions, and the other Protestant electors discovered that they did not, after all, wish to take on the all-powerful Habsburgs at this time and perhaps risk armed intervention from Spain. On August 28, ballots were cast, and all but the envoys for the Palatinate voted for Ferdinand (including, of course, Ferdinand, who as king of Bohemia was allowed to vote for himself). In the second round, fearing reprisals against their master if he should remain the one holdout, even Frederick's agents ignored their orders and cast their ballot in favor of the obvious victor.

And then came word that two days earlier, on August 26, 1619, the Bohemian aristocracy, by an overwhelming ballot of 110 to 3, supplemented by a unanimous vote by the middle-class burghers, had deposed Ferdinand of Styria and elected Frederick V, Elector Palatine, as king of Bohemia in his place.

ALTHOUGH THIS FLATTERING EXPRESSION of trust was almost certainly the outcome he'd hoped for, Frederick did not rush to accept the throne offered to him. Faced suddenly with the reality of so important and dangerous a commitment—for the Elector Palatine was well aware that Ferdinand would contest the legality of this referendum and would defend his right to the sovereignty of Bohemia by arms, if necessary—Frederick, who had only just turned twenty-three, tried to act in a conscientious and deliberate manner. He sought the counsel of the other Protestant barons. He asked for specific commitments from allies and called a meeting of the

Defensive Union for September. And, most important, as English support was deemed essential to the undertaking, he immediately apprised his father-in-law of the situation and asked James for his opinion as to whether the offer should be accepted.

Actually, the first notification came from Elizabeth, who had no doubt at all what decision her husband should make, and what they had been led to believe England would do for them. If her brother Henry were still alive, she knew he would have been at her front gate at the head of an army, ready to escort her and Frederick to Bohemia before she had time to order a suitable coronation gown.* She understood that James was not Henry, that he was older and more cautious, but she was sure that ultimately he would not fail them because he was her father and he loved her and he had already demonstrated that he wanted this. Of these facts she was certain, just as she was certain that it was James who had set them on this path in the first place, who had married her to this man, so inferior to her in station, in the expectation that Frederick would rise to her level by achieving the very throne he had now been offered. This had been the plan all along; it was merely a matter of having the courage to see it through. She was determined that she and Frederick do their parts.

Elizabeth had been absent from England for six years, but she had prepared for this day by keeping herself well informed of the nuances of her father's court. Consequently, she sent her letter not directly to James—Frederick would do that—but by special messenger to George Villiers, the seductively handsome duke of Buckingham who was the king's reigning favorite and the man most likely to have His Majesty's ear and sympathy.† "This worthy bearer will inform

---

* This would not be the only time that the loss of Henry due to premature death would have a significant impact on English and European history.

† When Elizabeth's mother, Queen Anne, had died six months previously, on March 2, 1619, without leaving a written will, James had taken the opportunity to bestow many of her finest jewels, as well as her primary residence and other holdings, on Buckingham. The father did not set aside a single gem or other property of his wife's, even as a token of remembrance, for his daughter, although Elizabeth grieved deeply at the loss of her mother. The rest of Anne's estate went to Charles, who was present at her deathbed and was her vocal heir.

you of a business that concerns his master [Frederick] very much; the Bohemians being desirous to choose him for their King, which he will not resolve of till he know his Majesty's opinion in it," she wrote from Heidelberg on September 1. "The King hath now a good occasion to manifest to the world the love he hath ever professed to the Prince here," she reminded Buckingham. "I earnestly entreat you to use your best means in persuading his Majesty to show himself now, in his helping of the Prince here, a true loving father to us both."

Sentiment in England overwhelmingly favored seizing this opportunity to extend Protestant influence abroad. "It is much debated here . . . whether it be fit the Prince Palatine should accept the crown or not; and I find it by most concluded that, since the revolutions of the world will in all likelihood . . . forcibly carry us out of this peaceable time, it is better to begin the change with advantage," reported one of James's ministers to a compatriot at The Hague. "If the Bohemians be suffered to be oppressed, the consequence of their loss will fall upon their neighbors, whose defense [a reference to England's obligations under the treaty James had signed with the German Protestants] is like to cost as much blood and with much less fruit than this acquisition."

"God forbid he [Frederick] should refuse it, being the apparent way His Providence hath opened to the ruin of the Papacy," exhorted another member of the English nobility to the same ambassador. "I hope therefore that his Majesty will assist in this great work . . . For my part most willingly I here offer both life and fortunes to serve his Majesty in this or any way I may be of use."

Frederick, meanwhile, was in Rothenburg, about 150 miles east of Heidelberg, addressing the Princes of the Union, his fellow Protestant members of the German defensive league. He knew that he could not even think of accepting the Bohemians' offer without the full support of this group. Ferdinand was vindictive enough to retaliate against the Elector Palatine for his presumption by attempting to annex his ancestral properties. Frederick needed to ensure that his

Protestant neighbors would defend both the Upper and Lower Palatinates against any imperial incursions while he was away in Prague. As Frederick's request was clearly covered by the terms of the Defensive Union, the signers all agreed to abide by their obligations and protect his territory in his absence. They naturally expected England, also a participant in this agreement, to honor the terms as well.

Ironically, among the many and varied parties involved in these events, including the members of his own Privy Council, James alone believed he had not encouraged his daughter and son-in-law's ambitions or committed himself to defending their property in any way. Of course, he had *said* he expected that Frederick would one day be king of Bohemia, and he had signed the treaty obliging him to send money and troops in specific amounts to Germany in case of a Catholic attack, but that didn't mean he thought he'd ever have to really do it! He was extremely irritated to be forced by Elizabeth and her husband to act on what he had always considered to be the usual vague promises. James had very high hopes that his one remaining son, Charles, now nearly nineteen years old and of marriageable age, might be wedded to the king of Spain's daughter, and of course Philip III was unlikely to be cajoled into an alliance with a suitor whose family was actively engaged in undermining Habsburg rule in Bohemia. The very first thing James did was dash off an obsequious note to Spain swearing that he'd had absolutely nothing to do with his son-in-law's enterprise and offering to mediate. After that, he did his best to stall and went out hunting in the hopes that it would all just go away.

But time had run out. The Bohemians, anxious to settle the matter, sent an urgent embassy to Frederick, threatening to withdraw the offer if he did not give an immediate answer. Around the third week of September, still having heard nothing from James and fearing to lose so great an opportunity, Frederick agreed to become king of Bohemia and sent a messenger to England informing the court of his decision.

The envoy arrived in London in the middle of a council meeting, where the news of Frederick's acceptance was greeted with great excitement by the ministers of James's government. The Spanish ambassador was quick to inform Madrid of the general approbation and celebratory atmosphere. "The greater number of the councilors... were inclined to persuade the King that he was under an obligation to help and succor his son-in-law on such an occasion; and they wished for an illumination [fireworks] and other demonstrations of joy, in order that the news of the Palatine's becoming a King might obtain the more credence, and that they might in this way entangle the King the more," he wrote worriedly to Philip III on September 27, 1619. But the analysis of the Venetian ambassador, who did not fail to note James's obvious reluctance to commit himself to the undertaking, was more astute. "The hope of making his daughter a Queen, and of giving his son-in-law two votes in the election of the next Emperor, the obligation under which he acknowledges himself to be from nearness of blood, and as the head of the Princes of the Union, incite him to a generous resolution," the envoy observed to the doge. "On the other hand, the desire of living without trouble, his disinclination to incur expense for the sake of others, and especially devotion to the friendship of Spain, are enough to keep him amused," the Venetian predicted.

But the newly elected king and queen of Bohemia, unaware of the character of the man in whom they and all of Protestant Germany had placed their trust, and perhaps not giving proper consideration to the obstacles that might be involved in governing a realm that resolved its differences by throwing the opposition out the window, forged ahead. On the very day that the diplomats from Spain and Venice informed their governments of developments in England, Frederick, along with a heavily pregnant Elizabeth, left their two youngest children, Karl Ludwig and Elizabeth, in Heidelberg with his mother (who had counseled strongly against the move), packed up their eldest son, Frederick Henry, and 135 cartloads of luggage, and set off for Prague.

4

Queen of Bohemia

ELIZABETH AND FREDERICK LEFT HEIDELBERG in the company of an extensive entourage designed to signal the seriousness of their commitment to Bohemia politically, ceremonially, and, most important, militarily. "The Prince and Princess Palatine are going with as much speed as such a train can admit," reported an ambassador from England, who had been sent specifically by James to appraise the situation. "For they have a fair representation of court, and a fair representation of an army together (her guard being of 800 horse)... I daresay he goes...truly with such a zeal in weighing the cause, such a magnanimity in pursuing it, and such a providence for the safety of the country which he leaves, as may well become a person of that rank to which God had brought him," the envoy observed with frank admiration. Along the way, the couple picked up a further escort of some three thousand foot soldiers and an additional thousand horsemen levied from Frederick's possessions in the Upper Palatinate, another show of strength designed to impress not only their new subjects in Bohemia but their imperial opponents as well. Both Frederick and Elizabeth were well aware that their every move was under scrutiny by Ferdinand and the other European powers and that it was necessary to behave in a way that instilled confidence in their allies and uncertainty in their enemies, although with so much at stake, it was unfortunately sometimes very difficult to tell who was who.

By the middle of October, they had arrived at the outskirts of Bohemia, where an official delegation, representing all of the most distinguished noblemen of the realm, waited to greet them. A short ceremony ensued in which the Bohemians formally offered Frederick the crown, and he accepted, and pledged to abide by the all-important Letter of Majesty. Then, one by one, his new subjects went down on one knee and paid homage first to their new king, and then to his queen.

Elizabeth was aware that her presence by Frederick's side was of enormous assistance to her husband, and this was one of the reasons she had insisted on accompanying him. Afraid for her safety and that of the child she was carrying, he had at first suggested she stay home,

Frederick V in his coronation robe

but she had rejected the idea absolutely, and he now reaped the benefits of her decision. The Bohemian delegation, as well as the crowds of ordinary citizens who thronged the streets of Prague eager for a view of their new sovereigns, adored Elizabeth. Young, beautiful, and glamorous, she provided exactly the diversion the kingdom needed from its troubles. "The queen's free and gracious demeanor doth win as much love as was lost by the Austrian [Ferdinand]," declared an eyewitness to these events. Even better, the fact that she was seven months pregnant and had elected to have her baby in her new realm bespoke a tremendous trust in her husband and his allies, particularly England. For what father would allow so ethereal a creature, his only daughter, in her vulnerable state, to enter into so dangerous an environment if he were not determined to protect her?

The procession made its way to the great castle of Prague, long the majestic residence of the Habsburgs, now home to the newly elected king and queen. A tour of the château's numerous apartments was conducted with pride by a local nobleman the very next day. Rudolf's extensive collection of art and curiosities, untouched since his death, was a natural focus of interest. "Their Majesties are very cheerful," this courtier reported in a letter to the English ambassador stationed in Holland. "I showed them the day before yesterday the chamber of rarities of the emperor. The queen was much pleased with them, and said to me smiling, 'Really, Ferdinand has left us a great number of fine things.'" To which her tour guide, charmed to be treated as a familiar by royalty, chivalrously assured her that "they were not his [Ferdinand's] at all."

The coronations—first Frederick's on October 25th, followed by Elizabeth's on the 28th—were conducted with solemnity and splendor. Where traditionally an archbishop would have officiated at the ceremony of a Habsburg, Frederick, a Calvinist, received his crown and scepter from the aged hand of the senior member of the Protestant ministry, a Moses-like figure whose long white beard and stern appearance were considered testament to his moral authority. The same elderly minister was employed to inaugurate the queen, whose coronation ceremony was a replica of her husband's except that the guests and witnesses were the highborn women of the kingdom rather than the men.

For the occasion, Elizabeth wore a coronation robe and gown magnificently adorned with pearls, with matching pearl earrings and a similarly ornamented comb to pin up her hair. She sat on a throne of velvet; her crown was gold, as was her scepter; a Te Deum was chanted, the bells of the city were rung, and the cannons fired. It was all as legitimately regal as if it had been conducted at Westminster, and Elizabeth's satisfaction was obvious. She was, after all, only twenty-three years old and may perhaps be forgiven for wearing her crown a little longer than was strictly necessary. "The queen appeared very joyous in going to the church and in the street leading from the palace, having the crown on her head, as she was also at table, and at the royal banquet in the great chamber of the palace; where, instead of the great lords, the great ladies filled the offices worthily, and in such fine order, that never before had anything more fine or magnificent been seen," enthused a newsletter describing this event.

Even better, the diadem had no sooner settled on Elizabeth's brow than news arrived of a promising Protestant offensive against the emperor. The kingdom of Hungary, taking its cue from Bohemia, had *also* deposed Ferdinand, selecting instead a Transylvanian prince by the name of Bethlen Gabor. Like Frederick, Bethlen Gabor had taken up the challenge, but this time Ferdinand, who'd had enough of his subjects giving away his thrones, sent troops to discourage his opponent from accepting the crown. Unfortunately for the emperor, he had chosen the wrong man to confront. Bethlen Gabor turned out to be a violent and experienced warrior who went to claim his realm at the head of a fearsome force of cavalry. "Bethlen Gabor hath made a great progress in Hungary, having cut in pieces 1000 foot and 500 horse which were sent by the count of Bucquoy [the general in charge of Ferdinand's army]," reported the English ambassador at The Hague. The diplomat further noted that

Bethlen Gabor had seized Pressburg, the capital, "and possessed himself of the crown of Hungary: which whether he will put upon his own head, or make other use of it...is very doubtful...some saying that he will make presentation thereof to the new King of Bohemia."

Bethlen Gabor's success was greeted with great excitement by Frederick's government, particularly when the Transylvanian let it be known that he wished to form an alliance with Bohemia against the emperor. Suddenly, with the Protestants of Hungary, Silesia, Moravia, Germany, Holland, the Netherlands, and England all allied against him, it was Ferdinand, and not Frederick, who seemed vulnerable. With pride, Elizabeth could assure herself that the risks she and her husband had taken in accepting the Bohemian throne had been entirely justified. Frederick was now not only the established ruler of a kingdom but also the acknowledged leader of a united Protestant movement against the Habsburgs. She and her husband were finally of equal rank, so there were no more uncomfortable episodes regarding precedence when they went out in society. More important, their children's standing had improved. When, on November 26, 1619, Elizabeth was delivered of a healthy son, whom the couple named Rupert, the bells in Prague rang out with joy at the birth of a royal prince.

BUT THE DANGER OF success is that it hardens opposition and provokes counterattacks. Just how close Frederick, Elizabeth, and their Protestant allies were to subverting the empire may be measured by the seriousness with which Ferdinand, and indeed the entire Habsburg dynasty, took the threat. And the resources that this family could call upon, especially when they were united, were formidable.

After the defeat of the imperial forces by Bethlen Gabor, Ferdinand took the precaution of appealing to his cousin Archduke Albert, who ruled the Spanish Netherlands (on the northern border of France). Albert in turn wrote to his brother-in-law, the king of

Spain, asking for help. Philip III's response was a model of what can be achieved by a veteran sovereign acting with decision. "By your Highness's letter of the 28th of last month," he wrote briskly on November 5, 1619, "I have received information of the bad state of affairs in Bohemia...and, considering how important it is that there should be no failure in the application of a remedy...I have resolved and ordered that seven thousand infantry...are to start at once for Alsace...and until the arrival of the provision of money which will be needed to support the troops which will from henceforward be maintained in Bohemia on my account...I have directed that 200,000 ducats...shall be immediately sent." On January 2, 1620, Philip again contacted the archduke. "I have resolved and given orders that...two thousand other soldiers of the Spanish infantry who are present in Naples, and four thousand Neapolitans who are also there, may be sent to you, as well as the regiment of Lombards... all of them being veteran and serviceable troops...Arrangements have been made to provide 1,000,000 ducats...besides the 130,000 ducats of ordinary supply for that army...that there may not be a moment lost in getting together the money and men, and in setting to work in the Spring." Then, just to make sure his brother-in-law understood that he would countenance no excuses and that no expense was to be spared, on February 3, 1620, the king of Spain again took pen to paper. "I have wished here apart to charge your Highness seriously, as I now do, to direct that there may be much haste in carrying out the invasion of the Palatinate. Everything that is possible will be done here for the provision of money for this object in time, so that there will be no failure."

Nor was there any secrecy surrounding the movements of these troops or the magnitude of the funds that had been allocated for their maintenance. As early as November 28, 1619, an English ambassador wrote to the principal member of James's government that "this last week's letters out of Germany...all of them, as well as those out of Italy and other parts, mention the sedulous care there is of raising men by the Catholic king and Catholic league against the next Spring." Another English envoy in Germany warned the same minister on January 20, 1620, "In our neighboring provinces... there are levies made daily both of horse and foot...to succor the Emperor and invade the Inferior [Lower] Palatinate." And, finally, from the English ambassador in Turin came the information on March 4 that "this last week...he [the Duke of Savoy] received order from the King of Spain to require...passage through his State for two regiments of Napolitans and one of Lombards, which the said King did pretend to send into Burgundy, and from thence to Flanders." The diplomat went on to report that this was so patently a ploy, and that the soldiers were so clearly intended to be used against Bohemia, that the duke of Savoy had requested that the king of England be made aware of this development.

In vain did the members of James's own government, overwhelmingly in favor of defending Frederick and Elizabeth, urge the need for speed in responding to this ominous massing of Catholic forces. "For commonly he that is first in the field, hath the advantage of that year; and the first year, though the quarrel may last longer, will in all reasonable conjecture either settle the crown forever on the new king's [Frederick's] head, or bring that kingdom, as a kingdom of conquest, into perpetual subjection under the house of Austria," admonished the English representative stationed at The Hague. "All of his Majesty's ministers except three or four, as I have already told you... [and] the whole nation takes the same side [Frederick's], and all the kingdom declares its impatience of this prolonged irresolution," the Venetian ambassador reiterated in a report to the doge from London on January 30, 1620.

But James stubbornly refused to commit himself to his son-in-law's defense. Intimidated by Spain, whose friendship he craved, and vexed at Frederick and Elizabeth for forcing him to depart from his comfortable position of detached neutrality, he took a scholar's refuge in disputation and minutiae. He demanded detailed evidence, supplemented by reams of written depositions from the various participants, that the election in Bohemia had been legitimate and not the work of a single faction. He parsed the clauses of the defensive treaty he had signed with the Princes of the Union to prove that he was not, after all, obligated to honor the terms that he himself had provided. He refused to refer to Frederick publicly as a king or to allow anyone else in England to do so. And he deliberately ignored the evidence of Spanish armament, observing to the Dutch ambassador as late as January 24, 1620, "his belief that, now that his son-in-law...was, as he understood, tolerably well established, he could not be in any need or danger for a year to come."

So concerned was James with projecting an image of strict impartiality so that Philip III would not think that he had anything to do with his daughter and son-in-law's advancement that he even declined to mark the birth of Rupert, his latest grandchild, by the ringing of church bells, a departure from tradition that caused the prince of Orange, who *had* agreed to honor his defensive commitments, to despair aloud that "he is a strange fellow that will neither fight for his children nor pray for them!"★

But of course James wasn't being impartial or statesmanlike or above the fray. He was taking a side — the imperial side — and everybody knew it. "If the cause had been good, the King...would have declared himself before now," the duke of Guise stated flatly, and France went to the empire. The duke of Savoy "doth still profess that if his Majesty will command him to stop the passage [of Spanish troops], he hath both the means and the will to do it," the English ambassador at Turin reported as late as March 4, 1620. "But because that cannot be done but by violence...before he do embark himself, he would gladly be assured of protection against the Spaniards." When no such promise was forthcoming, Savoy too, however reluctantly, sided with Ferdinand. In the absence of leadership or any

---

★ James's excuse for this behavior was "that his subjects were as dear to him as his children, and therefore he would not embroil them in an unjust or needless quarrel." But surely the time to have expressed this sentiment would have been *before* he signed the German defensive treaty. James had been happy enough to take on the role of the dominant Protestant power and leader of the Princes of the Union during peacetime.

encouragement whatsoever from England and faced with the certainty of an imperial onslaught, Protestant Germany also reneged on its agreement with Bohemia, especially as it was well known that Spain intended not simply to oust Frederick from Prague but also to annex his home territory of the Palatinate as a warning to others of the consequences of defying the Habsburgs. No one wanted to give Ferdinand an excuse to turn his army loose on one of *their* duchies.

It didn't have to be this bad. There were ways of keeping the enemy guessing, so that Frederick did not lose so many allies so quickly, or at least of providing funds toward the war effort. But even when it came to finance, James managed to sabotage his son-in-law's standing. When Frederick applied for a loan of £100,000 from the City of London, James refused to assist him. At this, even Bethlen Gabor, understanding that it took money to wage battle, gave up and made a side deal with Ferdinand. The king of England could not have been more destructive to Elizabeth and her husband, or to the cause of Protestantism in Europe in general, if he had been in the pay of Philip III. Indeed, the Spanish ambassador was so emboldened that, to the great bitterness of the members of the English government, he openly canvassed James's Catholic subjects for donations to support the imperial cause.

Rarely in history has an experienced ruler of mature years deliberately allowed himself to be manipulated so obviously by a foreign power.* Philip III knew that he had only to question England's neutrality to send James scurrying to refute the charge. The king of Spain could blithely deny that he was levying troops to invade Bohemia and the Palatinate, and his English counterpart would take him at his word and continue his round of hunting, refusing to credit the communiqués of his own agents. With disgust, the Privy Council realized that the Spanish ambassador could say anything,

---

* Woodrow Wilson's similarly studious insistence on neutrality and naive handling of the Germans in World War I comes to mind.

no matter how ridiculous, and the king would swallow it, as was witnessed in September 1620 when the news arrived that the Palatinate had been invaded by an imperial army led by a general named Spinola. The Spanish ambassador, called in and confronted with the charge of breach of promise, responded fatuously that "he was glad of it, and wished Spinola had all the rest, that his Majesty might see his power in having it released and restored!"★

ALL THROUGH THE WINTER and into the spring and summer of 1620, aware that Ferdinand and Philip III were at work assembling an army with which to take back Bohemia, Frederick and Elizabeth did what they could to prepare for an attack. Frederick made a progression throughout the realm and into Silesia and Moravia to recruit soldiers and raise funds. He secured a commitment from Bethlen Gabor (who, uncertain which side would ultimately prevail, was hedging his bets) to send a troop of Hungarian cavalry to supplement the Bohemian army. At a meeting of the diet in Prague in April, Frederick gave the prince of Anhalt, the general in charge of the Bohemian forces, 200,000 florins out of his own pocket to pay the soldiers' wages. As a result of these efforts, when the general left the capital on May 15, 1620, he had an impressive army of 30,000 men under his command with which to defend the kingdom.

For her part, Elizabeth sent a flood of letters to England pleading for aid, if not for Bohemia, then at least for her husband's home territory of the Palatinate, which had been left in the care of her mother-in-law. "My only dear brother," she wrote to Charles in a missive that demonstrated her understanding of the deteriorating diplomatic and military situation she and her husband faced, "I...beseech you earnestly to move his Majesty [James] that now he would assist us...for, to speak freely to you, his slackness...doth make the Princes of the Union slack too, who do nothing with their

---

★ In other words, the Spanish were not invading for their own conquest but only so they would have the pleasure of giving it all back to James.

army; the King hath ever said that he would not suffer the Palatinate to be taken; it was never in hazard but now...I doubt not but you will do it, since you have hitherto solicited his Majesty for us... which I beseech you to continue to her that is ever...your most affectionate sister." But cautious Charles was no Henry. Although he supported his sister and brother-in-law and even contributed his own funds to their defense, he was unwilling to cross James.

This was all very worrying, of course, but Frederick and Elizabeth were both still in their early twenties, with the natural optimism that accompanies youth, and neither had any experience of war. The Bohemian army had already demonstrated its ferocity by trouncing Ferdinand's troops the previous year, when they had far fewer regiments at their disposal. And then again, everything felt so *normal* in Prague. Ambassadors and friends came and went; the royal couple picnicked in the summer with Frederick's mother, who arrived for a short visit to see her new grandchild. There were the usual rounds of hunting and dinners. Elizabeth found herself pregnant again. Frederick rather scandalized his subjects by his habit of bathing naked on hot days, and Elizabeth's fashionable gowns were considered to show a little too much décolletage, but these were minor irritants. The greatest controversy to erupt in the first nine months of the year was when Frederick ordered the religious statues that adorned the main bridge in Prague destroyed as idolatrous, but he quickly reversed his decision when he saw the outcry this caused among the citizenry. In truth, Frederick and Elizabeth were much more concerned about Frederick's home territory of the Palatinate than they were for themselves. *They* had an army of 30,000 war-hardened troops standing between them and the empire, more than enough to handle anything Ferdinand could throw at them. The Palatinate, which they had left to the good offices and army of the Princes of the Union, did not.

Frederick's mother knew better. On August 17, 1620, as the Spanish soldiers mustered by Philip III descended on the Lower Palatinate, she sent an urgent letter to James. "My Lord," she wrote, "seeing the necessity to which my children, who are also those of your Majesty, are reduced...it is impossible that this should not touch your Majesty's heart, mine being so smitten with grief...I supplicate you most humbly to look at the peril in which they are, and to hasten a signal aid, by money or some diversion; otherwise it will be impossible for us to...preserve your dear children from the bloody hand of our enemies." And as if this were not enough to send a chill through any parent's soul, she continued forcefully: "Your Majesty will also know in what pain is the queen your daughter, and that she is about to be entirely surrounded with enemies; indeed the state in which I lately left her [a reference to Elizabeth's pregnancy] makes me doubly pity her."

It had begun.

THE IMPERIAL ATTACK PLAN was straightforward. Ferdinand had done everything he could in advance of the actual invasion to isolate Bohemia and the Palatinate and limit the scope of the war. Toward that end, he had offered incentives to Frederick's German allies to switch sides, or at least remain neutral during the conflict. To the Protestant electors and the Princes of the Union, he promised that none of their lands would be touched by imperial forces, nor would their past support for Frederick be held against them if they remained loyal to the empire. So when the 24,000 Spanish troops under General Spinola destined for the Lower Palatinate began pouring into Germany in August, the army Frederick had solicited to protect his homeland before he left for Bohemia never materialized. Similarly, Ferdinand cleverly offered Frederick's neighbor, the duke of Bavaria, the Palatinate itself, including the coveted title of elector and its concomitant imperial voting rights, as a reward if he would command the Catholic forces allied against Bohemia. This proposition turned out to be too tempting to resist, so the duke of Bavaria set out for Prague with a force of 22,000 men, intent on joining with the imperial army under General Buquoi, which was already marching through Austria on its way to Bohemia.* He sent a further 7,000 soldiers to the elector of Saxony, who had also taken the imperial side against Frederick, to be used in an attack from the north.

The duke of Bavaria's army crossed into Bohemia at Linz, on the border with Austria, on September 8. They met so little resistance that they caught up to Buquoi's forces by the 20th and together the two generals converged on Budweis, about 150 miles south of Prague. The imperial soldiers, resolved on looting and murder, were brutally merciless to the civilians who stood in their path. Even their commanding general was appalled. "I cannot conceal from your Imperial Majesty that, notwithstanding my many well-intended admonitions, this army has spread along the line of its march robbery, plundering, fire, and the indiscriminate slaughter even of innocent Catholics of both sexes, attended with demands of ransoms from the loyal, seductions of matrons and maidens, and the most ruthless plundering of churches and monasteries," the duke of Bavaria wrote grimly to Ferdinand. "The common people are ruined, and driven to the extreme of desperation, and will not in many years be able to recover themselves." So destructive were the invaders, and so intent on stealing everything they could lay their hands on, even to stripping the houses of wood, that an eyewitness described the villages left in their wake as so empty that they looked as though they had been "swept with a broom."

The progress of the enemy troops was carefully monitored in Prague, and by the second week of September the situation was

---

* There is no reliable data on the size of Buquoi's force, as it had been skirmishing in the field during the summer and its numbers were probably diminished and then refilled with recruits over that time. However, Buquoi was upset that he had not been named supreme commander and had wanted the duke of Bavaria's army to go in a different direction in order to split the Bohemian forces, believing that he could then easily defeat his half. If true, this means he must have had at least 20,000 soldiers under his command, which in turn meant that, once Buquoi and the duke of Bavaria met up, Frederick's army was looking at a combined imperial opposition force of over 40,000 men. And this was without the regiments advancing under the leadership of the elector of Saxony.

regarded as sufficiently threatening that Elizabeth's guard recommended that the queen retire from the capital and seek the safety of friendly territory. This Elizabeth adamantly refused to do. Frederick was preparing to join the army and she knew that if she abandoned Prague, it would be taken as a sign of impending defeat; it was her task to stay behind and keep up the morale of the citizenry. The couple did, however, manage to smuggle six-year-old Frederick Henry out of the country and all the way to Holland, one of the few principalities that had remained resolutely loyal to their cause. This journey was undertaken with the utmost stealth, as it meant traveling through enemy lines where, if the child's identity were known, he would surely be apprehended and held for ransom—or worse. Frederick and Elizabeth were extremely fortunate that he got away safely. At almost the same time, Frederick's aging mother, faced with the prospect of invasion by the Spanish soldiers under the command of General Spinola, gathered up three-year-old Karl Ludwig and one-year-old Elizabeth and fled south to Stuttgart, to the duke of Württemberg, the only member of the former Princes of the Union willing to offer her protection.*

But all was not completely lost. The Bohemian army still stood between the emperor and Prague. A decisive victory against Ferdinand's forces could yet turn the momentum of the war in Frederick and Elizabeth's favor, and all the allies they had lost would come rushing back. When at the end of September, with everything at stake, Frederick mounted his horse, kissed his wife good-bye, and left to join his troops in the field, Elizabeth, despite an acute understanding of their isolation, refused to give in to despair. "Spinola is still in the Low Palatinate, fortifying those places he hath taken, and the Union looks on and doth nothing," she reported in a letter to England. "The king is gone to the army...you see we have enough to do, but I hope still well, in spite of all," she ended courageously.

---

* The duke of Württemberg also levied a small force from within his duchy and conducted it personally to Bohemia to aid Frederick. He would later pay dearly for this demonstration of loyalty.

★   ★   ★

A MILITARY UNIT OF 30,000 well-maintained seasoned soldiers fighting to preserve their homeland and equipped with artillery was indeed a formidable force in the seventeenth century. Unfortunately for Frederick, this was not the condition in which he found his army.

He caught up with them at Rakovnik, about thirty-five miles southwest of Prague, hunkered down behind the medieval walls of the citadel. Having spent the summer hunting and skinny-dipping with his wife and friends, and not with his troops in the field, he must have been somewhat shocked to discover the quality of the divisions upon which he had been relying for his defense. On the day he arrived, his army—what was left of it, at any rate—was in full mutiny. It was difficult to blame them; they had not been paid for months. The 200,000 florins that Frederick had advanced out of his own funds in May had never arrived, having been stolen by highwaymen, who operated with impunity on the roads. His soldiers had been forced to plunder the stores of their own countrymen in order to eat, and even that was insufficient. Between starvation, illness, desertion, and skirmishes with Buquoi's troops over the summer, Frederick had already lost somewhere between 8,000 and 10,000 men (although these numbers were mercifully supplemented by the arrival of 8,000 Hungarian horsemen sent by Bethlen Gabor). Those who remained were refusing to fight at all unless their wages were paid.

This revolt was quelled by assurances that the promised money was on the way, a necessary imperative, as the enemy, which had met no resistance on its drive toward Prague and had consequently made excellent time, had discovered the Bohemian position and was eager to give battle. Frederick's troops were rather less enthusiastic, and in one of the first forays, he was treated to the sight of a regiment of 250 of Bethlen Gabor's much-heralded dragoons abandoning their posts in panic at an energetic charge conducted by eighteen imperial cavalrymen. Frederick immediately wrote home to his wife, who was nearing her seventh month of pregnancy, and told her to get out of Prague.

But Elizabeth wouldn't leave. She was expecting a party of English ambassadors sent by her father to negotiate for peace to pass through Prague on their way to see Ferdinand. She was determined to stay and convince the diplomats, and by extension England, to enter the war on her husband's behalf.

Frederick did not insist, because after the initial clash, the situation stabilized (as his general, the prince of Anhalt, who *was* experienced and knew that the medieval fortress of Rakovnik that he had chosen to occupy was very difficult to assail, had assured him it would). Despite their numerical superiority, the imperial troops under Buquoi and the duke of Bavaria were unable to dislodge the Bohemian army. The Hungarian cavalry even redeemed themselves and scored a decisive victory over a squadron of Buquoi's men, forcing them to retreat. A stalemate of sorts went on all through the month of October, as the imperial army, which *did* have the money to feed its soldiers, was obliged to call for new supplies, and Frederick began to take heart.

But once the carts bearing the requested provisions had arrived, and their troops had rested, the imperial generals adopted a new strategy. They might not be able to capture the fortress of Rakovnik quickly, it was true, but with the Bohemian army ensconced inside, the capital itself lay open to them, and this was of far more value as a strategic target. Accordingly, Buquoi and the duke of Bavaria broke camp on November 5 and headed toward Prague.

Again, the prince of Anhalt reacted with an alacrity that demonstrated that he had prepared for this contingency. No sooner were the enemy soldiers observed to have departed than he ordered his army to pack up and speed toward the unprotected capital. He was far more familiar with the roads and terrain than his imperial counterparts, and he knew exactly where he wanted to go to set up the defense of the city. It was to White Mountain, three miles from Prague, where he could command the high ground.

He arrived on the afternoon of Saturday, November 7, 1620, just ahead of his adversaries, in time to deploy his few cannons and position his men. The imperial soldiers, whose progress had paralleled the Bohemians' course, could occasionally be glimpsed through the trees. As it had been a long march, the general was satisfied that no battle was imminent. Darkness was falling and the imperial troops would need rest. There might not even be a battle once the sun rose and Buquoi and the duke of Bavaria had a chance to evaluate the advantage the Bohemians held in having secured the high ground. The prince of Anhalt encouraged Frederick, who had accompanied his troops, to leave camp and ride on into the city itself, in order to beg for much-needed new funds for his soldiers from the diet and the visiting English embassy staying with Elizabeth. Frederick, who had learned to trust his commanding officer, left in high spirits. "His Majesty coming to court on the Saturday, at 3 of the clock, with a countenance of glee, told his queen that the enemy was come within two Dutch miles of the city, which is eight English, but his army of 28,000 was betwixt them and it. That night we slept securely, as free from doubt as we supposed ourselves quit from danger," affirmed one of the English ambassadors staying at the royal castle in Prague.

But the prince of Anhalt had underestimated the determination of the imperial generals. Although the duke of Bavaria's force had sustained significant losses in October due to fighting and disease and now numbered only about 12,000 men, and Buquoi's troops too were down to an estimated 15,000 soldiers, leaving the imperial and Bohemian armies of roughly equal strength, the invaders were healthier and better fed than their Bohemian counterparts. Also, while it was true that the prince of Anhalt held the high ground, the emperor's forces had managed to surround the mountain—actually, it was more of a hill—so they were not limited to a frontal assault but could attack their opponents from either side, or both if necessary.

And that is exactly what they did. At noon on Sunday, the imperial cavalry charged from the left while its infantry stormed from the right. The prince of Anhalt's son managed to beat back the enemy horsemen, and the Bohemian cannons scattered the first wave of foot soldiers. But when this was not enough to discourage their adversaries—when both cavalry and infantry regrouped and forged ahead for a second thrust—the Hungarian dragoons stationed at the bottom of the hill, remembering that they still had not been paid, decided that they were not, after all, willing to lay down their lives for the bankrupt king of Bohemia, and fled. Their departure caused a general panic among the remaining troops, who fell back before the second onslaught. In a matter of minutes, the Bohemians had lost their small store of artillery. Despite the prince of Anhalt's desperate commands to hold their posts and strike back, his divisions scattered in all directions. The battle was over in less than an hour—and, with it, the war.

FREDERICK HAD HAD A busy Sunday morning. He had been in conference for several hours with the English ambassadors, arguing as forcefully as he could for aid from his father-in-law. Just before noon he received a summons from the prince of Anhalt, alerting him that a battle was imminent after all and requesting his presence to help inspire the troops. But lunch was just about to be served and it seemed rude not to dine with his guests, so he stayed to eat. Afterward, he put on his uniform, mounted his horse, and set out for White Mountain.

He had barely made it out of his own front gate when he met the soldiers from his army escaping pell-mell into the city, apparently followed in close pursuit by the enemy. Astonished, he learned that he had lost his crown at White Mountain sometime between the apéritif and the fish course. There was nothing to do but turn around and follow the example of his fleeing army. The castle was evacuated, the used luncheon dishes still on the table. Elizabeth, seven months pregnant, hurried into a carriage, and with Frederick on horseback beside her they retreated across the river. They left so quickly they almost forgot the baby, Rupert.

A member of the officers' staff bravely stayed behind to try to gain time by defending the bridge against the enemy soldiers, a hopeless task. By nightfall, the duke of Bavaria had moved into the imperial palace, and Ferdinand's forces occupied Prague.

5

The Winter Queen

IT TURNS OUT THAT QUEENS are not made with crowns and scepters after all. They are made with adversity.

After their alarming departure from the castle of Prague, Elizabeth and Frederick (along with the visiting English ambassadors, much startled by this turn of events) took refuge briefly in the home of a loyal member of the Bohemian aristocracy at the edge of the city. They were soon joined by what remained of Frederick's government and supporters, including his general and many of his officer corps. One small solace of this otherwise crushing loss was that the imperial troops had managed to slay only about 1,600 Bohemian soldiers at White Mountain—the rest had scrambled away too quickly to be killed. This left open the prospect of a counterattack. "I have learned from the English agent...that the defeat will not bring ruin. The slain were not numerous and if they had money they could easily gather their forces together again," the Venetian ambassador in Savoy reported to the doge. The English diplomats recovered sufficiently to volunteer to negotiate with General Buquoi and the duke of Bavaria, and sent letters asking to arrange a meeting. When they received no answer, it was determined to fall back on Silesia, which still held out against Ferdinand, in order to regroup.

By this time Frederick and Elizabeth had accumulated quite an entourage. Those of the Bohemian aristocracy most closely allied with the couple feared to stay behind and face the violence of imperial retribution.★ They had packed up what they could of their household belongings, which meant that the procession of refugees from Prague was encumbered by some three hundred wagons and carts. It was a harrowing journey, as the exact position of the enemy was unknown, so the king and queen were often forced to take back roads too rough for the wheels of Elizabeth's carriage, necessitating that she ride horseback behind a soldier in her heavily pregnant state. The baggage carts were preyed upon by thieves; the royal attendants were menaced by small bands of roving dragoons; the entire party feared capture by imperial forces sent to overtake them. Throughout this ordeal, neither Frederick nor his wife gave in to despair and in fact made a point of projecting an aura of calm good humor. The English ambassadors who accompanied them part of the way were struck particularly with the courage displayed by Elizabeth, "who truly saw the state she was in, [yet] did not let fall herself below the dignity of a queen, and kept the freedom of her countenance and discourse, with such an unchangeable temper, as at once did raise in all capable men this one thought — that her mind could not be brought under fortune."

Within a week they had made it to the relative safety of Breslau, where Frederick established an interim court in an attempt to reunite and augment his forces. But Silesia was under attack from the elector of Saxony. There was no way to know how long it could hold out, and Elizabeth was rapidly approaching the time of her confinement, during which she could not travel. She had to leave her husband and find a safer place to have her baby, and she had to find it fast. She decided to try for Berlin, where Frederick's sister, married to the elector of Brandenburg, lived. But to get there she was going to have to slip past the elector of Saxony's army.

She took one-year-old Rupert and a small personal guard of

★ This turned out to be a prudent move. Of Frederick's supporters who remained behind, more than forty of the leading aristocrats were rounded up, and a mass execution was held in the public square by direct order of the emperor, to discourage future rebellions.

horsemen. Baron Dohna, the Bohemian diplomat who had served as Frederick's loyal ambassador to England and one of the few members of his court familiar with the terrain, courageously volunteered to lead the way. It was winter, with snow and frigid temperatures. Elizabeth was already exhausted from the flight from Prague and ill from her pregnancy. She had to stay off the main road and often traveled by night to take advantage of the darkness. She didn't know the local language; she could have been betrayed at any time; she didn't know whom to trust and whom to fear. It must have been terrifying.

Somehow, she and her retinue escaped enemy notice and arrived at Frankfort-on-Oder on November 25. Two days later she approached Berlin, only to discover that her sister and brother-in-law were away from home. Upon appeal, the servants and town council refused to risk imperial wrath by offering her hospitality. With everything that had happened to her, this was probably her most desolate moment.

She couldn't go back and she couldn't go forward. The elector of Brandenburg owned an isolated fortress, the château of Custrin, about fifty miles east of Berlin. Since it was primarily used as a summer residence, it was currently uninhabited. "They shall find neither food nor fuel for man, nor fodder for horse—no wine in the cellar—no corn in the granary—nothing but misery and starvation," the elector of Brandenburg warned Frederick grimly in a letter. But this was the only option available to her, and so it was to this cold, lonely manor, miles from civilization, that Elizabeth and her small entourage trudged.

NEWS OF THE IMPERIAL victory at White Mountain and the subsequent flight of Frederick and Elizabeth from Prague spread rapidly through Europe. "This be the fifteenth day since the date of that victory in Bohemia, which hath filled all this Court and town with jollity," the English ambassador at Vienna, assigned to negotiate with the emperor, glumly wrote home to London on November 22.

Ferdinand was indeed in high spirits. In his hurry to evacuate Prague, Frederick had left behind his crown and insignia as well as many important government papers. The duke of Bavaria had exultantly forwarded these items to the emperor as spoils of the campaign. The very first thing Ferdinand did with his loot was to locate the signed Letter of Majesty, the legal document ensuring the religious freedom of the kingdom, and tear it in two.

Throughout Germany, especially in those areas where Catholicism dominated, Frederick and his wife were derided and lampooned in cartoons, songs, and pamphlets; they were labeled the Winter King and Queen for having ruled only a single season. The Lutherans too joined in the general mockery, and for this reason the imperial victory has long been interpreted not simply as a political triumph but more generally as a wholesale rejection of Calvinism. Of course, the Lutheran reaction may have been genuine, but with Ferdinand's troops hovering close by, ready to quash any resistance, it is just possible that, given the vulnerability of their position, the other Protestant sects were simply doing their best to distance themselves from so pathetic a failure. If Frederick had triumphed instead of folding up ignominiously at White Mountain and had chased down and destroyed the imperial forces, it is difficult to see the Lutheran majority of Germany voluntarily choosing to scorn him and side with Ferdinand.

By contrast, the loss of Bohemia and the Palatinate was greeted in England with profound grief, followed quickly by anger. "Everyone laments the misfortunes of the King Palatine, and the unhappy fate of the beloved queen, who in her flight never had a helping hand from her father to protect and accompany her," reported the Venetian ambassador on December 11, 1620, in a letter to the doge. "Tears, sighs, and loud expressions of wrath are seen and heard in every direction." Even James was sufficiently afflicted by the plight of his daughter and her family to take the unusual step of deviating from official routine. "Whereas, on the preceding days, without any concern about the bitter weather prevailing he could not have enough hunting of the hare in that cold and wind ridden country, he has since then remained constantly shut up in his room in great sadness and dejection, forbidding the courtiers any kind of game or recreation," the envoy noted.

And now at last the situation seemed dire enough to provoke the king to action. A parliament was called for January 30, 1621, the first in seven years, to determine the English response to the crisis. (James, still wedded to the principle of the divine right of kings, did not think much of representative government, but in this case he had no choice; he had overspent his income and needed the support of the assembled legislators to raise funds.) Although in his opening statement, the king refused aid for the recovery of Bohemia, claiming that his son-in-law had gone against his advice by accepting the crown of that realm, he did vow to see the Palatinate returned to his grandchildren, who were the legitimate heirs "and had never offended anyone." He would begin as always by negotiating, but this time if the talks did not yield progress, he committed himself to raising an army of 30,000 men and taking back the property by force, even if it meant "to imperil his three kingdoms and risk his own life and shed the blood of his own son," and he laid his hand upon Charles's bowed head in a particularly dramatic gesture to underscore his sincerity. The king's initiative was hailed by the majority of the representatives present, although they rather balked at the expense and voted to raise only £160,000, nowhere near the sum necessary to provision the number of troops requested. Still, it was not an insignificant pledge of support and certainly an encouraging move after the months of indecision.

Unfortunately, it arrived too late to help Frederick recover his regiments in Silesia, forcing him to abandon the hope of a swift counterattack. By December Buquoi's men had reached Moravia, and despite Frederick's appeals to hold firm, the local government capitulated and went to the emperor. Faced with advancing imperial troops from the north, south, and west, the Silesians knew themselves defeated and advised their king to withdraw in the hope that he would return at some future date to liberate them. Frederick reluctantly departed Breslau and joined Elizabeth in her isolation at Custrin, arriving on December 21, 1620. Less than a month later, she gave birth to her fifth child, a boy whom the couple named Maurice after her husband's uncle the prince of Orange, renowned for his martial abilities, because, as his mother observed, when he grew up he would "have to be a warrior."

As soon as Elizabeth was well enough to travel, she and Frederick made plans to leave Custrin. This was out of necessity as much as desire. Ferdinand, who would have liked nothing better than to capture his adversary, had issued an imperial decree forbidding any German prince from providing shelter to the couple and their followers. The elector of Brandenburg, Frederick's brother-in-law, had so far resisted complying, but he did not have the resources to hold out should the emperor decide to send an army to punish him for his disobedience and seize the helpless king and queen. Once again, they had to flee.

But where to go? There is no question that Elizabeth, exhausted and frightened, wanted England. She had not been back since her marriage although she had expressed a longing to return as early as 1617, after the birth of her second son, Karl Ludwig. "The Lady Elizabeth, we hear, makes great means to come over hither...and is so bent to it that she will hardly be stayed," a member of the English court had reported at the time. Now, especially, after such a traumatic episode, spiritually wounded by deprivation, hardship, and humiliation, she craved the solace of safety, familiarity, and love that she associated with England and home.

It must therefore have come as a particularly cruel disappointment to discover that, despite her father's having sent her an emissary with £20,000 to help defray the costs of travel, he refused to see either her or her husband, or indeed any member of her family. On

January 25, 1621, just nine days after the birth of Maurice, James instructed his ambassador at The Hague to prevent Frederick and Elizabeth from returning to England at all costs. "So great is our mislike of such a course...as we do hereby command you, in case he [Frederick] pass by that way with an intention to repair to this place...to divert him by good persuasions from proceeding any further in that journey...and if our daughter also do come into those parts, with any intention to transport herself hither you do use all possible means at this time to divert her; and rather than fail, to charge her, in our name and upon our blessing, that she do not come," the king wrote in a panic.

Although James gave his customary worry of compromising the negotiations for the return of the Palatinate as the official reason for refusing his daughter and her family access to England, his true motivation was more complex. Above all, he feared the political power of his daughter's popularity. There was a strong feeling against Catholic Spain in England, particularly among the growing Puritan party, and despite everything that had happened, James still cherished the idea of marrying his one remaining son, Charles, to the daughter of the Spanish king. Elizabeth's magnetic presence in England could only aid her cause and stiffen the resistance against a Catholic alliance; should she take up permanent residence in her homeland, it was even possible that the kingdom might choose Elizabeth over Charles as its future sovereign. "I think they have reason there [Spain], if they love themselves, to wish you and yours rather to succeed unto me than my daughter and her children," James would later write tellingly to Charles. In fact, it was not Spain who cared to prevent Elizabeth or her family from inheriting the throne of England—it was her father. So apprehensive was James about Elizabeth's potential influence in the government that he would not allow any of her sons to visit or be educated in England, *even for their own safety.*

But it went deeper than mere fear for Charles's ascension or the defense of his own policies. Possibly to distance himself from any lingering guilt he might have felt over his role in their humiliation, James blamed the disastrous Bohemian campaign on Frederick and Elizabeth alone. By this time, he had convinced himself that they had deliberately and maliciously set themselves in opposition to his express wishes, and his resentment was palpable. As he saw it, he had been forced into the position of having to defend Frederick's claim to the Palatinate; that's why he spoke only of his grandchildren's rights, and not his son-in-law's. "You speak to me of Italy, Bohemia, Germany, Flanders and the whole world. I cannot do everything!" James whined at his councillors.

Despite his talk of war, the king didn't care if the Palatinate was returned promptly; he was willing to let the emperor have it during his lifetime in exchange for a promise that ultimately, after Ferdinand's death, it would revert to Frederick's children. Coincidentally, this line of thinking fed nicely into James's natural inclination against spending money or raising troops. Having had many years of experience with the king of England, the Venetian ambassador was able to recognize this truth instantly. "His Majesty fears the troubles and the burdens of war more than any prince who ever lived and his real idea is to patch things up as best he may," he observed bluntly to the doge in a letter of March 5, 1621. It would obviously be much more difficult to break this news to Elizabeth and Frederick in person, or to ignore their plight if they were a presence at court, where his ministers and the general population would see their faces and be reminded daily of the human cost of their suffering.

James did not even have the courage to tell his daughter and son-in-law that they were not welcome in England directly by letter or messenger; they had to find out through back channels. Although Elizabeth held her head high and pretended that she had never had any intention of availing herself of her father's hospitality, she must have felt this final mortification keenly. They had already packed up their few belongings at Custrin and arranged to leave the new baby, Maurice, barely two months old, with Frederick's sister in Berlin.

For one long, dark moment, it must have seemed to Elizabeth as though she and her husband were all alone in the world.

And then her new son's namesake, Maurice of Nassau, prince of Orange, stepped gallantly into the void left by her father and invited Elizabeth and Frederick to take up residence in The Hague in a house provided by the governing body, the States General.★ This offer was gratefully accepted and by the first week in April 1621, the deposed king and queen of Bohemia, with one-and-a-half-year-old Rupert in tow, had reached Holland. There "they were met by the Prince of Orange and all his court, and so conducted to this town in coaches; the whole way, as well by water as land, betwixt this and the entrance into Delft, by reason of a great concourse of people coming from all parts, being like a continued street," the English ambassador to The Hague reported. "And their being saluted here, since their coming, by all the councils and assemblies, is an argument [that] the affection of this state, from the highest to the lowest, is not changed by the change of these princes' fortune." After all that she had been through, the adoration of the crowd, and especially the couple's reception as visiting royalty, must have cheered Elizabeth and somewhat eased the ache in her heart.

But there is no doubt that she had been wounded, and despite her efforts to hide her feelings behind a mask of dignity, the hurt and bitterness crept out in her private correspondence. "I have seen a genuine letter of the Queen of Bohemia, written to one of the leading Countesses here, an intimate friend of hers, saying how she has reached The Hague after a long and toilsome journey, where she enjoys more popularity among the people, with her husband, than she has ever experienced anywhere else, and where she will stay awhile, seeing she cannot come where she ought," confided the

---

★ Maurice of Nassau was Frederick's mother's half brother. Frederick's extended family was impressively confusing even by the standards of the day owing to his maternal grandfather, William the Silent, having had fifteen children by four wives. This was the same Maurice, prince of Orange—middle-aged and balding—who had once been a suitor for Elizabeth's hand.

Venetian ambassador to the doge on April 30. "She adds: Everyone is awaiting some good resolution from his Majesty [James]; for my part I expect very little, but it will only redound to the triumph of our enemies who mock and jest at him."

THE PRINCE OF ORANGE was as kind as her father was callous. At public expense, Elizabeth and Frederick were given a grand residence, one of the finest in the city, in which to live; it was even redecorated so that the rooms would reflect their kingly status. The couple was further allotted an allowance of 10,000 florins a month to help with the housekeeping. Reunited with their eldest child, seven-year-old Frederick Henry, who had been living in Holland with his father's relatives since his escape from Prague the previous September, Elizabeth and Frederick and their two small sons moved into their new home in The Hague, and with renewed determination they set themselves to the task of recovering all that they had lost.

And there was reason for optimism. The Spanish troops had not, after all, succeeded in occupying all of the Palatinate—the couple's beautiful ancestral home in Heidelberg was yet under the control of patriots loyal to Frederick, supplemented by a small remnant of his Bohemian forces, who had regrouped under the direction of one of his former commanders, General Mansfield. Even better, the hated king of Spain, Philip III, had died on March 31, just as Frederick and Elizabeth were making their grand entrance into Holland. The exiled king and queen of Bohemia took this news as something of a good omen; his successor, Philip IV, was only sixteen, and the kingdom might be weakened by the transition. "You will have heard of the death of the king of Spain," Elizabeth wrote coolly to a friend in England upon receiving this intelligence. "May all his race perish so, especially the women."

But as both his daughter and the Venetian secretary had so astutely predicted, despite his theatrics at Parliament, James was not in fact enthusiastic about sending soldiers into battle, especially when it was *so* much easier and less expensive to dispatch yet another emissary to negotiate with the emperor. This new English envoy duly arrived in Vienna in May. Ferdinand, who had no intention of reinstating Frederick as elector of the Palatinate—he informed the Spanish secretly by letter that he "would rather cherish a crushed snake in his bosom"—pretended to consider James's proposals, one of which involved Frederick's publicly getting down on his knees and begging the emperor's forgiveness. The bargaining was not without its compensations, however, at least from Ferdinand's point of view. He was able to use the time consumed by these negotiations to advantage, surreptitiously directing ever more imperial troops, now under the command of a general named Tilly, into the Palatinate to try to dislodge Mansfield's forces.

By August, Frederick, who understood very well what was happening, could stand it no longer, and with his wife's aid took action. Elizabeth, who like the emperor had also used the past few months productively by actively soliciting allies to her husband's cause through letters and heartfelt personal appeals, had succeeded in recruiting a particularly helpful young partisan by the name of Prince Christian of Brunswick. Christian was twenty-two years old, devoutly Protestant, an enthusiastic warrior, and much taken with the beautiful dethroned queen of Bohemia. In the chivalric spirit of the age, he devoted himself to her service, dramatically taking possession of one of her gloves as a token of her favor and promising, with a grand flourish, "Madam, I will give it you in the Palatinate!"

To this end, the prince gallantly mustered a cavalry of a thousand knights and offered to help Frederick lead them to Heidelberg to shore up Mansfield's defenses and retake his inheritance. This was exactly what Frederick, who had no money for troops on his own, had hoped for; even if he did end up having to negotiate with Ferdinand, it would be from a much stronger position if he won back his territory or held on to at least part of it.

He had already agreed to this proposal and left The Hague to meet up with Christian's forces in Germany when James was alerted to his son-in-law's intentions. Incensed that Frederick had undertaken an initiative without consulting him and fearful yet again of jeopardizing the endless negotiations in Vienna, the king demanded that his son-in-law remove himself from the battlefield. "The commandment I have from his Majesty is this, that...it is his pleasure that you deal roundly with his son-in-law...giving him to understand that his Majesty will not only quit him absolutely, *but give direct assistance against him*, unless he continue constant to all of his Majesty's desires," the English secretary in charge of transmitting these singular orders wrote to his counterpart in Holland. Frederick, faced with the prospect of losing all help from England in the future or perhaps even having his powerful father-in-law turn against him altogether, was forced to decline Christian's offer and return to The Hague. Two months later, the English envoy in Vienna gave up in disgust at Ferdinand's duplicity and returned to London. Even James had to admit that the emperor had not been negotiating in good faith.

That was 1621.

In 1622, Frederick and Elizabeth tried again. After the failure of James's diplomatic initiative in Vienna, a parliament was called in England and an additional £30,000 allocated to prosecute the war in the Palatinate, a sum that the exiled couple took, not unreasonably, as a sign of encouragement. While James continued to lobby for a negotiated settlement — this time dispatching an emissary to Spain in the hopes that the government there would exert pressure on the emperor to compromise — he did send this money to his daughter and son-in-law. But by that point, Elizabeth and Frederick were so heavily in debt that they had to use it to pay off their creditors rather than give the money to help protect Heidelberg. With no funds with which to keep his army together, Mansfield, Frederick's general in the Palatinate, was in danger of having to surrender what was left of the family estates to the emperor.

Frantic to prevent the complete forfeiture of their remaining property, at the end of March, a once-again heavily pregnant Elizabeth sent her husband off to Germany through hostile territory on yet another daring mission. So great was the risk of capture that Frederick shaved off his telltale goatee and adopted the dress of a humble merchant. In this disguise he was able to pass discreetly from town to town, although occasionally he was forced to stay in inns frequented by imperial soldiers. He played his part so well that none around him realized that the unassuming man in the common room of the tavern lifting his glass to the health and success of the emperor and the ignominious defeat of the Elector Palatinate was in fact the Winter King.

By April 17, 1622, just as Elizabeth was giving birth to the couple's sixth child, a daughter (whom she christened Louise Hollandine in grateful acknowledgment of all the Dutch had done for her), Frederick had arrived in Germersheim, about thirty miles southwest of Heidelberg. His general was already engaged in surrender talks with an imperial envoy; there was no time to lose. Like a cinema star in a 1930s adventure film, Frederick abruptly flung away his merchant's cloak and revealed himself to Mansfield, who immediately withdrew from the negotiations and renewed his commitment to his liege lord to defend the Palatinate.

And now, at last, through this bold initiative, Frederick's cause gained momentum. The news of his arrival spread quickly through the countryside, revitalizing his campaign and brightening the hearts of his subjects. On April 27, just ten days after his daughter's birth, he and Mansfield, in the company of an army of some 17,000 men, scattered the imperial forces under General Tilly, and Frederick had the intense satisfaction of reclaiming the city of Heidelberg as his own.*

Even better, Prince Christian of Brunswick, who had not forgot-

---

* Approximately seven thousand of these soldiers were Englishmen who had volunteered for this assignment under the command of Sir Horace Vere. The force was a far cry from the 30,000 promised.

ten his promise to Elizabeth, had raised an additional ten thousand men and was leading this battalion south from Westphalia to join with Frederick's army. The prince's progress was slowed somewhat by his acute need for money to pay his soldiers. Toward this end, he had developed an effective, if unique, method of fund-raising. Stopping at every city and town he came to, Christian delivered letters on scorched paper that read simply, "Fire! Fire! Blood! Blood!" He clearly had a flair for catchphrases, as the citizens who received this cryptic communication knew to hand over piles of silver to make him go away.

It was this fondness for specie that was to be Christian's—and his patron's—downfall. After the imperial defeat at Heidelberg, General Tilly had replenished his army with Spanish soldiers, and now strove to intercept Christian's forces on their way to rendezvous with Frederick's. The prince could have waited for Mansfield's army to give battle, but fearful of losing his treasure, he instead engaged the enemy. He saved his loot but lost his soldiers, an action for which he was roundly condemned by Frederick and Mansfield.

As a result of this loss, Frederick and his generals, who now no longer had the men needed to confront Tilly, were obliged to fall back to Alsace. Along the way, Mansfield and Christian quarreled, refusing to cooperate with one another; nor could either stop his soldiers from looting and ravaging the local villagers. In despair, Frederick saw all the goodwill he had engendered by liberating his subjects from the imperial forces disintegrate in the frenzy of carnage. The only way to prevent further destruction to his countrymen was to dismiss his generals and their unruly recruits from his service. This he did in August, in the most tactful way possible: "Be it known to all," Frederick published in an official decree, "that the Elector Palatine...being destitute of all human assistance, he perceives it impracticable to make farther use of them [his army], except to their own great inconvenience and detriment: he, therefore, with all due resignation of mind...like a friend, with all imaginable tenderness and humanity, not only absolves them from the oath they have taken to him, but permits them to consult their safety and interest, as far as may be possible, elsewhere."

With no organized force to oppose him, Tilly immediately went back to besieging Heidelberg, and on September 21, 1622, the town surrendered. Frederick was devastated by this loss, particularly as the imperial soldiers inflicted their customary vengeance on the local population. "My poor Heidelberg taken!" he wrote to Elizabeth on September 30. "All sorts of cruelties have been exercised there: the whole town pillaged, and...the handsomest part of it, burnt. God visits us very severely: I am sadly distressed, at the misery of these poor people." By October 19 he was back once more with his wife in The Hague, where, to add insult to injury, he was greeted with the news that Ferdinand intended to formally invest the duke of Bavaria as elector of the Palatinate at a grand ceremony in Vienna, now that Heidelberg was back under imperial control.

In England, this depressing turn of events prompted a new outpouring of public sentiment in Elizabeth's favor. Prince Charles, now nearly twenty-two years old and recovered from all of his childhood maladies, begged his father to be allowed to lead an army to his sister's defense; there was call for another parliament to raise new funds for the war effort and possibly even an authorization for the navy to become involved. But James remained committed to a negotiated settlement, particularly as the Spanish government, to keep England out of the war, tantalizingly held out the prospect of a match between the still unmarried Charles and the Infanta Maria Anna, the seventeen-year-old sister of the young Philip IV. James leaped on this possibility, believing that a wedding between England and Spain would solve all of his problems at once: Charles would be married magnificently, as befit his rank, and could start a family, thus ensuring his (and not Elizabeth's) succession to the throne, while the return of the Palatinate could be incorporated into the nuptial agreement as part of Maria Anna's dowry. So appealing was this alternative that the king once again refused to listen to the information gleaned by his own agents. "We have here at present a sudden strong noise (derived as they say by express intelligence from the court of Spain) that the Infanta Maria hath...besought the King of Spain not to press her any further about the match of Prince Charles," the English ambassador stationed in Venice had reported earlier that year. "And this very week I am advertized from home that the ambassador of the State of Venice did confidently affirm that the Infanta Maria was otherwise to be disposed." James's refusal to surrender the dream of a prestigious Spanish marriage for Charles capped another year of profound frustration for his daughter. "The king, my father, is cozened and abused, but will not see it till it be too late," Elizabeth wrote in despair to a friend on December 5.

That was 1622.

Matters came to a head in 1623. This time it was Charles who, emulating his brother-in-law, donned a disguise in order to slip unnoticed into Spain, in a last-ditch effort to secure the fair Maria Anna's hand in marriage. On February 19, he and his father's favorite, the handsome duke of Buckingham, who had helped hatch this novel plot, donned large hats and provincial attire and sailed for France; in these outfits they arrived in Paris two days later, where they fooled no one. By March 7 they were in Madrid, the French government having discreetly looked the other way as they journeyed south through the countryside sampling the local fare, collecting souvenirs of rustic life, and generally behaving like tourists on holiday.

Their bucolic merrymaking must have made them slightly more conspicuous than they'd planned, because the Spanish government seemed not much surprised when it was eventually revealed that the heir to the throne of England had taken it into his head to drop by for an impromptu visit. Eighteen-year-old Philip IV and his advisers were astute enough to treat this romantic escapade for the foolish political maneuver it was, and played along with straight faces.

Charles and the duke of Buckingham were entertained as honored guests, and the conditions of a possible marriage between the English prince and the Spanish Infanta were duly considered and consigned to the usual negotiations. These discussions, touching as they did on such critical subjects as the difference in religion between the bride and groom (she was a devout Catholic, he an equally pious Protestant) and the return of the Palatinate, naturally took time, particularly as the Spanish mediators loaded on all sorts of conditions sure to be repugnant to England, such as freedom of worship for all English Catholics and permission for Maria Anna to raise her children according to her religious beliefs and not Charles's. The days stretched to weeks, the weeks to months, during which time Charles was treated to only fleeting glimpses of his prospective fiancée.

Committed to the success of the alliance, to aid his son's cause, James raided the crown jewels and sent an astonishing array of precious stones to be given as presents to Maria Anna, in the hope of bribing her to acquiescence.* The ardent bridegroom himself, convinced that love would conquer all, even climbed a wall and waylaid his shy sweetheart, going down on his knees to propose while she was out in the privacy of her garden. This contrivance, while suitably quixotic, did not, alas, elicit the desired effect; rather, it caused the Infanta to immediately go down on *her* knees in front of her brother the king and beg to be allowed to go into a nunnery rather than marry Charles.

Lacking money and troops and so helpless to affect their fate, Elizabeth and Frederick were reduced by Charles's Spanish adventure to the role of sidelined spectators. It is a sign of how deep their resignation was, and how little hope they had of a successful conclusion to their struggle, that in April they accepted yet another gift

---

* "Ye shall present her with two fair long diamonds...and a fair pendent diamond hanging at them; ye shall give her a goodly rope of pearls, ye shall give her...thirteen great ballas rubies, and thirteen knots or conques of pearls, and ye shall give her a head-dressing of two and twenty great pear pearls...and three goodly pear pendent diamonds, whereof the biggest to be worn at a needle in the midst of her forehead, and one in every ear," read a partial list of the rare gems dispatched to Spain in pursuit of the Infanta, as elucidated by James to Charles in a letter of March 17, 1623.

Charles in his wooing days

from the prince of Orange—the use of a second house, this one in Leyden, for the purpose of rearing their children. Elizabeth was pregnant again and they needed more space. Also, she was used to the idea of guardians, and parents living apart from their offspring, as this was how she had been raised. She and Frederick were still divided from three of their children: Karl Ludwig and Princess Elizabeth (neither of whom had seen their parents in four years), and Maurice, the baby born at Custrin. These children were all together at a country house outside Berlin, where his mother had eventually found her way after Bohemia fell. The residence in Leyden was a first step toward perhaps one day soon reuniting the family. In the meantime, nine-year-old Frederick Henry, four-year-old Rupert, and one-year-old Louise Hollandine, as well as the new baby, whom they named Louis, after the French king (as a snub to Spain), moved into the country house that summer.*

By July, Charles, bored with wooing and ready to go home, abruptly gave in and agreed to a marriage treaty that was notable for its utter absence of any mention of the Palatinate and that gave the Spanish government everything it wanted, including a clause allowing Maria Anna to leave her husband and the marriage at any time to enter a convent if she so desired. On September 18, he sailed back to England without his bride (another condition of the agreement; the Infanta would remain in Spain until the pope issued a dispensation allowing the two to marry). By the time he landed it had occurred to Charles that he had been used badly by the Spanish and that perhaps he did not really want to be married to a woman so fond of nuns. Accordingly, he reneged on the treaty. For once, Elizabeth's ordeal came in handy: to save his son from acute embarrassment over his role in this foreign-policy fiasco, James pretended that the agreement had been scotched because "I like not to marry my son with a portion of my daughter's tears" (although he, too, had signed the original wedding contract).

And with this final if reluctant surrender of the dream of the Spanish match, the pendulum of fortune swung ever so temptingly in Elizabeth's direction once more. Because both Charles and his traveling companion the duke of Buckingham attributed their humiliation in Spain to the mendacity of their hosts—"There is nothing but trickery and deceit in the whole business!" the duke of Buckingham fumed, conveniently forgetting that it was Charles who had broken his word—they sought vengeance by threatening once again to have England intervene militarily in the Palatinate. "Since my dear brother's return into England all is changed from being Spanish in which I assure you that Buckingham doth most nobly and faithfully for me," Elizabeth wrote exultantly to a friend on March 1, 1624.

James tried to resist, but the king was old and sick. The years of

---

* Louis was sickly from birth and would die the following year. He "was the prettiest child I had, and the first I ever lost," Elizabeth would later write sadly.

heavy eating and drinking had taken their toll. "I remember Mr. French of the spicery, who sometimes did present him with the first strawberries, cherries, and other fruits, and kneeling to the King, had some speech...that he did desire his Majesty to accept them, and that he was sorry there were no better, with such like complimental words. But the King never had the patience to hear him one word, but his hand was in the basket," reported a bishop of James's acquaintance. Corpulent, afflicted with gout and arthritis, James was often confined to bed that winter. Early in the spring of 1625 he tried to make his usual hunting progression and came down with a fever. "Yet now, being grown toward sixty, it did a little weaken his body, and going from Theobalds to Newmarket, and stirring abroad when, as the coldness of the year was not yet past almost, it could not be prevented but he fall into a quartan ague," the bishop continued.

It was at his Theobalds estate at the beginning of March that the illness really took hold. James did not do much to help himself, continuing to drink heavily and refusing to listen to his doctors. By March 24 it was clear that the king was dying. He asked for Charles, and the two were alone together for several hours. So private was this conference that no one was allowed into any of the surrounding rooms for fear that their secrets might be discovered.

Three days later, in the early morning hours of March 27, 1625, James cried out for his son again. Charles came in his nightgown but his father had already lost consciousness. James I, king of England, died near noon that day, the new king by his side. He left no message for his daughter, not a single trinket or kind word for her or any member of her family. He departed life without ever having seen even one of his grandchildren or making any provision for them.

"He enjoyed life for fifty-nine years, for fifty-eight of which he was King of Scotland, and for twenty-four he governed the whole of Great Britain," the Venetian ambassador wrote home to the doge by way of a eulogy. "He spent his days in study, in peace, and in hunting."

James might have spent his days in peace but he left behind a war that would last for thirty years.

6

Queen of Hearts

ELIZABETH WAS TWENTY-EIGHT YEARS OLD, the mother of a large and still growing brood—her sixth son and eighth child, Edward, had been born the previous October—when she received the news of her father's death. She would not have been human if her grief was not tinged with a hint of relief. She and Frederick were by this time living under such straitened conditions that Charles, as one of his first acts, had to send his sister's family the black clothing necessary to outfit them during the official period of mourning. "You may easily judge what an affliction it was to me to understand the evil news of the loss of so loving a father as his late majesty was to me," Elizabeth wrote to an English diplomat of long acquaintance on April 11, 1625. "It would be much more but that God hath left me so dear and loving a brother as the king is to me, in whom, next God, I have now all my confidence," she added candidly.

Even better, this time Charles would not be laboring alone in his effort to restore the Palatinate to his sister and her husband. In the ever-shifting minuet that represented seventeenth-century European politics, a new and completely unexpected partner had suddenly emerged from the wings to help lead the next promenade around the dance floor. A prominent Catholic at the court of Louis XIII of France, this new ally's name was Armand Jean du Plessis, although he is much better known by his title Cardinal Richelieu.

The immense popularity of Alexandre Dumas's swashbuckling

historical romance *The Three Musketeers*, which cast Richelieu firmly in the role of archvillain, has assured the cardinal of the reprobation of millions of ardent readers over the centuries. But in fact, Louis XIII and France were in many ways, most particularly in regard to foreign policy, extremely lucky to have him. Part statesman, part soldier—for Richelieu had attended the top military academy in France before abruptly switching to theology at the University of Paris in order to take advantage of the opening of a lucrative bishopric that fell within the province of his family's estate—the cardinal had started his political career in the service of Louis's mother, Marie de' Medici, widow of Henry IV. But he soon advanced to a position of national prominence on the council of state and from there to chief adviser to the king himself.

Richelieu's great insight was that, although a staunch Catholic himself, he did not perceive the world in terms of religious dogma but instead focused on power. He could not help but notice, for example, that the Habsburgs were becoming something of a problem for France. It was perhaps not the best idea, the cardinal reasoned, to let the armies of Spain and the empire, Catholic though they might be, win quite so convincingly over their Protestant opponents. They were getting a little too ambitious. Already, Spanish forces were beginning to encroach on key mountain passes through the Alps that had traditionally been allied to France. To lose this territory made the kingdom much more vulnerable to attack. What Richelieu needed was something to divert Spain's and the emperor's attention and military away from Italy so that France could reclaim that property.

Charles's repudiation of the Spanish marriage and his subsequent ascension to the throne of England was coincident with the cardinal's rise to power. So when Charles, still looking for a suitable bride, inquired through intermediaries about the possibility of his marrying Louis XIII's youngest sister, fifteen-year-old Henrietta Maria, and tying this alliance to a French promise of help in retrieving the Palatinate for Frederick and Elizabeth, his proposal was met with approval,

Cardinal Richelieu

pending favorable resolution of a few niggling details. It was twenty-four-year-old Charles I and his favorite, the duke of Buckingham, negotiating against twenty-three-year-old Louis XIII and *his* favorite, Cardinal Richelieu. This cannot really be called a fair fight.

Louis XIII and the cardinal proved to be every bit as intractable and indefatigable in negotiation as the Spanish. In exchange for a league dedicated to the recovery of the Palatinate, they insisted that all the discriminatory laws currently enforced against English Catholics be rescinded; that Henrietta Maria be allowed to worship publicly in a chapel; that she be allowed to raise her children as Catholics; and that her household be made up of French Catholic attendants. (Luckily, the princess was not interested in going into a convent, so Charles was saved from that condition.) And, since the marriage was tied to a military alliance, the French also demanded the loan of

English ships. For this, Louis XIII was willing to give his sister a dowry of £120,000, to help defray the expenses of a war for the Palatinate and to supply Frederick's commander, General Mansfield, with funds for six months.

Charles accepted all of these conditions, although he kept the terms a secret, knowing they would be unpopular in Protestant England, and sent the duke of Buckingham to France in May with instructions to bring his bride to him as quickly as possible.* Henrietta Maria and her escort arrived in Dover on June 12 and the marriage was consummated the next day (they had been wedded by proxy in Paris). By June 17, 1625, they were in London, where Charles's new French Catholic wife was greeted by a traditional English downpour.

And with this marriage and the league with France, for the first time in years, Elizabeth allowed herself to feel hope. "The comforte of my deare brother's love doth revive me," she wrote excitedly in a letter to an English friend. "He hath sent to me Sir Henry Vane, his coferer [treasurer], to assure me, that he will be both father and brother to the King of Bohemia and me. Now, you may be sure, all will goe well in Englande; for your new master will leave nothing undone for our good. The great fleet is almost readie to goe out. [Charles had promised to bring the English navy into the war to help retrieve the Palatinate.]...My uncle, the King of Dennemark, doth beginne to declare himself for us, and so doth Sweden...I have the best brother in the worlde."

That the return of the Palatine to Frederick would even be considered to be an important international issue after so many years was due almost entirely to his wife's efforts. It was spirited, engaging Elizabeth who, by the sheer force of her personality, drew supporters to their small court in The Hague and made it a center of influence

---

* It was during this trip that the duke of Buckingham took it into his head to try to seduce Louis XIII's wife, Anne of Austria, queen of France, a diplomatic initiative of questionable value. This is the source of the liaison depicted in *The Three Musketeers*. Unlike the character of the French queen portrayed in the Dumas novel, however, Anne of Austria definitely rejected the duke's overtures.

in Holland; Elizabeth who charmed and cajoled, both by personal appeal and letter, all who might be of service to their cause, frequently bestowing drolly affectionate nicknames on her correspondents; Elizabeth (unlike her husband, who often gave in to depression, although who could blame him) who recognized that allies come to those who remain positive and refuse to surrender to despair. "Though I have cause enough to be sad, yet I am still of my wild humor, to be as merry as I can, in spite of fortune," she wrote. The English ambassador in Holland agreed. "I know not so great a lady in the world, nor ever did—though I have seen many courts—of such natural affection," he observed. Even the prince of Orange, though related to the husband, took the wife's part. "The Queen of Bohemia is accounted the most charming princess of Europe, and called by some the queen of hearts; but she is far more than that,— she is a true and faithful wife, and that, too, of a husband who is in every respect her inferior," he concluded frankly before his death in the spring of 1625. Unlike her father, he persuasively demonstrated his high opinion of her by leaving her valuable shares in the Dutch East India Company in his will. Her brother Charles, upon his ascension to the throne, made it clear that he too believed Elizabeth's political acumen to be more acute than her husband's. "I send you herewith letters of my sister and brother. I place them so because I think the gray mare [Elizabeth] is the best horse," read the new king's instructions to the duke of Buckingham when he sent him off to The Hague for an official state visit.

But it was not for her admirers alone that Elizabeth was known as the queen of hearts. No woman in Europe could boast a more tangibly affectionate husband than Frederick. No year passed without Elizabeth's either becoming pregnant, preparing for labor, or just getting over a delivery. On July 7, 1626, she gave birth to her ninth child and third daughter, whom she and Frederick christened Henrietta Maria as a gesture of respect to her new sister-in-law. On September 27 of the next year came Philip, number ten. Philip was followed in December 1628 by another daughter (who sadly did not survive childhood) but who was in any event almost immediately replaced by Sophia, number twelve, born on October 14, 1630. The arrival of Gustavus Adolphus on January 14, 1632, made for a whopping baker's dozen.

All of these children lived away from their parents under the care of a variety of tutors and governesses at the house in Leyden. In 1624, Karl Ludwig, the king and queen of Bohemia's second son, had been sent from Berlin to live with his brothers and sisters, but it wasn't until 1628 that the remaining two children, Princess Elizabeth and Maurice, who had been left in the care of Frederick's mother and sister in Germany, joined the rest of the family in Holland.

Of all of their many offspring, Elizabeth's and Frederick's highest hopes for the future naturally settled on their eldest, Frederick Henry. Frederick Henry was not only heir to the Palatinate and crown prince of Bohemia, he was third in line (after Charles I and Elizabeth, so long as Charles remained childless) to inherit the thrones of England, Scotland, and Ireland. Moreover, he was a bright, attractive boy, affectionate to his siblings, and showed great promise of developing into a strong and noble statesman. He was very attached to his sister Princess Elizabeth, who was only a baby when he left Heidelberg but whom he associated with his happy childhood days in Germany before the war. He sent letters to his grandmother in Berlin asking after her welfare and sometimes enclosed little gifts. "I wish for nothing so much that I may see her again, with all happy things around her, at dear Heidelberg," ran one of these compositions. "I beg your Highness to accept with this a pair of gloves and a silver pen... I beseech you to present... to my sister Elizabeth a true-hearted brotherly kiss, to whom I send also the enclosed trinket—a little heart—in token of my fond, faithful, fraternal love." With his brothers Karl Ludwig and Rupert (the others were too young), he attended the University of Leyden, where he mastered several languages, including French, English, German, and the inevitable Latin. His military training was not neglected and he took a keen interest in sports and particularly in the navy. His father was extremely proud of him, and took Frederick Henry with him on excursions and brought him to The Hague whenever he could to expose him to state business and diplomacy.

In her insistence that all of her children become fluent in English as well as French and German and that they be trained in English composition so that they would become accustomed to writing letters, Elizabeth ensured that, should all else fail, her progeny would at least have a future in her native land. Judging by the disastrous results of the efforts ostensibly waged on her behalf by her brother in the first few years of his rule, this would turn out to be a worthwhile endeavor.

IN HIS EXUBERANCE AT being crowned king, Charles—egged on by his most influential adviser and best friend, the duke of Buckingham, a man of large vision if somewhat questionable abilities—had made a great many promises. Among the more significant were his pledge to provide Mansfield, Frederick's general, with £240,000 (of which £120,000 was supposed to come from his wife's dowry) to support enough soldiers to take back the Palatine; another £300,000 to help his uncle Christian, king of Denmark, field an army against the Spanish troops who had remained in northern Germany in order to protect Holland and the Netherlands from imperial encroachment; and a further £300,000 to refurbish the mighty English fleet, which had been sadly neglected during James's reign, and which Charles and Buckingham, still nurturing hurt feelings over the humiliating Infanta episode, intended to use to attack Spain outright. These expenses were over and above the amounts Charles would also need to pay for his father's funeral, his own coronation, and his and his wife's household living allowances. A quick examination of the royal treasury confirmed a substantial deficit between the new king's expectations and the funds available at the time of his ascension, so Charles called a parliament in order to petition the kingdom's legislators to supply the difference.

Beginning one's reign by presenting one's subjects with a bill several times larger than any in recorded history was perhaps not the optimal way to establish a long and fruitful relationship. Not unreasonably given future events, Parliament balked and instead chastised Charles for agreeing to all the tolerant Catholic clauses in his marriage contract, forcing him to renege. They then went on the offensive and tried to impeach Buckingham for, among other transgressions, agreeing to lend Protestant English ships to the Catholic king of France, who, it turned out, intended to use them to help subdue their coreligionists, the Huguenots, who were rebelling at La Rochelle. To save his favorite from disgrace, Charles was forced to dismiss Parliament without obtaining anywhere near the amount of money needed to accomplish his objectives.

A lack of sufficient funds did not, however, dissuade Charles and the duke of Buckingham from going ahead and putting their ambitious war program into action anyway. Buckingham, after spending years first as James's favorite and then his son's, was by far the richest man in England. He bought himself the title of lord admiral, made a cut-rate attempt to spruce up the navy, pronounced the fleet seaworthy, and in October 1625 sent it off to attack the Spanish coast and hopefully bring back some pirated treasure. It was only after the fleet set sail that the commanding officer noticed that there wasn't nearly enough food or weaponry to support a military operation of any length and that in any event the ammunition supplied didn't fit the gun barrels. By November they were already on their way back to England, having achieved nothing beyond the loss of four ships and the sacrifice of a significant proportion of English sailors, many of them forced recruits, to storms, disease, and privation.

The outcry over this disastrous expedition served only to amplify the demands for Buckingham's censure and removal from office. To counteract this unfortunate trend, Charles, again on the advice of his favorite, decided to embark on an innovative new war strategy. Despite Elizabeth's and Frederick's pleas that the promised money and soldiers be sent to help retake the Palatine, the duke of Buckingham instead insisted that the best way to proceed (and, coincidentally, appease his parliamentary critics) was to come to the aid of the rebelling French Protestants at La Rochelle, who were under siege by Louis XIII's Catholic troops. The fact that this meant attacking *his own ally*, with whom he had just signed an extensive military treaty whose sole purpose was to return his sister and her husband to their property in Germany, seems not to have occurred to Charles.

So what remained of the fleet was once again patched up as best it could be, this time on monies raised through forced loans. (Those of Charles's subjects who refused to contribute were imprisoned, a novel if not particularly effective financing strategy.) By June 1627, the ships were pronounced sound, and the squadron set sail for France with Buckingham personally in command.

Despite the invigorating presence of the lord admiral, the mighty British fleet had much the same experience fighting the French as it had had with the Spanish. Determined to seize an enemy fort located on the Isle of Rhé, a small landmass just off the coast of La Rochelle, Buckingham launched an assault, only to discover that the scaling ladders he had brought along to scramble over the walls were too short to reach the top. He sent back messengers to England begging for money and reinforcements, but Charles, an art connoisseur, instead used what funds he could scrounge to purchase a collection of paintings by Old Masters (a once-in-a-lifetime opportunity, his Italian dealer assured him), so Buckingham was forced to retreat through a narrow strait that allowed the French to decimate the English soldiers with impunity. The entire operation was such a debacle that Louis XIII was able to joke about it. "Alack," he told the ambassador from Savoy, "if I had known my brother of England had longed so much for the Isle of Rhé, I would have sold it him for half the money it hath cost him."

By the time he and his ships limped back to England, Charles's lord admiral and chief adviser was the most detested man in the realm. ("Who rules the kingdom? — The king. Who rules the king? — The duke. Who rules the duke? — The devil" ran a popular London ditty.) Nonetheless Buckingham refused to admit defeat and convinced Charles to make yet another attempt to relieve the siege of La Rochelle. However, the lord admiral's luck ran out on August 23, 1628, when he was stabbed to death in Portsmouth, where he had gone to inspect the inevitable repairs on the fleet. The assassin, one of Buckingham's own seamen, a veteran of the catastrophic Isle of Rhé operation, was regarded as a hero by the general populace, who lit bonfires and proclaimed public prayers in his name when a shattered Charles had him executed for the crime.

Charles sent the naval force to France anyway, where it sat in the harbor of La Rochelle and watched as the Huguenot inhabitants slowly succumbed to the French Catholic troops under the generalship of Cardinal Richelieu—"in the sight of the English fleet which did effect nothing for them," as a French Protestant observed bitterly to a member of Charles's government. The English commander was moved by the suffering of the citizens, but Richelieu's army and defenses were so daunting that he dared not intervene. On October 18, 1628, the Protestants of La Rochelle surrendered. "There died in this siege, of famine, 16,000 persons. The rest endured a wonderful misery, most of their food being hides, leather, and old gloves," read the official report from the fleet.

Such were the results of the confident promises and resolutions, the carefully arranged alliances and military operations undertaken by Charles I on behalf of his sister. And while the king of England busied himself with a futile war against his French ally, the imperial army racked up victory after victory, dealing out death and destruction indiscriminately to all who stood in its path, burning, looting, and savaging the terrified civilian population, as Ferdinand tightened his hold on Germany.

ONCE AGAIN, ELIZABETH AND FREDERICK could only stand by and watch in dismay as their hopes and prospects were blighted by a lack of support from England. Elizabeth's uncle the king of Denmark bravely took to the field in a three-pronged, coordinated attack with General Mansfield and Christian of Brunswick (who had already lost an arm in service to the queen of Bohemia), but without English soldiers or money, the effort was doomed. Mansfield flung twelve thousand men over a bridge in Dessau, in northern Germany, about eighty miles southwest of Berlin, only to see nearly half of them brutally cut down by the far superior imperial artillery under the direction of General Wallenstein, Ferdinand's new, highly competent commander. Christian of Brunswick, who had so bankrupted himself in his lady's cause that his soldiers were reduced to fighting with iron rods, died despondent and forlorn at the age of twenty-eight of wounds received in battle at Wolfenbüttel, also in northern Germany. The king of Denmark was defeated in a pitched battle with General Tilly's Catholic forces at nearby Lutter, where six thousand Danish corpses littered the field and all of his artillery was lost before he sounded the retreat.

It wasn't until November 1628, just after the French Protestants at La Rochelle surrendered to Cardinal Richelieu's army, that a stroke of good luck actually fell Elizabeth's way. Ships from the Dutch East India Company suddenly appeared off the coast of England on their way to Amsterdam, and it was immediately apparent that Holland had been the beneficiary of an unprecedented (if pirated) windfall. "The great prize taken in the West Indies by the Hollanders amounts... to £870,000 or thereabout," a correspondent from London enthused. "They have also taken the Brazilian fleet, laden with sugars. In that West India Company of Holland, the Queen of Bohemia hath one-eighth part left her by the late Maurice, Prince of Orange, in his last will and testament."

One-eighth of nearly £900,000, a small fortune! Enough to try again, to raise a new troop of soldiers with which to pry Heidelberg from Ferdinand's grasp at last, with maybe even some left over to pay down their household debts! Elizabeth had (of course) just given birth again and couldn't make the trip, but she sent Frederick to Amsterdam, where the ships were harbored, to inspect the bounty. The treasure had excited the interest of the general population; many people took time to visit and marvel at the haul, and Frederick knew that his eldest son especially would enjoy the spectacle, so on

January 7, 1629, he took Frederick Henry, who five days earlier had just turned fifteen, with him.

Father and son boarded a small sloop with about twenty other people to sail from The Hague to Amsterdam. It was a bitterly cold day, with a strong wind. The sea was crowded with shipping vessels in a hurry to make port, which made it difficult to maneuver. The afternoon light was failing—night comes early in January in Holland—when suddenly out of the gloom came a much larger craft carrying a full cargo of beer. There was no time to get out of the way. The beer-laden galleon struck the boat carrying Frederick and his son with such force that it split it in two. In minutes, it had filled with water and sunk, its passengers pitched into the sea, screaming for help and clinging to the debris as best they could. According to a letter of January 21 reporting these events, "The murthering boat, having a fair wind, would have left them all there; but a skipper of the King's boat being gotten into it, did with his dagger threaten death to the master thereof, if he would not presently save the King of Bohemia, to whom a cable being cast, he was by that means saved, together with a woman and a lackey that took hold thereof with him."

But the other passengers were not so lucky. Frederick could hear his son's cries—"Save me, father, save me!"—but could not find him in the darkness, though with their last energies, the members of the drowning crew had hoisted the boy to the ship's mast, which yet stood above the water. The galleon on which the rescued king of Bohemia stood was forced, despite his entreaties, to give up the search. Nineteen people died that night in the frigid sea. The next morning, when Frederick came back to search for bodies, he found his eldest son's corpse bobbing in the water, the boy's cloak still wrapped around the mast of the ship and "his cheek fastened by the frost to the said pole."

This tragedy, the correspondent continued, "hath been such a wind to the poor father's and mother's hearts, as it is much feared that…(she being newly brought to bed, and he much bruised and distempered with that miserable accident) it may endanger their lives."

⋆　　⋆　　⋆

THE COUPLE SURVIVED, but Frederick, who had stood wet and shivering on the deck of the rescue ship in the bitter wind listening to his child's desperate pleas for help and whose grief must consequently also have carried with it the heavy burden of guilt for having exposed the boy, however unconsciously, to danger, never fully recovered his health and spirits. And the next two years were as dark and discouraging as any Elizabeth had known. Frederick was frequently ill with a nagging cough that the doctors feared was consumption. In the spring of 1630, Charles, whose military ambitions had died with the duke of Buckingham, sent a messenger to his sister and her husband at The Hague to break the news that he had agreed to a peace with Spain that did not include a return of the Palatinate.⋆ The ambassador reported back that thirty-three-year-old Frederick broke down in tears at this interview and threatened to send Elizabeth on the next boat to England to beg alms from her brother "for that he [Frederick] was not able to put bread into her mouth." In January 1631 they buried their second-to-youngest daughter, the child who had been born just before the terrible episode with the treasure ships, in the tomb next to their eldest son.

So when later that year the Swedish king, Gustavus Adolphus, onetime suitor of Elizabeth, decided to enter the war in Germany on the side of the Protestants, nobody gave it much thought.

Improbably, it was again Cardinal Richelieu who acted as catalyst. Although he had briefly reclaimed the vital passages through the Swiss Alps for France, these had reverted to Spain when the cardinal had been forced to redeploy his army to subdue the rebellion at La Rochelle. Now he needed another means by which to divert imperial attention and troops (as, clearly, based on recent experience, Charles I was neither competent nor reliable in this regard). After some contemplation, Richelieu looked around and settled on Gustavus as the man for the job. On January 23, 1631,

---

⋆ He had already signed a peace treaty with France the previous May.

France and Sweden signed the Treaty of Bärwalde, which, in addition to the usual smoke screen of trade and defensive language, specified that Gustavus, a Lutheran, was to lead an extensive army of some thirty thousand men, to be funded by Richelieu, into Germany against the Catholic emperor.★

This turned out to be an inspired move. Gustavus Adolphus, without question the finest commander of his age, known admiringly as "the Golden King" or "the Lion of the North" for his Nordic coloring and general ferocity in battle, was definitely a man worth backing. Unlike his opponent General Tilly, who was older and not particularly innovative when it came to tactics, the king of Sweden, who had begun fighting as a ten-year-old child in his father's army, had propelled himself enthusiastically into the study of combat and made it his life's work. Gustavus saw the various military units—cavalry, infantry, artillery—not as separate battalions but as interlocking gears in a precisely driven machine that he orchestrated and drilled incessantly, like a master conductor rehearsing a particularly complex and strenuous symphony. Before landing in northern Germany, he had the foresight to raise an army of over 40,000 men—not the usual motley conglomerate of enthusiastic but inexperienced knights supplemented by forced recruits, but skilled soldiers, trained in small groups to shoot and reload lightweight muskets so quickly and continuously that the effect was not unlike modern automatic weaponry. Nor did Gustavus bring this vast force over all at once, where there was the chance its ranks would be diminished by lack of food or illness. Instead, he had them shipped over in stages when he knew supplies were adequate, so they arrived fresh and strong.

The king of Sweden was also shrewd enough to recognize that

★ That the cardinal and Louis XIII feared Ferdinand's ambitions would eventually lead to an invasion of France if not checked was well documented. "They say the French king—though not yet in print, yet in words to those ambassadors and agents that are about him, and in deeds to all the world—hath now professed enmity more than ever against the house of Austria [the Habsburgs]: the main reason whereof is because he knows well enough that if he had not called that...king [of Sweden] into Germany, the Austrians had poured some four armies into France at one clap," reported a member of the English government.

Gustavus Adolphus, the Lion of the North

his prospects for a successful invasion would increase substantially if he could pry allies away from Ferdinand by convincing the Protestant members of the German ruling class to support his efforts. Luckily for Gustavus, he held clout with one such baron who was perfectly situated to assist him in his endeavors: his brother-in-law, the elector of Brandenburg.

The elector of Brandenburg, a man who seemingly could be cowed by a strong breeze, whose one ambition had been to pass through life in the comfort and safety of out-of-the-way, provincial Berlin, had had the misfortune first to marry Frederick's sister and then to have his own sister marry the fearsome Gustavus. Try as he might to wiggle out of it, this put him squarely in the middle of the conflict. With Frederick he had been firm—he would allow the deposed king of Bohemia's children to remain in Berlin until provision could be made for them in Holland, but he would not take his part against the emperor, and Frederick, having no choice, had acquiesced in this decision. But Gustavus was a different story. The Swedish king had an army, and on June 19, 1631, when the elector of Brandenburg peeked out the window of his safe, comfortable manor house, he saw himself and his family surrounded by some 27,000 shockingly well-armed and obviously able-bodied Swedish soldiers. Of course, he did the only thing he felt he could do under the circumstances—he sent his mother and wife out to negotiate with Gustavus while he hid inside. The result of this parlay was that the elector of Brandenburg abruptly switched sides and agreed to give the king of Sweden everything he wanted.

Gustavus's recruiting efforts were also given a strong boost at this critical juncture by the unfortunate actions of the imperial army. While the king of Sweden and his men were marching on Berlin, about 100 miles to the west, Ferdinand's commander, General Tilly, and *his* forces were busy attacking the Protestant city of Magdeburg. After a short siege, Tilly's army of nearly 30,000 men overcame the Magdeburg defenses and stormed the wall, swarming into the city. The slaughter was horrific. Even members of the Catholic minority (who had been living in the city in peace with their Protestant neighbors) were exterminated where they stood. So dire was the situation—so many terrified women, children, and innocent civilians were abused and butchered in the first hours of the attack—that the local burghers decided it was better to die by flames and so set fire to the town rather than allow the imperial soldiers to loot and find shelter among them. "A conflagration arose during the storming, which the enemy, according to the universal testimony of the prisoners, intentionally and wickedly kindled, 'in order that the city might not bring us any good,'" General Tilly complained to the imperial government in his official report.

The resulting inferno and destruction shocked even a country already inured to the carnage of over a decade of war. In the aftermath of the tragedy, the elector of Saxony, who had heretofore been bribed by Ferdinand to stay loyal to the empire, and who, with the duke of Bavaria, had been one of the Protestant barons who had originally turned against Frederick, suddenly offered to help the king of Sweden fight against Tilly, giving as his reason the brutalities committed at Magdeburg.

In August, Gustavus marched his 27,000 Swedes south from Berlin, and by September had met up with the elector of Saxony, who had marshaled a force of nearly 20,000 German soldiers and who had even thought to supply his own artillery. Tilly, aware of the threat, had spent the summer adding to his ranks, so he had somewhere around 42,000 experienced troops under his command. On September 17, 1631, the opposing armies met on a dry, dusty hillock called Breitenfeld, close to Leipzig, and fell on each other with "great fury." Such was the zeal exhibited by the imperial troops that the elector of Saxony and his men, whose previous military experience had been against the hapless Silesians, bolted almost immediately. It was reported that the elector of Saxony, who had a flashy new uniform for the occasion and whose movements were consequently easily discernible, did not stop galloping for fifteen miles, until he was safely back in his home territory. Although he could not prevent a portion of his army from chasing after the fleeing soldiers and so lost some men that he could have used on the field, General Tilly did manage to capture and turn the elector of Saxony's artillery around so he could use it, as well as his own, to fire on Gustavus and his Swedish troops.

In any battle that had come before, this dispiriting opening would have been enough to destroy the morale of the remaining combatants and with it their chance for victory. But Gustavus Adolphus was unlike any opponent Tilly had faced. He did not give up and he did not allow his soldiers to give up, even under the pressure of the heavy guns. His muskets kept firing, regularly, ceaselessly, over the course of hours; his cavalry, used to working in small groups, could turn in an instant to protect the infantry; and Gustavus was always in the lead where the fighting was thickest, driving his stallion from one hot spot to the next. The imperial army fought bravely but charge after charge was beaten back until by the end of the day it was the Swedes who were charging, recapturing the artillery that had been used against them. It was a battle for the history books; Napoleon would later cite it with admiration. When it was over, 15,000 imperial soldiers lay dead on the field, with another 7,000 taken prisoner, and Tilly was so severely wounded that he was forced to retreat. As night fell, the king of Sweden, who had lost only 1,200 men that day, held the field.

The news spread rapidly through Europe and a messenger was dispatched from Gustavus to Charles I in London. The envoy brought with him "a letter from him [Gustavus] to his Majesty [Charles]... of the great and complete victory which God had given him against his enemies," reported a member of Charles's government in amazement, "and withal to represent unto him the fair opportunity which now was offered of restoring the King of Bohemia to his estate."

AFTER SO MANY YEARS of raised hopes followed by crushing disappointment, Elizabeth could hardly credit the news. "They talk much of a letter from that king [of Sweden] to my brother, where all is promised; yet since we cannot have a sight of that letter I fear there is nothing in it," she wrote guardedly to a friend. But this time, unbelievably, it *was* true. Gustavus followed up his mighty victory by marching farther south into Germany, taking first Erfurt, and then Würzburg, which was only a little more than fifty miles from Heidelberg itself. Even better, to redeem himself and his men after their somewhat less than stalwart behavior on the battlefield at Breitenfeld, the elector of Saxony agreed to send some of his soldiers into Bohemia to capture the capital, an assault made significantly easier by the fact that the imperial troops charged with defending the city decamped before they got there. "I am this week to present you with the joyful news of the winning of Prague, by Count Thorne, who, upon his arrival in Bohemia with some of the Duke of Saxony's and of the King of Sweden's forces, the country people flocked unto him; and he no sooner appeared before the city but it yielded without any blows," an English envoy reported to Charles's secretary of state in a letter of November 29, 1631.

All through that glorious autumn and winter, the Protestant cause, crushed for over a decade under Habsburg rule and thought irretrievably lost, rebounded under the king of Sweden's potent dynamism. (So much for Lutherans preferring Catholics to Calvinists. What Lutherans preferred was what everyone prefers—to *win*.) And Gustavus seemed absolutely committed to returning Frederick's property to him. When Charles, pleading poverty (but actually worried about breaking his peace with Spain and hoping, like his father, to rely solely upon negotiations to settle the matter), refused to help his sister and her husband outfit a force that would allow Frederick to aid the effort to retrieve the Palatinate, Gustavus insisted that the king of Bohemia join him in Germany anyway, even if he could not contribute a single soldier. "When the King of Sweden first sent for him [Frederick] thither, he made answer . . . he had neither men or money," a legislator reported from London. "'No!' said the King. 'What, a brother of the King of Great Britain, and protected by the States, and must he come to me in his doublet and hose! Let him come, howsoever, and I will do my best to restore him to his patrimony.' To which end, I hear, that incomparable King hath sworn all the towns he hath taken in the Palatinate to the service of their original master, the Palsgrave [Frederick]. And I am told also that he hath given order to the Duke of Saxony once more to proclaim him King of Bohemia," the English correspondent added with awe.★

Elizabeth couldn't go—she had just (what else) given birth, on January 12, 1632, to her thirteenth child, a son whom the couple gratefully named Gustavus Adolphus—but she sent Frederick into Germany to meet with his benefactor. He left The Hague on January 26, but before setting off in earnest, made sure to visit the family house in Leyden to say good-bye to his children. On February 10 he was in Frankfort-on-the-Main, where the king of Sweden had set up his winter camp. By the time he got there, Gustavus was supreme commander of some seven armies incorporating approxi-

---

★ And this was the prince Elizabeth's parents wouldn't let her marry! What a couple these two would have made.

mately 80,000 men. A dozen Protestant German barons had joined him and were serving in his various armies. Ambassadors from every power in Europe thronged his court.

Finding the king of Sweden out with his troops, Frederick went after him into the countryside. "My Lord of Canterbury told me, yesterday, from Sir Francis Nethersole's mouth, that the Kings of Sweden and Bohemia...met...in a great field between Frankfort and Mentz," reported a member of Charles's government. "When they approached, the armies making a stand, the kings met on horseback, and, having saluted each other, dismounted and embraced; but he of Sweden the other with such joy and affection as he lifted him upon high, which was apprehended for a good omen to the King of Bohemia by all that saw it." Although Heidelberg was still held by Spanish troops, much of the rest of the Lower Palatinate was already under the king of Sweden's control and the inhabitants turned out in large numbers at the news of Frederick's arrival. "Wonderful welcome, was this prince to his own subjects of the Palatinate," exclaimed an English envoy, "who everywhere ran out to see his majesty, with infinite expressions of joy and contentment, with many a hearty prayer, and tear, and high-sounding acclamation." Such a reception could not help but lift Elizabeth's and her husband's spirits. "I think that the King [Charles I] will one day recognize the mistake he made in not giving military assistance to the King of Bohemia," Frederick wrote tellingly to his wife from Frankfurt.★ Back in The Hague, Elizabeth, giving herself over to joy and hope, had a commemorative medallion struck and engraved with the motto "The setting sun rises again."

But where Frederick's priority was to expel the remaining Spanish soldiers from Heidelberg and reestablish himself and his family in his ancestral territory, this was in no way Gustavus's primary concern. The king of Sweden had a major war to run, which was spread out

---

★ Frederick had an unfortunate habit of referring to himself in the third person, as "the King of Bohemia," even in his personal letters to Elizabeth.

across the Habsburg empire, and which obliged him to move swiftly from place to place. Nor could the king of Bohemia convince Gustavus (who was nonetheless unfailingly warm and polite to his guest) to let Frederick break away from the rest of the army and raise his own troops to take on the Spanish himself. "My dearest heart," Frederick was soon complaining by letter to Elizabeth, "I know not what I am about; I see clearly that the King of Sweden does not desire *me* to have *troops*; he said that if *I* raised any, it would ruin *his army*—I know not therefore what *I* shall be good for…If there be nothing more to do than what I see as yet, *I* had better have stayed at *the Hague*."

What really seemed to have happened was that Gustavus's head had been turned by all the attention, and whereas before he might have been content with just the territory he had already conquered in northern Germany, by the time Frederick joined him he had enlarged his vision significantly, to the point where he felt himself deserving of an empire, in which all the Protestant barons, including the king of Bohemia, would comprise so many vassals. "The appetite has been so sharpened in Gustavus Adolphus by the conquests which he has achieved that it *already has no bounds*," the French ambassador warned bluntly in a report to Paris, "and his confidence in his fortune has risen to such a height that he no longer doubts in regard to any supposable success, and regards assault and victory as of one meaning to him…He desires to rule the whole course of the Rhine, occupy Coblentz and Mannheim, extend aid to the Hollanders, and to cut off our access to Germany."

Frederick, not truly understanding this and believing that Gustavus would eventually get around to retaking Heidelberg, felt more or less obliged to stick around and sort of trail after Gustavus in his martial wanderings. They went from Frankfurt to Aschaffenburg, from Aschaffenburg to Nuremberg. Their destination was Augsburg, where Tilly, although clearly still damaged both physically and spiritually from the earlier battle at Breitenfeld, had been pressured by Ferdinand to regroup and mount an offensive. (During a military strategy meeting the veteran general shocked the duke of Bavaria by suddenly breaking down into uncontrollable sobs.) On April 15, Gustavus's soldiers surprised Tilly's in a morning skirmish. Tilly was shot in the leg in the first wave and had to be hurriedly evacuated by litter from the field; the rest of his army retreated with him. The aged and broken general died two weeks later, on April 30, 1632, of his wounds. Gustavus, with Frederick still part of his entourage, went on to take Munich.

By the end of the summer it was clear that the king of Sweden did not intend to reinstate his good friend and ally the king of Bohemia in the Palatinate except at a very great price, the terms of which were drawn up in Latin. Frederick would have to pay an exorbitant sum to Gustavus (whose soldiers, in fairness, would be doing all the work) and he would have to ensure that those of his subjects who were Lutherans could practice their religion without prejudice (Frederick was a very devout Calvinist). Even then, Gustavus did not agree to give back that part of the Palatinate that he had already conquered, although he gave lip service to the condition that Frederick's sons would inherit in full after his death. "I never did think that the King of Sweden would proceed honorably," Frederick fumed in a letter of September 29 to Elizabeth. "I saw clearly that he had designs on freedom." Thoroughly depressed, and suffering from an ear infection, he left Gustavus's army and headed back on his own toward the Lower Palatinate, intending to stop at the small village of Alsheim, near Mainz, to recover. "I will be miserable at Alsheim, where I shall be entirely alone," he confessed despondently to his wife. "I will not fail to write to you from there every week. Believe me that my thoughts are continually with you, whom I love with all my heart."

Back in Holland, Elizabeth did everything she could to raise her husband's spirits and forward his cause. No secretary of state or cabinet minister displayed more energy or ability than she. She secured audiences, drew important emissaries to her house at The Hague, and once again directed reams of letters to every member of her wide acquaintance, alternately coaxing, humoring, entreating, or bargaining. She was in direct correspondence with the English ambassador assigned to Gustavus's court, and he frequently replied to her before reporting to London. Charles's envoy to Brussels was also a regular correspondent, as was one of her brother's closest advisers in London. She lobbied endlessly for funds and sent a personal messenger to her uncle the king of Denmark, and thereby succeeded in soliciting a promise that Elizabeth would receive a share in the inheritance of her maternal grandmother to be used to help reclaim the Palatinate. To Frederick she wrote loving, encouraging missives two and sometimes three times a week: bright, chatty notes filled with news about his sons and daughters or entertaining gossip (any important information relating to the war or the Palatinate was communicated by cipher). Along with her letters, she often attached portraits of the children, for which in his forlornness he thanked her profusely.

And while Frederick made his weary, despondent way west toward Mainz, and Elizabeth strove to manage their affairs and infuse their prospects with new buoyancy, Gustavus Adolphus moved forward relentlessly.

A METEORIC SUCCESS of the kind achieved by the king of Sweden inevitably provokes pushback. In this case, Ferdinand, watching first in disbelief and then in desperation as town after town fell to the enemy, understood that this was a challenge that must be met immediately. Consequently, after Tilly's death, the emperor appointed his former commander General Wallenstein as well as Tilly's second-in-command, Count Pappenheim, to recruit a new army. It took all summer, but by the fall they had assembled a new imperial fighting force of approximately 26,000 soldiers.

Aware of Gustavus's superior numbers, Wallenstein wisely chose not to engage his opponent in open battle but instead to go wherever the king of Sweden was not. With so much territory to cover, Gustavus obviously could not be everywhere at once and so Wallenstein began to retake the towns and cities, beginning with Prague, which had been captured by the Swedes but then left sparsely defended. This strategy resulted in Gustavus's having to chase after the imperial army all over Germany. It wasn't until the second week in November that he caught up with them in Lützen, not very far from Breitenfeld, site of his original triumph.

Wallenstein knew himself to be in trouble. Not expecting to meet the enemy, he had sent Pappenheim's divisions north and so found himself left with only about half his soldiers. He sent an urgent message ordering Pappenheim's return and did what he could to prepare for the onslaught. He dug a ditch to protect his musket men and supplemented his meager 14,000 troops by pressing into service his cooks and baggage handlers. Gustavus had only 16,000 soldiers with him — he had been waiting for reinforcements — but when he was apprised of the thinness of the imperial numbers, he knew he could take them. On the morning of November 16, 1632, the king of Sweden called his troops together, bent his head in prayer, and attacked.

An early morning fog hung over the battlefield, which initially helped obscure the imperial position, but by late morning the Swedish cavalry had overrun the ditch and had only the small store of imperial artillery with which to contend. Alarmed, Wallenstein set fire to the town to have the cover of smoke in the event of a retreat when suddenly hurtling out of the north came Pappenheim and his troops. And sometime after that, as the smoke began to clear, Gustavus's stallion was observed to be running loose with no sign of the king in the saddle. The rumor ran frantically through the Swedish army that the Lion of the North had fallen.

By nightfall Wallenstein was forced to concede the field and retreated with the remains of his army, leaving the artillery and camp stores to the victor. But he also left behind the corpse of Gustavus Adolphus, the greatest warrior of his time or perhaps of any time. The body was found on the enemy's side of the ditch, and it was clear that the king of Sweden had not succumbed easily. He had been shot four times: once in the head, twice in the arm, and the last, ominously, in the back.

NEWS OF GUSTAVUS'S DEATH reverberated through Europe. No one was more shocked or disappointed than Elizabeth, who had clearly held out hope that after some negotiation, the king of Sweden and Frederick would come to terms and that they would soon be able to return to their home in Heidelberg. "The loss...doth not a little trouble me, considering in what estate the King [Frederick] is now left," she confessed to an English cousin. Her husband was still in Mainz, where he had been waiting for a messenger from Gustavus in response to his latest overture. He had recovered from his ear infection but still felt unwell; in addition, he was depressed and lonely. There was plague at Mainz but he couldn't sit still, and against his doctor's orders he went to a crowded church to pray for guidance. That evening, he went to bed with a headache.

During the night, he had a fever and a little swelling in the neck, but his secretary wrote reassuringly to Elizabeth that he had seen "his majesty of Bohemia, in his bed in the morning; and he told me that his fever had quite left him, but that the swelling in his neck troubled him a little, and he hoped when that had burst, he should be cured. For the rest, he spoke of business, and smiled at the physicians who wanted to charge him with the plague." But that evening the fever returned in force, and he was delirious. The telltale marks of the fearful disease began to appear on his body.

On November 17, Frederick rallied sufficiently to be able to write Elizabeth a short note. Not wanting to worry her, he did not mention his illness. But he knew he was failing. "I will not make this any longer except to assure you that I shall be until my grave my dear and only heart, your most faithful friend and most affectionate servant," he scribbled.

It was to be his last letter to her. In the early morning hours of November 29, 1632, just two weeks after the slaying of Gustavus in battle, thirty-six-year-old Frederick, onetime king of Bohemia and Elector Palatine, summoned witnesses to his bedside. His final thoughts were with his wife and children. He pleaded for their care and protection by the prince of Orange, the king of England, and the States General of Holland.

He died at daybreak.

PART II

≈

The Daughters of the Winter Queen

Princess Elizabeth, Louise Hollandine, Henrietta Maria, and Sophia

The Court of the Prince of Orange at The Hague

Princess Elizabeth

...at age twelve

7

A Royal Refugee

PRINCESS ELIZABETH, BORN IN HEIDELBERG on November 27, 1618, during the fleetingly gentle time that preceded her father's election as king of Bohemia, was her parents' third child and eldest daughter. When her mother and father left for Prague that fateful autumn, she and her older brother Karl Ludwig were left behind in the care of her grandmother, Frederick's mother, Louise Juliana. Elizabeth was ten months old. She was not yet two when the Spanish troops under General Spinola invaded the Lower Palatinate, and Louise Juliana, fearing capture, gathered her two small charges and, together with her unmarried daughter Catherine, who had also been living in the ancestral castle in Heidelberg, fled first to Stuttgart and then, the following year, to another of Louise Juliana's daughters, the electress of Brandenburg, in Berlin.

Grandmother, spinster aunt, and children arrived to find that the deposed king and queen of Bohemia, who were wanted by the emperor, had accepted the prince of Orange's invitation to establish themselves at Dutch expense in The Hague and had already moved on, leaving the infant Maurice with the electress. With nowhere else to go, the four of them — forty-five-year-old Louise Juliana, twenty-seven-year-old Catherine, four-and-a-half-year-old Karl Ludwig, and two-and-a-half-year-old Elizabeth — settled down in a country manor belonging to the elector and electress in out-of-the-way Krossen, about forty miles south of Berlin, to try to ride out the war.

And so Princess Elizabeth's earliest years—though likely she did not remember them—were marked by upheaval, fear, and loss. But she most certainly would have remembered when her brother and closest childhood companion, Karl Ludwig, was sent for by her parents to come live with the rest of the family in the nursery in Leyden in 1624, leaving behind Elizabeth and Maurice. She received letters from Karl Ludwig and from her eldest brother, Frederick Henry, as well as little gifts that were intended to build affection between the siblings despite the distance that separated them, but it is difficult to believe that she was not in some way conscious of having been left out. Luckily, whatever disappointment the princess might have felt was compensated for by her grandmother and aunt, who provided both love and stability.

By the time the king and queen of Bohemia *did* call these final two children to Holland, in the fall of 1628, Elizabeth was nearly ten and her brother seven. Neither had seen their parents since infancy. The only mother they had ever known was Louise Juliana, supplemented by the maternal efforts of their aunts, the electress of Brandenburg and the unmarried Catherine. The only home they knew was Germany. And now, suddenly, they were instructed to go off to Leyden to become part of a dauntingly crowded family they were aware of only through an intermittent correspondence. It must have felt a little like being unceremoniously shipped off to the doubtful care of a headmistress at a foreign boarding school.

And Elizabeth could not have arrived in Holland at a worse moment. She'd barely had time to make the acquaintance of her siblings and have her first Christmas away from her grandmother when her eldest brother, Frederick Henry, who had so sweetly attempted to keep up a relationship with her all those years in Krossen and who was so clearly adored by everyone, died tragically, and the strangers who were her parents went into a paralyzed mourning. Thirteen-year-old Karl Ludwig, the new heir to the Palatinate (and the only sibling, other than Maurice, whom she vaguely knew), was brought to The Hague to live. At least initially, Elizabeth seems to have been left with the other children, but within two years, following the English tradition, she as well as Rupert would also be summoned to live at their parents' court as each came of age.

These were the years of the Winter King and Queen's deepest depression, and their eldest daughter, sensitive and bookish, could not have helped but be affected by the general despair. Frederick was often ill, and no sooner had he recovered than he left to join the king of Sweden in Germany, in early 1632. Her mother remained but had an uneasy relationship with her eldest daughter. Their personalities were very different. The queen of Bohemia complained in a letter that Princess Elizabeth was too easily swayed by anyone who showed her affection, and questioned her daughter's judgment and attitude. For her part, Princess Elizabeth, bereft of her devoted grandmother, felt that her mother was cold and critical to her and far more loving to her brothers and sisters. The glamorous court at The Hague with its endless stream of accomplished and witty visitors, so different from the quiet backwater of Krossen where she had grown up, made the adolescent Elizabeth feel awkward and self-conscious. She was plagued by her looks, as teenage girls often are, although but for a prominent nose, she seems to have been very attractive. Her youngest sister, Sophia, reported that Elizabeth "had black hair, a dazzling complexion, brown sparkling eyes, a well-shaped forehead, beautiful cherry lips, and a sharp aquiline nose, which was rather apt to turn red." This nose was evidently the bane of the princess's existence. Whenever it turned red, "she hid herself from the world," Sophia continued. "I remember that my sister, Princess Louisa, who was not so sensitive, asked her on one such unlucky occasion to come upstairs to the Queen [her mother], as it was the usual hour for visiting her. Princess Elizabeth said, 'Would you have me go with this nose?' The other replied, 'Will you wait till you get another?'"

It is perhaps not surprising then that Princess Elizabeth, who was highly intelligent, should turn to the one pursuit at which she excelled: scholarship. And in this area, at least, her new home in The Hague offered educational resources and opportunities far superior to any she would have been exposed to had she stayed in Berlin. Wealthy and tolerant (by seventeenth-century standards), Holland was a magnet for academics and artists alike, some of them religious exiles from their native lands. The Hague was bursting with experts in navigation, engineering, and mathematics, all on the cutting edge of science, as well as humanists and historians, and many found their way to the queen of Bohemia's drawing room; even the younger children at the house in Leyden had regular dinners with visiting professors. As she became more familiar with her surroundings, Princess Elizabeth, whose former studies had been weighted heavily toward Calvinist religious training, was exposed to first-rate tutors with access to sophisticated books and papers in exciting new fields.

And then, just two days after her fourteenth birthday, the father she had barely known died.

THE BEREAVEMENT WAS SO unexpected, coming as it did on the heels of Frederick's letter confidently predicting that all was well, and such a catastrophe to the family's hopes that it was judged best to have a doctor communicate the news to his widow, in case she should break down completely. This Elizabeth nearly did.* "It was the first time that ever I was frightened," the queen of Bohemia confessed in a letter to one of her oldest and dearest confidants. "I... could neither cry nor speak nor eat nor drink for three days." In fact, she stayed in bed for eight days. By her own admission, she had lost her best friend.

But when she emerged from her darkened room, she did so with an unshakable purpose—to defeat her enemies and install Karl Ludwig, Frederick's heir, in her husband's homeland and reclaim his inheritance. Her first move was to secure the alliance with Sweden. Even before she answered her brother Charles's heartfelt letter of

---

* I know it is difficult to keep the different Elizabeths straight but I will try very hard to make it clear when I am talking about the mother and when the daughter. This Elizabeth is Frederick's widow. As a rule, I will endeavor to always refer to her eldest daughter as Princess Elizabeth to avoid confusion.

condolence—"Never did I rail at any opportunity for writing to you excepting this one," he penned sadly—she wrote to Axel Oxenstierna, chancellor of Sweden, who had assumed command of the Swedish military effort in Germany after Gustavus Adolphus's death. She entreated him to continue with the plan to retake the Palatinate, and received in reply the assurance that Sweden remained faithful to the goal of returning her children's legacy. She saw to it that sixteen-year-old Karl Ludwig inherited all of his father's titles, and sent representatives to the Protestant barons in Germany urging them to continue to fight until all of her son's property in the Palatine was restored and certainly not to allow any peace that did not include the recognition of his right to the title of elector. She reached out to the States General of Holland, composing an emotional address, which was read out in assembly, thanking the legislators for all they had done for her family in the past and pleading for their continued support.

In the first wave of grief, Charles generously insisted that his sister come home, and sent a delegation to The Hague to hasten her journey. So sincere was the king of England in his desire to have Elizabeth return that he ordered her old rooms prepared for her at Whitehall and additional accommodations made ready for her children at one of his own country houses. But as much as the queen of Bohemia had longed for such an invitation from her father when she and Frederick had fled Prague, she now refused this kind offer. Although she politely gave as her reason the specious excuse that the German custom of mourning forbade the widow from leaving the house for an extended period, what Elizabeth really seemed to want was to stay close to the prince of Orange, who was ever her mainstay and whose interests were much more allied with hers, and to keep her independence, a condition that promised to be somewhat trickier at her brother's court.★

★ In light of future events, staying out of England would prove to be a very wise decision.

The results of the queen of Bohemia's first flurry of diplomacy after her husband's death were extremely promising. For by spring 1633, the Swedish army had actually retaken Heidelberg, and Chancellor Oxenstierna, true to his word, was ready to deliver it to Karl Ludwig, provided that Sweden was compensated for its expenses in driving out the Spanish troops. Elizabeth immediately dispatched an ambassador to Charles to beg for the requisite funds and arranged to send Karl Ludwig (along with his thirteen-year-old brother Rupert, who was very precocious when it came to swordplay and other martial games and who begged to go so relentlessly that she finally gave in) to Germany in the care of the prince of Orange because "I think he cannot too soon be a soldier."

Nothing bespoke the success of the queen of Bohemia's efforts, or the perception that this time her brother, the king of England, would honor his promise to defend the Palatine, more than the advantageous marriage alliances that suddenly seemed possible for her children. To draw England into the war in Germany on the side of the Protestants, there were rumors that Chancellor Oxenstierna was willing to marry Gustavus Adolphus's only child and heir, six-year-old Christina, to Karl Ludwig, provided that Charles I would furnish his nephew with the money and troops necessary to continue the struggle against the Habsburgs. As early as June 1633, the English secretary of state proposed to Elizabeth that she wed her second daughter, eleven-year-old Louise Hollandine, to the son of the elector of Saxony, whose allegiance was (rightly) feared to be wavering. And it was also at this moment that the new king of Poland, who had ascended to the throne the year before during that same fateful month of November that had seen the deaths of the kings of Sweden and Bohemia, began a determined campaign to win the hand of the Winter Queen's eldest daughter, Princess Elizabeth.

WLADYSLAW IV, THE PROSPECTIVE bridegroom, was thirty-seven years old when his father died and he replaced him as king of Poland.

His grandfather had once ruled Sweden, and the new sovereign felt that he had strong claim to that throne as well. He judged that now might be a good time to go after it, what with Gustavus Adolphus dead and his daughter, Christina, installed as queen. Six-year-old Christina didn't seem like she'd put up nearly as robust a fight as her fearsome parent.

But even up against a child, he was still going to need allies, and the king of England (about whom Wladyslaw seemed to know very little) was high on his list. If he married the queen of Bohemia's eldest daughter, Wladyslaw reasoned, he might be able to lure Charles, her uncle, to his side in his contest for the Swedish throne. Surely the king of England would want to see his niece crowned queen of both Poland *and* Sweden. Of course, Princess Elizabeth would have to convert—Poland was an overwhelmingly Catholic country and the governing Polish aristocracy would never accept a Protestant as queen—but the hopeful suitor was confident that this could be arranged.

Accordingly, Wladyslaw sent an ambassador to The Hague in the summer of 1633 to obtain a portrait of the fourteen-year-old princess and assess her mother's probable reaction. The queen of Bohemia, who would have fought with her life any attempt to convert her daughter to Catholicism, clearly did not take the prospect of a union with Poland seriously. "It is meant...only for a show to get friends against Sweden," she sniffed dismissively to a friend.

But Wladyslaw was not to be swayed. Having gotten nowhere with the mother, he now determined to go behind her back and send an emissary to the English court—specifically, to Princess Elizabeth's aunt Henrietta Maria, the queen, whom he knew to be Catholic. The sovereign's instructions to his envoy on this occasion were very precise. "When he has had his official audience of the King, the ambassador must ask for a private one from the Queen, and to her majesty must say that the King of Poland has by no means given up the idea of uniting himself to the eldest daughter of the late Elector," the envoy's commission read. "The King of Poland consequently hopes in the Queen of England for obtaining from her niece, the Princess Palatine, the conversion of the latter to the Catholic faith; and suggests that, to facilitate matters, her Majesty should, under some pretext that may appear natural to the Queen of Bohemia, invite the young princess upon a visit to her uncle. The conversion would then doubtless follow easily enough. If the Queen of England could only give the simple assurance that her niece would abjure her heresy, without further binding herself, it might be possible at once to commence the matrimonial negotiations."

Alas for Wladyslaw and his innovative (if unscrupulous) approach to lovemaking, the Polish king had seriously misread the appetite of the English court at this juncture for meddling in European affairs. For although in spirit Charles sincerely wished his sister and her children well and desired his nephew's reinstatement in the Palatine, in practice he found that he did not after all wish for it sufficiently to take the unpleasant steps necessary to secure it. In fact, since the duke of Buckingham's death, Charles, like his father before him, had embraced the charms of peace. He found that he loved his wife, who had already given him a son and heir, Charles, born on May 29, 1630; a daughter, Mary, on November 4, 1631; and, most recently, a second son, James, on October 14, 1633.* He had a new adviser, Bishop Laud (again like his father, Charles allied himself with the Anglican Church, which recognized the king as the ultimate authority, and not with the unruly Puritans, who believed that they, as members of the elect, had the right to tell the sovereign what to do), as well as a new treasurer, whose job it was to find the revenues necessary to run the kingdom without ever having to call another parliament. For Charles had discovered that he disliked parliaments every bit as much as his father had and was determined to rule without them. The last one, in 1629, had descended into such

---

* It is interesting that the queen of Bohemia, whose children's names read like a litany of whoever happened to be helping her at the moment, never named any of *her* sons James.

a rout that he'd had to dissolve the proceedings by fiat and have the most outspoken of its members imprisoned.

So when the queen of Bohemia sent her secretary to London to beg for the funds Chancellor Oxenstierna had demanded in order to secure Heidelberg for Karl Ludwig, Charles found himself unable to comply publicly with her request, as only by convening parliament could he hope to raise the necessary sum, and this, of course, he refused to do. Secretly, he gave his approval to try to raise the money from private sources, but Elizabeth's secretary was overly zealous in her cause and made so many enemies at court that the attempt failed. And when by the next year it became clear that England was not, after all, going to tangibly aid the anti-imperial cause in Germany, the Swedes and their Protestant allies looked around for someone who would. And there was Cardinal Richelieu, who was still funding the Swedish army and willing to make a deal.

The upshot of these negotiations was that Louis XIII raised a force of some 35,000 Frenchmen, who crossed into Germany through Lorraine and into Alsace in September of 1634. By December they occupied Heidelberg. And on April 30, 1635, the French king and Chancellor Oxenstierna signed the Treaty of Compiègne, which split the west bank of the Rhine between France and Sweden, prompting the elector of Saxony and the elector of Brandenburg to go over to the imperial side. Everybody changed dance partners all over again except that this time, the queen of Bohemia and her family were left on the sidelines as wallflowers.

The atmosphere of defeat associated with the court at The Hague, the sense of having been outmaneuvered by Richelieu and betrayed by Oxenstierna, and the attendant loss of prestige and influence were unmistakable.

The king of Poland shrugged his shoulders and married the emperor's daughter.

Louise Hollandine

A seventeenth–century Dutch artist in his studio

8

Child of Light and Dark

THE WINTER QUEEN'S SECOND DAUGHTER, vivacious, free-spirited Louise Hollandine, whom everyone called Louisa, inherited her mother's fun-loving outlook and easy temperament, qualities that were only enhanced by her childhood experience. In contrast to her older sister, Princess Elizabeth, who had been hurried from place to place and left out of the larger family circle, Louisa's early years had been stable and placid. As the first child born in her parents' adopted country, she felt no pull, like her older siblings, to Germany; nor did she have to overcome linguistic or cultural differences in order to assimilate to her surroundings. Born on April 17, 1622, she was not yet two years old when the prince of Orange provided her parents with a residence in Leyden specifically to house their children, and, with Frederick Henry and Rupert, she moved in as the nursery's first female occupant. She was already comfortable with its routines and safely established as head girl when every year or so a new sibling arrived.

The security of her childhood expressed itself in her personality. "Louisa was lively and unaffected," her youngest sister, Sophia, reported. She was "not so handsome" as the eldest, Princess Elizabeth, "but had, in my opinion," Sophia continued, "a more amiable disposition."

But what really contributed to Louise Hollandine's vitality and set her apart from the rest of the family was the joy she took in art.

"She devoted herself to painting, and so strong was her talent for it that she could take likenesses without seeing the originals," Sophia marveled. When immersed in front of a canvas, Louisa was apt to lose herself in concentration, an idiosyncrasy for which she was often teased by the rest of the household. "While painting others she neglected herself sadly," Sophia remembered with amusement. "One would have said that her clothes had been thrown on her, and this caused [a visitor to the court] to compare her...to a painter who, failing to paint a horse's foam, threw his brush at the picture in a rage, and by this chance succeeded to perfection."

Not only was Louisa blessed with obvious talent, but she also had the spectacular good fortune to have been born at exactly the right moment and in exactly the right place to take advantage of one of those rare seismic shifts in perception in the history of art: the emergence of the Dutch school of painting.

A NUMBER OF FACTORS are said to have contributed to the flowering of Dutch art during the first half of the seventeenth century. The profits pouring into Holland from the East India Company and other shipping ventures are usually cited first, for it is true that wealth and art go hand in hand, the one to buy, the other to produce. Then, too, with the fighting centered in Germany and Belgium, Holland was for the most part able to avoid the ravages of war—the atrocities committed by occupying enemy soldiers, the famines and diseases that haunted the rest of Europe. This in turn allowed those of its citizens so inclined to concentrate on more peaceful artistic pursuits.

But surely the defining impetus for the magic that gleamed softly from Dutch palettes was the exhilaration that came with finally squirming out from under the centuries-old strictures of the Catholic Church with its emphasis on the same repetitive biblical stories, and the ensuing opening up of subject matter. Protestant Holland had no soaring cathedrals whose oversize walls required decoration with images of penitent crowds surrounding John the Baptist's head on a platter. Large paintings went instead to town halls, whose members clamored for more secular scenes of banquets and battles. And there was a whole new market—here's where the wealth comes in—in smaller pictures, which were much in demand by the burgeoning upper middle class, whose taste ran to portraits (usually of themselves) and scenes of domestic life. These more intimate, interior paintings demanded a high degree of detail as well as a complex handling of light and dark.

The king and queen of Bohemia arrived at The Hague just in time to get a firsthand look at the exciting new developments in art. They were a little too early for Rembrandt—in 1621 he was only sixteen and was apprenticing in his hometown of Leyden—but they, like everyone else in Holland, were very impressed by the work of a thirty-year-old master who had just returned from an extended period of study in Rome. His name was Gerrit van Honthorst.

HONTHORST WAS BORN IN Utrecht, less than fifty miles east of The Hague, in 1592. He demonstrated an early talent for sketching and was apprenticed under a local painter. Wanting a wider artistic experience, by the age of twenty-four he had found his way to Italy. It was to be the making of him.

Honthorst settled in Rome and was for the first time exposed to the genius of the Renaissance. He learned the difficult technique used to produce frescoes and studied the masterworks on the walls of St. Peter's. He was particularly impressed with the paintings of Raphael, who employed multiple sources of light in a single canvas, and of Caravaggio, whose style he at first sought to emulate and later incorporated into his own approach. He stayed for several years, working for a prince and honing his skills by painting religious scenes. His twist was to portray a familiar story but set it at night, which altered the effect. He did this so often that his contemporaries called him "Gherardo delle Notti" (Gerrit of the Night).

By 1622 he had returned to Utrecht, where he produced, among other works, *The Dentist,* which depicted a man having his tooth pulled by candlelight. The novelty of the subject matter, the intensity of the light on the faces of dentist and patient, the shadows on the small circle of men observing the operation with interest, and the darkness beyond all combined to recommend Honthorst to the public and his peers alike. He was elected dean of his local guild and came to the attention of Elizabeth, who was looking for an art instructor for her children. He quickly became her official court painter, specializing in portraits of the Winter King and Queen and their many children. He was also employed by the prince of Orange and his wife, and Elizabeth even sent him to England in 1628 to paint portraits of Charles I and Queen Henrietta Maria.*

By 1629 Honthorst was back in Holland and engaged as instructor to those of Frederick and Elizabeth's children who were old enough to take lessons, and Louisa was soon included in this group. To have such a teacher must have been a gift indeed. It's no wonder that Louisa was passionate about her painting.

But a royal princess could not, as Rembrandt did, perfect her talents by spending all of her time sketching in the streets or in her room at home painting her own face in the mirror. ("He never left off working in the house of his parents while daylight lasted," a contemporary asserted.)† By 1635, Louisa was old enough to be moved out of the Leyden house and into the court at The Hague, where her mother and elder sister resided. She still took lessons from Honthorst and did as much painting as she could, but her days were bound by other obligations, such as helping to entertain the many

---

* The prince of Orange's wife, Amelia de Solms, one of the queen of Bohemia's former ladies-in-waiting, branched out a little and had *her* portrait painted in 1631 by the popular new young artist Rembrandt van Rijn. But Rembrandt, with his keen observation and emphasis on detailing every wrinkle, painted her in profile, giving special attention to her double chin, so after that she stayed with Honthorst.

† If you want to see what Leyden looked like while Louise Hollandine and her siblings were growing up, you have only to glance at Rembrandt's work before 1630. He took all of his subjects (except for his many self-portraits) from the streets of the town. After that he moved to Amsterdam, where the demand for his portraits was so great that "he had not only to be paid but to be prayed" to take on a subject, a local wag quipped.

visitors who flooded her mother's court and participating in whatever amusements had been scheduled for the evening. And of course, her principal duty was to attract a suitor, preferably one who could help promote the family's single, overriding interest: to have Karl Ludwig reinstated as elector, and secure the return of the Palatinate.

WHEN IT BECAME CLEAR to the elector of Saxony that France and Sweden had come to an agreement to more or less divide up Germany between them (leaving him out), his enthusiasm for his former allies, never particularly strong to begin with, waned considerably. He might do better, he began to think, if he offered his services and allegiance to the emperor. At least it was worth talking about. So in the spring of 1635, he sent envoys to Ferdinand to open up a channel of negotiation.

Ferdinand, to his credit, jumped at the chance to come to terms with one of his Protestant opponents. Fifteen years of watching the brutal impact of war on his formerly prosperous empire had sickened him. He'd seen beautiful, centuries-old cities and towns destroyed, and farmland ruined by battle. Thousands died every year in the fighting and thousands more from the disease and famine that were the inevitable by-products of the movement and quartering of large armies.

The resulting treaty, ratified on June 15, 1635, and known as the Peace of Prague, was clearly intended to end the war for good. By its terms, the emperor volunteered (with one exception) to turn the clock back to 1620, before the start of hostilities. He offered full amnesty to all the Protestant Germans currently fighting against him, and agreed to allow them to practice their religion within their various territories without fear of imperial reprisal. No longer would Protestant churches or any of their other property be appropriated for Catholic use, nor would a Protestant area be put under the administration of a Catholic governor. But the emperor went even further in his concessions. By this contract, he formally committed himself to ensuring that an equal number of Protestants and Catholics served as judges on the high court and even accepted that this same religious quota would apply to the members of his own private council.

The really unique aspect of this agreement was that this time, he meant it. The Catholic Ferdinand, once rigidly intolerant, no longer sought to eradicate his otherwise loyal Protestant subjects or degrade their rights as citizens of the empire simply on the basis of their religious beliefs. In his revised and far more temperate approach to rule may be discerned the first precious seeds of the Enlightenment.

The emperor's one caveat was that the duke of Bavaria, who had remained loyal to him from the beginning, should retain the Upper Palatine and the title of elector, leaving only the Lower Palatine to the queen of Bohemia's family, although he did offer to bestow a small monetary compensation on Elizabeth's children, provided they came before him and humbled themselves properly.

The publication of these peace terms caused a sensation. Protestant Germany, with no desire to give itself over to France and Sweden, looked to its own interests and overwhelmingly followed the elector of Saxony's lead. By August of 1635 nearly every German member of the former anti-Habsburg alliance had taken advantage of Ferdinand's offer of amnesty and defected to the emperor's side. Nobody cared that the duke of Bavaria was going to keep the Upper Palatinate.

Nobody except Elizabeth, who fought this new development with everything she had. She fired off letter after letter to Bishop Laud, whom she knew to be the man most likely to influence her brother Charles, denouncing the terms of the Peace of Prague and begging for English help against it. She lodged an official protest with the Protestant German barons who had formerly been her allies. She put pressure on the prince of Orange to add his own voice—and ambassadors—to hers to oppose the peace, characterizing it as a victory for Catholicism. She even had Karl Ludwig, who at nineteen had come of age and was at least nominally the head of the family, issue a public manifesto entitled "Charles Lodowicke, by the Grace of God, Count Palatine of the Rhine...and Prince Elector of the Sacred Empire," and addressed to "his Imperial Majesty and to all Kings, Potentates, Electors, Princes and Estates within the Empire and Whole Christendom" (Elizabeth wasn't taking any chances on leaving anybody out), in which he traced his claim to the Palatine to a bull issued in 1356 by the then Holy Roman emperor Charles IV, which stated that "hereafter, no dispute nor dissension arise between the sons of the said Electors, and Princes temporal, and that the public good and tranquility suffer no stop nor detriment. We, desirous to remove all such impediments, do by this present Act, *never to be repealed*, declare, will, and ordain, by our Imperial Authority; that when any of the said Electors shall decease, his Right, Vote, and power Elective shall descend to his eldest Son...without any opposition."

As a final, lasting illustration of her defiance of the Peace of Prague, in 1636 Elizabeth threw down the gauntlet in the most visceral way possible by commissioning Honthorst to paint a massive group portrait, fifteen feet long by ten feet wide, of every member of her immediate family (including the dead ones, who were portrayed in a corner window bathed in celestial light, looking down benevolently and sort of cheering on the live ones). Called *The Triumph of the Winter Queen*, it featured a larger-than-life Elizabeth riding over her crushed enemies in a Roman-style chariot harnessed to a set of lions (most likely representing England, a nice mix of symbolism and wishful thinking) and surrounded by her children.*

Fourteen-year-old Louisa, posing for this picture (that's her in salmon pink with a chaste veil over her head, standing behind the lions and holding the palm frond; her older sister, Princess Elizabeth, as the eldest daughter and leading nuptial candidate, holds a position of prominence in the foreground in blue), could not have helped but been aware of the political implications of the painting. By the summer of 1636, her two eldest brothers (pictured on

---

* It's hanging in the Museum of Fine Arts in Boston, where it was recently restored. Go see it.

horseback behind their mother, Karl Ludwig in kingly ermine, Rupert on his right dressed as a Roman soldier) were both away in England. The visit represented something of a milestone for the family. None of the queen of Bohemia's children had been allowed to set foot in Britain while their grandfather was alive, but they had heard their mother's stories of it and knew it to be a place of great wealth and ease. They were all naturally very curious about it (all those English lessons!), and it seems to have grown in their minds into a kingdom of fairy-tale dimensions. Elizabeth, fearing rejection, had not even bothered to ask her brother's permission to send her sons but had used the occasion of Karl Ludwig's coming of age to establish the precedent that he might, as a sovereign in his own right, travel freely on state business, and would naturally want his first official act to be to pay his respects to his uncle Charles.

It was a gambit that paid off. Both boys were warmly received by the king and queen and became great favorites of the court. Karl Ludwig, conscious of the heavy responsibility he had inherited, was cautious and staid, but his manners and English were perfect, which helped a lot. He made a very persuasive advocate for his cause. Elizabeth had been right: Charles found it much more difficult to turn down an entreaty for money and soldiers when it was delivered in person by such an obviously respectable young nephew. And sixteen-year-old Rupert, all fire and energy (the family nickname for him was "Le Diable"—the devil), the polar opposite of Karl Ludwig, only added to his brother's appeal. A superior sportsman, constantly in motion, quicksilver Rupert was irresistibly charismatic. Both Charles and Henrietta Maria found him enormously entertaining and encouraged his fearless, adventuresome nature—Charles even went so far as to consider sending Rupert off to conquer Madagascar until his mother, hearing of this wild scheme, put a stop to it. For their part, Karl Ludwig and Rupert, used to the genteel poverty of the household in The Hague, were dazzled by the magnificence of their uncle's court and felt that England more than lived up to their childhood imaginings.

Prince Rupert at twelve

While they were away, Louisa and her two older siblings, Princess Elizabeth and fifteen-year-old Maurice (who always seems to have been left behind), had a visitor: her sixteen-year-old cousin Frederick William, eldest son of the elector of Brandenburg. A bright boy, Frederick William had been sent by his father to study at the University of Leyden with Maurice and Maurice's two brothers, eleven-year-old Edward and nine-year-old Philip. (Gustavus Adolphus, the baby of the family, was still too young to attend school.)

Frederick William evidently enjoyed this, his first visit to Holland, every bit as much as Karl Ludwig and Rupert relished their time in England. The Hague might not be as overpoweringly vast as London, nor his aunt's court as grand as Charles I's, but it was a pinnacle of commerce, culture, and sophistication as compared to

Berlin. The trip made a big impression on him. He was fascinated by the ships and bustling streets; he found himself drawn to the art and intellectual life of the Dutch; he took pleasure in participating with his older cousins in their various amusements — riding and hunting at his aunt's summer house in Rhenen, as well as the usual diversions of parties, concerts, and plays. But what really seems to have recommended The Hague to him and made his time there so delightful was his cousin Louisa. Teasing and talented, she was unlike any girl he had met. It soon became obvious that he was smitten with her.

This was a very good match for Louisa. Frederick William stood to inherit his father's lands and titles, and he was just the right age for a bridegroom. Even better, as a Calvinist, he passed the Winter Queen's all-important Protestant test. And although there is no record of her response, Louisa seems to have reciprocated his affection — or, at least, she made no objection to a wedding. As for her mother, the queen of Bohemia welcomed the idea of a marriage alliance with her brother-in-law the elector of Brandenburg, especially as it would make it more difficult for him to side with the emperor against her.

It is a measure of just how toxic a union with the queen of Bohemia and her family had become in the wake of the Peace of Prague that the instant the elector of Brandenburg was alerted to his son's romantic inclinations, he had Frederick William recalled to Berlin. Young love being a potent impulse, Frederick William at first tried to rebel against his parent and remain in Holland, but he was at length compelled to obey. No sooner had he arrived back in Berlin than he mysteriously took ill at a dinner given by the minister who had negotiated his father's return to the imperial alliance, giving rise to widespread rumors that he had been poisoned to prevent his speaking out against the Peace of Prague and allying himself with the queen of Bohemia and her family. Certainly Elizabeth always believed this to be the case. Although Frederick William eventually recovered from this indisposition, and the allegations were never proved (they were never denied either), it does give a sense of the intensity of the debate in Germany over whether or not to adhere to the emperor at this pivotal moment.

For although the elector of Brandenburg and the other Protestant barons had agreed to the terms of the Peace of Prague, that did not mean the war was over. There was still the little problem of the Swedes, who, having invested so many lives and so much time and money in Germany, were unwilling to accept peace terms unless they were bought off with a large parcel of land (preferably in northern Germany, close to Sweden, which meant the elector of Brandenburg's territory, something he was obviously reluctant to relinquish, another reason he had gone over to the imperial side). And the Swedish troops were perfectly capable of holding their own with or without the presence of their former German allies, a point that was driven home on October 4, 1636, when they decimated a superior imperial force under the command of the elector of Saxony, leaving 8,000 of his men dead and thousands more prisoners, and taking all of his artillery. This victory was sufficiently impressive to cause several of the Protestant barons to change their minds about the Peace of Prague and re-ally with Sweden (although the elector of Brandenburg, who had the most to lose, was not among them).

And then, early the next year, came the final blow to those who had hoped to see the seemingly interminable struggle end. On the morning of February 15, 1637, fifty-eight-year-old Ferdinand, who had never ruled a moment in peace and had in the end learned to yearn for it, died a broken man, and was immediately replaced as emperor by his firebrand son (named—what else?—Ferdinand; well, at least it's consistent), thereby guaranteeing that the war would go on.

That summer, Elizabeth, eager to capitalize on these events, recalled her two eldest sons, to their great disappointment, from their English visit. "Both the brothers went away unwillingly, but Prince Rupert expressed it most," wrote an English correspondent, "for being ahunting that very morning with the King, he wished that he might break his neck, so he might leave his bones in

England!" But there was no help for it; all the dance partners had changed again. The prince of Orange had made a new alliance with the French against the Habsburgs, and Charles had at last agreed to provide Karl Ludwig with his own force.

And back at The Hague, Louisa, now fifteen, poor and single, her prospects for love and marriage dwindling with each twist and turn of the war, went on with her painting.

Henrietta Maria

Lilies and roses in a seventeenth-century Dutch painting

9

Lilies and Roses

By the beginning of 1638, Henrietta Maria, the Winter Queen's third daughter, had already moved out of the Leyden house. Born on July 7, 1626, she was only eleven—slightly younger than her elder sisters had been when they were deemed old enough to attend their mother at her court in The Hague. Her progress had been accelerated not because she was particularly mature—she wasn't— but because of a public scandal involving her brother Maurice. Apparently Maurice, who at sixteen was old enough to feel himself somewhat neglected as compared to his two older brothers, had done what teenage boys sometimes do and expressed himself in a destructive way. Specifically, he had stepped out with two of his mother's pages for a night on the town, during which time the small band managed to insult the Portuguese ambassador, and then compounded this crime by attacking some innocent passersby on the street. The police had been called in and Maurice and his accomplices were arrested.★

His mother, judging that it might be best to get him out of Holland while the resulting furor died down, had the happy thought to combine his exile with the schooling of her younger sons, thirteen-year-old Edward and nine-year-old Philip, and so make it less

---

★ There's no hard data on what caused this behavior but somehow I suspect that excessive alcohol consumption was involved.

obvious that Maurice was being packed off in disgrace. She was afraid to send the three boys to England—she could not afford to have her family's image tarnished in any way lest Charles I withdraw his support for Karl Ludwig, and she could not take the chance that Maurice would relapse into impropriety, or that one of his younger brothers would get into trouble and embarrass her. So she looked around and settled on Paris as the next best place to educate her sons and perhaps improve their manners.

Her choice reflected not only her desire that her children acquire some aristocratic polish but her grudging recognition that, as a result of Cardinal Richelieu's policies, France now exercised significant power in Germany and it behooved her to cultivate their friendship. Louis XIII had no more liking for the Peace of Prague than she did and had already allied himself with the prince of Orange to fight against the Spanish in the area around Flanders and Belgium, on the northern border of France. The prince of Orange was Elizabeth's most trusted friend and adviser, even more than her brother Charles, and if he thought it was a good idea to work with the French despite their being an overwhelmingly Catholic kingdom, then probably she should do that too. Perhaps Maurice, or even Edward or Philip, once accustomed to the ways of the French, would make inroads into Louis XIII's court and eventually help negotiate a settlement that restored the Palatinate to the family. And if they misbehaved, well, the French weren't doing anything for Karl Ludwig at the moment anyway, so the damage to her foreign policy would be minimal.

The departure of the brothers meant that only three children— Henrietta Maria, seven-year-old Sophia, and six-year-old Gustavus Adolphus—were left at the nursery in Leyden. There being a considerable gap in age between Henrietta Maria and the two youngest, it was decided that the society of her older sisters would be more beneficial to her upbringing. And so the Winter Queen's third daughter came to live at the house in The Hague.

Her mother would not have hesitated to bring her out into society, for Henrietta Maria was the acknowledged belle of the family.

Sophia described her, somewhat in awe, as having "fair flaxen hair, a complexion, without exaggeration, of lilies and roses, and a nose which, although well shaped, was able to resist the cold" (a mischievous comparison to Princess Elizabeth's). "She had soft eyes, black well-arched eyebrows, and an admirable contour of face and forehead," Sophia continued, "a pretty mouth, and hands and arms as perfect as if they had been turned with a lathe."

But beauty doesn't always know its own power. Coming to her mother's court on the cusp of adolescence, still a child in many ways, Henrietta Maria seems to have been somewhat intimidated by her new surroundings. She had not Princess Elizabeth's intelligence nor Louisa's artistic ability and wit. Instead, she was sweet, delicate, and gentle. Henrietta Maria did not compete with her sisters and was in no way ambitious. ("Her talents, by which I chiefly profited," Sophia reported, "lay in the direction of needlework and preserve-making.") Rather, she looked up to her older siblings, particularly Princess Elizabeth, whom she regarded almost as a second mother. Fittingly, she appears in the oversize Honthorst family portrait *The Triumph of the Winter Queen* as a small, soft-colored presence, a child dressed as an adult, clutching an open book so heavy and unwieldy that she can barely stand upright (most likely a Bible, burdensome symbol of the family's commitment to Protestantism, an unintended irony), trailing behind the prominent royal-blue figure of her eldest sister.

Henrietta Maria's appearance at her mother's court coincided with a glittering extravaganza that, like almost all the queen of Bohemia's social engagements, had a significant political dimension. In February 1638, Elizabeth organized a jousting tournament followed by a grand feast and dancing, ostensibly to celebrate the marriage of the princess of Orange's sister but which she in fact used to showcase Karl Ludwig's and Rupert's military prowess. The two young men, back from England, were mounted on pure white stallions and costumed as Saracen warriors, complete with flowing robes and scimitars. They paraded around the ring at the head of a procession of thirty knights to open the competition while Henrietta Maria and her sisters watched from the stands. Rupert, as always, particularly distinguished himself, winning his joust with ease to the loud approval of the Dutch public, who had been invited to observe the games.

The reason behind this unusual display of pomp and optimism (not to mention expenditure of scarce resources), what the family was really celebrating, was Charles I's sudden, unexpected decision to provide Karl Ludwig with his own army. "I am so much over-joyed with this...that it seemth to me as a dream," Karl Ludwig exulted when he heard the news. His mother's enthusiasm matched his own. "The king my dear brother was pleased to write to me himself, that he doth approve of my son's intentions, and with so great a favor as the bestowing his money towards the levies. You may easily imagine how much contentment it brought to us both... the levies are already begun; I hope shortly he will be ready to go himself into the field," she wrote to Bishop Laud, Charles's chief adviser, on April 12, 1638.

Henrietta Maria, observing the jubilant bustle surrounding her brothers' preparation for battle all that spring and summer, could not have helped but be caught up in the general excitement. She had been only six when Frederick died—just old enough to remember him, but barely. She regarded Karl Ludwig, now twenty-one and head of the family, as a surrogate father and worshipped both him and the dashing Rupert as paragons of manliness. Of course they would win! How could they not, especially as the king of England had allowed Lord William Craven and a regiment of trained soldiers to join with Karl Ludwig and Rupert to assist in the retaking of the Palatine? This infantry was supplemented by three regiments of cavalry, one of which was led by Rupert, and two troops of dragoons, all paid for by Lord Craven and the English levies.

By the end of August, all was at last in readiness. The two broth-ers, splendid in their new white-plumed helmets and burnished armor, rode out of town at the head of their regiments. They must have made quite a stirring impression on the local population, and especially on their little sister.

★   ★   ★

KARL LUDWIG HAD ARRANGED to join forces with a small Swedish battalion at Bentheim, about 120 miles to the east, and this rendezvous was successfully accomplished on September 10. The heir to the Palatinate now had approximately 4,000 soldiers under his command.

The original plan had been to head immediately south to Heidelberg, but the commander of the Swedish warriors wanted to make a short stop first at the stronghold of Lemgo, about seventy miles to the east, which was then under siege by an undermanned imperial force. He argued that theirs was the only Protestant army in the area available to help and that the castle could be relieved so quickly that they would lose little time. This seemed like a laudable goal, so Karl Ludwig agreed to make the detour, and off they went.

Unfortunately, the commander's information had been somewhat dated. The army of the Palatinate arrived only to find that the original imperial troops had been supplemented by auxillary units and that they now faced an enemy force of some 8,000 soldiers. Nor could they strategically retreat, as they hadn't bothered to send a reconnaissance unit ahead to assess the situation. The imperial commanders had already spotted them and would have given chase. There was nothing to do but make the best of it and fight.

The battle took place on October 19, 1638, just outside Lemgo. On the advice of his more experienced warriors, Karl Ludwig arranged his army into four lines, the better to preserve strength, with the idea that each division would move forward to help as necessary. Rupert headed the third line, composed of cavalry. Karl Ludwig, as the commanding general, prudently took control of the rear guard, which was to be held in reserve and then unleashed at the critical moment.

Alas, the imperial soldiers did not feel the need to conform to their opponents' battle plan. They hurled eight regiments of armored knights, some four thousand men, at the enemy force. The sight of this crushing mass of iron weaponry approaching at full speed seemed to mesmerize Karl Ludwig's front line. Instead of galloping out to meet the attack as they were supposed to, they backed up, which got them sort of tangled up in their own second line. This did not last long, however, as the second line, noting the reaction of those in front, turned around in a panic and fled—right into Rupert.

For valiant Rupert, the athlete, was in his element. Tearing ahead, he charged his cavalry into the thick of the imperial troops, hacking away with his sword. He was joined by Lord Craven (who had promised the queen of Bohemia that he would watch out for her sons) and the English knights, and together they put up enough of a fight that the imperial army, which had also held back some of its troops, sent in reinforcements.

Now was the time for Karl Ludwig and his fourth line, left in reserve for this very purpose, to enter the fray! But when Rupert looked behind him to call for support, there was no one there. Like those in his advance line, Karl Ludwig had taken one look at the first tidal wave of imperial soldiers and fled the field, and with their commander gone, the bulk of his army had done the same.

Despite this disappointing reality, Rupert kept up the struggle for as long as he could. (He appears to have been aided in his efforts by the white plume in his helmet; unwittingly, Rupert had chosen the same insignia the imperial officers used, and in the confusion, it seems to have taken the enemy some time to figure out that he was fighting *against* them rather than for them.) But eventually even Rupert was forced to surrender, although he had to be surrounded and pulled down from his horse before submitting. Still undaunted, he refused to identify himself when ordered, so his adversaries pulled up his visor to see for themselves. "Sacrément! You are a young one!" the officer in charge exclaimed when he saw his seventeen-year-old captive.

It didn't take them long to figure out who he was, particularly as Lord Craven, loyal to the end, had been captured as well. Having a member of the Winter Queen's family in custody was a boon, as Rupert, a nephew of the king of England, could be held for ransom. He and Lord Craven (who was also recognized as a potential financial asset) were immediately packed off as prisoners of war to a castle in Austria for safekeeping.

His fellow recruits were not so lucky. Two thousand of Karl Ludwig's original four-thousand-man army, many of them members of Rupert's cavalry, died on the field that day. The commander himself just barely escaped alive when the carriage in which he had fled the scene tried to ford a fast-running river and flooded. Horses and driver drowned, but the heir to the Palatinate survived by seizing the overhanging limb of a well-placed tree and holding on with all his might until help arrived.

THE INTERMINABLE YEARS of struggle had clearly taken their toll; even inured to disaster as she was, Elizabeth's chagrin on hearing the news of her sons' defeat was very great. She tried as always to put as favorable an interpretation on the fiasco as possible, to limit the public damage to the family's reputation and cause, but could not fully control her anger and despair. "I am glad to hear the good opinion you have of [Karl Ludwig], though hitherto he has had but misfortune," she replied on November 1 to one of her closest friends, who had written to console her. "My comfort is, though he had the worse, yet he has lost no honor; and if I were sure where Rupert were, I should not be so much troubled. If he be prisoner, I confess it would be no small grief to me, for I wish [him] rather dead than in his enemies' [hands]," she ended apprehensively. She soon calmed down, however, and bent her energies toward trying to free the captive. Karl Ludwig had vigorously to dissuade her from launching a rescue attempt. "It will be in vain to send any gentleman to my brother Rupert...neither could I force any to it, since there is no small danger in it, for any obstinacy of my brother Rupert's, or venture to escape, would put him in danger of hanging," he warned his mother bluntly.

After his woeful performance outside Lemgo, it's reasonable to assume that Karl Ludwig might have had second thoughts about his proficiency as a military leader, but this was not the case. Instead, having lost one army, he simply looked around for another. Conveniently, a large force became available the following year when one of the few Protestant German barons who had not been lured back to the imperial side by the Peace of Prague died of fever on July 18, 1639, and left a battalion of some 16,000 soldiers without a commander. Even better, this army was stationed in Alsace, which was practically next door to Heidelberg. Karl Ludwig at once left for London to try to get his uncle to provide the funds necessary for him to purchase the loyalty of these regiments.

Unfortunately, the political environment in England had deteriorated alarmingly since his last visit. Charles I had only recently returned from Scotland, where the outcry over his decision to back the bishops over the obstreperous Presbyterians (which had taken the tangible form of replacing the old, humble Scottish prayer book with a new, much fancier version that followed the English Anglican model) had caused a rebellion. The king had been forced to lead an army into Scotland to quell the disturbance. No sooner had he left, however, than the Scottish Presbyterians went right back to their violent protests and civil disobedience.* Charles had consequently just spent a great deal of money for nothing and was not in a position to finance his nephew's newest scheme, particularly after the miserable showing associated with his prior cash outlay. "My son writes that the king continues to persuade him to go, but will give no money nor much hope of any hereafter, excusing all upon the business of Scotland," Elizabeth fumed in frustration.

Karl Ludwig, unwilling to let such an exceptional opportunity pass by without at least taking a crack at it, resolved to follow his uncle's advice and just show up in Alsace to see if, on the strength of his family's name and commitment to Protestantism, he couldn't convince the orphaned army to fight under his command. Time being of the essence, he felt he couldn't afford to take the long way around through Holland and Germany. But nor could he take the more direct route through France without applying for a safe passage from Louis XIII, which would take time and might raise uncom-

---

* Clearly, not much had changed in Scotland since the days when James had had to contend with his equally intractable subjects.

fortable questions about the purpose of his journey. So, emulating his father, who had once found himself in a similar predicament, Karl Ludwig decided to try to sneak through France in disguise. On October 4, 1639, again encouraged by Charles, whose fond memories of his own youthful escapade with the duke of Buckingham seems to have given rise to a somewhat unrealistic impression of the ease with which the French could be fooled by a change of clothing, Karl Ludwig sailed from England dressed as a valet.

Unfortunately for the success of this ploy, Cardinal Richelieu also wanted that army—had, in fact, already bribed its officers to accept a French commander—in order to secure Alsace for Louis XIII. The cardinal was aware, too, of Karl Ludwig's desire to use this force to fight for the Palatinate—he'd made no secret of it—and through an extensive spy network had been keeping an eye on his competitor. He let his prey get as far as Moulins, about 200 miles south of Paris, before swooping down and having Karl Ludwig arrested on October 14. The captive was subsequently transferred to the castle of Vincennes, which functioned as a prison near the capital, where he was held under close guard.

The uproar at the family court at The Hague caused by this inhospitable treatment of the Winter Queen's eldest son may well be imagined. Henrietta Maria now had *two* brothers incarcerated by enemies, and Maurice, Edward, and Philip were all still in France, which clearly could no longer be considered friendly territory. It must have been a very frightening time for her. Her mother, determined to get her sons out, was grimly consumed by her correspondence. Elizabeth called on everyone in her wide acquaintance—English, Dutch, Swedish, Danish, German—to exert pressure on the French court to release Karl Ludwig, and she demanded that Maurice, Edward, and Philip be allowed to return to her immediately. "I do pity, and shall pity all my life, the misfortunes of this noble princess," wrote one of her secretaries in a letter of November 21, 1639, "and shall not less admire her firm constancy, by which she remains unmoved, by the sad attacks of a fortune which has made her, like another Niobe, fruitful only for misfortune."

The resulting deluge of protests from foreign courts was sufficient to give even a man of Richelieu's equanimity pause. The younger children being of no interest to him, a safe passage was immediately granted to all three boys. To the great relief of his mother and sisters, Maurice was back in The Hague by January 1640, followed two months later by Edward and Philip.

But Karl Ludwig was a different story. The best the cardinal would offer his captive was an improvement in accommodations: he would release the heir to the Palatinate from his cramped prison cell and allow him to live in comfort with the English ambassador in Paris, but *only* if Karl Ludwig swore that he would not leave France without permission and under no condition approach the army in Alsace. To sweeten this deal, Richelieu shrewdly promised to enter into negotiations to help the younger man to recover his inheritance by providing money and arms—*if* he could convince his uncle the king of England to do the same. Karl Ludwig, faced either way with a prolonged stay on French soil, on the whole much preferred Paris to prison, and accepted the cardinal's terms.

Although Richelieu's posture seemed reasonable, even generous, it was only for show. The cardinal knew that there was no danger of having to make good on his offer to help as long as Charles I's participation was also required. The king of England, under pressure from his Scottish Presbyterian subjects, who had put together an army and were threatening to invade from the north in order to achieve their political and religious objectives, had been forced to call a parliament in order to raise enough money to meet this crisis. This was the first time in eleven years that Charles had called a parliament, having previously met his financial needs through the expedient of forced taxes and loans and throwing the people who refused to pay them into prison. As might be expected, the assembly did not go well. The Puritan legislators, who were in the majority, turned out to be in sympathy with the Scottish Presbyterians. They, too, resented the influence of the bishops, particularly Laud, over the king, and they were none too fond of Charles's Catholic queen either, who was rumored to be conducting secret negotiations with the pope for money and soldiers to help her husband. This defiant congress, which opened on April 13, 1640, concentrated on voicing its grievances rather than approving the necessary funding and was consequently speedily dissolved by the king on May 5, earning it the apt if not particularly inventive nickname of the Short Parliament.

In the wake of this unhelpful exercise in representative government, Charles, who believed that the Puritans, for all their loud troublemaking, were in the minority and that his subjects would rally to his side in the event of a Scottish invasion, sought to assert his royal prerogative. He turned as always to Laud, now archbishop of Canterbury, who on May 16 arranged a gift from his fellow bishops of £20,000 a year to the Crown. Laud also threw the power of the pulpit behind the throne by ordering that the doctrine of "the most high and sacred order of kings is of Divine right" be read out four times a year in church.

The Puritans, with whom the Winter Queen and her family were still wildly popular, fired back by inciting violence in the streets and by etching "God Save the King, confound the Queen and her Children, and give us the Palsgrave [Karl Ludwig] to reign in this kingdom" into a window at Whitehall with a diamond blade, an inscription that did not improve Charles's relationship with his nephew. In fact, by August, when the Scots invaded and took Newcastle, on the coast in northern England, Richelieu was so confident that the king of England's troubles would engulf him that he let Karl Ludwig go home to The Hague on the condition that he promise not to interfere in Germany without French permission.

Henrietta Maria's and her sisters' relief at having their eldest brother home and safe was very great. Although the family continued to worry about Rupert, who was still incarcerated in faraway Austria, there had been talk that he would be freed soon in exchange for a Polish prince who had been taken prisoner by the French. It seemed as though the family's prospects, if not entirely cheerful, had at least stabilized. But unlike her daughters', Elizabeth's joy was tempered by the news of the Scottish invasion of England. The Winter Queen, forced by circumstance to be more of a politician than her brother, followed Charles I's combative policies at home with some alarm. "The distractions of my own country doth so much trouble me as I know not what to write," she confessed in a letter to a friend on October 11, 1640. "By your own you may guess my sadness, all true honest hearts here wish the king would call a parliament and there let them find out who have done ill or well."

His sister's political insight proved astute. Charles, unable to turn back the Scots by force of arms due to a lack of funds, soldiers, and morale and fearing that if they remained unchecked, they might well advance all the way to London, at length agreed to call for another parliament to consider the Scottish demands. And so, on November 30, 1640, the governing body representing England came together again in a session that, in direct contrast to its predecessor, would forever be known, ominously, as the Long Parliament.

It is highly unlikely that Henrietta Maria, only fourteen, would have understood the significance of these events. In any case, she would have been far more concerned that winter with the health of her youngest brother, Gustavus Adolphus, a charming little boy, very good-looking, who had been sickly from birth and who that Christmas had become seriously ill. The type of infection was not recorded but whatever it was, the child was in acute pain and "died soon afterwards in such terrible suffering that one shudders to think about it," her younger sister, on whom this trauma clearly made a deep impression, remembered half a century later.

In her grief at her son's death, the Winter Queen made the decision finally to disband the royal nursery at Leyden. In January 1641 the servants were dismissed and its last remaining occupant, her fourth daughter and youngest child, Sophia, was transferred to the court at The Hague.

Sophia

Sophia's aunt, Queen Henrietta Maria, by Van Dyck

10

A Royal Education

"I WAS BORN, THEY TELL me, on October 14, 1630," Sophia would later recall in her memoirs. "Being the twelfth child of the King my father, and of the Queen my mother, I can well believe that my birth caused them but little satisfaction. They were even puzzled to find a name and godparents for me, as all the kings and princes of consideration had already performed this office for the children who came before me." Consequently, "the plan was adopted of writing various names on slips of paper and casting lots for the one which I should bear; thus chance bestowed on me the name of Sophia," she revealed.

The twelfth child! It must have felt rather like being the runt of a litter. Sophia certainly perceived herself as being shortchanged of her parents' attention. When she was an infant, "the Queen my mother sent me to Leyden, which is but three days' journey from the Hague, and where her Majesty had her whole family brought up apart from herself," she observed tartly, not understanding that this was how Elizabeth herself had been raised.

Unfulfilled childhoods might be uncomfortable, but in the right hands they make for excellent literature, and clever Sophia, an extremely talented writer, left a memorable portrait of life at the nursery. "At Leyden we had a court quite in the German style," she explained. "Our hours as well as our curtsies were all laid down by rule." Her governess "had held the same post with my father when he was a child, and from this fact her probable age may be guessed." The governess had two daughters "who looked older than their mother...I believe that they prayed to God, and never disturbed man," she continued, "for their appearance was frightful enough to terrify little children."

The training of a royal princess, even a five- or six-year-old princess, was taken seriously in the Leyden household. The children were roused at seven o'clock each morning. "I was obliged to go every day *en déshabillé* to Mlle. Marie de Quat [one of the governess's daughters], who made me pray and read the Bible," Sophia reported. "She then set me to learn the 'Quadrains de Pebrac,' while she employed the time in brushing her teeth; her grimaces during this performance are more firmly fixed in my memory than the lessons which she tried to teach."★

By eight thirty, little Sophia was dressed and ready to receive a series of professors in English, French, and German (being a girl, she was mercifully spared Latin); religion ("I learned the Heidelberg catechism in German, and knew it by heart, without understanding a word of it"); and the humanities. "They kept me busy until ten o'clock, except, when to my comfort, kind Providence sent them a cold in the head," she observed. Academic studies were relieved by a pleasant hour with the dancing master, where she could at least move around a little, and was immediately followed by dinner with her siblings, which seems to have been as much an extension of the ballroom as it was a culinary experience. "This meal always took place with great ceremony at a long table. On entering the dining-room I found all my brothers drawn up in front, with their governors and gentlemen posted behind in the same order side by side. I was obliged by rule to make first a very low curtsy to the princes, a slighter one to the others, another low one on placing myself opposite to them, then another slight one to my governess, who on

---

★ *Fifty Quatrains, Containing Useful Precepts for the Guidance of Man* by Gui de Faur Pibrac, a sixteenth-century author, was considered a standard educational text for the period.

entering the room with her daughters curtsied very low to me."
Even then, protocol was not yet satisfied: "I was obliged to curtsy
again on handing over my gloves to their custody, then again on
placing myself opposite to my brothers, again when the gentlemen
brought me a large basin in which to wash my hands, again after
grace was said, and for the last and ninth time on seating myself at
table," she recalled mournfully.

Dinner—"so arranged that we knew on each day of the week
what we were to eat, as is the case in convents"—was followed by
a short period of rest. Then came the afternoon's instruction, which
lasted until six o'clock. Her teachers "believed that I should turn out
a prodigy of learning because I was so quick, but my only object in
applying myself was to give up study when I had acquired all that
was necessary, and be no longer forced to endure the weariness of
learning." At six she had another, less formal meal, and was in bed
by eight thirty, "having said my prayers and read some chapters in
the Bible."

Sophia, spirited and precocious, chafed under these conditions,
particularly as she was well aware that there was a colorful world
beyond Leyden accessible to her siblings but denied to her. "Suffice
it to say that, as my brothers and sisters grew up, the Queen withdrew them from Leyden. The princes she sent to travel, and kept
the princesses to live with herself at the Hague," she wrote. Her few
appearances at her mother's court as a child did not seem to have
been entirely successful. She was once invited to visit so that she
could be shown off, "as one would a stud of horses," to some cousins, one of whom pronounced, after scrutinizing the eight-year-old,
that " 'she is thin and ugly; I hope that she does not understand
English.' To my vexation I understood but too well, and was deeply
distressed, believing that my ill-fortune was past all remedy," Sophia
confessed.

But of course she wasn't ugly—none of them were. By her own
account, she had her mother's long curly brown hair and a well-
proportioned figure (although she wasn't as tall as she would have

liked, height being prized). But what Sophia lacked in stature she more than made up for in demeanor, for she had "the bearing of a princess." All those deportment lessons, tiresome though they might have been, had clearly paid off.

When her younger brother, Gustavus Adolphus, died on January 9, 1641, it seemed a superfluous expense to keep the Leyden house open just for one little girl, so Sophia was transferred to the capital to live with her older sisters. Elizabeth's youngest daughter was absolutely delighted by the change of residence. "I was...ten years of age when I came to live at my mother's court at the Hague, and I was lost in an ignorant admiration of all that I beheld," she marveled. "To me it was the joy of Paradise to see such varying kinds of life, and so many people; above all to behold my teachers no more. I was not at all abashed by meeting with three elder sisters, all handsomer and more accomplished than myself, but felt quite pleased that my gaiety and wild spirits should serve to amuse them."

The Winter Queen's court was unused to younger children, and at least in the beginning many of the adults seem to have treated Sophia like one of her mother's pets. But Sophia gave as good as she got ("I made it my business to tease everyone," she declared), and demonstrated an admirable self-confidence and toleration of raillery. At one point, one of the courtiers, "in order to amuse the Queen, wrote a letter in the name of all her Majesty's monkeys, electing me to be their queen," Sophia remembered. "This letter was handed to me in a large company, to see how I would take it. I was too much amused to be angry, so laughed with the rest."

But the witty, jesting nature of the court at The Hague, so appealing to little Sophia, was only the mask her mother donned to disguise a period of mounting anxiety. For the arrival of the youngest daughter of the Winter Queen in January 1641 coincided with increasingly alarming news out of England, as reflected by the sudden determination of Charles I to marry his eldest daughter, Mary, to William, son of the prince of Orange.

★　　★　　★

WHEN CHARLES, CONFRONTED BY the invasion of a large and proficient Scottish army, was forced to call the Long Parliament to gather the funds and soldiers necessary to meet the crisis, he did not have high hopes of success. After all, he'd had plenty of experience with discordant representative government (which was why he generally tried to rule without one). But even with these reduced expectations, it still came as something of a shock to him to realize in the opening days of the assembly that many of the legislators, particularly those in the predominantly Puritan House of Commons, were actually *on the side* of the Presbyterian Scots and wanted to keep the invaders in England in order to pressure the king to yield to their demands. In fact, they were willing *to pay the expenses* of the Scottish army to stay right where it was. To top it off, they immediately charged both Laud, archbishop of Canterbury, and the earl of Strafford, Charles's top military adviser, with treason and had both men arrested and confined to the Tower.

It was Charles's (and his kingdom's) great misfortune that he and his forceful wife, Queen Henrietta Maria, upon whom the far weaker Charles was rapidly becoming almost totally reliant, were both great believers in the art of the shortcut. Neither saw any reason to rebuild trust or grind out what they could of their objectives through an extended and tiresome negotiation, especially with antagonists whom they saw as beneath them. "I see that all these... tumults and disorders have only risen from the meaner sort of people," Charles would later assert. "I am ready to obey the king, but not to obey 400 of his subjects [the parliament]," Queen Henrietta Maria observed scornfully. The shortcut, in this case, was to bring in funds and soldiers from somewhere outside England to overwhelm the Parliament, dispense with the Scots, and reassert the king's undisputed authority over his realm.★

★ In Charles's defense, he genuinely believed that all of his problems were the work of a few troublemakers and that overall his subjects supported him. Richard Nixon,

But where to obtain these soldiers and funds? Charles's first thought was Spain, and to this end secretly offered all sorts of inducements—a military pact, a marriage alliance between his eldest son and Philip IV's daughter, the promise of future naval aid in exchange for a large loan to be paid as soon as possible. But Spain, at war with France and Holland, had no resources to spare and turned him down. Queen Henrietta Maria then applied to her brother Louis XIII in France, but Cardinal Richelieu, whose focus was on the war in Belgium and Germany and whose ends were served nicely by an England in debilitating turmoil, denied her request, going so far as to send an ambassador to her court specifically to make his refusal clear. Undaunted, the queen next entered into secret negotiations with the pope, promising that once back in power, Charles would restore his Catholic subjects to full religious freedom; but the pontiff would only agree to consider sending military aid if the king first converted publicly to Catholicism, a condition that would have ensured Charles's immediate dethronement in Protestant England and Scotland.

Having run through the most obvious candidates on his list, Charles was forced to broaden his search to the lesser powers, and among these, Holland caught his attention. The prince of Orange was an experienced military commander who took the field regularly and was beginning to score successes in Flanders in combination with his French allies. And Charles could hardly have failed to notice the strength of the Dutch navy, which had recently chased down and destroyed a fleet of some seventy Spanish ships right off the coast of England. Even better, the prince of Orange's family was stalwartly Protestant, so there could be no objection from Parliament on the basis of religion. Accordingly, on January 6, 1641, Dutch ambassadors arrived in London, and Charles formally agreed

---

another leader inclined toward expedience, famously labeled this helpful population as "the great silent majority" and also used it to justify his actions.

to wed his eldest daughter, nine-year-old Mary, to fourteen-year-old William, son of the prince of Orange.

The announcement of this marriage pierced his sister Elizabeth's vanity like a well-aimed sword thrust. Not knowing Charles's true motivation behind the alliance, she could not fathom it. Yes, of course, the prince of Orange was her dear friend and most trusted ally; yes, his family had been staggeringly generous and supportive throughout her steady, unrelenting misfortune; but it was always understood, at least from her point of view, that she was his social and political superior. She had graciously arranged a match between him and one of her ladies-in-waiting, for goodness' sake! Now that woman's son was to ally himself with the royal family of England? It wasn't possible! "I cannot see what the king can gain by precipitating this marriage," the queen of Bohemia complained to a confidant at Charles's court. "They [the Dutch] seek to get my eldest Niece but that I hope will not be granted it being too low for her...I pray you do your best in this... you may think what interest I have in it both for my Brother's honor, my Niece's good, and my children's," she wheedled.

Plans for the marriage went forward despite her objections, and in April the young groom left for London at the head of a large retinue to which Karl Ludwig (who was just hanging around The Hague anyway, not doing very much and sponging off his mother) was attached. His mission was both to try yet again to get military aid to take back the Palatinate and to act as an eyewitness and report to Elizabeth about the true state of her brother's affairs in England. Although it was traditional for the bride's family to provide a dowry, in this case it was the Dutch wedding party who brought £200,000 to the king of England as a gift. The marriage was celebrated at Whitehall on May 2, 1641. Charles, grateful for the cash infusion and still hoping that his new in-laws would agree to lead an army into England to rescue him from his own subjects, made a point of raising William above his own nephew in a matter of precedence. Karl Ludwig was so insulted by this breach of etiquette that he refused to attend the nuptial feast.

William II, prince of Orange, and Mary on their wedding day

But he stayed on in England as a member of his uncle's court after the wedding and so was in a position to appreciate firsthand the escalating political crisis as well as his aunt and uncle's rapidly declining popularity. It must have been quite an education. On May 9, violence in the streets of London threatened to spill over into Whitehall, forcing Charles to sign the earl of Strafford's death warrant. His chief military adviser and loyal friend had been found guilty of conspiring to bring an army over from Ireland to initiate a Catholic overthrow of the realm in support of the king and the bishops. " 'If my own person were only in danger, I would gladly venture it to save Lord Strafford's life; but seeing my wife, children, and all my kingdom are concerned in it, I am forced to give way unto it,' " Karl Ludwig reported his uncle as saying as he signed the order. "And he cried as he said these things," he added in his letter to his mother. In August, after the Scottish army had finally been bribed to return home, Karl Ludwig accompanied Charles to Edinburgh, where the king, at the queen's urging, went to try to get a new army of Scottish troops together, this time to fight *for* him. They refused in spite of Charles's giving in to every one of their demands. The prince of Orange, too, declined to participate in the English king's wild military schemes, and by November 25, 1641, Charles and Karl Ludwig were back in London, having accomplished nothing beyond reducing the royal prerogative in Scotland and making the representatives of the Long Parliament, who were still in session, even more suspicious of their sovereign's intrigues than before.

By this time Karl Ludwig, whose family had lost everything and who had grown up in straitened circumstances struggling for opportunity, and who was consequently far more pragmatic and circumspect than his uncle, had seen enough, and did his best to intervene, but to no avail. "The Queen doth all," his mother lamented to her contact at the English court that November. "My son advised [the King] to reconcilement with the Parliament; but the Queen wouldn't hear of it."

With the troubles of England in mind, the close of Sophia's first year at her mother's court held the promise of yet another gloomy, worry-filled Christmas. And then, the mood at The Hague was suddenly lifted by an unexpectedly cheerful event. Out of the blue, on December 20, 1641, her brother Rupert came home.

FOR SOMEONE WHO HAD just spent three years in an imperial fortress in Linz, Austria (about a hundred miles west of Vienna), Rupert certainly looked hale enough. "Prince Rupert arrived here in perfect health, but lean and weary, having come... from Hamburg since the Friday noon," the English ambassador to Holland informed his government. "Myself, at eight o'clock in the evening, coming out of the court gate, had the good luck to receive him first of any; no other creature expecting his coming so soon. Whereby himself carried the news of his being come to the Queen, newly set at supper. You may imagine what joy there was!" the ambassador exclaimed.

How eleven-year-old Sophia must have loved hearing the story of this dashing, grown-up brother's adventures! For Rupert's captivity had been far from dull. He had hardly ever been confined to his cell except for a few brief periods when the emperor made a series of futile attempts, first, to convert his prisoner to Catholicism; second (when the first failed utterly), to get him at least to apologize for rebelling (another suggestion that Rupert coolly rebuffed); and third, to persuade him to fight on the imperial side. To this last offer, the twenty-year-old stalwart retorted that "he received the proposal rather as an affront than as a favor, and that he would never take arms against the champions of his father's cause."

But Rupert, tall and darkly good-looking, had an insolent charm that his imperial hosts admired. The owner of the castle in which he was confined had a *very* pretty daughter ("one of the brightest beauties of the age," one of her contemporaries confirmed), and she interceded on Rupert's behalf and seems to have helped him to while away the hours in a pleasant fashion so that "the Prince's former favors were improved into familiarities, as continued visits, invitations and the like."* In those interludes when he was not fully occupied with amour, Rupert had been allowed to ride, play tennis, draw (Louisa was not the only member of the family with artistic talent), and even hunt. He had also acquired a white poodle, whom he named Boye, and who became his constant companion, as a gift from the English ambassador at Vienna.

But a cage—even one as delightful as this one appears to have been—is still a cage, and Rupert chafed to get out. Here he had help from an unlikely source: the emperor's younger brother, Archduke Leopold, recently promoted to commander in chief of the imperial army. Leopold, who was only six years older than Rupert, had heard much about the prisoner and, curious to meet this charismatic man of action, came for a visit. The two became fast friends.

---

* He seems really to have fallen in love with her. Rupert "never named her after in life, without demonstration of the highest admiration and expressing a devotion to serve her," a chronicler of the period observed.

Soon Rupert was going on extended hunting parties and was invited to all the fashionable houses in the vicinity. He was "beloved by all," an imperial soldier confessed. "His behavior so obligeth the cavaliers of this country that they wait upon him and serve him as if they were his subjects."

Archduke Leopold spoke to his brother, and the emperor softened sufficiently that the English ambassador attached to the imperial court, who happened to be one of Elizabeth's closest friends, was able to arrange for Rupert's release — provided that he agreed never to fight against the empire again. Although this precluded him from any future military action to restore the Palatinate to his family, Rupert, who was tired of his prolonged stay in Austria and wanted to go home, agreed. The emperor still required a sign of the prisoner's submission, but even this was disguised to accommodate Rupert's acute chivalric sensibilities. An imperial hunting party was arranged to which the captive was invited, and when, as expected, he led the field, he was given the hand of the emperor to kiss as a mark of favor — and just like that, he was free. Even then, he was so popular he could not get away without spending a week in Vienna, where, according to a courtier, "There were few persons of quality by whom he was not visited and treated . . . the ladies also vied in their civilities, and labored to detain him . . . by their charms."

Elizabeth was very happy to have Rupert (along with Boye the poodle) home and safe, but she soon wondered what she was to do with him. He had given his word of honor that he would not fight against the emperor in Germany, and this was the focus of all of her energies, the only arena in which she had some influence and could help place her sons. So where was fiery Rupert, who clearly belonged in an army, to go?

And then, as if on cue, civil war broke out in England.

THE CONFLICT BETWEEN CHARLES and the Long Parliament, which had simmered along for over a year, was by Christmas 1641 so fraught that it was clear to court observers that it would take only the slightest impetus to break out into open hostilities. This push was obligingly provided at the start of the new year by Queen Henrietta Maria.

Henrietta Maria, who despite having lived in England for sixteen years was still rigidly, royally French Catholic to her core, could not understand why her husband did not simply stand up to the mulish members of the opposition, who were just a lot of vulgar commoners in her opinion. It was she who kept coming up with one improbable scheme after another to raise a foreign army to force the kingdom to submit to Charles's authority. As she was not very discreet about her intrigues, intelligence about her plots seeped out to the legislators, often through the medium of her good friend, the duplicitous Lady Carlisle, who happened also to be intimate with one of the opposition leaders in Parliament. As a result, on January 2, 1642, Charles was informed by reliable sources that five members of the House of Commons had gotten together, reviewed the evidence, and concluded that there were sufficient grounds for concern. They were therefore intending, at the earliest possible moment, to accuse his wife of treason.

Having just gone through all of this with his close friend and adviser the earl of Strafford, Charles well knew what that meant. First would come the accusation, then the arrest. Henrietta Maria would be consigned to the Tower. There would be a trial, followed immediately by a guilty verdict. And then Charles would be obliged to sign his wife's death warrant.

Henrietta Maria was the dearest person in the world to him, his rock, his soul, the mother of his children. They had two choices: the queen could flee the kingdom, or Charles could turn the tables by preemptively raiding the House of Commons in the company of an armed guard, charging and arresting the five ringleaders for treason, and putting *them* in the Tower. His wife had no doubts about which alternative she preferred. "Go, you coward, and pull these rogues out by the ears, or never see my face more," she screeched at him two days later on the morning of January 4.

So Charles went. But he didn't go right away. He had to get an armed guard together—some three or four hundred men—which took time; and then he had to go find Karl Ludwig, whom he wanted to accompany him; and so it wasn't until about three o'clock in the afternoon that Charles and Karl Ludwig, yet again an eyewitness to his uncle's somewhat peculiar governing methods, actually climbed into a coach stationed outside the door at Whitehall. At which point Charles cried out, "Let my faithful subjects and soldiers follow me!" and took off toward the House of Commons with hundreds of armed men behind him.

Unfortunately, by that time his wife, who had assumed he would leave that morning right after she told him to, had already triumphantly let Lady Carlisle in on the secret that the king had gone off to storm the Parliament and arrest the five traitors. Lady Carlisle, in turn, had managed to smuggle a message to her contact at the House of Commons, warning the victims to flee. So when Charles and his mob of soldiers arrived, entered the building, and demanded that the members turn over the five ringleaders, they weren't there. He and his men were forced to back down and leave empty-handed.

It was a very big deal for a king to break into the House of Commons in this way. No sovereign had ever attempted it before. And now Charles had done it—and come away with nothing. The doctrine of the divine right of kings, embraced by James the century before and handed down lovingly to his son, was dealt a deathblow in that instant by the long, sure lance of representative government. Charles's blunder was obvious, and it turned the people against him. "Parliament! Privilege of Parliament!" they jeered at him in the streets on his way back to Whitehall.

"Never did he treat me for a moment with less kindness than before it happened, though I had ruined him," Henrietta Maria confessed later to a friend.

NOW THE QUEEN REALLY did have to flee. The royal family retired to Windsor so quietly that even their servants were unaware of their plans and did not have the castle ready for them. The queen had taken the precaution of smuggling as many of the crown jewels as could be comfortably transported out with her, in case it should be necessary to pawn them for future expenses. Charles appealed to the prince of Orange again for help and arranged for a ship to be prepared on the pretext that the queen had decided to escort her ten-year-old daughter, Mary, to her new husband at The Hague. On February 12, 1642, Charles and Henrietta, with Mary and the jewels in tow, made for Dover "in such post-haste that I never heard the like for persons of such dignity," reported a member of the court. On February 23, Charles said good-bye to his wife and daughter. They sailed that day for Holland.

The queen of Bohemia and her daughters were at Elizabeth's hunting lodge in Rhenen when the news arrived of their relatives' flight. The entire family at once changed their plans and hurried back to The Hague in order to be present when the queen of England and her daughter arrived. To her great delight, Sophia was singled out to be among the first to welcome the visitors as they docked at port. "The Queen my mother went to meet her [Queen Henrietta Maria]...and I was chosen out from among my sisters as being the fittest companion for the young princess [Mary], who was but a little younger than myself," Sophia remembered with pride. Her initial impression of her aunt was somewhat muted, however. "The fine portraits of Van Dyck had given me such an idea of the beauty of all English ladies, that I was surprised to find the Queen (so beautiful in her picture) a little woman with long lean arms, crooked shoulders, and teeth protruding from her mouth like guns from a fort," Sophia confessed.

But the fugitive queen, reliant on the goodwill of her hosts and knowing how important it was to appear charming and sympathetic to her husband's family, exerted herself in her cause and at least succeeded in winning over her twelve-year-old niece. "After careful inspection, I found she had beautiful eyes, a well-shaped nose, and an admirable complexion," Sophia conceded. "She did me the honor to say that she thought me rather like her daughter. So pleased was I, that from that time forward I considered her quite handsome. I also heard the English milords say to each other that, when grown up, I should eclipse all my sisters. This remark gave me a liking for the whole English nation," she admitted merrily.

Her mother was not so easily taken in. Although the English ambassador stationed at The Hague reported that outwardly the Winter Queen and her sister-in-law were "very kind, one to another," privately Elizabeth expressed strong reservations about Charles's wife. "I find by all the Queen's and her people's discourse that they do not desire an agreement between his Majesty and his Parliament, but that all be done by force, and rail abominably at the Parliament. I hear all and say nothing," she wrote grimly to her closest correspondent.

Meanwhile, back in England, the king gathered his two sons, twelve-year-old Charles and eight-year-old James, and, with Karl Ludwig still by his side, made for York, in the north, where his strongest supporters resided. Although Parliament took control of the navy and began to raise its own militia, there were yet trained troops that remained loyal to the monarchy, and Charles spent all that spring and early summer recruiting men and arms in preparation for civil war. For her part, Queen Henrietta Maria, from her exile in The Hague, commissioned Rupert to be commanding general of her husband's Horse (the cavalry) and sent him and his younger brother Maurice, along with a large cache of weapons, mostly musketry and shot, to England. They arrived on August 22, 1642, just in time to join Charles and his two young sons at the top of a hill in the town of Nottingham. There, in the midst of a driving storm, the king had the royal standard, ancient symbol of war, unfurled, and by a proclamation read out to the heraldry of trumpets, officially called upon his loyal subjects to fight for king and country against the Parliament.

Significantly absent from this lofty scene, however, was Karl Ludwig, who had been his uncle's constant companion for over a year and who had no doubt gleaned enough from the experience to anticipate how it was all going to turn out. His fight, he knew, was in Germany, where Charles, despite his many protestations of support, had in fact been of minimal aid to him in the past and certainly could in no way be counted upon for the foreseeable future. And so Karl Ludwig had prudently decided to slip away and sail back to The Hague just as his younger brothers were enthusiastically approaching. They might have waved to each other from their passing ships.

Princess Elizabeth

...at The Hague

11

The Visiting Philosopher

"In my time, which was 1642," reminisced a French physician who settled in Leyden and eventually became dean of the College of Orange, "there used in Holland to exist the following custom: the ladies of the Hague used to delight in going in boats from the Hague to Leyden or to Delft; they were dressed as women of the burgher class and mixed in the crowd so as to hear all that might be said upon the great ones of the earth, touching whom they tried to provoke all present to converse. Often they heard much that concerned themselves, and even—their manners being something rather extraordinary—they seldom returned without some cavalier having offered them his services. The said cavaliers, however, were, for the most part, terribly disappointed in their hopes of having made acquaintance with females of a certain kind, for when they landed from the boats, there was invariably a coach in waiting, which carried the fair adventuresses all alone," the doctor snickered. "Elizabeth, the eldest of the Bohemian princesses, would sometimes join these parties," he noted.

By the time Karl Ludwig returned to The Hague, in the fall of 1642, Princess Elizabeth was nearly twenty-four years old. It had been seven long years since the king of Poland had actively solicited her hand, and except for a brief scheme floated by her mother to marry her eldest daughter to a German duke in order to help Karl Ludwig's war effort—a plan that unfortunately had to be abandoned when the prospective bridegroom died of fever before anyone had a chance to sound him out on the subject—she had had no other proposal. A highly intelligent woman, Princess Elizabeth must have known that her principal asset had always been her position as the niece of a rich and powerful uncle who might be coaxed to do something for his only sister's eldest daughter, and that consequently her chances for marriage had decreased even more with the recent outbreak of civil war in England. Without the promise of English money or influence, she was simply one of four poor, landless sisters of superior breeding but dubious title whose religious affiliation precluded any alliance with a Catholic, a proviso that unfortunately significantly reduced the pool of potential suitors. Princess Elizabeth would have been starkly aware that she was rapidly approaching an age where, youth and childbearing being prized, she would no longer be considered desirable, and so she must steel herself to spinsterhood.

And this cannot have been a happy prospect for her, as Princess Elizabeth does not seem to have fit in particularly well at her mother's court. The numerous responsibilities, both social and political, that daily claimed her attention seemed only to irritate her. "The life which I am obliged to lead, leaves me hardly disposition nor time to acquire the habit of meditation... Sometimes the interests of my family which I ought not to neglect, sometimes conversations and complaisances which I cannot avoid, lower this weak mind of mine with weariness or vexation that it is rendered useless for a long while," Princess Elizabeth once confided in frustration. Translation: she often found herself bored into a stupor.

Small wonder, then, that she took whatever opportunity she could to escape into the outside world, to blend in anonymously dressed as someone other than herself. But it is highly unlikely that Princess Elizabeth took these boat trips simply to engage in some surreptitious coquetry. Rather, she used the barges as other people did, as the quickest means of getting to Leyden or Utrecht, where the elite universities in Holland were located.

For Princess Elizabeth had made herself into a scholar of note.

Even the French doctor admitted it. "Wonders were told of this rare personage; it was said, that to the knowledge of strange tongues she added that of abstruse sciences; that she was not to be satisfied with the mere pedantic terms of scholastic lore, but would dive down to the clearest comprehension of things; that she had the sharpest wit and most solid judgment...that she liked surgical experiments, and caused dissections to be made before her eyes...her beauty and her carriage were really those of a heroine," he revealed.

Reports of the princess's intellectual accomplishments were in no way hyperbole. Nor was she the only woman in Holland to have succeeded in infiltrating the heretofore almost exclusively male world of scholarship. In her pursuit of learning, Princess Elizabeth had obviously been inspired by the achievements of her good friend, the remarkable Anna Maria van Schurman.

Anna Maria was a prodigy. She was a gifted artist and singer as well as a voracious reader and formidable intellect. She had been taught Latin and Greek as a child by her father, who early recognized her abilities and encouraged her in her studies. Later, the rector of the University of Utrecht, impressed by her erudition, allowed her to attend lectures (although she was required to sit separately from the rest of the all-male class, in a small alcove shielded by curtains) and personally instructed her in Hebrew and theology. "Desire for knowledge absorbed me," she confessed simply.

Princess Elizabeth met Anna Maria through Gerrit van Honthorst, who, impressed by her artistic talent, brought her into his school, where she took lessons with the queen of Bohemia's children. Eleven years older than Princess Elizabeth, Anna Maria had already mastered Ethiopian and produced a grammar as a study guide for others, and was renowned throughout Europe for the publication of a Latin treatise in defense of women's higher education. "My deep regard for learning, my conviction that equal justice is the right of all, impel me to protest against the theory which would allow only a minority of my sex to attain to what is, in the opinion of all men, most worth having," she wrote in 1637 in a letter to an eminent theologian, explaining her motivation in writing the pamphlet. "For since wisdom is admitted to be the crown of human achievement, and is within every man's right to aim at in proportion to his opportunities, I cannot see why a young girl in who we admit a desire of self-improvement should not be encouraged to acquire the best that life affords," she concluded. Princess Elizabeth, whose passion for learning was considered excessive by her family (they signaled their amusement by assigning her the nickname "la Grècque," the Greek), recognized Anna Maria as a kindred spirit and looked up to the older woman as a role model. "Despising the frivolities and vanities of other princesses, she raised her mind to the noble study of the most lofty science; she felt herself drawn to me by this community of tastes and interests, and testified her favor as well by visits as by her gracious letters," Anna Maria remembered.

Her eldest daughter might have disparaged the diversions of the Winter Queen's court—the endless rounds of hunting, balls, and concerts that defined the upper echelons of Dutch society—but in fact, her mother's presence at The Hague, along with the household of the prince and princess of Orange, contributed greatly to the blossoming intellectual environment. The encouragement and patronage of these two courts attracted some of the best minds in Europe to Holland. The prince of Orange's secretary was an accomplished poet and scholar, and although he referred to his position as "his golden fetter," it nonetheless provided not only his livelihood but also access to and influence within the international academic community. The queen of Bohemia, too, was known to take an interest in all the latest developments in the arts and sciences, and hosted many of the leading intellectuals at her salons. "This town [The Hague] can certainly compare with the first towns in Europe," boasted the same French physician, "and in my time was proud of possessing three Courts: firstly, the Court of the Prince of Orange, a military court, where might be seen above two thousand noblemen and their suite of soldiers decked out in buff doublets, with orange scarves, high boots, and long sabers, and who were this Court's chief ornament; secondly, the Court of the States-General, full of provincial deputies and bur-gomeisters, and representatives of the aristocracy, in black velvet coats, broad collars, and square beards; lastly, the Court of the Queen of Bohemia, which seemed that of the Graces, seeing that she had four daughters, at whose feet all the *beau monde* [fashionable society] of the Hague came to depose their homage, and whose talents, beauty, and virtues were the subject of all men's talk."

And so it was that when the eminent French philosopher René Descartes, looking for the solitude necessary to his work and an atmosphere of intellectual freedom, decided to move to Endegeest, right outside Leyden, in the early 1640s, it was more or less inevitable that he would one day end up on the Winter Queen's doorstep.

PHILOSOPHY IS ONE OF those subjects, like astrophysics and neuro-surgery, that are not for the fainthearted. To delve into the absolutes of the human experience, to seek to advance the progress of enlight-enment first expounded by the likes of the revered Aristotle and Plato, to search for the answers to the profound questions of the universe, often at the risk of deadly reprisal from entrenched powers, requires not only brilliance and tenacity but a deep sense of purpose. But even among this select fraternity, Descartes stands out. From him did we get practical discoveries like coordinates in geometry and the law of refraction of light. But what he really did was to shake loose the human mind from the shackles of centuries of stultifying religious orthodoxy by creating an entirely original approach to reasoning: the Cartesian method. You *know* you've gotten some-where when they name a whole new branch of science after you.

René Descartes was born into a family of minor regional nobility in a small town in western France near Poitiers in 1596, which made him only a year or so older than the queen of Bohemia. He had been quite sickly as a young child, so when he was nine and his father sent him to the nearby Jesuit school, he instructed the headmaster, who was a close friend, to have a care for his son's health. Conse-quently, Descartes's academic experience fell quite outside the boundaries of traditional instruction for the period. Where his fellow students were required to awaken early each morning and attend classes led by dreary masters who often resorted to scoldings or beatings if a pupil failed to absorb the material, Descartes was allowed to sleep late and stay in bed reading as long as he liked, a privilege of which he took full advantage and which instilled in him the lifelong habit of rarely rising before the noon meal. As a result, and possibly alone in the entire history of Jesuit school training, Descartes actually *enjoyed* his years at the seminary and always remembered them fondly. As he was a brilliant student who was particularly gifted in algebra and geometry, this innovative approach produced a higher-quality education than what he would have received if he had been subjected to the usual routine. "I had been taught all that others learned," he observed, "and, not contented with the sciences actually taught us, I had, in addition, read all the books that had fallen into my hands... [It was like] interviewing the noblest men of past ages who had written them."

He left school at the age of eighteen and, intent upon experiencing "the great book of the world," as he called it, determined to travel. Somewhat inexplicably for a young man whose talents tended so obviously to the cerebral, he chose to satisfy his craving for new people and places by enlisting in foreign armies. Again, his sojourns in the military, like his time spent at the Jesuit school, differed substantially from that of the common soldier's. While there is evidence that he could handle his sword, he does not seem to have used it very often. It's also unclear how frequently (if ever) he actually went into battle, although he was usually stationed near one. Moreover, as a gentleman knight of small but independent means, Descartes considered his valet to be as vital a component of his equipage as his bayonet, and generally camped out in a warm, comfortable room at a local inn where he could keep to his preferred regime of ten uninterrupted hours of sleep, followed by lying in bed and thinking until noon. Nor during those rare periods of the day when he condescended to dress and go out did Descartes waste much time on military affairs. Dismissing his fellow officers as dissolute louts, he instead made a point of seeking out all the leading mathematicians and academics in the area and dazzling them with his knowledge of algebra and geometry, and in this way obtained an ever-increasing circle of learned friends and admirers.*

It was in November 1619, during one of these intervals of semi-active service (when, ironically, he was attached to the imperial army under General Buquoi, who was fighting *against* the king and queen of Bohemia), that Descartes had his great epiphany. It came to him (where else?) in bed as a dream that most of what he had learned in school was incorrect and that in order to rectify these errors, it was going to be necessary to start all over again from the beginning, this time using the sort of rigorous proofs that worked so well in logic and mathematics. "As for the opinions which, up to that time, I had embraced, I thought I could not do better than resolve at once to sweep them wholly away, that I might afterwards be in a position to admit either others more correct, or even perhaps the same when they had undergone the scrutiny of Reason," he later wrote. From that moment on—and here was the big break with accepted wisdom—Descartes would apply this objective, logical approach to *every* aspect of life, including the really tricky ones, like the existence of God, the relationship of the mind to the body, and the nature of consciousness.† This is where *Cogito, ergo sum* ("I think, therefore I am") comes from; his ability to reason was, to Descartes, the one irrefutable truth that he could rely upon and on which he would in the future strive to rebuild all human knowledge, "like one walking alone and in the dark."

Descartes spent the next period of his life, through his twenties and into his thirties, refining his methodology with the intention of publishing his doctrine. Although he gave up the life of a soldier, he continued to wander restlessly across Europe, seeking out

---

* It has been suggested that Descartes was in fact a spy, not a soldier, and this theory has merit in my view.

† An approach that later became known as the Cartesian method.

René Descartes

mathematicians and philosophers wherever he went and working on his treatise. He had completed a first draft and was just about to send it off to a publisher in France when the news broke that the astronomer Galileo had been condemned by the Inquisition for supporting the thesis, first advanced by Copernicus, that the earth went around the sun, and not the other way around. Despite going down on his knees and recanting his views, the distinguished scientist had been sent to prison, where, as part of his punishment, he was required to repeat seven psalms of contrition aloud every week for the next three years.

Galileo's conviction came as a terrible shock to Descartes, who, as a devout Catholic and a great admirer of the Jesuit order, had been hoping to use the principles of logic and mathematics to reconcile the Church to scientific inquiry. "I could hardly have believed that an Italian, and in favor with the Pope, as I hear, could be considered criminal for nothing else than for seeking to establish the earth's motion," he wrote, almost in despair, to the friend in France to whom he had been about to entrust his own manuscript. "I thought I had heard that...it was constantly being taught, even at Rome; and I confess that if the opinion of the earth's movement is false, all the foundations of my philosophy are so also, because it is demonstrated clearly by them. It is so bound up with every part of my treatise, that I could not sever it without making the remainder faulty," he concluded despondently. Descartes was so terrified of courting a similar fate that in the immediate aftermath of Galileo's condemnation in 1633, he seriously contemplated destroying all of his notes and papers.

But despite his fears, he couldn't let it go, and in 1637 he summoned up the courage to publish his first major work, *A Discourse on the Method of Rightly Conducting the Reason and Seeking Truth in the Sciences*, which he followed up in 1641 with a second volume, *Meditations Concerning the First Philosophy in Which Are Demonstrated the Existence of God, and the Immortality of the Soul*. Both tracts were widely circulated throughout Europe, but it was the first, *A Discourse on the Method*, that vaulted Descartes into the public consciousness and made his name as a brilliant philosopher.

And so it was as something of an international celebrity that he first walked into the queen of Bohemia's drawing room and there met her eldest daughter, Princess Elizabeth.

THERE IS NO RECORD of what occurred during this first interview, but by the spring of 1643, forty-seven-year-old Descartes, who had been made aware through an intermediary that twenty-four-year-old Princess Elizabeth had read his work and wished to discuss it with him, was sufficiently interested to make an impromptu visit to The Hague specifically to talk to her. Unfortunately, the princess was with her mother at the royal hunting lodge in Rhenen on the day the philosopher chose to call, an oversight that prompted a gracious note of apology from his absent hostess. "Monsieur Descartes," Princess Elizabeth wrote on May 6, 1643, "I have learned with much pleasure and regret the intention you had of seeing me a few days ago, and was equally touched by your kindness in wishing to converse with one so ignorant...and by my misfortune in losing so profitable a conversation." She went on to say that she had questions about some of his theories and had been encouraged by her tutor to approach him directly. In particular, she had trouble understanding how metaphysics controlled emotions and bodily functions, and so, "I have driven from my mind all other considerations than that of begging you to tell me how the soul of a man can determine the motions of the body to perform voluntary actions (being but a thinking substance). For it seems that all determination of movement comes from the force exercised on it... Therefore, I ask for a more particular definition of the soul...that is to say, of substance separate from its action, thought."★

Although this was clearly not the ordinary "So sorry to have missed you!" society missive, Descartes, in his response, seems to have assumed that her position outweighed her intellect, and he elected to toady rather than teach. "The favor with which your Highness has honored me in allowing me to receive your commandments by letter is far greater than I could ever have dared hope," his fawning reply began. "And it makes my defects easier to bear than the one event that I would have fervently wished for, to have received them from your own mouth...seeing a discourse more than human come from a body so like those painters give to angels, I would have been in the same rapture it seems must be those who, coming from earth, enter for the first time into heaven," he continued, before fobbing her off with an answer that even he noted was not "entirely satisfactory."

He was right; it wasn't. "Your kindness is shown, not only in pointing out and correcting the faults of my reasoning, as I had expected," Princess Elizabeth shot back on June 10, "but also to render their recognition less vexatious you try to console me — to the

---

★ Please don't be concerned if you don't understand this question, or the material in any of the other letters that follow. Personally, I've no idea what the two of them were talking about either; what seems to be important here is that *they* understood each other.

prejudice of your judgment—by undeserved praises, which might have been necessary...if my being brought up in a place where the ordinary style of conversation had not accustomed me to hearing of them from people incapable of estimating them truly, and made me presume myself safe in believing the contrary of what they said," she observed drily. (Translation: *I expected more from you than sycophancy. I don't have to consult a renowned philosopher to hear cheap compliments, I get them at home for free all the time.*) "But as you have undertaken to instruct me I assure myself that you will explain to me the nature of immaterial substance and the manner of its actions and passions in the body." (In other words, *Take me seriously or not at all.*) Signed (to take the sting out of it), "Your very affectionate friend, Elizabeth."

It was some time before Descartes responded to Elizabeth's letter. Possibly he was pondering how best to approach her. But in the end he evidently decided to take her at her word, because, through an intermediary, he sent her a math problem.

And not just any math problem: a lulu, one of those that had stumped mathematicians from the beginning of recorded time, one that had never before been solved. Except that Descartes had just solved it.

It's called the kissing circles problem. There are three tangent circles (that is, all touching each other). Solve for a fourth circle that touches all of the other three.

He didn't expect her to answer it. In fact, he almost immediately regretted sending it to her. "For the rest, I have much remorse for proposing the problem of the three circles to Madame the princess

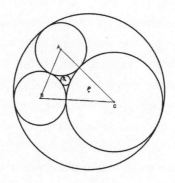

of Bohemia, because it is so difficult that it seems to me that an angel who had only the algebra taught her by [her math tutor] would not be able to solve it without a miracle," he wrote on October 21 to the friend he had used to forward the puzzle in the first place. He knew that by sending it he'd been showing off a bit—he probably couldn't resist—but it was also the gesture of respect that she had asked for. Mathematics was the measure by which Descartes judged the world. Those who grasped its principles and appreciated its beauty he held in high regard and counted among his intimate friends; those who did not were simply not taken as seriously.

And then she solved it.

It wasn't an elegant answer, like Descartes's, that solved for all possibilities, but she'd managed to work out a specific case. Princess Elizabeth herself was aware of this defect but decided to send her answer along anyway, "as a young angler might show an old fisherman his catch...For I know perfectly well that in my solution, there was nothing clear enough to result in a theorem," she admitted in a letter of November 21, 1643. This problem, and Descartes's solution (which was shown to her only afterward), "taught me more than I would have learned in six months with my tutor. I am very indebted to you...there are few things that I would not do to obtain the effects of your good will, which is infinitely esteemed by your very affectionate friend at your service, Elizabeth," she concluded.

It was the turning point in their relationship. From a rocky start—condescension on his part, pride and frustration on hers— there now developed a warmth and closeness that rivaled physical intimacy. Descartes eventually took her step by step through his own solution to the kissing circles and used her queries to sharpen and refine his theories concerning the mind and the soul. "I have never met anyone who could so thoroughly understand all that is contained in my writings," he enthused. "For there are many, even among the best and most highly instructed minds, who find them obscure, and I observe that almost all those who understand readily those things that pertain to mathematics are not capable of comprehending those that belong to metaphysics, and I can say with truth that I have met none except your Highness to whom both are equally easy." He dedicated his next work, *The Principles of Philosophy*, published the following year, to her, and the inscription was so obviously heartfelt that it prompted comment. "Bless the good man!" the chatty French doctor said of Descartes. "He thinks only one man and one woman capable of entering into his doctrines, the physician Regius and the Princess of Bohemia."

As for Princess Elizabeth, it would not be an exaggeration to say that the friendship she shared with Descartes—a friendship of ideas and analysis, a melding of minds and souls so different from the shallow pretense of her daily existence—was the most precious relationship in her life. To have secured the regard and affection of such a man, to have *earned* it through her own efforts, to be esteemed for who she was on the inside and not for her title, breeding, or connections—this was a source of great solace. There was no question of physical intimacy between a middle-aged Catholic philosopher and a Protestant princess twenty-three years his junior whose virginity might yet secure her an appropriate husband, but what they had together was more than most marriages could boast and that can only be described, without irony, as metaphysical love.

It was well for Princess Elizabeth that she managed to forge this intimacy with Descartes when she did, that she had someone she could trust to turn to during periods of sorrow or hardship. For life at her mother's court at The Hague, never easy for her even in the good times, was about to become extremely challenging.

WHILE PRINCESS ELIZABETH WAS wrestling with algebra and geometry, the rest of Europe continued its armed struggles over religion and power. In the winter of 1642 again occurred one of those seminal events that resounded through the theater of war and that caused the dancers to pause momentarily in their steps. It was a loss not on the battlefield but in a quiet bedroom in Paris. There, on December 4, 1642, the architect of the French entrance into the German war, the man who had successfully, almost single-handedly, guided the kingdom through nearly two decades of serpentine political turmoil, Cardinal Richelieu, died at the age of fifty-seven.

He'd been sick for a long time, getting steadily weaker, as was true also of his sovereign, Louis XIII. The previous June both men had been so ill that the only way they could meet were in rooms that contained a bed for each to lie upon. By November Richelieu was coughing blood, and his physicians knew his end was near. "I pray God to condemn me, if I have had any other aim than the welfare of God and the State," the cardinal was reported to have avowed just before his demise. At the time of his death, France, once apprehensive of being crushed between all-dominant Spain and the Empire, stood as the ascendant power in Europe. In nearly every direction — to the north, south, and east — the French had wrested territory away from the Habsburgs and pushed back their borders as a result of Richelieu's tactics.

"A great politician has departed!" mourned Louis XIII when he was informed of the cardinal's passing. Less than six months later, he too was dead, and the future of France — and, by extension, Europe — was left to his widow, the queen mother, Anne of Austria, who was regent for her two young sons, four-year-old Louis XIV and his younger brother, two-year-old Philippe, duke of Orléans.

But of course it was not France that occupied the thoughts and prayers of the queen of Bohemia's court at The Hague at this time. It was to England and the civil war between Charles I and Parliament that the family's anxious eyes were turned. They were right to worry. Charles's war effort, feeble from the start, would likely have collapsed with the first battle were it not for the industry of one man whose exploits and expertise were so vital to the royal cause that they were analogous to possessing a secret weapon (or perhaps, more aptly, employing a ringer) — the king's twenty-four-year-old nephew, Rupert.

THE ENERGETIC RUPERT'S EFFECT on his uncle's military affairs was immediate and electric. No sooner had he and Maurice (who had accompanied his older brother to England to serve as his right-hand man) rendezvoused with Charles at Nottingham for the inauspicious planting of the royal standard, than Rupert, used to continental warfare and shocked by the overall lack of supplies and general ineptitude of the king's troops, began to take over. The first order of business was obviously to train the cavalry they already had and then use them to secure additional men and armaments. This Rupert did so quickly that Charles made him not simply commander of the King's Horse but general of the whole army. "That brave Prince and hopeful soldier, Rupert, though a young man, had in martial affairs some experience, and a good skill, and was of such intrepid courage and activity, that—clean contrary to former practice, when the King had great armies, but no commanders forward to fight—he ranged and disciplined that small body of men [Rupert had only 800 cavalry to begin with]—of so great virtue is the personal courage and example of one great commander. And indeed to do him right, he put the spirit into the King's army that all men seemed resolved," observed a member of Charles's circle.

Having whipped his small team of men into shape in record time, Rupert, along with his white poodle, Boye, who was so intelligent that the opposition Parliamentarian soldiers believed the dog to be possessed by the devil, conducted a whirlwind tour through the countryside.★ All those years of English lessons his mother had insisted on came in handy, as is evident in the letter he sent to the mayor of Leicester in advance of his arrival, which was typical of his approach. With great decorum, in the king's name, he asked for £2,000, promising that it would be repaid at a more convenient period; signed the note "Your friend, Rupert"; and then added a postscript: "If any disaffected persons with you shall refuse themselves, or persuade you to neglect the command, I shall tomorrow appear before your town in such a posture, with horse, foot, and

---

★ To the great amusement of the royal forces, Rupert taught Boye to lift his leg whenever the name Pym (head of the House of Commons) was mentioned.

cannon, as shall make you know it is more safe to obey than to resist his Majesty's command." In this way, Charles's 800 ragtag cavalry troops grew to 3,000 well-supplied horsemen in a single month.

As a result of his high spirits, military expertise, and seemingly limitless energy, Rupert very soon became the public face of the royal army to the rest of the kingdom, and particularly the enemy. The stories of his escapades were legion. It was said that he could travel fifty miles in a single day through hostile territory, win a battle, take prisoners, and be back at base camp by dinner. Once, interrupted at shaving by an enemy attack, he simply shrugged into his shirt, leaped onto his horse, and routed the opposition before returning calmly to his washbasin. A Puritan soldier reported that Rupert, out on a sur-veillance mission, met an apple peddler on the road near the enemy camp, bought the man's entire stock on the spot, exchanged his coat and horse for the apple seller's costume and cart, and arranged to meet him again later in the day. The prince then drove the cart to the heath where the Parliamentarian soldiers were stationed, sold them the apples, counted the number of their forces, perused the quality of their artillery, and then returned to the peddler. He rewarded the man with a golden coin and instructed him to go back to the opposition troops "and ask the commanders how they liked the fruit which Prince Rupert did, in his own person, but this morning sell them."*

Rupert's innovative methods, while condoned on the Continent (whose inhabitants had been at war for over two decades and who were therefore much more inured to intimidation), were considered highly unorthodox by his English victims. "The two young Princes, Rupert especially, the elder and fiercer of the two, flew with great fury through divers counties...whereupon the Parliament declared him and his brothers 'traitors,'" affirmed a chronicler of the period.

---

* Rupert apparently inspired as much admiration for his good looks as he did for his derring-do. A memoir by a gentlewoman who lived through the civil war affirmed that "when the Prince broke up his quarters, the neighboring ladies not only went to see him march out of the town, but some of them were actually gone along with him!"

Unfortunately, her younger sons' highly public intervention in English affairs, so necessary to her brother's war effort, put great stress on the queen of Bohemia and her court. Since his ascension to the throne, Charles I had been helping to support his sister and her family with an annual stipend of £12,000—not sufficient for grandeur but enough to cover basic expenses and keep food on the table. But with the advent of the civil war, Parliament held the purse strings, and its members declined to support the mother of the commander of His Majesty's forces. Instead, through Puritan spies, they put the court at The Hague under surveillance.

This dilemma appears to have been anticipated by Karl Ludwig (whom Charles had also supported financially) and had in fact been at least partly responsible for his leaving England when he did. But despite Karl Ludwig's attempts at neutrality, no money was forthcoming. The court at The Hague entered a period of increasing austerity. "We were at times obliged to make even richer repasts than that of Cleopatra, and often had nothing at our court but pearls and diamonds to eat," Sophia recalled. To help cut expenses, the queen of Bohemia once again sent her two youngest sons, twenty-year-old Edward and sixteen-year-old Philip, to live with relatives in France, taking the risk that, with the reviled Cardinal Richelieu safely in the grave, there would be no plots against them.

She was right—in a way. Under the new regime, the queen of Bohemia's younger sons were perfectly safe from the threat of espionage, prison cells, and sword thrusts. But not, as it turned out, from Cupid's arrows.

LIKE HIS OLDER BROTHER Rupert, Edward had grown into a very attractive young man. He had long, flowing dark locks, a little pencil mustache, and a muscular body. He spoke French to perfection, having spent much of his later childhood and adolescence in France. He knew the manners and customs of Paris better than those of Holland. He liked the fashionable pleasures of the capital, which were much more sophisticated and entertaining than life at The

Hague, but, alas, he had not the financial means to pursue them as fully as he would have liked. Still, as a nephew of the queen of England, herself a member of the French royal family and aunt to the boy sovereign Louis XIV, Edward managed to get around a little, and was invited to dinners. At one of these soirees he met a force of nature by the name of Anna de Gonzaga.

Anna was born in 1616, which made her nearly eight years Edward's senior. She was both highly political and notoriously passionate and was as a result in possession of a reputation sorely in need of rehabilitation. The second daughter of the count of Mantua, Anna had been raised in a French convent where she and a younger sister were enjoined to take the veil by their father, who wanted to put all his resources into obtaining an advantageous marriage for his beautiful eldest daughter, Marie.* But the count of Mantua died before he could force his middle daughter to say her vows, and at twenty-one, Anna exchanged the nunnery for the French court. There, she met Henri, duke of Guise,† with whom she fell instantly, hopelessly, recklessly in love. "M. de Guise had the figure, the attitude and the manners of a Roman hero," she sighed in her memoirs. Henri reciprocated her passion and shortly thereafter seduced her, promising her marriage in a letter signed in blood. His mother tried to put a stop to it by using her influence to promote him to archbishop of Rheims, a position he accepted. His new life in the Church did not, however, get in the way of his torrid affair with Anna, although it did come in handy, as he was able to bully a priest into marrying them secretly in a private chapel with no witnesses. Anna was so infatuated that she disguised herself as a man in order to follow her lover wherever he went, and she referred to herself as the duchess of Guise in letters

---

* Marie de Gonzaga would fulfill her father's wishes by becoming the second wife of Wladyslaw IV, king of Poland, Princess Elizabeth's old beau, after the death of his first spouse, the emperor's daughter.

† Grandson of Henri, duke of Guise, with whom Marguerite de Valois, youngest daughter of Catherine de' Medici, fell in love before being forced instead to marry her cousin Henry, king of Navarre (the future Henry IV of France). It would appear that virile good looks and outstanding physiques were part of the genetic makeup of the family.

to friends. It therefore came as something of a shock when Henri suddenly eloped with a French countess, whom he (legitimately) married in Brussels. By 1643, Anna was back in Paris, devastated and seriously on the rebound, when she met Edward.

She was wealthy in her own right but wanted respectability and a title; he was young, penniless, and malleable. He never had a chance.* "This princess," reported another lady of the French court, "did not despise the conquests of her eyes, which were in truth very beautiful; but besides that advantage, she had that which was of more value, I mean wit, address, capacity for conducting an intrigue, and a singular facility in finding expedients for succeeding in what she undertook." But of course Anna was a Catholic and Edward was a Protestant, and this wouldn't do—to have the marriage accepted by French society, he would have to convert. As a matter of fact, it would be much to Anna's credit if she could get the son of the queen of Bohemia, who was widely recognized as one of the staunchest Protestants in Europe, to accept the Catholic faith, and this may have contributed something to his allure. Edward weighed the advantages of a marriage to Anna—a brilliant life in Paris, money, a worldly, fascinating wife—against those of his religion—poverty, rootlessness, a mother he barely knew, and the generally uncertain existence that could be expected by the middle son of a deposed king—and took the deal.

They were married in April of 1645 and afterward Edward very publicly converted to Catholicism, accepting Communion at the hands of a popular priest in Paris. Anna was given the credit for this coup, and her career at court was assured. She and Edward set up housekeeping in Paris as the prince and princess of Palatine, where they were accorded honors and a status comparable to those assigned to foreign dignitaries, and Edward would go on to watch his wife become a political force in France. "She had so much intelligence,

---

* To give a sense of what Edward was up against, the most powerful man in the kingdom, Cardinal Mazarin, would later take on Anna de Gonzaga—and lose.

Edward and his new wife, Anna de Gonzaga

and a talent so peculiar for business, that no one in the world ever succeeded better than she did," a French statesman concurred.

The news of Edward's conversion and marriage fell upon the family court at The Hague like one of the ten plagues called upon the pharaoh by Moses in the Bible. His mother would have preferred that he take out his dagger and plunge it into her breast than to suffer the humiliation of having raised a traitor to the Protestant cause. Karl Ludwig, who had gone back to England, not to support his uncle's cause, but to personally assure Parliament of his goodwill and lobby for the reinstatement of his income, was equally incensed, as Edward's rejection of Protestantism played directly into Puritan fears that Charles I would call on Catholic forces to invade the kingdom. Moreover, as the nominal head of the family, Karl Ludwig should have been consulted before his brother entered into a marital alliance. To prevent further damage, he immediately ordered his youngest brother, Philip, to leave Paris, "where were only to be found either Atheists or hypocrites," as he scornfully avowed, and return to the vigilant orthodoxy of The Hague.

Princess Elizabeth was, if possible, even more distressed than the rest of the family by what she considered to be a betrayal on Edward's part. The sensational tidbit was picked up by the Dutch papers, and as might have been expected, they had a great deal of fun with it. The princess was used to adversity, even tragedy, but had always been firm in the family's cause and clearly took her religion very seriously. The very public nature of the scandal mortified her. So used to turning to Descartes was she that, despite his being a devout Catholic who could not help but rejoice at Edward's conversion, she poured out her heart to him. After first apologizing for not having answered an earlier letter as promptly as usual, "It is with shame that I confess the cause, since it has overthrown all that your lessons seemed to have established in my mind," she continued, distraught. "I believed that a strong resolution only to seek happiness in the things which depend on my will would render me less sensitive to those which came from without, before the folly of one of my brothers made me feel my weakness. For it has disturbed the health of my body and the tranquility of my soul more than all the misfortunes which have yet happened to me.* If you take the trouble to read the gazette you must be aware that he has fallen into the hands of a certain sort of people who have more hatred to our family than love of their own worship, and has allowed himself to be taken in their snares to change his religion and become a Roman Catholic, without making the least pretence which could impose on the most credulous that he was following his conscience. And I must see one whom I loved with as much tenderness as I know how to feel, abandoned to the scorn of the world and the loss of his own soul (according to my creed)." Then, as if suddenly remembering that Descartes was a Catholic, she added quickly, "If you had not more charity than bigotry it would be an impertinence to speak to you of this matter, and if I were not in the habit of telling you all my faults as the person most able to correct them."

This humble disclaimer notwithstanding, her correspondent took

---

* Interestingly, she seems to have turned to metaphysics as a way for her mind to control her body and emotions and lead to inner peace, something like the seventeenth-century version of yoga.

offense; the letter that came back was a very long, full-on defense of Edward's conversion to Catholicism, for Descartes was as passionate about his dogma as she was about hers. "I cannot deny that I was surprised to hear of your Highness's anger, even to the inconvenience of her health, by a thing that the greater part of the world finds right [bonne], and which for many forceful reasons render it excusable to the rest," he began coldly. He then went on to scold her for her reaction and to put Edward's behavior, and that of those who had advised him to convert, in the best possible light, although at the very end, possibly realizing that he had been harsh, he added: "It is with the ingenuousness and frankness that I profess to observe in all my actions that I also particularly profess to be, etc." (which was the way he signed all his letters, implying yours truly, in your service, and so forth).

She had asked him always for honesty, and that is what he gave her: there was nothing of the courtier in *this* letter. Nonetheless, it took Princess Elizabeth several months to renew the correspondence. The reason for this is unclear, as certainly the events of 1646 were sufficiently distracting to take up so much of her attention that there was no time to dally in the world of metaphysics. Or it could have been that truth is subjective after all.

Louise Hollandine

Portrait of Boye the dog, by Louise Hollandine
(Photographic Survey, The Courtauld Institute of Art, London)

12

A Scandal in Bohemia

LOUISE HOLLANDINE WAS APPROACHING HER twentieth birthday in
the spring of 1642, the year that Princess Elizabeth began her friendship with Descartes. Dark-haired, pretty, and lively, with an artist's
aesthetic and *joie de vivre*, she seems to have had none of her older
sister's complaints about the tedium of life at court; but this might
have been because her future at this stage looked far rosier than that
of the scholarly Elizabeth. The year had started with an extremely
encouraging sign: an exploratory probe from Berlin indicating the
renewed interest of Louisa's old beau Frederick William, eldest son
of the elector of Brandenburg, in marrying her. "I will acquaint you
with a business which I pray take no notice of to anybody till I desire
it," wrote the queen of Bohemia conspiratorially to one of her closest friends in England on January 6. "The Elector of Brandenburg
hath designe to match with Princesse Lewisse [Louisa], he hath had
it ever since he was here but now it begins to come out, and hath
made [his] grandmother to write of it to me," she continued, fluc-
tuating between caution and exultation.

The Winter Queen's enthusiasm was not misplaced: her second
daughter (and, indeed, the family as a whole) could not have hoped
for a more appropriate or advantageous match. Frederick William
was twenty-two to Louisa's twenty; he was a staunch Calvinist who
had remained faithful to her family and supported her brother's
claim to the Palatinate over that of the duke of Bavaria; he was

intelligent and energetic; and he loved her. Even better, the objections Frederick William's father, the elector of Brandenburg, had originally raised to the match were no longer relevant, as the elector had fortuitously died two years earlier. Frederick William, as head of the family, was now in control of his own affairs.

And unlike his father, Frederick William possessed courage, determination, and a political acumen astonishing in so young a ruler. Within two years of his ascension to the electorate, to protect his subjects from the ruin of war, he had concluded an armistice with Sweden in which, for a lump-sum payment of 140,000 crowns and a thousand bushels of corn a year, the Swedes agreed not to violate Brandenburg territory; he deposed his old nemesis, the Catholic minister who had tried to poison him when he had been recalled from The Hague the first time, clearing the way for a change in policy; and he had declared himself and Brandenburg neutral in the conflict against the emperor, pending the restitution of the Palatine to Karl Ludwig. In addition to all of this, he had martial experience, having served, like the queen of Bohemia's own sons, in the army of the prince of Orange during his stay in Holland. He was what has been recognized throughout centuries of matchmaking as a catch.

But then again, so was she. For by this time Louisa's renown as an artist rivaled that of her sister for scholarship. Richard Lovelace, one of seventeenth-century England's foremost lyricists, who was in Holland during this period, was so captivated by Louise Hollandine that he wrote a long poem about her, in which he painted her portrait in words. Entitled "Princesse Loysa Drawing," it began: "I saw a little deity,/Minerva in epitomy,/Whom Venus, at first blush surpris'd..." In a series of stanzas, Lovelace compared the princess's skill at bringing her subjects to life to the power of various Greek gods and goddesses. "To live, and love, belov'd again:/Ah, this is true divinity!" ran one line; and in another, Venus chided Adonis: "See here a pow'r [Louisa's] above the slow/Weak execution of thy bow." The poem ended tenderly, "See, see! The darts by which we burn'd/Are bright Loysa's pencills turn'd;/With which she now enliveth more Beauties,/then they destroy'd before."

Although ostensibly extolling her talents as an artist, there is no mistaking the poem's romantic undertone; Lovelace had clearly been inspired by more than his subject's pencils. And he was no tongue-tied courtier. Described by an English politician of the period as "the most amiable and beautiful person that ever eye beheld...much admired and adored by the female sex," Lovelace had sufficient experience with women to be a shrewd judge of feminine charms. That he would be so taken with the Winter Queen's second daughter is indicative of the sort of frank admiration she aroused in members of the opposite sex. No wonder, then, that her cousin Frederick William, smitten, remembered her from his teenage years at The Hague and wished to marry her.

Wasting no time, by March 1642, an envoy from the queen of Bohemia had arrived in Berlin charged with negotiating the terms of the marriage alliance. The talks were already well under way when the news broke that Charles I had planted his standard at Nottingham and declared war against his own Parliament.

AT FIRST, THE REPORTS coming out of England were heartening. On October 23, 1642, the royal army had its first major engagement with the opposition forces at the tiny hamlet of Edgehill, about a hundred miles northwest of London, at which Rupert and his cavalry distinguished themselves, causing the enemy troops under an obscure Parliamentarian leader by the name of Oliver Cromwell to break ranks and flee. If Rupert had not chased after them, leaving the rest of Charles's divisions unprotected, the battle would have been a resounding success. As it was, although the losses were severe, the royal army held the field and the victory, and if his uncle had agreed, as Rupert urged, to push on immediately to Westminster, the war might have been over and the throne secured through a position of strength. But Charles had cautiously demurred. The enemy was able to regroup, and the chance was lost. Worse, Oliver

Cromwell had learned from his stinging defeat at Rupert's hands. "Your troops," he informed his superior commander after the battle, "are most of them old decayed serving men, and tapsters, and such kind of fellows, and their troops are gentlemen's sons, younger sons, and persons of quality; do you think that the spirits of such base and mean fellows [the Parliamentarian troops] will ever be able to encounter gentlemen [Rupert's cavalry], that have honor and courage and resolution in them? You must get men of a spirit…that is likely to go on as far as gentlemen will go; or else you will be beaten still." And Cromwell was commissioned at once to go and begin recruiting and training a new kind of army.

Still, there was no denying that with his nephew's help, the king had won the first round against the enemy. And the following year, the royal army received a big boost when his wife, Queen Henrietta Maria, managed to raise enough money on the jewels she had smuggled out of England to buy herself an arsenal—among which were six badly needed cannons—along with some 2,000 infantry and 1,000 cavalry. By February 1643 the queen of England had left The Hague to sail triumphantly back to her husband at the head of this impressive force, just in time for the spring campaign.

The additions helped—the offensive was sporadically successful, with Rupert's taking of the city of Bristol in July as a high point— but there was no real forward movement, no one victory that could be capitalized on to overwhelm the opposition. And with the passage of time, momentum began to shift slowly toward Parliament, which had spent most of 1643 productively mounting a force specifically designed to combat Rupert's cavaliers. "My troops increase," Cromwell crowed that year to his superiors. "I have a lovely company. You would respect them did you know them."

And then, in the summer of 1644, the pendulum swung decidedly against Charles I with the entrance of the Scottish army into the English war—on the side of Parliament. Henrietta Maria, weakened by a recent pregnancy and fearing capture by the invaders, was compelled to flee the kingdom so quickly that she did not even have time to name the daughter she gave birth to on June 6.★ (This time, the queen of England eschewed Holland in favor of her homeland of France, where her sympathetic sister-in-law Anne of Austria, the queen mother, took her in.) Charles sent Rupert and an army of some 17,000 men to meet the threat, commanding him to attack the Scottish troops, who had rendezvoused with Cromwell's divisions for a combined enemy force of nearly 28,000 soldiers.† On July 2, 1644, the two opposing battalions met at Marston Moor, about seven miles west of Charles's home base of York.

It was late in the day, in a driving rain, when Rupert and his men finally reached the battleground, and by the time they had organized and set up their artillery and defenses (which as usual had the cavalry in the front line, just behind a ditch, the better to seize the offensive), it was close to seven in the evening. Between the rapidly failing daylight and the darkly overcast sky it was concluded that there would not be enough time to prosecute a battle before nightfall, and so the attack was put off until the morning. Rupert, with his men, had just settled himself on the ground with a plate of food for supper when suddenly came the ominous sound of the drumming of hoofs, and without further warning Cromwell burst out of the rain and gloom, thundering down on them at the head of an imposing cavalry division.

Rupert was on his horse in an instant and managed to summon his front line for a counterattack. But his opponent, by taking the offensive, had deprived Rupert of his customary tactic. The royal army, already severely outnumbered, was forced to fight a defensive

---

★ Charles called the child Henrietta Maria after his wife, who in the urgency and danger of her departure had been forced to leave the baby behind in the care of a trusted lady-in-waiting.

† "Wherefore I command and conjure you, by the duty and affection which I know you bear me, that...you immediately march...with all your force to the relief of York...You may believe that nothing but an extreme necessity could make me write thus," implored Charles in a letter of June 14. "Had not [the king]...this year given a fatal direction to that excellent Prince Rupert to have fought the Scotch army, surely that great Prince and soldier had never so precipitately fought them," a Royalist officer who knew Rupert well concluded.

action. And this time, Cromwell's troops did not turn and run from the cavaliers' swords as they had in the past but stayed resolutely in place and fought so doughtily that Rupert later nicknamed them "Ironsides" (for the iron caps, back, and breastplates, rather than knightly armor, that they wore). "Whereupon followed a very hot encounter for the space of three hours," the Parliamentarian generals reported in their official dispatch of these events to London on July 5. "Whereof by the great blessing and good providence of God the issue was the total routing of the enemy's army, with the loss of all their ordnance to the number of 20 [pieces], their ammunition... and 10,000 arms. There were killed on the spot about 3,000 of the enemy, whereof many were chief officers, and 1,500 prisoners taken." By contrast, the Parliamentarian army lost only a handful of officers and less than three hundred foot soldiers.

It was Rupert's first serious defeat. He survived, "escaping narrowly, by the goodness of his horse," but he lost more than his army on that dark night. Left on the field among the dead, many of whose bodies, having been stripped of all of their possessions by the victors, gleamed whitely in the moonlight, was also to be found the still, lifeless form of Rupert's beloved poodle Boye, who had been the prince's brave and constant companion since his imprisonment in Austria. The animal had obviously been specifically targeted for death. "Here also was slain that accursed cur, which is here mentioned...because the Prince's dog hath been so much spoken of, and was prized by his master more than creatures of much more worth," gloated another Parliamentarian report in the aftermath of the fighting.

The battle at Marston Moor marked the beginning of the end for the Royalist cause. Rupert realized this. Although he managed to reunite with what was left of his cavalry after this fiasco and continued to prosecute the war as best he could, he counseled his uncle to come to terms with Parliament. Peace negotiations did in fact commence but Charles never had any intention of compromising; rather, egged on by Henrietta Maria, with whom he was in constant (and damning) correspondence and who was doing all she could from her position in France to raise funds and recruit Catholic allies to provide reinforcements, he was intent upon regaining his throne and all of his former sovereign powers by force. In the spring of 1645, just as Rupert's brother Edward was getting married to Anna de Gonzaga in Paris, Charles insisted that Rupert and his brother Maurice (who had not been present at the battle of Marston Moor) bring what troops they still had to Northampton, in central England, about sixty miles north of London.* They complied, and on May 9, 1645, they rendezvoused with Charles at the town of Naseby to meet the enemy. The Royalist forces had managed to scrape together just 11,000 men. Their adversaries could count on twice that number.

The outcome was predictable. Although Rupert, stationed on the side, succeeded in cutting through the enemy's left flank, Charles, in the center, was less successful. "One charge more, gentlemen! One charge more and the day is ours!" the king called out, positioning himself at the head of the infantry—but instead of charging forward as these brave words would indicate, he instead allowed himself to be turned away at the last moment by a solicitous courtier who, concerned for his sovereign's safety, grasped the bridle of his horse and *led him off the field*. The infantry, correctly inferring that this was not a good sign, also tried to turn back and was cut down in its confusion by the opposing army. There was nothing Rupert, who was furiously trying to fight his way to his uncle, could do to help. Five thousand of Charles's soldiers, nearly half his forces, were killed or captured that day. In addition, all of his armaments and luggage were taken, including the royal standard. More important, the king lost all of his private papers, including his wife's letters. When these were subsequently made public, it was clear to all

---

* Rupert was apprised of his brother's marriage by a letter from an English correspondent in Paris dated May 5, 1645. "Your Highness is to know a romance story that concerns you here, in the person of Prince Edward. He is last week married privately to the Princess Anne...[His new wife] is very rich; six or seven thousand pounds a year sterling is the least that can fall to her, maybe more: and is a very beautiful young lady."

of England that the king had been duplicitous about the peace negotiations and had merely been stalling for time.

And now, at last, Rupert saw what had become obvious to his brother Karl Ludwig during the time that he had spent with the king just before the outbreak of hostilities and the most likely reason that he had not stayed to fight beside him: his uncle was not competent to prosecute a war. He was too easily led astray by optimistic dreams that resulted in impractical strategies; he refused to face harsh realities. Even after the bloodbath at Naseby, Charles persisted in believing that he could still win if only he could raise more soldiers. He had a new fantasy that involved retreating to Scotland, of all places, and there regrouping. This was for Rupert the last straw. "My Lord," he wrote bluntly on July 28, 1645, to one of his uncle's council, "it is now in everybody's mouth, that the King is going for Scotland. I must confess it to be a strange resolution, considering not only in what condition he will leave all behind him, but what probability there is for him to get thither...If I were desired to deliver my opinion what other ways the King should take, this should be my opinion, which your Lordship may declare to the King. His Majesty hath now no way left to preserve his posterity, kingdom, and nobility, but by a treaty. I believe it a more prudent way to retain something, than to lose all," he concluded grimly.

For daring, swashbuckling Rupert, the warrior whose greatest pleasure was in the fight, who almost from childhood knew no more glorious existence than to charge forward at the head of a line of cavalry into battle to write such a letter tells more of the story behind the outcome of the civil war than mere speeches or statistics ever could. As he gave up all hope in his uncle the king, so did England—and, with it, the rest of Europe.

As it became increasingly obvious that Charles I would not prevail in his struggle to regain his throne, the pressure on his sister's court at The Hague intensified. It had been four years since Parliament had cut off funding to the queen of Bohemia, and what credit she had managed to scrape together on the promise of future repayment dried up completely once the outcome of the battle at Naseby was made public. She was responsible not only for herself and her four daughters but also for her youngest son, Philip, who had been hurriedly recalled from France after Edward's marriage. (Karl Ludwig remained in London in the hopes of getting his income reinstated, but although he did manage to convince Parliament of his fidelity, they declined to support him beyond the token disbursement of a few hundred pounds.) To limit expenses, Princess Elizabeth undertook negotiations to send eighteen-year-old Philip to Venice as a mercenary soldier. The queen of Bohemia disapproved of this sort of employment, but in light of the dire nature of the family's finances and the willingness of the Venetians to pay up-front for military service, there seemed little choice. Still, hammering out the details of the contract, which of course had to be conducted by letter, took time, and for the moment Philip was stuck at home.

Worse, to compound the Winter Queen's distress, the opposition sent spies into Holland to monitor her court's every movement and intercept her mail. Being under such close surveillance only heightened the tension and created an atmosphere of fear and suspicion of which innuendo and gossip were the natural by-products. "Slander just then was very prevalent at the Hague," Sophia remembered. "It had become a kind of fashion for the wits to sit in judgment on everybody's words and actions."

And into this already fraught environment, in the spring of 1646, came a man.

He was a Frenchman of an uncertain but debonair age, good-looking, sensual, and polished. Much about his background remains murky. A stranger in Holland, he gave his title as the marquis d'Epinay, and let it be known that he was a Huguenot—the name by which Protestants were called in France—who had quit his homeland after his fiancée had had her head turned (and apparently the rest of her body with it) by an unscrupulous prince of the blood, a member of the extended French royal family. But there were also reports that he was merely Monsieur Epinay, a captain in the army, and that it had been he who had seduced the prince's mistress, not the other way around; and who, after having been discovered, felt the most prudent course was to emigrate quickly, so as to be out of his powerful rival's reach. Whichever of these versions was true, as a matter of course, he was attracted to the Winter Queen's predominantly female court, and being a Protestant, was naturally welcomed at her salon, where in a remarkably short space of time he managed to ingratiate himself with her. There is a name for gentlemen of this sort that has been handed down through the centuries and is entirely appropriate in this instance. The marquis d'Epinay was a cad.

As one, her children knew it and despised him, watching in mounting consternation his hold on their mother. But the Winter Queen, about to turn fifty, had been used to male attention all her life, and it had been fourteen long years since her husband died. The marquis, with his perfect French manners and worldly air, flattered and played up to her. Before long, she announced that she was considering attaching him to her household as a member of her private council and allowing him to advise her on financial matters.

What followed is a scandal as shadowy as the marquis's—or the monsieur's—background. Because this episode was seized upon with glee as propaganda in Europe's various power struggles, it was written up in several periodicals. These accounts support the general outline of the story but vary in the details. So, depending on whether the source was Dutch, German, or French, on the evening of June 20, 1646 (or perhaps the afternoon or night before), the queen of Bohemia's eighteen-year-old son, Philip, was out for a pleasant walk or some other form of after-dinner entertainment with his friends when he encountered the marquis d'Epinay, who was out for a similar purpose with some of his friends. There ensued an altercation during which the marquis, in an attempt to humiliate Philip, taunted him by claiming to have had "bonnes fortunes" with his mother, or with his sister Louisa, or with both (depending again on the source). Philip, as the man of the household, was beside himself and either challenged the marquis to a duel or rushed at him with his friends. He had to remain unsatisfied, however, as his tormentor, shielded by his entourage, managed to get away. But the next day, while out riding in his carriage, Philip saw him again on the street, and this time the marquis was alone. Ordering his carriage to stop, Philip leaped out, and rushed at d'Epinay. Again there is confusion among the accounts. Some report that the marquis was unarmed; some assert that he drew his sword and wounded his assailant first; but all agree that Philip pulled his hunting knife from its sheath, plunged it into the marquis d'Epinay's breast, and then threw it aside and escaped in his carriage, leaving his victim dead in the street.

To the great displeasure of her children, the queen of Bohemia took the side of the murdered courtier over that of her son and refused all communication with Philip, who had fled across the border; nor in the aftermath of the crime would she allow him to return to her court. She was reported to have "bowed weeping from her high sphere, bewailing the misfortune of having such a son." Philip appealed to Karl Ludwig, as the head of the family, to intercede on his behalf, which he did with alacrity. "Madam," wrote Karl Ludwig to his mother from England on July 10, 1646, "give me leave to beg pardon in my brother Philip's behalf, which I should have done sooner, if I could have thought that he had needed it. The consideration of his youth, of the affront he received, of the blemish had lain upon him all his life-time, if he had not resented it, but much more that of his blood, and of his nearness to you, and to him to whose ashes you have ever professed more love and value than to anything upon earth [Dad], cannot but be sufficient to efface any ill impressions which the unworthy representation of the fact by those who joy in the divisions of our family, may have made in your mind against him. But I hope I am deceived in what I hear of this...since I will still be confident that the good of your children, the honor of your family, and your own, will prevail with you against any other considerations," he concluded severely. His eldest sister, utterly appalled, confronted her mother indignantly to her face, asserting, "that Philip needed no apology," a verdict that provoked a quarrel of sufficient magnitude that twenty-seven-year-old Princess Elizabeth abruptly packed her belongings and went to live with her cousins in Berlin.

It seems likely from the violence of her children's reactions that the queen of Bohemia was guilty, at the very least, of the appearance of indiscretion. Her affections had been so far engaged that it was certainly possible she had been intimate with d'Epinay and so was at least partially responsible for the tragedy. But what held for the mother does not seem to have been true for her daughter. For nowhere is there a mention that anyone in the family ever censured Louisa for her role in these events, and unquestionably Karl Ludwig, had he been informed of any impropriety on her part, would have seen it as his duty to write and reprimand her. Nor would Princess Elizabeth have focused her anger solely on her mother had Louisa been complicit in a love affair with the marquis. Princess Elizabeth had long since taken over the maternal duties of the household, and watched over her younger sisters with a sharp eye. Louise Hollandine seems to have been guilty of nothing more than being a beautiful twenty-four-year-old princess at the height of her powers to attract men, and she had indeed attracted the attention of a roué like the marquis d'Epinay. Of course it is impossible to know for sure, but certainly he would not have been the first man in history to have seduced the mother in an attempt to divert suspicion from his true designs on the daughter.

But it didn't matter that Louisa was no more than an innocent bystander in this episode. Between her brother's turning Catholic, her uncle's dispossession, and now this new notoriety, she was caught up in the wreckage of her family's reputation. Frederick William, who would go on to a brilliant career and become famous in the annals of history as the Great Elector, the founder of Prussia, and the great-grandfather of Frederick the Great, reluctantly decided that he needed a wife who brought money, the prospect of military aid, and an unblemished dignity to the table. Negotiations with the queen of Bohemia's emissary were broken off, and the coveted suitor entered into an alternate nuptial alliance.

Later that same year, Frederick William and his entourage arrived in great state at The Hague. There, on December 7, 1646, he married his far less attractive cousin, the daughter of the prince of Orange. As a matter of course, the Winter Queen's family was invited to the festivities, so Louisa had the singular privilege of witnessing her former suitor wed her cousin of lesser rank but better prospects and of rising with the rest of the company to wish the couple joy.

Marriage portrait of Frederick William, the Great Elector of Brandenburg, and the princess of Orange

Princess Henrietta Maria

...as a young woman of marriageable age

13

Honor and Duty

OF ALL OF HER SIBLINGS, pretty, bright-haired Princess Henrietta Maria was perhaps the most fragile, not simply in health but also in spirit. She had just turned twenty in the summer of 1646 and she was deeply affected by the divisions in her family caused by the murder of d'Epinay. Her brother Philip was nearest to her in age — less than fifteen months separated them — and she was closer to him than to any of the other children save Edward, with whom (as a Catholic) she was now not allowed to communicate. Her eldest sister, Princess Elizabeth, upon whom the preponderance of household responsibility had long since devolved, had from childhood been more of a mother to Henrietta Maria than had the queen of Bohemia.

Now both were gone: Philip to Karl Ludwig in England as a prelude to his employment as a mercenary soldier in Venice, a project over which his eldest brother voiced concern — "I could wish my brother Rupert or Maurice would undertake the Venetian business, my brother Philip being very young for such a task," Karl Ludwig warned his mother by letter — and Princess Elizabeth to her cousins in Berlin, where she clearly intended to stay for as long as possible. "I must remind you of the promise you made me of quitting your agreeable solitude to give me the happiness of seeing you before my departure deprives me of the hope of it for six or seven months, which is the longest time which the queen, my mother, and my brother, and the opinion of the friends of our family prescribe for my absence," she wrote to Descartes just before she left.

Princess Henrietta Maria held out for as long as she could, but when December came and her eldest sister still showed no signs of returning, she took the opportunity of Frederick William's marriage to the princess of Orange (who was only a year younger than Henrietta Maria and had been one of her closest friends since childhood) to accompany the bridal couple back to Berlin so she could be with Elizabeth. It was the first time the princess had ever been out of Holland or on any kind of a long journey at all, and the upshot of this was that she no sooner arrived than she fell sick. "My sister Henriette has been so ill we thought we should have lost her," Princess Elizabeth confided to Descartes in a letter of February 1647.

But under the care of her older sister, who had nursed her before and knew how best to restore her, Princess Henrietta Maria made a full recovery and was soon on her feet again and out enjoying the rounds of sleighing parties and evening balls that characterized fashionable society in Berlin. She was regularly in the company of Frederick William's family, and his mother, the dowager electress (the queen of Bohemia's sister-in-law), became particularly fond of this shy niece. Such a sweet, pretty girl should not go unmarried like her elder sisters, the dowager electress thought, and she was determined to do something for her.

And astoundingly, in one of those abrupt, head-shaking turnarounds in history, the dowager electress's ambition of a prestigious match for her niece, which would have been nearly impossible six months earlier, seemed suddenly plausible. For by 1647, the emperor was on the cusp of signing a general peace that included a settlement for Karl Ludwig and the Palatinate. As a result, for the first time in decades, the prospects of the family of the Winter Queen genuinely seemed to be on the rise.

THE PEACE PROCESS IN Germany, like the war itself, was an exceedingly complex and extended affair. Originally scheduled to begin in

1642, it took the 135 participating delegates, each with his own staff, nearly three years just to decide where the talks should be held and a further six months to straighten out life-and-death issues like which ambassadors had the right to be referred to as "Excellency." In the end, it was decided that the province of Westphalia, in northern Germany, was the most convenient spot to hammer out a treaty, but even then they could not locate a town large enough to accommodate everyone, so the French ambassadors held their deliberations in the city of Münster while the Swedish diplomats convened in the town of Osnabrück, a day's carriage ride away. This forced the imperial envoy, who had to come to terms with both these powers before any general peace could be signed into law, to engage in the seventeenth-century version of shuttle diplomacy for the duration of the negotiations, an additional three years.

That a gathering this crowded and fractured would succeed in coming to any agreement is testament to the collective public exhaustion brought about by the seemingly interminable decades of wholesale slaughter and destruction. So many people had been killed, so many towns leveled and fields burned over and over, that there really wasn't much territory left that could sustain the armies that swarmed to conquer it. The duke of Bavaria in particular—he who had been accorded the Palatinate and the coveted title of elector by the emperor in exchange for originally ousting Frederick and Elizabeth from Bohemia—now found himself presiding over a desolate wasteland and was so desperate to stop the carnage that he was even willing to give back some of his lands if it would mean an end to the fighting. Ferdinand, the emperor, having already lost key regions to the armies of France and Sweden, was also eager to achieve a political solution before more of his hereditary estate could be occupied and annexed. In Sweden, Gustavus Adolphus's daughter, Queen Christina, had recently come of age and taken control of her government, and she, too, strongly desired peace, provided that Sweden was adequately compensated for its efforts. Even in France, Cardinal Mazarin, who had succeeded Richelieu as chief adviser to the Crown, recognized that the time to make peace was from a position of strength, a status that a string of recent French victories, including a battle at Rocroy on the border with Belgium that decimated the Spanish army, had helpfully provided.

Karl Ludwig, still in England, was not present at these negotiations. But his cause was upheld by the Protestant Germans and Swedes, not out of any sense of loyalty but from religious self-interest. If the duke of Bavaria was allowed to keep the Palatinate *and* the title of elector, that would mean that of the six German electors, four would now be Catholic and only two Protestant, with the kingship of Bohemia (held again by Ferdinand, the emperor) as the seventh. The Catholics would thus hold a decisive majority where before the war the German electors had been split evenly between the religions, three and three. This the Protestants could not allow. Yet the duke of Bavaria, while willing to return some of the Palatinate to Karl Ludwig, was adamantly opposed to yielding his rank as elector, an impasse that called for some creative problem-solving. By the summer of 1646, the delegates had come up with what they felt was a workable compromise, which they forwarded to Karl Ludwig in London just as the civil war in England seemed to be winding down.

As RUPERT HAD PREDICTED, the later stages of combat had not gone at all well for Charles I. After the disastrous battle at Naseby, the king had refused to listen to his nephew's advice to treat for peace and instead sent him to hold the town of Bristol, the last Royalist stronghold. But no sooner had Rupert arrived than the city was surrounded and attacked by a Parliamentarian army substantially larger and better equipped than the prince's forces. He could have fallen back upon the castle and withstood a siege for several weeks, but that would have left the town itself undefended, and he could not in good conscience do this in the absence of "any probability of relief in any reasonable time," as Rupert reported in his official declaration of these events. As it was, "the city had thereby been exposed to the spoil and fury of the enemy, so many gallant men who had so long and faithfully served his Majesty, whose safeties his Highness [Rupert] conceived himself in honor obliged to preserve as dearly as his own, had been left to the slaughter and rage of a prevailing enemy." So instead of fighting to the death, Rupert surrendered Bristol on terms that guaranteed that no harm would come to its inhabitants.

Charles was furious and accused Rupert of high treason, claiming that he had been in the process of raising a new army and hurrying to his nephew's aid when he was given the news of the capitulation. To this allegation Rupert pointed out that as the Scottish army had already taken Gloucester, through which Charles would have had to march to get to Bristol, "can any rational man imagine them [the Scots] so stupidly inactive, as to suffer his Majesty to pass so near them without opposition, considering what effective forces they had, and their commanders neither ignorant or idle to entertain opportunities for action?" To clear his name, Rupert, along with his brother Maurice, fought their way back to Oxford, Charles's home base, and demanded a hearing. A court-martial was held at which Rupert argued his case and was declared innocent, and Charles forgave him.

The king then decided that his best option was to slip away from Oxford in disguise and give himself up to the Scottish army rather than Parliament, another course of action against which Rupert argued so vehemently that to console him, Charles signed an official document relieving the prince of any responsibility for the decision. Then, clothed as a servant, the king of England stole away from Oxford with a small party to try to surrender himself to the faction that he considered the lesser of two evils.

After Charles decamped, Rupert and Maurice agreed to relinquish Oxford to Parliament without a fight provided that they were allowed a safe passage to leave the kingdom, a condition that Parliament granted. Here the prudence of Karl Ludwig's having refused to support his uncle's position when he believed the Crown to have been in the wrong and instead allying himself with Parliament was made manifest, for it is doubtful that the commanding general of the Royalist army would have gotten away so easily had not his elder brother been trusted by the government. Karl Ludwig was even allowed to meet with his younger siblings before they left. "Having received information from Münster and Osnaburgh [Osnabrück], that in whatsoever shall be agreed at the general treaty concerning my interests, the consent of all my brothers will be required, I am desirous to confer with my brothers Rupert and Maurice, afore their departure out of this kingdom, about this, and other domestic affairs which do concern us," he wrote to Parliament on June 30, 1646. "Whereby I do not at all intend to retard my said brothers' journey; but shall endeavor to efface any such impressions as the enemies of these kingdoms, and of our family beyond seas (making use of their present distresses), may fix upon them, to their own and our family prejudice."

The brothers met at Guildford, about thirty miles southwest of London, on July 1, and clearly more than just the negotiations at Westphalia were discussed. The disagreement over English politics aside, Karl Ludwig, nearing his thirtieth birthday, asserted himself as head of the family. The reacquisition of the Palatine, in whatever form that took, came first, and both of his younger brothers consented to accept whatever terms and conditions came out of his negotiations with the empire. There was then the problem of what to do in the wake of d'Epinay's murder. The family simply could not afford another scandal at this delicate time. Someone was going to have to go back to The Hague to babysit the queen of Bohemia and her court and ensure that there was no repetition of this sort of behavior in the future. Maurice, as the junior member of the company, was assigned this unenviable task. Rupert, who was now prohibited from combat in both Germany *and* England and who was consequently rapidly running out of places where he was allowed to fight, was sent to Queen Henrietta Maria's court in exile in France, where Charles I's eldest son, the Prince of Wales, had also fled.

There he was made a field marshal and recruited by the French to fight the Spanish in Flanders. Karl Ludwig remained in England to try to salvage relations with Parliament in the hopes of getting those all-important bequests restored, and to keep an eye on developments.

Such was the stern reaction of her eldest son to his mother's midlife flirtation with the marquis d'Epinay. The Winter Queen did not know it yet, but among her children she had just been dethroned.

It was a condition that seemed to run in the family. For just at that moment, Charles I was facing the capitulation of his own sovereignty to Parliament.

ALTHOUGH THE KING'S RUSE of disguising himself as a servant had succeeded, and he was able, once he had stolen away from Oxford, to surrender himself to the protection of the Scottish army, this scheme, like so many of Charles's other undertakings, had not worked out quite according to plan. Rather than coming to an arrangement with their sovereign against Parliament, as Charles had hoped, the Scots instead came to an arrangement with Parliament against their sovereign, Parliament having had the advantage of being able to underscore any commitment to their mutual religious objectives with a payment of hard cash. Accordingly, after extended negotiations and a bribe of £100,000, the Scottish army agreed to hand Charles over and withdraw from England. By August of 1647 the king was under house arrest at his wife's castle at Hampton Court, about fifteen miles west of London.

But his cause was by no means lost. In fact, ironically, Charles was actually in a stronger position than he had been since the war started. Five years of opposition rule had not endeared Oliver Cromwell and the other Parliamentarian leaders to the English citizenry. Sympathy had swung in the other direction; the king was now far more popular than his jailers. There were Royalist uprisings all over England, and more than half of the navy rebelled, their captains and crews pledging allegiance to the king and fleeing with their ships to

The Hague to organize a counterattack. Even the Scots repented their decision and actually sent emissaries to Charles assuring him of their loyalty and support and offering to invade England again in order to rescue him!

Under the circumstances, Cromwell, upon whom, as a result of his storied military successes, the leadership of Parliament had devolved, was ready to make a deal that would return Charles, in some fashion, to his throne. Accordingly, the king was treated not as a prisoner of war but as an honored guest who, although he could not leave Hampton Court, was allowed to have servants and company. Even better, negotiations to bring the war to a peaceful conclusion, which was clearly the optimal solution for the kingdom, commenced in earnest.

Karl Ludwig was among those who visited his uncle that fall, no doubt to encourage Charles to make the compromises necessary to end hostilities, and his account of their interview is revealing. "His Majesty, upon occasion, doth still blame the way I have been in all this time," he complained to his mother, referring to his having taken the side of Parliament over that of the king. "I do defend it as the only shelter I have, when my public business, and my person, have received so many neglects at Court. Madame, I would not have renewed the sore of his ill-usage of me since the Queen hath had power with him, but that he urged me to it, saying that I should rather have lived on bread and water, than have complied with the Parliament, which, he said I did 'only to have one chicken more in my dish,' and that he would have thought it a design more worthy of his nephew if I had gone about to have taken the crown from his head...Neither do I know of anyone, but Our Saviour, that would have ruined himself for those that hate me [Queen Henrietta Maria]," he finished bitterly.★

Just as it is clear from this letter that Charles's opinions of his

---

★ Karl Ludwig has been treated rather unfairly by historians who uniformly accuse him of abandoning his uncle in order to obtain money from Parliament. But it is clear that Karl Ludwig, who was the only member of his family actually present in England during the run-up to the civil war, consistently gave the king solid advice to moderate

The Court Paintings of Gerrit van Honthorst

The Winter Queen and King…

Elizabeth Stuart, Queen of Bohemia
(Royal Collection Trust © Her
Majesty Queen Elizabeth II, 2017/
Bridgeman Images)

Frederick V, Elector Palatine and King of Bohemia
(Heeresgeschichtliches Museum Wien)

And Their Children, in Order by Birth

Frederick Henry, the eldest son
(Ashdown House, Berkshire, UK/
National Trust Photographic Library/
Bridgeman Images)

Although it says "Maurice," this is
actually a portrait of Karl Ludwig. It
was mislabeled in a later century.
(Ashdown House, Berkshire, UK/
National Trust Photographic Library/
Bridgeman Images)

Princess Elizabeth, "*la Grècque [the Greek]*"
(Ashdown House, Berkshire, UK/
National Trust Photographic Library/
John Hammond/Bridgeman Images)

Rupert, "*le diable [the devil]*"
(Ashdown House, Berkshire, UK/
Photo © National Trust Images/
John Gibbons/Bridgeman Images)

This is Maurice.
(© Sotheby's 2017, Private Collection
of James Stunt of Stunt Acquisitions)

Louise Hollandine, "Louisa"
(Lobkowicz Palace, Prague
Castle, Czech Republic/
Bridgeman Images)

Edward
(Private Collection/
Johnny Van Haeften Ltd.,
London/Bridgeman
Images)

Henrietta Maria
(Ashdown House, Berkshire, UK/
National Trust Photographic Library/
Derrick E. Witty/Bridgeman
Images)

Philip
(© Sotheby's 2017, Private Collection by
courtesy of the Hoogsteder Museum
Foundation)

Sophia, the youngest daughter
(Royal Collection Trust © Her
Majesty Queen Elizabeth II, 2017/
Bridgeman Images)

In the upper left-hand corner, the deceased family members: Frederick V, Elector Palatine and King of Bohemia; his eldest son, Frederick Henry; and two children who died
as toddlers. The living members, from left to right: Philip; Edward; Gustavus Adolphus;
Princess Elizabeth; Louise Hollandine; Henrietta Maria; Elizabeth Stuart, Queen of
Bohemia; Sophia (flying overhead); Rupert; Karl Ludwig; Maurice. Notice that, even
though Karl Ludwig had by this time come of age and was the ostensible head of the
family, he is not the one driving the chariot!

(Oil on canvas/Museum of Fine Arts, Boston/Private Collection/L-R 12.2011/Photo © 2018
Museum of Fine Arts, Boston)

Selected Art of Louise Hollandine

The Finding of Erichthonius, an allegorical painting. The woman on the far right in the gold dress is almost certainly Louisa's first cousin Mary, daughter of Charles I and princess of Orange, which means that the baby pictured is very likely Mary's son, William III, prince of Orange and future King of England.
(Private Collection/Photo © Christie's Images/Bridgeman Images)

Self-portrait by Louisa as a young, unmarried woman living at her mother's court at The Hague
(© Sotheby's 2017)

Self-portrait of Louisa as a nun at the abbey of Maubuisson
(© Sotheby's 2017, Private Collection by courtesy of the Hoogsteder Museum Foundation)

eldest nephew's behavior had not changed, so did the king remain committed to the policy of recovering his throne without yielding to parliamentary demands. He was particularly inflexible on religious issues. "As the Church can never flourish without the protection of the Crown, so the dependency of the Church upon the Crown is the chiefest support of regal authority," he opined to his eldest son, the Prince of Wales, in a letter of August 26. "This is that which is so well understood by the . . . rebels, that no concessions will content them without the change of Church government."

Emboldened by the pledges of support from Scotland and the navy and riding the tide of his restored popularity, Charles believed if only he could muster the forces for a new invasion, he would win. To buy time, he went through the motions of negotiating without ever intending to treat it seriously, all the while continuing to intrigue surreptitiously through ciphered letters to Queen Henrietta Maria in France, a subterfuge that Cromwell, who had spies planted all around, soon discovered. Tipped off on November 18, 1647, that the king had smuggled out one such missive by having it sewn into a messenger's saddle, Cromwell and one of his compatriots rode swiftly to intercept the document. "As soon as we had the letter we opened it," Cromwell later revealed. "We found the King had acquainted the Queen that he was now courted by both the factions, the Scotch Presbyterians and the army, and which bid fairest should have him, but he thought he should close with the Scots sooner than the others. Upon . . . finding we were not likely to have any tolerable terms from the King, we immediately, from this time forward, resolved his ruin."

But of course Charles didn't know this, and continued to plot and make plans to escape. He managed with the help of a loyal colonel

---

his approach and was frustrated at every turn by the outlandish schemes of the queen, whose counsel Charles took instead. Karl Ludwig, whose father had precipitated the Thirty Years' War, viewed his uncle's behavior as similarly self-destructive and refused to encourage him. To paraphrase Oscar Wilde, for the family to lose one kingdom (Bohemia) may be characterized as misfortune; to lose two (England) seemed to Karl Ludwig like carelessness.

in the army to steal away from Hampton Court, intending to take a ship to France, but the boat was delayed and he ended up a prisoner again, this time on the Isle of Wight, off the southern coast of England. But there was yet reason for optimism. To the west, Royalist supporters in Wales were in full rebellion, forcing Cromwell to once again take the field. By May 1648 a Scottish invasion was expected daily by the Parliament, and in July, Rupert and the Prince of Wales left France to join Maurice at The Hague, where Rupert was named commander of the royal navy in Holland. By fall, a fleet was in readiness to sail to Charles's rescue.

And then, on October 14, 1648, a momentous event occurred on the Continent. An accord had finally been reached, and a peace treaty signed by all the combatants in Germany. The Thirty Years' War was over.

THE AGREEMENT, KNOWN AS the Treaty of Westphalia, was as comprehensive and far-reaching a document as has ever been produced in Western civilization. The 135 squabbling delegates had somehow managed to address not simply political and territorial issues but religious divisions as well. The first order of business, of course, had been to come to an understanding with the two occupying foreign powers, Sweden and France. This was accomplished through bribery. Sweden received a cash payment of five million thalers and the province of Pomerania, in northern Germany on the Baltic Sea, which is what it had always wanted. As Pomerania had formerly been part of the electorate of Brandenburg, Frederick William had to be compensated for the diminution of his property. He reluctantly agreed, in the interest of peace, to take two million thalers, the cities of Halberstadt and Herford, and the promise of Magdeburg in the future in exchange for ceding part of his homeland to the Swedes.

France got an even bigger prize: Ferdinand, bowing to realities (the French army was in possession of these anyway), formally surrendered the region of Alsace-Lorraine, as well as the towns of

Breisach, Benfeld, Neuenburg, and Saverne, all of which had for centuries owed allegiance to the emperor. It was a reward of immense proportions; it gave France control of a hundred miles of the Rhine that had formerly served Germany as protection from invasion; it changed the equation of Europe.★

Of the many participants in this horrific, decades-long war, by this settlement there is no question that France emerged the clear victor. Never again would the Habsburgs achieve the power or greatness they had assumed at the start of the century was theirs by birthright. Although he did not live to sign the papers, Richelieu's handprint was nonetheless all over the Treaty of Westphalia—so much so that it might well be considered his last will and testament, his legacy to France.

The foreign conquerors having been satisfied, the delegates then turned to the problems of Germany and the empire. A general amnesty was declared, and as had been promised earlier in the Peace of Prague, the emperor agreed that 50 percent of the judges and advisers to the imperial court would be Catholic and the other 50 percent Protestant. But he went even further: By the Treaty of Westphalia, no matter how many times Church property had changed hands from Protestant to Catholic or vice versa over the course of the war, everything was thereby ordered to go back to the way it was on January 1, 1624. For nonreligious property, ownership went back to the way it was in 1620, before the war had even begun.

Except for the Palatinate. But even here there were concessions. The duke of Bavaria got to keep the Upper Palatinate and the title of elector, it was true, but Karl Ludwig was given back the Lower Palatinate, which included the family estate at Heidelberg, and an eighth electorate was created specifically for him. As a further incentive to take the deal, Ferdinand agreed to pay the queen of Bohemia's younger sons a total of 400,000 thalers, and to provide a

---

★ This ceding of Alsace-Lorraine would contribute to hostilities between France and Germany for the next two and a half centuries, up to and including the two World Wars.

marriage portion of 10,000 thalers to each of her daughters as compensation for the loss of the Upper Palatinate. To these terms, Karl Ludwig agreed.

And so the war ended. Upon the signing of the treaty, trumpets were sounded and heralds sent in every direction to proclaim that all fighting was to cease immediately. Every prisoner was to be set free, and any towns, villages, and castles that had been captured were to be returned.

There was great rejoicing throughout the empire but the cost of the fearsome struggle remained. In 1619, when Frederick and Elizabeth first entered Prague so hopefully in state, the kingdom of Bohemia, the epicenter of the conflict, had boasted a population of two million subjects. At the time of the signing of the Treaty of Westphalia, the citizenry had been reduced to 700,000. Half of the houses in the realm were vacant or destroyed, and 50 percent of the farmland, scorched by combat, lay fallow. The statistics for central Germany were even worse: there, the duchies lost 75 percent of their inhabitants, 66 percent of their homes, and 80 percent of their livestock. On average, as a whole, Germany lost 50 percent of its population in the Thirty Years' War, either through carnage, disease, or starvation. It represented the worst holocaust in the history of the world to that date. Even the plague was not so thorough.

ALTHOUGH THE QUEEN OF BOHEMIA and her family had been forced by the Treaty of Westphalia to cede the Upper Palatinate to the elector of Bavaria, the agreement was nonetheless cause for rejoicing. At least now they could safely return to their beautiful castle in Heidelberg, and Karl Ludwig would still wield some influence in Germany as an elector (although not nearly as much as before). But the news of the signing of the historic agreement had barely had time to sink in before the family was confronted with yet a further ominous development in the struggle for power in England. For on December 15, 1648, exactly two months after peace was declared in Germany, it was resolved by Parliament "that the King be forthwith sent for to be brought under safeguards to Windsor Castle, and there to be secured in order to the bringing of him speedily to justice."

The timing of this decree was not coincidental. With the conclusion of the war in Germany, the Puritan leaders of Parliament were concerned that the French court would now turn its attention (and its victorious army) toward England. Certainly this was what Queen Henrietta Maria, who had established herself at St. Germain so as to be near her sympathetic sister-in-law Anne of Austria, was clamoring for. Charles I's eldest son, the prince of Wales, had already (unsuccessfully) attempted a rescue mission by sea, using the decamped ships of the royal navy. Cromwell and his supporters felt they could not take the risk that the king would escape only to return at the head of a large foreign army that would impose unpalatable conditions on a defeated Parliament. To prevent this possibility, they had determined on an extreme and savage course of action.

On December 23, Charles was brought under heavy guard from the Isle of Wight to London. There, on January 20, 1649, in an eerie replication of the proceedings against his grandmother Mary, queen of Scots, the king of England stood trial for high treason in front of English judges at Westminster Hall.

And just as Mary had protested that as a queen, she could be tried only by a gathering of her peers (other members of royalty), so Charles argued that the parliamentary action against him was illegal, as his judges did not have the standing necessary to pass judgment on a king. "It is not my case alone: it is the freedom and liberty of the people of England; and do you pretend what you will, I stand more for their liberties; for if power without law may make laws, may alter the fundamental laws of the Kingdom, I do not know what subject he is in England that can be sure of his life, or anything he calls his own," he asserted eloquently.

But of course it didn't matter, and the trial continued inexorably along its grim path. Again like Mary, the king was not allowed to speak in his own defense. His inquisitors wanted only to hear him confess to his crimes, and when Charles refused to do so and tried to answer the charges, they shouted him down. His trial was concluded more quickly than his grandmother's, in a mere six days, but the same preordained, pitiless verdict was handed down: that Charles, "as a tyrant, traitor, murderer, and public enemy to the good people of this nation, shall be put to death by the severing of his head from his body."

On January 29, the day before his execution was scheduled to take place, his persecutors allowed him to say good-bye to two of his children: his second daughter, thirteen-year-old Elizabeth, and his youngest son, eight-year-old Henry, both of whom were still in England. It was a heartbreaking scene. The children, frightened and bewildered, cried and clung to their father, and Charles in turn had to be strong for their sakes. He spoke gently but as an adult to his daughter to console her, but then had to face the boy. He put Henry on his knee and, perhaps remembering the plan of the conspirators in the long-ago Gunpowder plot, spoke lovingly but firmly to him. "Sweetheart," he said to his youngest son, "now they will cut off thy father's head; mark, child, what I say: they will cut off my head and perhaps make thee a king; but, mark what I say: you must not be a king so long as your brothers Charles and James do live; for they will cut off your brothers' heads when they catch them, and cut off thy head too at the last, and therefore I charge you do not be made a king by them." "I will sooner be torn in pieces first!" promised the child bravely through his sobs.

On the morning of the next day, January 30, 1649, Charles was brought to Whitehall. As with Mary, the public was invited to witness the fruits of justice, and so the scaffold had been set up outside the Banqueting House. The execution ceremony was short. The king's hair was gathered into a white satin nightcap, the better to expose his neck to the ax, just as Mary's hair had been gathered up and her neck laid bare some sixty years before; he, too, knelt on a cushion and laid his head upon the block. Then, by prearranged signal, he stretched out his arms, indicating his readiness to receive the blow.

The executioner's aim was sure. In this one detail did Charles's experience of death differ materially from his grandmother's. His life was severed with the first stroke. "Behold the head of a traitor!" came the cry as the evidence of the executioner's handiwork was held aloft for all to see.

Monarchs had died on the battlefield but never before in the history of the realm had a sitting English king been tried, convicted, and sentenced to decapitation. It was a shocking and brutal act from which there was no turning back.

AT THE HAGUE, THE queen of Bohemia was in the middle of a public holiday celebrating the end of hostilities in Germany and the return of the Lower Palatinate when Karl Ludwig suddenly turned up with the news of her brother's beheading. Stunned and grief-stricken, she immediately canceled the festivities, and from then on she set apart January 30 as a day of mourning every year until her death.

Rupert, too, took the news hard. In one of his last letters to his nephew, smuggled out during the period when he still believed the Scottish army would come to his rescue, Charles had written him that "since I saw you, all your actions have more than confirmed the good opinion I have of you. Assuring you that, next my children... I shall have the most care of you, and shall take the first opportunity either to employ you or have your company. And, be confident that this shall be really performed by your most loving Uncle, and constant faithful Friend," the king had closed with genuine affection. "The bloody and inhumane murder of my late dread uncle of ever renowned memory hath administered to me fresh occasion to be assistant, both in Counsel and to the best of my personal power, to my dear cousin [Charles's eldest son, formerly the Prince of Wales], now Charles II of England," read Rupert's grim response to the execution in a proclamation issued on March 9, 1649.

Again, it was Karl Ludwig alone among the family who had witnessed Charles's trial and execution, and brought back a lock of the king's hair for his mother, which she had set in a ring and wore every day to remind her of the manner of his death. Although as a

German elector, he had heretofore striven to maintain friendly relations with Parliament and stay neutral in the civil war against the king, whose impetuous behavior he condemned, the barbarity of his uncle's decapitation had torn the mask of sobriety off the Puritans' intentions, and Karl Ludwig had fled London for The Hague, no doubt concerned for the safety of his own head. He continued to blame Queen Henrietta Maria for her role in convincing her husband to initiate a civil war over his own more sedate advice—he absolutely refused to write her a letter of condolence despite his mother's entreaties—but he switched sides and offered his allegiance to Charles II. "Dearest brother," eighteen-year-old Sophia wrote to Rupert on April 13, 1649, "my brother the Elector is now here, and cares no more for those cursed people in England, for he has paid his duty to the King [Charles II]."

And so was the queen of Bohemia's family brought together again. Even Edward penned a heartfelt condolence letter to his mother—"I should die happy if I could steep my hands in the blood of those murderers!" he fumed—and was forgiven. But this time the sorrow was lightened by hope. For by October of 1649, Karl Ludwig, for the first time in thirty years, had entered triumphantly into Heidelberg and reclaimed his birthright.

And with the Elector Palatine's return, the conditions of the Treaty of Westphalia became generally known, not simply to the immediate family but to their extended relations in Berlin, where Princess Henrietta Maria was still a guest. There, her aunt the dowager electress of Brandenburg, with the single-minded clarity that had allowed her to survive for so long and through so many challenges, focused in on the one clause she considered most pertinent out of the myriad terms in that complicated peace agreement: the 10,000-thaler dowry allotted to her favorite niece.

THERE WAS NO NEED to cast around for a potential suitor. The dowager electress already had the perfect candidate in mind.

His name was Siegmund Rakoczy. The Rakoczys were the ruling family in Transylvania, having taken over the realm after the death of Bethlen Gabor, who had been the king and queen of Bohemia's ally against the emperor thirty years before, at the start of the war. As a second son, Siegmund's official title was prince of Siebenbürgen but he was in line for the throne should his older brother die without heirs. Even better, he was just the right age — four years older than Henrietta — Protestant, wealthy, and in the market for a bride. The empress dowager knew that an imperial dowry of 10,000 thalers, while respectable, wasn't sufficient in itself to draw the prince's attention, but her niece had other attributes that might be of interest to a young man looking to marry. Taking the initiative, she played her best card and sent the prospective bridegroom a portrait of Henrietta, most likely one that had been painted for just this purpose by Gerrit van Honthorst.

The empress dowager knew what she was about. The painting arrived and Siegmund immediately compared it to those he had already received from the other applicants for the position, most of whom were daughters of the regional nobility as depicted by local artists. Honthorst earned his stripes with this one: there was no contest. At a subsequent council meeting the prince was extremely forceful with both his family and prominent members of the ruling aristocracy about his choice of a bride. The upshot of this discussion was that an emissary was sent to Karl Ludwig (in his role as paternal head of the family) in Heidelberg in 1650 with a formal offer for Henrietta's hand in marriage.

Karl Ludwig, unsure of what to do and not wanting to be bothered with the tedium or expense of the negotiation, passed the emissary on to Berlin to treat with the dowager empress, and it was at this point that Henrietta evidently became aware of the machinations taking place on her behalf. "I wish your Highness could have seen the dearest niece when her name was mentioned, turning pale and the tears coming into her eyes," the dowager electress wrote with satisfaction to Karl Ludwig, of the Transylvanian ambassador's arrival at her court.

But those were not tears of modesty or joy. They were of fear. It wasn't that Henrietta didn't want to get married. She knew it was the best choice both for her and her family. If she did not wed, she would remain a financial burden on those she loved most dearly for the rest of her life. But Transylvania! Siegmund's hometown of Sarospatak, where she would live, was so far from Berlin that no one she or anyone else she knew had ever been there.* To marry a prince of Transylvania was equivalent to a sentence of exile. Even the dowager electress, while celebrating the fitness and generosity of Siegmund's offer—Henrietta, she knew, would want for nothing for the rest of her life—could not help but acknowledge that the distance was not optimal (although this in no way stopped her from strongly supporting the match). "Since the conditions appear so favorable I do not hesitate to recommend it to your Highness's best consideration, and I must say if it were not so far off it would be in my opinion an excellent thing," she continued in her letter to Karl Ludwig.

Shy, obedient Henrietta did her best to be brave but it is clear that she was praying that fate would somehow intervene and she would not have to go through with the marriage. "If she sacrifices herself for her relations, she feels sure they will be too kind to abandon her, should she have need of them," Princess Elizabeth, still in Berlin, informed Karl Ludwig. "These words were accompanied with such torrents of tears that they made me pity her," she added. Henrietta herself wrote to her eldest brother, whom she, like her younger sister Sophia, called Papa. "The highly honored Elector and gracious Herr Vater [father]...It seems rather too far away to be pleasant, and though I might have a little more money by it, I do not love myself so much that for the sake of that I would go so far from all my relations; besides I am used to doing with a little," she pleaded.

But the diplomatic machinery of an alliance of state had been

---

* In fact, it was 569 miles to the southeast, and this in a time when the roads were poor or nonexistent.

thrown into gear, and plans for the wedding moved relentlessly forward. There was simply too much evidence in the groom's favor to call a halt to the proceedings. Even given the need to woo by long distance, the prince could not have been more considerate. "I envy the fate of this letter, which will see your charming countenance sooner than I shall; though there are no words which would translate my feelings fully, I comfort myself that this will be the interpreter of my love," was the note Siegmund attached to the beautiful watch set in diamonds that his ambassador presented to Henrietta as an engagement gift. And although Transylvania was too far away for anyone in the family to actually meet the prospective bridegroom themselves, they had reports from reliable witnesses as to Siegmund's eligibility. The prince lived in his own castle, and not with his mother, and "keeps always two hundred men-at-arms and fifty gentlemen in his suite, and his household is served on vessels of silver," Princess Elizabeth confirmed to Karl Ludwig in a letter of December 24, 1650, adding that the governor of Lusatia had personally informed her that "the marriage was spoken of and everyone considered it very advantageous and by the Silesians from the frontier he was considered the richest and most desirable match that could be found amongst the Protestants."

That settled it. Even the queen of Bohemia, who had been deliberately excluded from the negotiations for fear she would "not consent out of crossness," as Princess Elizabeth put it, remembering the military aid Transylvania had brought to her husband's struggle against the emperor, approved of her daughter's impending marriage. There remained only the expense of the wedding, which would be held by proxy (again, it was too far for the bridegroom to make the trip to Berlin himself). Karl Ludwig was petitioned for funds many times—"Your daughter [Henrietta] says that if your Highness would give her a little something that she may appear among strangers without shame, she hopes not to be obliged to importune you any more, and she will repay it at a future time," Princess Elizabeth implored—but in the end it was the dowager electress of Brandenburg and her son Frederick William who bore most of the cost.

The wedding was a three-day affair that began with a great feast on May 13, 1651. Henrietta's wedding dress was embroidered with silver thread and lace from Holland; her train was held aloft by four maids of honor whose silver gowns were sewn from somewhat less expensive material. From her fond aunt, the bride received two silver candelabra and a hand basin, also of silver, as useful gifts with which to start her new life. Henrietta's meager trousseau — six nightgowns, three day-dresses, a dozen undergarments, and some embroidered handkerchiefs were all her eldest sister had been able to scrape together — was happily supplemented by the proxy's handsome gifts of jewels, golden chains, pearls, and sumptuous gowns befitting her status as the wife of one of the richest men in Transylvania. The marriage contract was signed on May 14, after which a Protestant service was performed. Finally, on May 15, the new princess of Transylvania bade a tearful farewell to her family, climbed into a coach-and-six provided by her husband, and, accompanied by a small entourage, began the long journey to Sarospatak.

The impatient bridegroom and his family met her halfway, at Breslau. Karl Ludwig had evidently commanded her to describe the manner in which she, as his sister, was treated by her in-laws, much as James I had once demanded that his daughter Elizabeth maintain her dignity as a princess of England among her husband's family. Henrietta hurried to set his mind at rest. "Because your Highness has bidden me to give an account of my position here I must say that both the Frau Mother and the reigning Princess [wife of Siegmund's elder brother] have greatly caressed me . . . and my lord is very good to me and sees that I have nothing to complain of except being so far from all my relations," she wrote bravely upon her arrival. "I wish I could have been so happy yesterday, that your Highness might have seen me in my Hungarian dress; I looked so pretty in it, my lord's mother could not express how delighted she was. Yet it is not at all a splendid dress, but quite bürgerlich [bourgeois], and all the women have one like the peasants, which would not please your Highness," she continued apologetically, striving for honesty. "But the men are very fine and mostly courteous people, amongst whom my lord is not the least well bred, as some had said and written of him. I wish my lord could be so happy as to be known to your Highness, for I feel sure you would like your brother-in-law," she recovered hastily.

The relief of the family upon receipt of this letter must have been very great. So, after all, they had done the right thing: Henrietta, while no doubt homesick, was nonetheless in good hands. And perhaps someday in the future Karl Ludwig would have need of an ally in Transylvania, and Henrietta and her husband, and maybe even her children, would arrive in state and be welcomed on a family visit, and they would all see each other again.

But this was not to be. Because, as had happened the last time she had taken a long journey, fragile Henrietta Maria fell ill soon after arriving in Transylvania. But this time there was no Princess Elizabeth, who knew her well enough to take great care, to nurse her. Instead, Henrietta, no doubt trying to please her husband and his family, exerted herself to go with them when they made their annual summer excursion to the Rakoczy country palace. By the time her mother-in-law realized her mistake and brought her back to Sarospatak, Henrietta was very sick indeed. "I found no fault in him [Siegmund] but that he loves me too much," she managed to scrawl in one of her regular reports to Karl Ludwig in August 1651. But she could not go on. "I am so weary that I can scarcely support myself upon my legs, and must beg leave to end this," she confessed.

Tragically, this would be her last letter home. For on September 18, 1651, twenty-five-year-old Henrietta Maria, beautiful daughter of the Winter Queen, died, most likely of a bacterial infection. Sometime between eight and nine on that sorrowful morning, far from all whom she loved, removed from every familiar face or surrounding, every affectionate word or gesture that might have brought a measure of comfort or soothed her terror, sweet, gentle Henrietta took her last breath. That she died a princess, obediently upholding the family honor, must have seemed of small moment to her anguished relations when they heard the terrible news.

Although they were together only a few short months, her new young husband, too, had truly loved her and was overcome with grief at her passing. "I hold my life for nothing worth," he wrote in despair in the letter announcing her death. He was evidently in earnest, for less than six months later, he too was dead—of fever compounded, it was said, by a broken heart.

Sophia

Karl Ludwig, Elector Palatine

14

Royal Sense and Sensibility

IN THE PERIOD IMMEDIATELY FOLLOWING the execution of Charles I in January 1649, while her sister Henrietta was yet alive and the negotiations for the disastrous Transylvanian marriage had barely commenced, clever eighteen-year-old Sophia, still at her mother's court at The Hague, found herself at the center of an unaccustomed swirl of political activity. The presence of the royal fleet had lured her penniless first cousin the Prince of Wales—now, in the aftermath of his father's death, designated King Charles II—to Holland to take advantage of his sister Mary's and her husband, William, prince of Orange's hospitality, and with Charles II came an entire court of some 300 dispossessed followers, as well as loyal champions who hurried to pay homage to the young monarch. Happily for Sophia, this swarm of visitors for a time also included her eldest brother, Karl Ludwig, whom she, like Henrietta, adored.

But Karl Ludwig was eager to reclaim his property under the terms of the Treaty of Westphalia, and all of her other brothers were away. Charles II had named Rupert lord high admiral (an impressive title for a very small navy, as by this time the royal fleet was down to five seaworthy vessels) and sent him to pirate ships along the Spanish coast to capture loot for the royal treasury. Maurice, considered too experienced a warrior in these troubled times to stay home and chaperone his mother's court, had been named vice admiral, under Rupert, and was out accompanying him on this fund-raising expedition. Edward was of course still in France living the life of a privileged married aristocrat, and Philip was by now in Italy under disgruntled contract to the Venetians. ("Unworthy pantaloons" was how he had contemptuously described his employers to his brother Rupert in a letter of the previous fall.) And so, in the summer of 1649, Sophia found herself alone at The Hague with her mother and elder sister Louisa, once again without the fond but stern protection of a male member of the family.

In fact, Karl Ludwig had no sooner climbed on his horse and trotted out of town in the direction of Heidelberg than rumors and intrigues began swirling around the Winter Queen's youngest daughter. The chief plot, sponsored by her mother's close friend William, earl of Craven*—an extremely wealthy admirer upon whom the queen of Bohemia was financially dependent—involved Charles II and had been in the works even before his father's execution. (This was the same Lord Craven who had participated in and helped fund Karl Ludwig's one disastrous military campaign during which the youthful Rupert had been captured.) "An old Englishman [he was forty-one at the time], Lord Craven took an interest in me," Sophia volunteered later in her memoirs. "There was an idea that I might some day marry the Prince of Wales [Charles II], who was a year my senior. My friends hoped for success, because the English desired for their prince a wife of his own religion, and at that time there were no Protestant princesses of birth superior to mine for him to choose amongst."

For most young women in Sophia's position, the prospect of being wed to Charles II, by right of birth the king of England, would have been irresistible. At twenty, Charles, with his long, coal-black hair and strong, lean body, made for an extremely attractive

---

* "Lord Craven was a very valuable friend, for he possessed a purse better furnished than my own from which to provide presents for my partisans. He always had refreshments standing ready, and used to give away quantities of little ornaments, such as would delight young people. He needed all these attractions to make him agreeable, and to enable us to tease him a little in private," Sophia observed.

marital candidate; he was described by a courtier who knew him as "very well made; his swarthy complexion agreed well with his large bright eyes...his figure extremely fine." He was also exceedingly tall—just over six feet—and energetic, particularly, apparently, when it came to lovemaking, as he had already fathered two children by two different women, out of wedlock.

But having lived through the scandal associated with d'Epinay and watched Princess Elizabeth's and Louisa's various engagements fall by the wayside, Sophia had the benefit of their experience and had learned to be prudent. "My manners and behavior had been so carefully watched over by my two elder sisters that I was even more commended for conduct than for beauty," she recalled. Shrewdly, Sophia sized Charles up as "a prince richly endowed by nature, but not sufficiently so by fortune to allow him to think of marriage." Despite being "much courted by the English nation [the Royalists who had fled with Charles II to The Hague], who took endless trouble to please me," Sophia also could not help but "notice other signs of weakness on the King's part." For example, "he and I had always been on the best of terms, as cousins and friends, and he had shown a liking for me with which I was much gratified," she reported. "One day, however, his friends Lord Gerit and Somerset Fox, being in want of money, persuaded him to pay me compliments on the promenade. Among other things he told me that I was handsomer than Mrs. Berlo [one of the women with whom he had fathered an illegitimate child; now there's a flattering comparison], and that he hoped to see me in England. I was surprised by this speech, and learned afterwards that Somerset Fox's object was to induce me to ask Lord Craven for money for the King, which he meant to share with his comrade, Lord Gerit. I was highly offended; but the Queen [of Bohemia, her mother], who had noticed his Majesty's marked attentions, was just as much delighted, and blamed me for not going to the promenade on the following evening. I made the excuse of a corn on my foot, which prevented me from walking. My real reason, however, was to avoid the King, having sense enough to know that the marriages of great kings are not made up by such means," she concluded sagely.

It's a rare gift, particularly when young, to be able to see into the future and anticipate the consequences of a reversal, but this Sophia, despite the determined fawning of the hangers-on around her, was able to do. "All these circumstances combined proved to me that my friends' plan [to marry her to Charles II] would come to nothing, and that, were I to remain in Holland, I should doubtless be subjected to the mortification of losing the esteem in which I was held; for those persons who paid court to me would do so no longer when they came to perceive that I was powerless to reward them," she worried. Luckily, due to the Treaty of Westphalia, she now had somewhere to go—back to the ancestral castle of Heidelberg, where Karl Ludwig had taken up permanent residence. To distance herself from the potential for scandal or notoriety that were the inevitable by-products of failed marital hopes, "it was agreed that I should go to the Palatinate on a visit to my brother the Elector Palatine, who had always favored me with his affection, even to the extent of calling me his daughter, for he was thirteen years older than I. Hearing that he had married a princess of Hesse Cassel, and knowing him to be a prince of great powers of mind, I felt sure that in so important a matter he would not have allowed inclination to overrule judgment, and that in the young and beautiful princess of his choice I was certain to find a delightful companion," she rejoiced.

And so, over her mother's objections (who was still hoping for a wedding with Charles), off Sophia went in the summer of 1650, escorted by two English ladies-in-waiting and the ever-useful Lord Craven, who footed the bill for the entire journey. She even sweet-talked the government of Holland into providing her the necessary transportation to Germany. "As I had never during my whole life stirred from The Hague—except once, when I went to Rhenen, and now and then in a canal-boat to Leyden or Delft—I dreaded the fatigue of a carriage, and therefore begged from the States General the loan of a pinnace, in which I was able with great comfort to sail up the Rhine," she admitted. Her journey took her through Dusseldorf, Cologne, and Rheinfels and finally to Mannheim, where Karl Ludwig and his new young wife, Charlotte of Hesse-Cassel, were waiting to escort her to nearby Heidelberg, her new home.

THE HEIDELBERG TO WHICH Karl Ludwig had returned after a thirty-year absence bore very little resemblance to the charming city he had been forced to flee with his grandmother at the age of three. Everywhere he looked he saw destruction: the houses burned and looted, the fields fallow, the much-reduced population poverty-stricken and starving. The beautiful castle he remembered from childhood had been hit particularly hard, its towers demolished and the roof caved in. "There is hardly a corner fit for habitation," he had written grimly to his mother upon his arrival in October the year before.

To recover from such ruin was a Herculean task, but it was a job he had been waiting to tackle all his life. To his very great credit, Karl Ludwig put his subjects' welfare ahead of his own and sought to rebuild the town itself before attempting to renovate his own property. The economic revival program the Elector Palatine put into place upon his arrival was astonishingly enlightened. Restore a house or farm in Heidelberg, and Karl Ludwig guaranteed the owner a two-year tax break; build a new home from scratch, and the tempting tax-free offer rose to three years. Anyone wishing to open a business or conduct trade was welcome in Karl Ludwig's domains, be they Calvinist, Lutheran, or Catholic; even Jews were tolerated and encouraged to settle in the city, as long as they brought along money to spend. Nor did the Elector Palatine omit the public sector from his agenda but made the reopening and staffing of the prestigious University of Heidelberg, which had been forced to shut down during the war, one of his top priorities.

The salutary effect of these new, pragmatically inclusive policies was remarkable. The town recovered so dramatically even within the first year that Karl Ludwig was able to begin renovations on the castle itself. Again, he proceeded cautiously, in stages, so as not to prove a burden to his subjects, and occupied a much less impressive house in town while his home was under construction.

Altogether, Karl Ludwig demonstrated a concern for his dependents, a commitment to financial responsibility, and a talent for leadership that won him the hearts of his people. The years of exile and struggle in Holland when he himself had known poverty and humiliation and perhaps also the example of his uncle's experience in England had not been wasted, but instead had clearly taught him the importance of thrift, moderation, and compromise. With such skills, he was on track to regain not only Heidelberg's former prosperity but also his family's prominent political position within Germany.

And then he got married.

HER NAME WAS CHARLOTTE, and she was the daughter of the landgrave (the German name for a count) of Hesse-Cassel. Karl Ludwig must have had his eye on her for some time, as it was the landgrave of Hesse-Cassel who had died and left the Protestant army that Karl Ludwig had wanted and tried to get to by crossing France in disguise (only to be captured and thrown into prison by Cardinal Richelieu) years before. Charlotte was a decade younger than her husband; he consulted no one in the family about his choice. They were married on February 22, 1650, four months after his arrival at Heidelberg.

They were still newlyweds when the queen of Bohemia's youngest daughter, away from home for the first time in her life, arrived at Mannheim later that summer and found them waiting for her. Eager to meet this new sister-in-law, Sophia left an indelible portrait of her in her memoirs. "The Elector, with his hearty manner, seemed delighted to see me," she recalled, "but Madame [Charlotte] assumed a doleful air, and hardly spoke during the whole day, thereby giving me the better opportunity of inspecting her at my leisure. She was very tall, with an admirable complexion and most beautiful bust. Her features were irregular, and her eyebrows, which were dyed black, struck me as forming too violent a contrast with her beautiful flaxen hair...she had beautiful sparkling eyes, full pouting lips, and very fine teeth; altogether she would be called a handsome woman." There can be little doubt from this description that Karl Ludwig, otherwise so prudent with money and public affairs, had splurged and gotten himself the seventeenth-century version of a trophy wife.

Despite her sister-in-law's unhelpful attitude, Sophia exerted herself to be pleasant. She even complimented the mode of transportation by which she was to be conveyed to Heidelberg—"I was so pleased to see in Germany a carriage which was assuredly much better built than any that I had yet encountered during my travels, that I praised its beauty," she remembered—only to have even this innocent comment fall flat. "A grimace on the part of Madame showed me to my surprise that my praise displeased her. I was not then aware that this, her wedding carriage, had excited her wrath, because she thought it inferior to the one with which her sister, the Princess of Tarentum, had been presented, and that Madame had therein considered her mother to show greater affection for her sister than for herself," Sophia explained. That evening, after they had arrived in Heidelberg, when she was alone in her room, Sophia could not help exclaiming in astonishment: "My sister-in-law is very stupid!"

Still, Sophia persisted. The next day being a Sunday, she sought out Charlotte in her room—the castle was still being repaired and they were all living at the house in town—when she was preparing to go to church. Charlotte was in a better mood and had evidently decided to be gracious to her houseguest by engaging her in conversation. "I found her with all her fine clothes spread out on a table, enumerating whence they came and how long she had had them. I took all this as a joke, it being the fashion then to have few dresses at a time, and to renew them frequently. When the catalogue of her clothes was completed we went to church," Sophia reported. This cozy tête-à-tête was picked up again after services. "On our return my sister-in-law confided to me that she had married the Elector against her will; that she had been sought in marriage by several other princes; but that her mother had chosen to make her marry a jealous old man [Karl Ludwig, age thirty-three]; that a duke of Würtemberg, named Frederick, had sighed for her, as had two dukes of Brunswick [Hanover], George William and Ernst Augustus, a prince, Philip Palsgrave of Sulzbach, and several counts. This conversation quite took me aback," Sophia revealed.

It soon became very clear that Karl Ludwig also wished to unburden himself to his sister and that one of the reasons he had acceded so quickly to Sophia's request to visit was that he expected her to act as a sort of marriage counselor. "The Elector on his part had matrimonial grievances to confide with regard to his wife's temper," a disconcerted Sophia continued. "He said that she possessed sterling worth, and many good qualities, but had been badly brought up; and he entreated me to cure her of all her affectation, and point out how unsuitable it was to a person of her rank." This state of affairs, which could hardly have been anticipated, was perhaps not the most comfortable way to begin an extended stay. "I wished myself a thousand times again at The Hague!" Sophia confessed.

Nor did the situation improve with time, as Charlotte and Karl Ludwig seesawed between love and hate with disturbing rapidity. "I could see that he idolized her, and I often felt ashamed to see him kiss her in public," admitted the poor put-upon houseguest. "There was continual embracing going on, and I have often seen him kneeling to her, or her to him. At that time one would have said that their love was likely to be of lifelong duration, but jealousy, the troublesome child of love, soon disturbed their peace. The Elector, believing that Madame could not look at anyone without lessening her affection for himself, often made accusations which she received with great indignation, and which were, indeed, very ill founded." But Sophia could not help but note that the fault was not all on the side of her brother, as Charlotte "loved to attract attention. There was more folly than evil in her; but the Elector, having great delicacy of feeling, wished her to be all in all to himself and nothing to others. The slightest word from him on this subject put her into a frightful rage, which usually lasted the whole day," Sophia reported. "I leave it to be imagined whether I was very happy at that time," she added drily.

She was just twenty years old and clearly out of her depth; what was needed were reinforcements. There was only one thing to do. "I wrote for my sister Elizabeth," said Sophia.

Princess Elizabeth

Queen Christina of Sweden

15

A Lesson on the Passions

THROUGH ALL THE YEARS OF turmoil—the murder of d'Epinay and the flight of her brother Philip; the seemingly endless up-and-down negotiations for the partial restoration of the Palatinate by the Treaty of Westphalia; the sudden, horrific execution of her uncle Charles I—Princess Elizabeth had clung to her special friendship with the philosopher René Descartes as her one refuge of joy and stability in an otherwise brutally unkind world. Even before she left for Berlin in the summer of 1646, she had turned to him time and again for strength and solace, and these he unfailingly attempted to provide through regular, affectionately reassuring correspondence. Princess Elizabeth was frequently ill and unhappy (who can blame her) and attributed her physical ailments, at least in part, to her emotional state. "Know then that I have a body imbued with a large share of the weakness of my sex, quick to feel the afflictions of the soul and without strength to rally from them, being of a temperament subject to depression," she observed in a letter to the philosopher. "I will go on to confess to you that even now, when I do not place my happiness in things which depend on fortune or on the will of others, and do not esteem myself absolutely miserable though I should never see my House restored nor my family out of poverty, I cannot but consider the injurious accidents that befall them as an evil nor the useless efforts which I make to help them without an anxiety that is no sooner calmed by reason than a fresh disaster provokes fresh trouble," she concluded despairingly.

But Descartes, refreshingly, would have none of it. "The difference between great souls and those which are low and vulgar consist principally in this: that the vulgar give way to their passions, and are happy or miserable according to whether the things that happen are to them agreeable or displeasing; while the others have reasoning powers so firm and so elevated that, though they also have passions and often stranger ones than the common herd, yet reason remains always the mistress and makes their afflictions serve them," he replied firmly. "I remark always in your letters thoughts so clever and reasoning so cogent that I can hardly persuade myself that the mind capable of receiving them is lodged in a body so feeble and sick... Consider all the advantages which may be drawn from the thing which yesterday appeared so irremediable a disaster, and turn your attention from all the evils which have been imagined or forecast," he suggested sensibly. "And your Highness may draw this general consolation from the buffets of fortune, that they perhaps contributed to make you cultivate your mind to the point which you have attained, and that is a good which might outweigh an empire." And to help distract her and keep her from fretting, he proposed that they start their own private book group, just the two of them, beginning with the Roman philosopher Seneca's *De Vita Beata* [*On the Good Life*], a work that attempted to provide a rational framework to emotions and the achievement of happiness.

If he had discovered penicillin, he could not have provided a more effective tonic for the ailing princess. They went back and forth in letters, first on Seneca, then Epicurus, and later Zeno and Aristotle (Elizabeth often quoting in Latin). "Monsieur Descartes," she wrote. "Your letters always serve as an antidote against melancholy, even when they do not instruct me, turning my mind from the disagreeable subjects which occur every day to make it contemplate the happiness which I possess in the friendship of a person of your merit, to whose counsel I can confide the conduct of my life."

His answers to her questions about Seneca's thesis were so penetrating and helpful to her that she encouraged him to publish his own work on the subject. So, in the spring of 1646, just before she left for Berlin, he summarized his thoughts in an essay entitled *On the Passions*, inscribing it "For the special use of the Princess Elizabeth."

Happily, Elizabeth's abrupt departure from Holland in the wake of d'Epinay's murder and her subsequent quarrel with her mother did not sever this connection. If anything, she relied on her relationship with Descartes even more once she had established herself in Berlin. "I only try to put in practice the rule you laid down at the end of your [last] letter, trying to take pleasure in present things, as much as I can," she wrote to Descartes on September 30, 1646, soon after her arrival. "Here I find little difficulty, being in a house where I have been cherished from my childhood, where everyone conspires to caress me, although they sometimes distract me from more useful occupations. I easily bear with this inconvenience for the pleasure of being beloved by my relations," she informed him, evidently a comparison to the manner in which she had been treated by the queen of Bohemia at The Hague. But if her relatives were warmer and more inviting, the town itself was not what she had hoped for, particularly in terms of education. "The people of this country and especially the learned... are even more pedantic and superstitious than any of those I knew in Holland, because the whole population is so poor and no one studies except to make a living by it," she complained. "I employ the little time that remains to me after the letters I must write...in rereading your works...But there is no one here with sense enough to understand them, though I have promised them to the old Duke of Brunswick to adorn his library. I doubt they will much adorn his rheumy old brains, already stuffed with pedantry," she observed drily.

But she did not feel the absence of the intellectual stimulus associated with her old life at The Hague so keenly as long as she had Descartes's letters to look forward to, and these continued to appear with a satisfying regularity. Soon after her arrival, they began the study of a new book, Machiavelli's *The Prince*, for, as Descartes wrote to her, "Happiness is dependent on the right use of reason; the study to acquire it is the most useful occupation one can have, as it is the sweetest and the best."

But the use of reason could be controversial in the seventeenth century, and there were signs of trouble for Descartes in Holland. The religious climate, reflecting the influence of the victorious Puritan movement in England, was becoming more repressive, especially against Catholics. The new rector at the University of Utrecht, a strict Calvinist, took issue with some of Descartes's writings and denounced him; the controversy spread to the University of Leiden, where his ideas were banned. Descartes was nervous enough about being subjected to a public trial and punishment that he suggested to Elizabeth that they write to each other in cipher, just in case their letters should go astray and be used as fodder against him. Elizabeth, whose entire family had been communicating in this manner for decades (in order that their various plans and political strategies not fall into the hands of the enemy, be they imperial, Spanish, Puritan, or French) had no problem with this, although ironically she did have to point out gently to the world-famous mathematician that the system he proposed was unwieldy. "I examined the number code you sent me and find it very good, but too prolix for writing all the meaning, and if one only writes a few words, one can find them by the quantity of the letters. It would be better to make a key of words by the alphabet, and then mark some distinction between the numbers which signify letters and the ones which signify words," she recommended diplomatically.

But although his university friends stood up for him, and the prince of Orange himself intervened in his favor, Descartes was sufficiently worried about being censored or even possibly condemned in the future to begin casting around for another, less threatening place to live. The obvious kingdom to turn to was his native France, and there his contacts and supporters tried to arrange a position for him at court. Unfortunately, this prospect failed to materialize. And then, just as he was getting over his disappointment at losing the opportunity in Paris, one of his closest friends and most ardent admirers, Pierre Chanut, was named ambassador to the court of Queen Christina of Sweden.

CHRISTINA WAS ONLY TWENTY years old when Chanut first arrived in Stockholm in 1646, but she had already won international renown for her scholarship and political acumen. The only child of the great warrior Gustavus Adolphus, Christina had evidently felt the weight of expectations all through her childhood and adolescence and had responded by pushing herself to excel both physically and intellectually. She reportedly had learned eight languages and was a voracious reader and supporter of the arts. Even better, she was in the process of recruiting scholars to come to Sweden to further her education and that of her people, and she was embarking on an ambitious program to organize schools and universities. She was the perfect solution to Descartes's problem, Chanut decided. There remained only the delicate task of bringing these two illustrious mortals together.

A diplomat by training, Chanut handled the negotiations brilliantly. Christina, who was under pressure to marry, was at that time debating the philosophic question of which was worse, to love or hate unwisely, and Chanut offered to write to his good friend the eminent philosopher René Descartes for enlightenment. Descartes responded in February 1647 with a short essay entitled "The Nature of Love"— love being defined by the philosopher as "the property of allowing each of its thoughts to associate itself with certain movements or dispositions of the body in such a way that the repetition of certain dispositions of either, causes a corresponding action in the other"— which he happened to have handy, as he had already worked this out with Elizabeth in his *Treatise on the Passions*. Chanut (wisely) read little bits of this to Christina, who then asked to see more of Descartes's work. Flattered, Descartes decided to crib from his earlier discussion of Seneca and send copies of the letters he wrote to Elizabeth for his *Treatise on the Passions*. But of course his correspondence represented only one side of the conversation; it would be *so* much better if he could include the princess's responses as well. Accordingly, in the summer of 1647 he wrote to Elizabeth asking her permission to send copies of her letters to Christina along with his. He must have been aware that this idea might not be entirely welcomed by Elizabeth, because he couched the request as a way to perform *her* a service by encouraging a friendship between the two women. "The portrait which Chanut draws of the Queen and the discourse he reports have given me such a high esteem for her, that it seems to me you and she would be worthy of each other's conversation," he volunteered disingenuously. "And since there are so few of the rest of the world who are worthy of it, it would not be unpleasant to your Highness to enter on a close friendship with her, and that besides the contentment of spirit you would find in it, it might be desirable for many reasons."

This letter was the first inkling Elizabeth had that Descartes admired the queen of Sweden and was trying to impress her. It must have sent a chill through her heart. Christina was younger, of higher rank, more powerful, and by all reports just as accomplished intellectually. Nor did it help that the man to whom she had poured out her soul in letters now wanted to use those very letters to entice another woman. It was like overhearing your lover use exactly the same pickup line he had once used with you, and then having him turn to you to ask for help in convincing his new quarry of his sincerity.

Elizabeth's training as a princess—her rectitude, her careful preservation of her dignity in the face of numerous humiliations—served her well in this challenge to her most prized relationship. She was warm in her response to Descartes, reminding him how much she valued his friendship and emphasizing her efforts to introduce members of the Berlin aristocracy to his work. She ignored completely his request to show her letters to Christina and indeed refrained from any mention of the queen of Sweden.

But of course this did not stop Descartes from sending *his* letters to Christina, who by this time had been primed by Chanut to receive them with great interest. "I had the honor two months ago to accompany the Queen on a journey to the silver and copper mines. In her leisure time in traveling she devoted herself entirely to her books. I carried with me your *Principles of Philosophy*. I read her the Preface. She opened the book at various parts, and remained very thoughtful for several days," he wrote to Descartes in December 1648. (I'll bet.) Soon after, Christina penned Descartes a short thank-you note for sending her his letters instructing her on the passions. Descartes, ever the courtier, was thrilled to receive a personal missive from a sitting monarch. "Had a letter come to me from heaven, and had I seen it descending from the clouds, I should not have been more surprised, and could not have received it with greater respect and veneration than that with which I received the letter it has pleased your Majesty to write," he rhapsodized in his reply. "It seems to me that this Princess is created in the image of God in a greater degree than the rest of mankind," he raved to Chanut in a subsequent note written in February 1649.

And so it came about that in the spring of 1649, Queen Christina of Sweden, through the medium of the French ambassador Pierre Chanut, formally invited René Descartes to Stockholm to take up a position as philosopher-in-residence at her court for the purpose of instructing her personally in the Cartesian method.

ALTHOUGH HE HAD CLEARLY been angling for just this invitation, once it actually arrived, Descartes hesitated. "I confess that a man born in the garden of Touraine [France], who is now in a country where, if there is not as much honey as God promised to the Israelites, there yet may credibly be discovered more milk [Holland], cannot so easily make up his mind to quit it for a land of bears between rocks and ice [Sweden]," he confided candidly in a letter to a friend in April 1649. But it was too tempting an offer to turn down, and he began making preparations for the journey, one of which was to break word of his new employment to Elizabeth.

No husband who had cheated on his wife and was trying to get out of it by pretending to be concerned for her welfare ever penned a guiltier letter. "I have put off this journey for many reasons," he finally wrote to Elizabeth, "but principally in order that I might have the honor of receiving your highness's special commands before my departure. I have so publicly and constantly declared my devotion and zeal for your service that it would be more natural to think unfavorably of me if I manifested any indifference to what touches you...Therefore do I supplicate your Highness most humbly to favor me so far as to instruct me on every point where you think I can be of service either to you or yours, and to be assured that you possess the same power over me as if I had been all my life your slave." This high-minded sentiment was rather spoiled, however, by his next line. "I entreat you also to let me know what you wish me to answer, if I should be put in mind of your Highness's letters...which I had mentioned last year in my correspondence, and which there might be some curiosity to see." Again, aware of how hurtful all this might appear, he could not resist throwing her a sop: "I intend to spend the winter in the country I am alluding to [Sweden]...if my desires are fulfilled I shall wend my homeward road through the spot where you may be in order to be able personally to reiterate to your Highness the expression of those sentiments I shall never cease to devote to you," he concluded, although he had not bothered to visit her once during the three years she had been in Berlin.

Poor Elizabeth! This letter hit her hard upon the heels of numerous ordeals. The previous year, she had just gotten over a bout with smallpox—"Though the fever has left me, and with it the peril of my life, I am still quite covered with it and can use neither my hands nor my eyes. They feed me like a little child," she had informed Karl Ludwig—when news came of Charles I's execution, a trauma that affected her so profoundly that she had again taken to her bed.★ She was also at this time in the midst of negotiations for Henrietta Maria's

---

★ Descartes, famously following his precept to always seek out the positive when dealing with adversity, had written to her in the aftermath of Charles's beheading: "Although the death we speak of, being so violent, may seem at first far worse...it is undeniable that without his last trial the gentleness and other virtues of the dead king would never have been so remarked and so esteemed as they will be in future by

unhappy Transylvanian wedding, the very mention of which caused her younger sister to burst into tears. And now the man she felt closest to in the world was leaving her for another woman. Although the letter she wrote him in answer has since been lost, she had sent an earlier one when he thought he might be taking a position in Paris, and it may be presumed that she reiterated the poignant sentiment expressed at that time: "Assuring myself that in changing your abode you will always keep the same charity for your very affectionate friend to serve you, Elizabeth."★

On September 1, 1649, Descartes embarked from Amsterdam to begin his journey to the Swedish queen's side. A number of his friends were present to see him off. It was remarked that Descartes had had his hair curled and donned his best clothes for the occasion. "He reminds me of that Plato who was not so divine that he did not wish to know what humanity was," reported one of the well-wishers with amusement, "[who was] going to Stockholm a courtier all shod and clad."

A month later Descartes arrived at Chanut's house, where he was lodged and treated as an honored guest, and the next day appeared before the queen.

HE MIGHT HAVE SAVED his fancy clothes. Sweden was no France, and Queen Christina was no fashionable lady. "As to the time she took to dress," observed a contemporary report, "it needed in no way to be counted in the distribution of her day. In a quarter of an hour all was over, and, unless on most solemn occasions, a comb and a bit of ribbon were her sole head-dress. Her hair, thus neglected, was not unsuited to her face, of which she took so little care, that neither in town or country, neither for wind nor for rain, did she ever use mask or veil. She wore on horseback nothing but a hat with feathers,

whoever shall read his history." How much consolation this view of Charles's sufferings, not to mention his minimal achievements, afforded Elizabeth is unclear.

★ To please Descartes, Elizabeth dutifully wrote a letter to Christina as a way of initiating a correspondence, but Christina, who was interested in Descartes, not a rival female disciple, chose not to answer her.

beneath which it was hard to discern her, when she added to it a mantle with a narrow collar like a man's. This absence of all attention to her person was excessive, and would even have threatened her health had she been less vigorously constituted."

Descartes might have overlooked his new patron's somewhat prosaic appearance if she had demonstrated a keen interest in his work, but this seems not to have been the case. Although their first interview began well, with Christina summoning the captain of the ship that had brought Descartes to Sweden to ask his opinion of the philosopher—"He taught me more in three weeks of the science of seamanship and of winds and navigation, than I had learned in the sixty years I have been at sea," the sailor reportedly declared—the rest of the audience seems to have been disappointing. In fact, Descartes realized almost immediately that he had made a mistake, as can be ascertained by the rapidity with which he sought to reestablish contact with Elizabeth. "I have been in Stockholm but four or five days, and among the foremost things to which I am in duty bound, stands the obligation to write and offer my homage to your Highness, in order that you may know how powerless is all change of land or scene to alter or diminish in any way my zealous devotion to you," he wrote humbly. Of Christina he reported, "She is extremely devoted to the study of literature, but since I do not know that she has done anything in Philosophy, I cannot judge of what her taste will be, nor if she will be able to take the necessary time to study it...Nevertheless," he continued, "though I have so great a veneration for her Majesty, I do not think anything would avail to keep me longer in this country than till next summer...I can only assure you that I remain all my life yours," he finished.

The receipt of this letter must have acted like a balm on Elizabeth's aching heart. She, who understood him so well, knew exactly what Descartes was saying to her. Christina, with her interest in literature, was no threat to Elizabeth. If he'd written that the queen of Sweden had a love of mathematics, well, that might have been a different story; but as it stood, the erring husband had discovered that he preferred his former soul mate after all. "I do not think anything would avail to keep me longer in this country than till next summer," was a particularly telling phrase — he had been there less than a week and was already talking about leaving!

Elated, she wrote back to him quickly to assure him that all was forgiven, and they could continue as before as though none of this had happened. Under the circumstances, she could afford to be generous. "It is proof of the continuance of your kindness to me, which assures me also of the happy success of your journey, since the object was worth the trouble, and you find still more marvels in the Queen of Sweden than her reputation had announced," she answered virtuously. "I feel however capable of a crime against her service in rejoicing that your veneration for her will not detain you long in Sweden," she continued merrily before offering to arrange a means by which to escape graciously, even naming a prospective guide to lead him to Berlin, as Descartes had earlier promised to visit her on his way back. "If you leave this winter I hope it may be in the company of M. Kleist, which will afford the opportunity of giving the happiness of seeing you again to your very affectionate friend to serve you, Elizabeth."

But of course he couldn't leave right away; he had to at least make an effort to instruct his royal pupil. The problem was, Christina had many duties to perform, and needed a clear head to tackle a subject as challenging as philosophy. She found herself most able to concentrate first thing in the morning, when she had just arisen, before the inevitable duties associated with her position began to descend upon her. For an old soldier's daughter like Christina, this meant five o'clock in the morning.

If the devil himself had been asked to devise a revenge that would most punish a man like Descartes, he could not have come up with a more miserable torment. For Descartes, who was used to his ten uninterrupted hours of sleep followed by spending most of the day either in bed or wrapped up in blankets in a cozy room near a cheerful fire, to have to throw off the warm covers and rise in the blackness of a winter's morning three times a week to ride in an open carriage through the howling winds and frigid temperatures of a Swedish winter to stand attendance in a drafty castle and try to instruct an unkempt twenty-three-year-old woman on the finer points of the Cartesian system taxed even the philosopher's cherished beliefs about always looking on the bright side of a situation. "It seems to me that men's thoughts freeze here during the winter, just as does the water," he groused in a letter to another friend written on January 15, 1650. "I assure you that the desire which I have to return to my desert increases every day. It is not that I have not great zeal in the service of the Queen, nor that she does not show me as great kindness as I can reasonably expect. But I am not in my element here," he concluded with uncharacteristic understatement.

The winter he had chosen to visit was particularly cold and cruel, even by Swedish standards. His good friend Chanut, with whom he was still staying, also unused to the extreme cold, fell ill that January with a fever and an upper respiratory ailment; Descartes volunteered to help nurse him. And then, just as Chanut began to recover, Descartes sickened, infected with the same disease.

All that January and February, Elizabeth waited impatiently for news from her friend, to hear how soon he might be leaving Sweden and coming to her; finally, it arrived. "Madame Elizabeth Palatine," wrote Chanut in a letter dated February 19, 1650. "The duty which I herewith tender to your Royal Highness is the very last by which I should have desired to testify my humble respects; but I think myself obliged to give an account of a person whom you so greatly esteemed for his rarement, and to inform you, Madame, with incredible grief that we have lost M. Descartes. We were both he and I attacked almost at the same time by a similar malady, a continuous fever with inflammation of the lungs; but since his fever was in the beginning more internal, he did not believe it dangerous, and would not allow himself to be bled for several days, which rendered the illness so violent that all our trouble and the continual care which the Queen of Sweden took in sending her own physicians could not hinder his decease...On the eighth day [he] told me that during the night he had made his account and was resolved to leave the world without grief and with confidence in the mercy of God... we were nevertheless deceived, both he and I, in the estimation of his strength, the end was nearer than we thought: the following night the oppression of his chest increased so as to hinder his breathing. He felt his end approaching without trouble and without fear; and not being able to speak, made signs many times repeated that he departed content with life and with men, and trusting in the goodness of God. I believe, Madame, that had he known the day before, while he could still speak, that his end was so near, he would have commended to me many of his last wishes, and would particularly have desired me to tell your Royal Highness that he died with the same respect he had always held for you during his life, which he had often testified to me in words full of reverence and admiration..."

Soon after this, Elizabeth, in response to her sister Sophia's urgent plea for help, left Berlin and traveled to Heidelberg to see if she could be of use in reconciling Karl Ludwig's marital discords with his new young wife. Their brother Edward was also visiting at the time and he and Sophia remarked on Elizabeth's surprisingly haggard appearance. "We thought her much changed, both in mind and person," Sophia reported in her memoirs. "Looking at her, Prince Edward whispered to me: 'Where has her liveliness gone? What has she done with her merry talk?'"

Louise Hollandine

...self-portrait at The Hague
(© Sotheby's 2017)

16

A Desperate Plan

ALL THROUGH THE TUMULTUOUS PERIOD following the murder of d'Epinay, which encompassed the Peace of Westphalia and the assassination of Charles I, Louise Hollandine, alone among her sisters, exhibited no inclination to leave her mother's court. The Hague, a center of both political and artistic activity, full of color and visitors, suited Louisa. Highly focused on developing her aesthetic, she had the freedom to spend hours sketching and painting while her mother, determined to do everything in her power to avenge her brother's death and regain the throne of England for her nephew Charles II, entertained a steady stream of ambassadors, displaced Royalists, and other politicians. To those who frequented the Winter Queen's court, this charming daughter, so vivacious in company and yet so serious about her work, must have represented an island of loveliness in the midst of a raging storm.

In 1649, Sophia, who had not yet left The Hague to go to live with Karl Ludwig in Heidelberg, and who was consequently in a position to observe these events firsthand, remembered one visitor in particular who had clearly fallen under her sister's spell: the marquis of Montrose. "Being a good general, and a man of great ability, he [Montrose] believed everything to be attainable by his courage and talent, and was certain of re-establishing the young King [Charles II] if his Majesty would appoint him Viceroy of Scotland, and after so signal a service, bestow on him the hand of my sister,

Princess Louisa," she reported. "The commission was granted by the King," she added.

Montrose! James Graham, the marquis of Montrose, in love with and engaged to marry Louisa! Americans have never heard of Montrose, but in Britain his name is still synonymous with the romantic ideal of true nobility. Born into a high-ranking Scottish family, gratifyingly handsome, a superb athlete and an even better general, Montrose was also a poet and statesman of no mean ability. His was a spirit that flamed bright and reached far, as these verses, penned when he was younger, attest: "He either fears his fate too much/Or his deserts are small/That dares not put it to the touch/*To gain or lose it all.*"

Although a Protestant, Montrose rejected the machinations of the Presbyterian ministers in Scotland against Charles I as self-serving and dangerous. "The perpetual cause of the controversies between the prince and his subjects, is the ambitious designs of rule in great men, veiled under the specious pretext of Religion and the subjects' Liberties, seconded with the arguments and false positions of seditious preachers," he argued as early as 1640. "Do ye not know, when the monarchical government [the king] is shaken, the great ones [the nobles] strive for the garland with *your* blood and *your* fortunes?" he demanded in a public document addressed to the citizens of Scotland. "Whereby you gain nothing... and the kingdom fall again into the hands of ONE, who of necessity must, and for reason of state will, tyrannize over you," he warned grimly.★

But Montrose had done more than simply stand up to Argyll and his Presbyterian cronies (known as the Covenanters, for a document they had drafted that would force the king to accede to all of their religious demands) in fine speeches. He had sworn undying loyalty to Charles I and undertaken almost single-handedly to restore him to the throne by leading the Royalist cause in Scotland. His military

---

★ Although the "ONE" to whom Montrose referred was his archenemy Archibald Campbell, marquis of Argyll, who led the Scottish Presbyterians during the years of the English civil war and joined with the Puritans in the rebellion against Charles I, he thus also correctly predicted the dictatorial rise of Oliver Cromwell.

exploits in this capacity were legendary. Having been declared an enemy of the state and excommunicated by Argyll, Montrose had been forced to sneak back into his own territory in the Highlands of central Scotland disguised as a servant. There, he had rendezvoused with a bedraggled troop of some 2,300 Irishmen recruited to the Royalist cause by another Scotsman. They had no artillery; three emaciated horses represented their cavalry; and those with muskets had only enough ammunition to fire a single round. As there weren't enough clubs, pikes, and swords to outfit every soldier, nearly a third of the company would have to resort to throwing rocks when they went into battle.

But Montrose was daring, he had surprise on his side, and he knew the surrounding area well. Moreover, the Irish were career soldiers and they were desperate. He fell with his ragtag force on the city of Perth, and although outnumbered four to one, succeeded in taking the town as well as all of the enemy's artillery, arms, ammunition, and supplies. From there he had launched a brilliant series of attacks against Argyll's personal lands, prompting his enraged adversary to offer a reward of 20,000 Scottish pounds for Montrose's head. By the winter of 1645, Argyll and his clan, the Campbells, had put together two armies of sufficient strength to trap Montrose's small regiment of men between them and crush it. But in a truly astonishing feat of military genius, Montrose, unable to move either forward or backward, chose instead to go—up. For two days he led his men, without food, in the dead of January, over the Lochaber mountains to Loch Ness, struggling through the snow and ice, then doubled back behind Argyll's men and overwhelmed the superior Campbell force in a surprise flanking assault. An onlooker memorialized the resulting struggle in verse:

> Heard ye not! heard ye not! how that whirlwind, the Gael
>   [Montrose];—
> To Lochaber swept down from Loch Ness to Loch Eil—
> And the Campbells, to meet them in battle-array,

Like the billow came on, — and were broke like its spray!
Long, long shall our war-song exult in that day...
Though the bones of my kindred, unhonor'd unurn'd
Mark the desolate path where the Campbells have burn'd, —
Be it so! From that foray *they never return'd!*

But after Rupert was defeated in England, and the king had given himself over to the Scottish army, Argyll insisted that Charles I order Montrose to lay down his arms and leave Scotland, and Charles had been forced to comply. Montrose, following the king's command, had sailed to France to confer with Queen Henrietta Maria. Then came word of Charles I's execution. Devastated, Montrose swore "before God, angels, and men, that I will dedicate the remainder of my life to avenging the death of the royal martyr, and re-establishing his son upon his father's throne," and wrote in a condolence letter to Charles II that "I never had passion on earth so great as that to do the King your father service."

This, then, was the caliber of man who knelt at Louisa's feet in the summer of 1649 and declared his love for her. True, at thirty-eight, he was a decade older than she was, and he was not of as high a rank as her former suitor the elector of Brandenburg. But as marital consolation prizes went, the marquis of Montrose was in a class by himself.

There was just one little thing he had to do before they could wed. He had to reprise his earlier exploits and win Scotland for Charles II.

THE VIOLENT OVERTHROW OF a legitimate authority, such as occurred at the time of the beheading of Charles I, is almost always accompanied by a struggle for power, as various factions compete for influence over the policies of any potential successor. This was especially true in the case of Charles II, who was only eighteen when his father died and obviously in need of experienced counsel to navigate the difficult path ahead. The problem was that even among his staunch-

Marquis of Montrose

est supporters, there was intense disagreement on how to proceed in the wake of the crisis. Almost immediately, two distinct camps emerged, one originating at his mother's court in France, the other at his aunt's in The Hague, each with its own plan for reclaiming the English throne. In the year that followed the king's execution, the rivalry between these two circles grew so acute that it would not be an exaggeration to characterize the conflict as in some form a contest for the young heir's soul.

At the heart of the argument was what to do about Scotland. Argyll was still in power and in March 1649 he sent an embassy to The Hague with an offer for Charles II. If the young king would promise to uphold the covenant and thereby place himself under the authority of the Scottish Presbyterian Church, Scotland would recognize him as king and fight to return him to the throne of England. As part of this deal, Charles would also be required to "abandon the Marquis of Montrose, as a man unworthy to come near his person, or into the society of any good men, because he is excommunicated," explained an observer with firsthand information about the Scottish propositions.

One of the chief advisers to Queen Henrietta Maria was another Scotsman, the duke of Hamilton, long a rival to the marquis of Montrose, and he strongly counseled both Charles II and his mother to accept Argyll's terms. But the opposing faction, led by the queen of Bohemia, argued just as strenuously against this alliance on the grounds that it had been Argyll and his Covenanters who had treacherously handed Charles I over to Cromwell for a bribe of £100,000 after the king had surrendered to the Scottish army and so were not to be trusted or dealt with on principle. The queen of Bohemia's faction proposed instead to send Montrose and as large a force as he could muster to Scotland, as their intelligence indicated that Argyll was very unpopular and that the opposition clans could be rallied to rise up in favor of Charles II. Indeed, an envoy, arriving later by ship, "in the name of the whole kingdom, did intreat and press Montrose, earnestly, to go to Scotland...for his presence was able to do the business, and would undoubtedly bring twenty thousand together for the King's service; all men being weary and impatient to live any longer under that bondage [Argyll's], pressing down their estates, their persons, and their consciences."

While he was with his aunt, Charles II agreed to reject Argyll's terms and instead concurred with the plan to send Montrose to Scotland. But in June he left The Hague to go to Breda, about fifty miles south, to meet with his mother's advisers. The queen of Bohemia, worried that, once out of her sight, the young king would vacillate, sent Montrose to Breda as well to ensure that her nephew stayed true to his former commitment. "My Lord," she wrote to the marquis on June 24, "I have found that the Prince of Orange will again extremely press the King to grant the Commissioners' desires, and so ruin him through your sides. I give you this warning of it, that you may be provided to hinder it...For God's sake leave not the King as long as he is at Breda; for without question there is nothing that will be omitted to ruin you and your friends and so the King at last." Then again on July 4, hearing that Queen Henrietta Maria's counselors continued to induce Charles II to accept Argyll's terms, she urged Montrose, "I do not desire you should quit Brussels while there is danger of change...I can add nothing but my wishes that you may persuade the King for his good."★

The Winter Queen's strategy worked: Montrose's presence at Breda secured the king's commitment to the Scottish expedition. On June 22, 1649, Charles II formally commanded Montrose to raise a force and invade Scotland in his name. Knowing his aunt's doubts, to reassure both her and his Scottish champion, the young king gave his word not to betray their trust. "Montrose: Whereas the necessity of my affairs has obliged me to renew your former trusts and commissions concerning the Kingdom of Scotland; the more to encourage you unto my service, and render you confident of my resolutions, both touching myself and you, I have thought to signify to you, that...I will not do anything that shall be prejudicial to your commission," Charles pledged in a private letter just before leaving for France to consult with his mother personally at her court in St. Germain. Yet even with this written guarantee, the queen of Bohemia, who shared the same disparaging view of her sister-in-law as did her eldest son Karl Ludwig, fretted. "I pray God keep the King in his constancy to you and his other true friends and servants," she affirmed to Montrose in a letter of August 4. "Till he be

---

★ It was during this period, while he was at Breda, that Montrose had his portrait painted and sent to the queen of Bohemia. "I give you many thanks for your picture," she added in a postscript to her letter of June 24. "I have hung it in my cabinet to fright away 'the Brethern.'" (The Brethern was the Winter Queen's scornful nickname for Argyll's Covenanters.) Her receipt of this portrait, combined with her many affectionate letters to Montrose, have led some historians to speculate that these two were having an affair. But there is no evidence of this; rather, the queen of Bohemia had portraits of all of her family around her, like a modern-day photograph album. That Montrose sent her this likeness could instead be interpreted as further evidence of his future role as the queen of Bohemia's son-in-law.

gone from where he is [Queen Henrietta Maria's court at St. Germain], I shall be in pain."

Montrose, having received his orders, left the king's side to begin the process of gathering an army of sufficient strength to achieve his objectives. He came back to Holland in August to confer with the Winter Queen at her hunting lodge at Rhenen (which also gave him the opportunity to visit Louisa and say good-bye), but by September he was in Hamburg and then Denmark and Sweden on a whirlwind tour of northern Europe to gain allies and purchase supplies. To encourage him and remind him of the steadfastness of his commitment, on January 12, 1650, Charles II sent Montrose the blue ribbon signifying the Order of the Garter, England's highest chivalric honor, and reiterated his command "to proceed vigorously and effectively in your undertaking... We doubt not but all our loyal and well-affected subjects of Scotland will cordially and effectually join with you, and by that addition of strength either dispose those who are otherwise minded to make reasonable demands to us in a Treaty, or be able to force them to it by arms, in case of their obstinate refusal."

But the queen of Bohemia had been right to worry; these commands were all for show. For while he was with his mother, she and the duke of Hamilton had convinced Charles to ally himself with Argyll and accept the Covenanters' terms, particularly after Argyll had offered the king not only the support of the realm but a hefty bribe of £300,000 if he agreed to sign a treaty—"otherwise, to give him no money at all," as an English observer familiar with these proceedings noted. Although the decision was made in January, it was judged best to let Montrose go on with his mission as a way to keep the pressure on Argyll and ensure that Charles II received the best possible terms (the "reasonable demands" alluded to in his letter awarding the ribbon of the Garter) during the negotiations.

It was an act of almost unfathomable perfidy. By April 12, 1650, when Montrose and his small force landed at the very northern tip of Scotland, the king's acquiescence to the Covenanters' terms was already widely known throughout the realm, and it was understood

Argyll

that Charles II had chosen Argyll over Montrose. Consequently, there would be no general uprising against the current government—no 20,000 Scottish troops would appear to rendezvous with the Royalist expedition. Instead, Argyll's troops would be waiting for him. Only Montrose did not know that he and his men were walking into a trap.

He might yet have succeeded—or at least held out—had the expedition gone as planned, but he had lost half his army, a thousand men, when their ships went down in a storm during the crossing. These he was forced to replace with green recruits from the island of Orkney, men who had never fought in battle before. Besides the Orkney conscripts, he had only some 500 experienced Danish and German troops, as well as fifty officers, nearly all of them friends and former comrades-in-arms, who made up his cavalry.

Still, Argyll took no chances. He sent no less than *three* armies this time to destroy his rival. On April 27, the Covenant divisions ambushed Montrose and his men at the pass at Caithness, on the northern coast. Over two hundred cavalry, sent from the first army, thundered down on their prey. The Orkney recruits panicked and fled and were cut down and massacred by soldiers and guns from the other two Covenant forces. Montrose's remaining 550 men were easily surrounded, overwhelmed, and compelled to surrender. As it became clear they were trapped, Montrose's men convinced him to try to get away to find reinforcements. Montrose, bleeding profusely from a number of wounds, escaped into the wilderness with a pair of his officers.

For two days they stumbled, lost, through the unfamiliar terrain. They separated to improve their chances of finding aid. His loyal companions were never heard from again and it is presumed that they perished of starvation. Montrose himself was reduced to gnawing his gloves to survive before happening upon an isolated farm, where he was given bread, milk, and a change of clothing to hide his identity. But he had a price on his head, and the next day he was spotted and given up by a laborer hoping to claim the reward (much to his disappointment, the informer ended up being paid in oatmeal). The day after he was taken, on May 1, 1650, Charles II officially signed the Treaty of Breda with the Scottish Covenanters. Four days later, Charles again wrote to Montrose, commanding him to lay down his arms as required by the treaty.

But by this time, Montrose, still in his peasant clothes, bleeding and ill from his untended wounds, was in the hands of one of Argyll's generals. In a chilling re-creation of the last journey of Christ, in this condition he was paraded south through Scotland all the way to Edinburgh. "The 7th of May, 1650, at Lovat, he sat upon a little shelty horse, without a saddle, but a quilt of rags and straw, and pieces of ropes for stirups," recorded an eyewitness. "His feet fastened under the horse's belly with a tether; a bit halter for a bridle; a ragged old dark reddish plaid; a montrer cap, called magirky, on his head [to further humiliate him, a sort of Scottish crown of thorns]; a musketeer on each side...Thus conducted through the country, near Inverness...where he desired to alight, he called for a draught of water, being then in the first crisis of a high fever." By May 18 he was outside Edinburgh, where he was transferred to an executioner's cart in which a special chair had been installed; he was bound with rope to this mock throne, and another demeaning form of headgear, this time the hangman's own red cap, placed on his head.

He was condemned to the gallows, after which his body was sentenced to be quartered, yet a further humiliation, as by right of birth and honor he ought to have been beheaded; hanging and quartering was for thieves and villains. On Tuesday, May 21, 1650, he was brought to the marketplace on High Street, where a scaffold had been erected. He was allowed a last speech— "I am sorry if this manner of my end be scandalous to any good Christian here. Doth it not often happen to the righteous according to the way of the unrighteous? Doth not sometimes a just man perish in his righteousness, and a wicked man prosper in his wickedness and malice?" he asked. Then, as a final indignity, his arms were tied behind his back and he struggled up the gibbet in this awkward position, "where, having freely pardoned the executioner, he desired him that, at the uplifting of his hands, he could tumble him over, which was accordingly done by the weeping hangman..."

They left his corpse to swing publicly for three hours, then cut up the body and sent his appendages to various cities as a reminder to the populace of the fruits of defiance. "I saw his arm upon the Justice-port of Aberdeen; another upon the South-port of Dundee; his head upon the Tolbooth of Edinburgh," reported a visitor. "Also, I saw it taken down and Argyle's head put up in the place of it," he added thoughtfully after the inevitable fall of that strongman, although this was still over a decade in the future and therefore of dubious consolation to Montrose and those who loved him.

On May 25, four days after the execution, the parliamentary annals of Scotland recorded that its officials had received "a letter from the King's Majesty [Charles II] to the Parliament, dated from

Breda, 12th May 1650, showing, that he was heartily sorry that James Graham had invaded this kingdom, and how he had discharged him from doing the same; and earnestly desires the Estates of Parliament to do himself that justice as not to believe that he was accessory to the said invasion in the least degree."

The gruesome details of Montrose's martyrdom were broadcast all over Europe. The queen of Bohemia, Louisa, and Sophia were all at Breda with Charles II when they discovered what had happened. "Montrose meanwhile went to Scotland, and the [Scottish] Parliament, dreading his influence and valor, sent deputies to the King at Breda — where I also was with the Queen my mother — offering the crown of Scotland on condition that he gave up Montrose, swore to the Covenant, and acknowledged the Parliament as lawful. The King suffered himself to be persuaded by the enemies of Montrose to grant all this in order to secure the crown for himself," Sophia reported in her memoirs. "I was deeply shocked; the more so on hearing that the gallant Montrose had been put to a cruel death, as may be read in the history of England."

Unlike Sophia, Louisa did not leave a record of her feelings regarding the torture and murder of her fiancé. But it may be presumed from her later actions that she considered his treatment at the hands of the Presbyterians to be far from God.

THUS BEGAN A PERIOD of escalating repression, privation, and sorrow for Louise Hollandine.

She had barely six months to mourn the loss of her lover when her family was forced to endure yet more tragedy. Her youngest brother Philip's experience with the Venetians having proved unsatisfactory, he had become involved in an uprising in France by some discontented noblemen seeking to unseat Cardinal Mazarin. On February 16, 1651, twenty-three-year-old Philip fell in battle during the siege of a fortress at Rethel, in northern France, about twenty-five miles north of Reims. His death was followed almost immediately by word that thirty-year-old Maurice had been lost at sea and presumed drowned in a hurricane somewhere near the coast of Anguilla on February 26.★ This degree of affliction (which would be followed that September by news of her sister Henrietta Maria's demise) was unprecedented even for a family as inured to adversity as Louisa's, and it provoked an unusual visit: her brother Edward, the reprobate Catholic, arrived at The Hague that summer to condole personally with his mother and sister.

It was the first time he had been back in Holland since his conversion and marriage. Two years younger than Louisa, Edward had been barely out of his teens the last time she had seen him; now he was wealthy, self-assured, and married with children of his own. In the shock and grief of having lost two sons in succession, the queen of Bohemia was more than prepared to forgive Edward his transgressions, and he was welcomed back into the family.

His stay coincided with the arrival in Holland of an embassy of some 250 functionaries sent by Cromwell to try to promote an alliance between the English Puritans and the Dutch States as a means of depriving Charles II of support. Despite her hatred of the faction that had assassinated her brother, the queen of Bohemia was nonetheless petitioning these envoys for payment of the over £100,000 she argued was owed to her by virtue of lifetime bequests made by the English government before the civil war, which had been withheld by Parliament for nearly a decade. Necessity drove her to this extreme; her credit had long since been exhausted and it was a daily struggle to put food on the table. Despite this, she refused to toady and communicated with Cromwell's ambassadors entirely through Dutch intermediaries, forbidding everyone in her household to come into direct contact with them.

But Edward had no compunctions about confronting the men he considered to be the enemy. Soon after his arrival, he and a few friends were out riding when they came upon a coach carrying

---

★ Rupert, who survived the storm, was so broken by his brother's death that for years he refused to believe it, and continued to hold out hope that Maurice had somehow escaped.

senior members of Cromwell's embassy. According to Dutch news reports of this event, they then blocked the carriage's passage, forcing it to stop, and taunted its occupants, calling them "rascals and dogs." As the coach was protected by an armed guard whose members substantially outnumbered Edward and his companions, the envoys were eventually allowed to pass without a struggle. But two days later Edward again accosted the parliamentary diplomats and their retinue, and this time he had over a dozen men carrying swords and daggers at his side. A clash ensued and several members of the English suite were wounded before Edward and his friends escaped. The envoys complained vociferously to their Dutch hosts. "It was England that received the affront done by the petty, paltry thing called Prince, whose very nursing was paid for out of the purse of England; and therefore we are confident those in power here among the Dutch cannot but consult so far with their own honors as to make a severe vindication, answerable to a crime of so high a nature," fumed one of the functionaries. The matter was referred to the Dutch court of justice, which did nothing beyond issuing a stern warning to Edward to have "a better tongue another time." Although it diminished her chances of recouping her income, his mother could not help but take great satisfaction at this insult to her brother's executioners. "You will have heard of the high business between my son and their pretended ambassadors, whom Ned called by their true names," she reported in a letter to Charles II soon after this incident. To further infuriate and demean the parliamentary delegation and demonstrate that he was not afraid of them, Edward prolonged his stay at his mother's house by an extra week before continuing with his planned itinerary of calling on Karl Ludwig in Heidelberg before returning home to Paris.

Louisa, too, applauded her brother's exploit and was happy to have him back as an accepted member of the family. Of all her male siblings, Edward was closest to her in age; she and he had been among the first occupants of the nursery at Leiden. They had been together all through childhood and into adolescence and this was a strong tie between them. And she could not have failed to note that alone at her mother's court, Edward, the Catholic, was not intimidated by the increasingly ominous atmosphere surrounding The Hague and had the courage to say and do what they all felt.

THAT CROMWELL'S AMBASSADORS WERE able to influence the political and religious environment in Holland was due almost entirely to a change in leadership in the house of Orange. Frederick Henry, the old prince who had ever been the Winter Queen's true friend and generous benefactor, had died in 1647 and been succeeded by his son William II, husband of Charles I's daughter Mary. But William II's tenure as prince of Orange had been extremely short as he, too, had died—of smallpox—in October 1650. Although his nineteen-year-old wife, Mary, delivered a son on November 4, a week after her husband's death, the infant was obviously too young to rule. This left a vacancy in leadership, and into this vacancy stepped the dowager princess of Orange, the queen of Bohemia's former lady-in-waiting Amelia de Solms, with the alacrity and determination of a bill collector holding a winning lottery ticket.

She had first to dispense with any possible competition from Mary, who, as the widowed mother of the heir to the house of Orange, was the natural claimant to her son's regency. The battle between these two began within weeks of William II's death with a bitter dispute over the naming of the infant; Mary wanted to call her son Charles, after his martyred grandfather, while Amelia insisted on William, after her beloved son. The struggle continued right up until January 5, 1651, the day of the baptism. The hundreds of assembled guests had to wait two hours at the church while Mary, under siege in the royal apartments, did her best to hold her ground against her relentless mother-in-law. In the end she was forced to give in, and her son was christened William III at a ceremony notable for his mother's refusing to attend.

But Amelia did not content herself with symbolic victories. She went after Mary's legal rights as well. She took the matter to court and had herself, along with her son-in-law Frederick William, the elector of Brandenburg, named as co-guardians with her daughter-in-law of little William III. As the elector lived in Berlin, this left Amelia in charge of her grandson's education, estates, and income. Small wonder that Mary spent the preponderance of her time in Holland in the company of her sympathetic aunt the queen of Bohemia and her cousin Louisa, and got away from The Hague altogether whenever she could.

Louisa was no politician—unlike her mother, she left no letters commenting on the feud between the princess of Orange and her mother-in-law. But her support of Mary may be discerned in a scene she painted during this period depicting the finding of Erichthonius. According to Greek mythology, Erichthonius, who would grow up to rule Athens, was the adopted son of the goddess Athena. Soon after his birth, to keep him safe, Athena hid Erichthonius in a box that she then bestowed upon the three daughters of the king of Athens, accompanied by strict instructions never to lift the lid and peek inside. Of course, curiosity overwhelmed the sisters, and they betrayed their commission and opened the box. There, they found a baby who was half serpent, a discovery that caused them to go mad. Rubens had famously painted this scene in 1632; Louise Hollandine no doubt was influenced by his work as she was by that of her mentor, Gerrit van Honthorst, who often composed allegorical portraits (like *The Triumph of the Winter Queen*) in which he depicted those who sat for him in classical costumes and attitudes.

But unlike the Rubens portrayal, in Louisa's hands, the scene has strong political overtones and could easily be interpreted as a metaphor for her cousin's predicament. The baby coming out of the box is Mary's son, William III; the female figure in the foreground, in the act of being pushed away by one of the other sisters, is Mary herself.* Although the women in the background look at the baby,

---

* This would not be the only time that Mary sat for Louisa. On August 6, 1654, Charles II wrote to his aunt that "I have now received my sister's picture that my dear

the baby reaches only for Mary his mother, while she in turn gazes out at the viewer with quiet, thoughtful dignity. The painting, one of Louisa's finest, is an example of how far she had progressed. The child has no father; he is compromised by a serpent; the woman at the forefront is beautiful and vulnerable. Knowing the circumstances under which it was painted, it is likely that this was intended as a political statement highlighting Mary's victimization.

Unfortunately, all of these factors—their public support of Mary and the Royalist cause, Edward's sneers and hostility toward the Puritan ambassadors, and the death of their longtime protector the prince of Orange—made Louisa and her mother easy targets for Cromwell and his agents. The simplest way to attack them was financially, and this the English Parliament did very effectively by charging the wealthy Lord Craven (who had essentially been supporting the queen of Bohemia for years) with treason, which conveniently allowed them to strip him of his estates and income. By November 3, 1653, the Winter Queen's situation was sufficiently dire for her to write that it was "as no parable but the certain truth, the next week I shall have no food to eat, having no money nor credit for any; and this week, if there be none found, I shall neither have meat, nor bread, nor candles."

Karl Ludwig was appealed to but he was in no position to underwrite a separate residence for his mother and rebuild Heidelberg at the same time. Moreover, he was already supporting his sister Sophia and was father to a son and daughter with another child on the way. His solution was to invite his mother to come live with him in Germany. This proposal the queen of Bohemia, in her midfifties and set in her ways, refused even to consider. She would not leave, she harrumphed to Lord Craven, "although she supposed he [Karl Ludwig] meant to starve her out of the Hague, as he would a blockaded fortress."

But it was becoming increasingly clear to Louisa that the situation

---

cousin the Princess Louisa was pleased to draw, and do desire your Majesty thank her for me, for tis a most excellent picture."

was untenable, and that as a thirty-one-year-old spinster whose last good chance for marriage had been massacred on the shores of Scotland, she was a financial burden on those around her. There were women who made a living painting in the seventeenth century, but they were not of royal blood like Louise Hollandine; this expedient was forbidden her by her rank. Already Princess Elizabeth, anticipating that something must be done to secure her middle sister's future, had taken it upon herself to write to a cousin who ran a Protestant women's abbey in Herford, Germany, some two hundred miles east of The Hague, asking if there was space for Louisa, and she urged her sister to contact the abbess directly and accept this vocation. "I have not before taken the liberty of troubling your Grace [the abbess] with my worthless writing," Louisa was forced to respond, "but now as I understand from my sister in Berlin that you have the kindness to wish me to have a place in your institution, for which I am very highly obliged to you...I beg you would further do me the kindness to let me know how I should pay over the three hundred rix thalers which one must give to purchase a position in the institution."

But the abbess was in no hurry to comply with her cousin's request. The negotiations dragged on for a year, then two, despite Princess Elizabeth's best efforts. "My sister could wait upon you for a day or for four days, and bring letters of recommendation," she petitioned the abbess again in 1655, "but if it is inconvenient or your Grace should have other views so that you do not wish it, write to me openly, for you know well that she [Louisa] cannot act otherwise than candidly and does not like others to act differently to her," she warned.

Princess Elizabeth no doubt meant well, as she had when she had helped to arrange the ill-fated Transylvanian marriage for Henrietta Maria. But although it is clear from these lines that she understood Louise Hollandine's character, she could not know the effect that the abusive political and religious climate at The Hague would have on her sister's conscience. For after a brief war over commercial rights, Cromwell had managed to persuade the Dutch that it was in the best interest of the two Protestant nations to ally, and a treaty was signed at Westminster. As a result, the Puritan movement in Holland was empowered and over the next few years, public conformity in religious practice — the necessity, for example, of proving loyalty by adhering to certain rites at Christmas — became a source of not-so-subtle intimidation. Even the queen of Bohemia, impoverished and harassed, gave up and accepted Karl Ludwig's invitation to Heidelberg, but when she and her daughter tried to leave The Hague, they were prevented by their many creditors.

And it was at this point that Louisa came to a decision that must have been building up inside of her for years. Turning secretly to her brother Edward and a mutual friend, the princess of Hohenzollern, Louise Hollandine began laying the foundation for a new life. It must have taken months to organize, but by the winter of 1657 she had gathered her nerve, and early on the morning of December 19, at the age of thirty-five, she crept quietly out of the house to the harbor, where a boat was waiting. Her mother rose several hours later and when she remarked on her daughter's absence was handed the following letter, which had been left behind for her: "Madam," Louisa had written, "the respect which I have for your Majesty is too great to permit me to do anything purposely to displease you; and God knows that no impulse, except that of His spirit, could ever have induced me to undertake any action, however reasonable, without having first communicated it to you; but in this contingency, the affair being...one in which I should doubtless have found your Majesty opposed to the guidings of Divine Providence in my behalf, I could not act otherwise...I must tell you, then, madam, that the Christmas festivals being so near, I have been obliged to withdraw from your Majesty, from fear of being desired to receive the [Protestant] sacrament against my conscience, since at length it has pleased God to discover to me the surest way to salvation, and to give me to know that the Catholic religion is the only way...I trust you will pardon me for a course which...I have only resolved to adopt from the pure motive of assuring the repose of my soul...that I have no other aim than that of securing a tranquil retreat, where I may have full leisure for the service of God, and to testify to you in all things that I am, and wish to remain all my life, Your Majesty's most humble and most obedient servant, Louisa."

Louise Hollandine was converting to Catholicism.

Her mother was naturally quite upset by this turn of events and searched her daughter's room, where she found two letters from the princess of Hohenzollern, herself a Catholic, containing helpful suggestions for how Louisa might make her escape. One plot had the runaway pretending that she wanted to visit Antwerp to see her brother Edward, who had taken it on himself to secure the necessary travel documents; the other was to steal away silently, leaving a letter explaining her motives. As Louisa had evidently decided on the second approach, the princess of Hohenzollern had arranged to bring the fugitive by barge to her own home in Bergen op Zoom, some fifty-five miles to the south. From there it was arranged that she would officially convert and then retire to a convent in Antwerp.

The queen of Bohemia's first step was to write an angry letter to the princess of Hohenzollern, accusing her of betraying her trust. To this, both the princess and Louisa replied that the desire to convert had been entirely Louisa's choice and that the princess had collaborated only after Louisa had confided this decision to her friend. But her mother, believing that her daughter could yet be brought back, applied to the governing Dutch States for satisfaction. They, in turn, stripped the princess of Hohenzollern of some of her privileges including her right to name the magistrates in her hometown of Bergen op Zoom, unless she could prove her innocence in the affair.

It was at this point that the story turned ugly. The princess of Hohenzollern, stung, wrote back sharply to the queen of Bohemia justifying her conduct by insinuating that Louisa had fled for reasons "highly prejudicial to her honor" (i.e., she was pregnant). The Winter Queen, displaying some truly questionable maternal judgment, showed the States this letter and demanded that the princess of Hohenzollern be censured for lying about Louisa's moral conduct. Of course, after that the newspapers got wind of it, the gossip became propaganda for the Parliamentary party, and that was the end of Louise Hollandine's reputation. She was gleefully painted as a fallen woman.

To console her aunt, Mary, princess of Orange, together with her brother, Charles II, offered to act as intermediaries. "The King and my niece...were at Antwerp, and went to see Louisa in the monastery," the queen of Bohemia reported to Rupert on March 4, 1658. "The king and my niece did chide Louisa for her change of religion, and leaving me so unhandsomely; she answered that she was very well satisfied with her change, but very sorry that she had displeased me...The bishop of Antwerp has written a letter to your brother Edward, where he clears Louise of that base calumny [the supposed pregnancy]; yet Ned is so willful as he excuses the Princess of Zollern," she fumed.★

Evidently it was perceived after this visit that Antwerp was rather too close to Protestant territory to ensure that the new convert would be safe from further entreaties or possibly even extradition, for within a month Edward had arranged for Louisa to come to France. "Your sister Louisa is arrived at Chaillot, her brother [Edward] went and fetched her from Rouen; the queen went to see her the next day; the King of France went thither the week after," the Winter Queen complained to Rupert. "They are very civil to her. The queen wrote to me that she will have a care of her as of

---

★ Edward was clearly invested in his sister's conversion. "Madam, I received yours of November 29 so late that I can give you but a word in way of return," he wrote to Louisa from Paris on December 31, 1657. "I am transported with joy concerning that which you write, and doubt not but God will bless your design...The Queen [of France] had already propounded Challiot, a nunnery of the order of St. Marie, whither the Queen of England doth continually resort, and there you may be instructed in the manner how to live in this condition without engaging yourself at all...there are many persons in convents to whom pensions are given, and they are respected as queens."

her own daughter, and begs her pardon; I have excused it as handsomely as I could, and entreated her not to take it ill, but only to think what she would do if she had had the same misfortune," she added bitterly.

On April 20, 1659, Louise Hollandine was officially accepted into the Catholic Church by the papal nuncio in Paris and was granted an income by the French Crown. A year later she took her vows as a nun and disappeared into the abbey of Maubuisson, about twenty miles northwest of Paris, one of the oldest and most prestigious convents in France.

Sophia

Heidelberg Castle

17

The Electress, Two Dukes, and the Lady-in-Waiting

WHILE LOUISE WRESTLED WITH WEIGHTY matters of spirituality amid the corruption and intimidation of The Hague, her younger sister Sophia, still ensconced with her brother's family in Heidelberg, faced a challenging home environment of her own, although on a rather less exalted plane. Specifically, she was forced to cope with the cascading domestic friction between Karl Ludwig and his wife, Charlotte. It was perhaps to be expected that a marriage that had begun so stormily would unravel still further over time; many do. But not like this. This was one for the history books.

The first two years had been rocky but manageable. Charlotte fulfilled the first obligation of wedlock by giving birth, on March 31, 1651, to a son and heir they named Karl and then followed up this achievement on May 27, 1652, with a little girl, christened Elizabeth Charlotte but whom everyone called Liselotte. Karl Ludwig, for his part, improved the economic environment in Heidelberg sufficiently to begin work on the ruined family castle and so had been able to move everyone into the renovated space in time for the birth of his son.

But this uneasy truce between husband and wife vanished abruptly in 1653 with an invitation to the imperial court. Karl Ludwig had already been formally received by the emperor (still Ferdinand) the previous year in Prague, a prestigious event that Charlotte had been unable to attend due to the birth of Liselotte.★ She had complained bitterly about being left at home, so Karl Ludwig thought to appease her by taking her, along with his sisters Sophia and Princess Elizabeth, who had also joined the household, to meet the emperor at Ratisbon, nearly two hundred miles to the east.

Charlotte, envisioning a social triumph, threw herself into preparations for this exciting round of festivities, ordering splendid gowns as befit her position as Karl Ludwig's wife. "The Electress, whose one thought during the whole expedition was how best to display her beauty before this great assembly, had sent to France for a Mme. La Prince to dress her hair, and nothing was omitted to show her off to the best advantage," Sophia remembered. All had been packed and sent when Charlotte, to her very great chagrin, discovered herself to be pregnant again. Her hair might have looked charming but her chic new gowns did not fit, and of course no one looks or feels her best with several extra inches around the waist. Ferdinand and his wife took pains to treat her with great respect, but it was no use; Charlotte was in "such a bad temper that her husband often took refuge in my rooms to escape from it," Sophia revealed.

Matters were not improved when the baby was born prematurely and died the next day, and Karl Ludwig accused his wife of having brought on the tragedy by insisting on accompanying the imperial court when it moved on to Augsburg rather than waiting quietly at Ratisbon for the birth. Charlotte retaliated by refusing to sleep with him. By the time everyone returned to Heidelberg it was all-out war: she threw the dishes at him, he slapped her so hard her nose bled. A further complication ensued when Karl Ludwig, denied the solace of his wife's bed, fell in love instead with Louise von Degenfeldt, Charlotte's sweet-tempered twenty-year-old lady-in-waiting.

Charlotte's first inkling that Karl Ludwig's attentions might be

---

★ "His Majesty [Ferdinand] received him at the Weissen Berg [White Mountain], where our father had been defeated by the late Emperor," Sophia noted. "This caused the courtiers to say that my brother gained there more than my father had lost."

wandering came in the summer of 1654 with the arrival of yet another member of her husband's family: his brother Rupert. Ill and exhausted from his years at sea, Rupert had given up pirating and was considering his options. Domesticity appealed to him (probably because he had no experience with it), and Karl Ludwig had generously agreed to give his brother a substantial plot of land out of his own holdings in the Palatine on which to settle. Naturally, Rupert stayed with Karl Ludwig and the rest of the family at the castle in Heidelberg while the details of this transaction were being finalized.

Unfortunately, during this visit, Rupert also met Charlotte's endearing lady-in-waiting Louise and, used to success in affairs of the heart and having no idea that he was trespassing on his brother's territory, made a play for her. When she rejected him, he passed her a note declaring his love and accusing her of coldness. To deflect suspicion, Louise in turn handed this incriminating document over to Charlotte, pretending it had been meant for her. Charlotte, thrilled to have attracted Rupert's attention, rushed to assure him of the warmth of her affections, a confession that caused her disconcerted brother-in-law to blush with embarrassment. Charlotte immediately perceived from his reaction that the note had been intended for her lady-in-waiting and not herself, and angry and humiliated, she tried to dismiss Louise, only to have her husband intervene and place the young woman under his protection, insisting that she stay. So besotted was Karl Ludwig with his new love that he rashly revenged himself on Rupert by reneging on the land-settlement deal. He even went so far as to shut the gates of Heidelberg against his rival, a gesture his brother found so hurtful that he left the city and never returned.*

In the aftermath of this debacle, the remaining household divided into two opposing camps. Princess Elizabeth, appalled at Karl Ludwig's

---

* Years later Karl Ludwig had real need of Rupert and begged him for help but was turned down in a way that indicated that the wound had still not healed. "Your Belovedness has caused me to take a solemn oath to God that I will never more set foot in the Palatinate; and my sworn, if regrettable, oath I will keep," Rupert responded with bitterness.

behavior, sided with Charlotte, while Sophia, always her brother's favorite, remained his ally. Her husband's fondness for his youngest sister excited Charlotte's wrath. "She tried to forbid the Elector's visits to my rooms, but this only made him more determined to come nearly every evening attended by his whole court, at which the anger of the Electress knew no bounds," Sophia admitted.

Unable to subvert her adversaries, Charlotte sought to divide them. The simplest way to accomplish this was to exile Sophia by marrying her off. To teach her sister-in-law a lesson, the electress, wretched with her own husband, thought to punish Sophia by arranging a similarly joyless match.

THE PROSPECTIVE BRIDEGROOM HAILED from the Swedish court. On June 6, 1654, just as Rupert was arriving for his turbulent family visit, Queen Christina, intent upon converting to Catholicism, famously abdicated her throne in favor of her cousin Charles X Gustav. Charles Gustav's wife, the new queen of Sweden, had a brother Adolf. Sometime toward the end of 1654, Prince Adolf arrived in Heidelberg on a diplomatic mission.

Sophia took an instant dislike to him. "His manner was good and his figure rather fine, but he had a disagreeable face with a long pointed chin like a shoehorn," she observed queasily. "After a short sojourn at Heidelberg he asked my hand in marriage; the Electress, wishing to be rid of me, had no small part in bringing this about. She contrived to conceal from the Elector and from me that this prince was so extremely bad-tempered—he had actually beaten his first wife, a fact the Electress knew full well." But the Swedes were allies of the Palatinate and Sophia knew herself to be in trouble. "The Elector was devoted to the King of Sweden, and therefore unwilling to refuse anything to his brother. He consented on condition that the King approved the match and ratified all the advantageous terms which the Prince had willing promised me," she despaired.

Luckily for Sophia, there's nothing like a firm bid to increase market value. Way over in Hanover, some two hundred and fifty miles due north of Heidelberg, Duke George William of Brunswick, the second eldest of four brothers, "heard the report of my engagement at the very time when, urged by his subjects to marry, he had promised to take the subject into consideration, if they on their part would increase his revenues," Sophia explained. Although he had never met her, "while in treaty with his subjects on this question, he could think of no princess more suitable than myself were he, indeed, forced to take a step to which he had always felt the greatest repugnance," she noted drily. As he customarily spent his winters in Venice, Duke George William decided to drop by Heidelberg on his way to Italy and, as part of his salary drive, see if Sophia's charms were really as advertised. He brought his youngest brother, Duke Ernst Augustus, with him on the inspection tour for moral support. Sophia had actually met Ernst Augustus several years earlier and enjoyed his company; he played the guitar, "which served to show off his exquisite hands; in dancing he also excelled," she remembered.

Duke George William, the older brother and hopeful suitor, turned out to be very nice as well, especially as compared to Sophia's Swedish conquest. "I infinitely preferred the Duke to Prince Adolf, to whom I had taken so great an aversion that only a strong effort of will could have overcome it," she confessed. Happily, the duke "at once attached himself to me, questioning me as to my reported engagement, and paying me numberless compliments, to which I was not backward in responding. At last he spoke the great word, asking if he had my permission to demand my hand of the Elector." Sophia's relief at having secured this second timely proffer for her affections was obvious. "My answer was not that of a heroine of romance, for I unhesitatingly said 'Yes,'" she declared forcefully.

There remained only the small problem of her previous commitment to Adolf, but again fortunately for Sophia, Duke George William was wealthier and, as sovereign of his own duchy, of higher standing than the prince. "I knew also that the Elector loved me well enough to approve my choice, especially as right was on my side, for this match was much superior to the other," she reported.

She was correct in her assessment. "The Elector did not wait to be asked twice, but at once gave his consent," she affirmed. By the time the duke and his brother left Heidelberg for Italy, the marriage contract had been drawn up and signed by all the relevant parties, although Duke George William, who was clear on his priorities, "enjoined the strictest secrecy on us, saying that, were his subjects to hear that he was already engaged, all hope of obtaining from them any increase of revenue would disappear."

Meanwhile, Prince Adolf, justifiably operating under the assumption that he and Sophia were getting married, had obtained the desired consent of his brother-in-law the king of Sweden to the match. This inconvenient fact was brought home to Karl Ludwig with the arrival of a Swedish ambassador bearing a letter from the monarch welcoming Sophia into the family and inquiring when would be the best time for Adolf to come collect his bride. With "the greatest gentleness," Karl Ludwig, without actually mentioning the other engagement, broke the news to the envoy that "the state of affairs was changed" and that "even were his sister not so fortunate as to become Prince Adolf's wife, he (the Elector) would all the same remain his obedient servant, ready and willing on all occasions to serve him to the utmost of his ability." Then he dismissed the ambassador "laden with fine presents."

This did not work. Adolf did not want fine presents or the elector's service; he wanted Sophia. He showed up in Heidelberg unannounced and tried to force the issue. "The idea that he was to possess me was so fixed in his mind as to become his prevailing passion, and he left no stone unturned to gain his object," Sophia recalled. "Sometimes he wept, at others flew into a rage." When these tactics failed, he rode off in a huff, "determined to go himself and persuade his brother [the king of Sweden] to take up his cause."

No sooner had Adolf departed than a new, and far more ominous, impasse occurred. Duke George William, enjoying his accustomed sojourn in Italy, which clearly included many pleasures not commonly associated with holy wedlock, "plunged in the dissipations of

Venice, ceased to think of me, nor had his subjects come to any conclusion as to the increase of his revenue," Sophia was forced to report. Worse, "he began to repent the promise, which bound him by word and deed to me, his letters grew colder, and he himself failed to appear at the appointed time. The Elector was very uneasy," she added, and it was clear her concern matched her brother's. If the duke backed out, she would have no excuse but to marry the obnoxious Adolf after all.

And just at this moment, with Sophia's fate hanging in the balance, Charlotte made a discovery.

ALL THROUGH THE EXTENDED process of negotiation with first Prince Adolf and then Duke George William, Karl Ludwig had been engaged in similar (albeit clandestine) bargaining for the affections of Louise von Degenfeldt, his wife's lady-in-waiting. To forward his suit—she obstinately resisted the ultimate surrender, holding out for marriage—he sent her love letters, which he took the precaution of writing in Latin, a language of which he knew Charlotte to be ignorant. But Karl Ludwig, like his grandfather James I before him, had been highly educated and was something of a snob about scholarship, and he made the mistake of bragging one night at dinner before guests that his wife employed a lady-in-waiting of such superior quality that she could read and write Latin.

Charlotte might not have been steeped in the classics, but she was sharp enough to have her suspicions aroused by this comment. And although it was true she herself could not read Latin, she knew someone who could—her sister-in-law Princess Elizabeth, who conveniently happened to be staying with them. The electress took the first opportunity to sneak into her handmaid's room, where she broke into the little box that held her correspondence. There she found several suspect letters from Karl Ludwig, which Princess Elizabeth confirmed to be love notes. A further frenzied search of Louise's quarters revealed that her errant husband had not confined his activities to pen and paper but had also urged his case with gifts of jewelry, including a ring "stolen from out of her [Charlotte's] drawer...given her by the Elector."

It was the jewelry that did it. Charlotte might have forgiven Karl Ludwig for adultery but not for adornment. She raised such a ruckus that Louise, forewarned, ran to get Karl Ludwig, who was followed by the rest of the household. "On entering the chamber we saw an extraordinary scene," read Sophia's report of this picturesque domestic interchange. "The Elector was standing in front of his mistress to protect her from his wife's blows; the Electress was marching around the room holding La Degenfeldt's jewels in her hands...the Elector said that she must give back the jewels to the one who owned them. She replied by throwing them all over the room. 'If they aren't to be mine, then *voilà!*' However, the Elector took his mistress and...lodged her in a fine apartment above his chamber where he made a hole in the ceiling through which he could climb by means of a ladder. The Electress soon discovered this route and would have climbed up the ladder with a knife in her hand if her ladies had not prevented her." Undeterred, by her own admission, Charlotte later availed herself of a gun, which she intended to use to "send a bullet through the ill-conditioned heart of the peace-destroyer [her husband]," but was again overpowered by a member of the household, who emptied the cartridges harmlessly by shooting out the window into the garden.

Under the circumstances, in the spring of 1657, Karl Ludwig decided it was best that he and Louise remove themselves from the castle at Heidelberg until such time as a more permanent solution to his marital troubles could be arranged. Being Protestant, he unfortunately could not avail himself of an appeal to the pope for an annulment, so he did the next best thing: he made a thorough investigation of German history and learned that one of Charlotte's own ancestors, a Lutheran who had experienced a similarly unhappy family situation, had been allowed to trade in one wife for another. He then used this discovery as precedent to begin divorce proceedings against Charlotte, a course of action that prompted his mother to observe that "if everybody could quit their husbands and wives for their ill humors, there would be no small disorder in the world."

And it was at this point that Duke George William, motivated by a similar yearning to be free of an unwanted commitment, came up with his own creative solution to the problem of his engagement. Only in his case, he aspired to swap not wives but husbands.

FACED WITH THE DILEMMA of how to maintain his treasured bachelorhood and get married at the same time, George William, after considerable thought, had the inspired notion of employing a surrogate. "The Duke of Hanover...perplexed how to find an honorable escape...hit on the expedient of proposing to his brother, Duke Ernst Augustus, that he, as his other self, should marry me," Sophia explained. So sincere (and desperate) was the older brother in his overture to the younger that he offered to make over all of his property to Ernst Augustus if only he would agree to take Sophia off his hands, "proposing to retain for himself only a liberal income sufficient for his private expenses. He also assured his younger brother that he would give him a paper, written and signed by his own hand, to the effect that he would never marry, but live and die a bachelor," Sophia continued. This was quite a good deal for a fourth son. "Duke Ernest Augustus listened with pleasure to this proposition," Sophia related.

Having settled the matter between them, there remained only the challenge of convincing the other interested parties to accept this somewhat unorthodox arrangement, beginning with their middle brother, Duke John Frederick. It must be confessed that his reaction did not bode well for the success of the initiative. "Duke John Frederick by no means relished this proposal, and replied to the Duke of Hanover: 'Why should you give the Princess to my brother and not to me? It would be absurd on my part to grant such an advantage to the youngest!'" But George William, who favored Ernst Augustus, had no intention of allowing sibling rivalry to undermine so excellent a solution to his predicament. "The Duke of Hanover was so enraged by this answer that he drove John Frederick in the rudest manner out of the palace," Sophia observed.

His advisers' views of this scheme were also given short shrift. The duke of Hanover, who had learned his lesson about asking for consent, simply presented the plan to them as a fait accompli. "George William announced to his Council that, being resolved never to marry, he had persuaded his brother Ernst Augustus to bear for him the burden which he could not bring himself to endure," Sophia recounted. "He, therefore, demanded that his brother's income should be so considerably increased as to enable him to maintain a wife. Though this speech was by no means to the taste of the audience, still they were forced to content themselves with it, and obey their master by raising the funds required."

There remained then only the necessity of informing the unwanted fiancée and her brother of the last-minute change of bridegroom. George William not having the courage to break this news in person, a messenger was accordingly dispatched to Frankenthal, about ten miles northwest of Heidelberg (where Karl Ludwig, "to avoid disturbances at home," had "taken refuge"). The envoy presented the details of the new plan, assuring Karl Ludwig that "I should be mistress at Hanover, for my children, should God grant me any, were to inherit all the Brunswick possessions, seeing that...John Frederick [the middle brother] was too stout ever to have any," Sophia reported. "I, therefore, should become mother to the family and country as effectually as though I had been made the wife of Duke George William. The Elector listened with considerable surprise to this discourse," she noted.

But being in the middle of his own highly irregular divorce and general marital finaglings, Karl Ludwig was hardly in a position to object. He did voice concern that Duke George William would later change his mind about remaining single, but, being "assured that he need entertain no apprehensions on that score," he agreed to write to Sophia to see what she thought of the substitution. With the detested Adolf still lurking in the background, Sophia answered "that a good establishment was all I cared for, and that, if this was secured to me by the younger brother, the exchange would be to me a matter of indifference," a demonstration of clearheaded reasoning worthy of the protagonist in a Jane Austen novel.

And so a new marriage contract was drawn up to which was attached a singular document, dated April 11–12, 1658, entitled *Renunciation of Marriage on the Part of Duke George William of Hanover.* "Having perceived the urgent necessity of taking into consideration how our house of this line may best be provided with heirs and be perpetuated in the future," it began, "yet having been and remaining up to the present date both unable and unwilling in my own person to engage in any marriage contract, I have rather induced my brother, Ernst Augustus...and he is prepared forthwith and without delay to enter into holy matrimony."

And this time, the duke was as good as his word. The wedding took place in Heidelberg on October 17, 1658. Ernst Augustus was a month shy of his twenty-ninth birthday; Sophia had just turned twenty-eight. "I was dressed, according to the German fashion, in white silver brocade, and my flowing hair was adorned with a large crown of the family diamonds," Sophia remembered with pleasure. "My train, which was of enormous length, was borne by four maids of honor...I was escorted by the Elector and my brother, Prince Edward; Duke Ernst Augustus by the little Electoral Prince [Karl Ludwig's seven-year-old son] and the Duc de Deux-Ponts. Twenty-four gentlemen marched before us, bearing lighted torches, adorned with ribbons of our armorial colors, blue and white for me, red and yellow for the Duke. Cannons were fired at the moment when the clergyman united us." The religious ceremony was followed by a splendid supper ball, where "we danced in German fashion, the princes dancing before and behind us with lighted torches in their hands." Best of all, Sophia's surrogate husband turned out to be just as charming, and certainly more enthusiastic, than her original intended. "I, being resolved to love him, was delighted to find how amiable he was," she observed with relief.

A few days later, Ernst Augustus left Heidelberg to arrange an appropriately elaborate welcome for his bride in her new home, and soon after an impressive retinue arrived to escort Sophia to her husband. She traveled by carriage from Mainz to Frankfurt, from Frankfurt to Cassel, and finally to Hanover, where both dukes—Ernst Augustus and his older brother George William, in whose house they would all be living together—were waiting for her.

CONSIDERING ITS UNUSUAL GENESIS, Sophia's marriage, at least in the beginning, was all she could have hoped for. No sooner had she arrived than "the Duke my husband, taking my hand, led me to a very fine room, which the Duke of Hanover [George William] had had built expressly for me," she reported with pride. The palace was full of aristocratic company who had been invited to meet the bride, and a second wedding ceremony took place in front of this august body, followed again by an evening ball. But best of all was the improbable exhilaration the newlyweds found in each other's company. "I take pleasure in remembering how rejoiced we were to be left to ourselves when all the guests were gone, and how great was the Duke's devotion to me," Sophia reminisced. "Marrying from interest only he had expected beforehand to feel nothing but indifference for me; but now his feelings were such that I had the fond conviction that he would love me forever, while I in return so idolized him that without him I felt as if I were lost. We were never apart," she recalled wistfully. But of course, they couldn't be completely by themselves, as Duke George William was living there too. "He took part in all our amusements, cards, hunting, and walking, and in return spared no pains to make himself agreeable to me," Sophia noted. "The Duke my husband, who knew him better than I did, began to be jealous; but of this I was wholly unaware."

In fact, in the face of so much obvious affection (not to mention sexual fulfillment), George William was clearly having second thoughts. Apparently, when debating the merits of man-about-town over matrimony, he had not sufficiently taken into consideration the concept of the honeymoon. Now he was forced to witness this seductive interlude from the unenviable viewpoint of the third wheel. "He actually told me one day that he much regretted having given me up to his brother," Sophia volunteered. "This speech I cut short by pretending not to hear it."

But try though Sophia might to ignore her brother-in-law, George William's attentions were sufficient to arouse the notice of her husband. They had a big fight, with Ernst Augustus accusing Sophia of preferring his older brother to himself. Shocked and in tears, she vehemently denied the charge. They made it up, but Ernst Augustus continued to maintain his suspicions. "I took pleasure even in his precautions to guard me, for after dinner, when he took a siesta, he would seat me opposite to him, and place his feet on the sides of my chair so that I could not stir; this would last for hours together, and to anyone who loved him less than I did, would have been very wearisome," Sophia admitted. She did everything she could to ease his mind, shunning George William's company except when absolutely necessary. "I now hardly ever saw his brother except at table, or, to speak more correctly, I sat at table without seeing him at all, having taught myself to turn away my eyes from him altogether, in order to avoid my husband's reproaches. Indeed, I can say with truth, that for years the Duke of Hanover handed me to dinner without my seeing so much as his shadow," Sophia observed wryly.

The awkwardness of her situation was somewhat alleviated in November of 1659 with the dukes' winter sojourn to Italy, an annual holiday that clearly neither brother had any intention of giving up just because one of them was now married. Sophia was by this time pregnant and unable to undertake a long journey, so Ernst Augustus proposed that she instead visit her mother in Holland while he and George William were away. Sophia agreed to this suggestion with alacrity, particularly as "he assured me . . . that he would never again be jealous, as I had entirely cured him of that fault." She took her seven-year-old niece Liselotte, Karl Ludwig's daughter, with her to The Hague as a treat.

In fact, owing to the strained relationship between her own parents, Liselotte was by this time living with her aunt Sophia in Hanover. Karl Ludwig, having obtained his divorce decree from the Diet of Ratisbon (the German governing body) in 1657, had the following year married Louise von Degenfeldt in a quiet ceremony, and by 1659 the couple, along with two children born to Louise, had moved back to Heidelberg. As Charlotte had declined to recognize the legality of the divorce and had adamantly refused to move out, *both* of Karl Ludwig's families were now living together in the ancestral castle. ("I have already ousted X [Charlotte] from the upper story and I have given her the old bedroom downstairs," Karl Ludwig reported to Louise before moving her in.)

As may be imagined, this arrangement was hardly conducive to domestic harmony. Matters were not improved by Karl Ludwig's strict approach to child rearing, which provoked many scenes. His son was timid by nature and submitted to his father's authority, but Liselotte, who naturally took her mother's side over that of Louise, had a strong character and often talked back or refused to retreat if she did not believe she was in the wrong.* To improve his daughter's manners and education (and punish Charlotte for her unwillingness to surrender her home and position as electress), in June of 1659 Karl Ludwig sent Liselotte to live with Sophia, whose judgment and erudition he trusted more than his first wife's.

Liselotte's removal was a great cruelty to Charlotte but an enormous relief to the girl herself, who adored her aunt Sophia and was thrilled to exchange her strict, unhappy home environment for the pleasures of Hanover. She loved the outdoors and was allowed the freedom to run where she chose and was even given her own pony to ride. Where Karl Ludwig, having grown up always having to beg for money, kept a firm hand on the household accounts, famously weighing the butter before serving it, the two dukes, George Wil-

---

* Karl, Liselotte's brother, would later say of his upbringing, "I carry with me the stigma of oppression. My young days were poisoned and I have known but little happiness in this life."

liam and Ernst Augustus, had the means to support a far more lavish lifestyle, and they took full advantage of it. At her aunt's house, Liselotte ate as much as she liked of the hearty German sauerkraut and sausages that comprised the dukes' steady diet and was so impressed by their Christmas celebrations that fifty years later she could still describe the scene as though it were taking place in front of her eyes: "The tables were dressed like altars and were laden with all sorts of things for every child, new clothes, silver ornaments, silk, dolls, sweets and all kinds of things," she recalled with awe.

Sophia was as happy to have her niece at her side as Liselotte was to be with her. "I shall watch over her as though she were my child," Sophia promised Karl Ludwig in a letter of April 18, 1659. She was especially gratified to be able to bring the girl with her to The Hague, although even here, Duke George William pursued her and threatened to ruin the visit. "I look for your sister here about Wednesday or Thursday," the queen of Bohemia observed to Karl Ludwig in December 1659. "Her brother-in-law is yet here, you may chance hear of some love and rumors of love, but do not believe it, for there is no show towards it." Luckily, Sophia managed to convince George William to carry on with his original plan to winter in Italy, so she and Liselotte were able to enjoy themselves in Holland. "After his departure, I spent my time very pleasantly with the Queen my mother, who graciously expressed great pleasure at having me once more with her," Sophia remembered. "I had also brought my niece...to whom the Queen was passionately attached, the more so, perhaps, because this princess was the only one of her grandchildren that she had seen."

"Her shape and humor make me think of my poor Henriette," the Winter Queen observed wistfully of the little girl.

And then, five months later, on May 28, 1660, Sophia fulfilled the purpose for which she had initially been recruited to Hanover by giving birth, after an extremely difficult delivery in which it was feared that either she or the child would die, to a son. "Great was the joy of the Duke and of all of his subjects when our son was born alive," she exclaimed. She and Ernst Augustus decided to name the child George, after their benefactor, the older brother who had made their happiness possible.

And then, just at the moment when it seemed that Sophia's life could not be more complete, as though it had been sent as an unlooked-for christening gift, came the astounding news that Charles II had been restored to the throne of England.

IT SHOULD COME AS no surprise that Charles II's cynical sacrifice of Montrose, intended to help him secure more advantageous terms in his negotiations with Scotland, had not achieved the desired effect. In fact, once his longtime nemesis had been dispatched, Argyll and the Covenanters had only increased their demands on the young sovereign. In order to be recognized as king of the Scots, Charles II had been instructed not only to swear to uphold Presbyterian rule in Scotland but to promise that it would also be imposed on England. Catholicism was to be outlawed in Ireland as well as in Scotland and England. Personally, Charles (who, like his father, was an Episcopalian) was to abstain from dancing and other forms of revelry, endure long sermons, and dismiss all but nine members of his retinue on the grounds that the rest were not considered sufficiently godly by the Presbyterian ministry. He was to take the oath of the Covenant and never issue a decree or conduct an action contrary to the interests or desires of the Scottish church. Although Charles, by his own admission, "perfectly hated the Presbyterians and all their ways," he nonetheless submitted to all of these terms on the advice of, among others, the prince of Orange and Queen Christina of Sweden, who told him to promise whatever was necessary and then just go back on his word later, "so that he may be in a capacity to recover all in the end."*

---

* His mother, Queen Henrietta Maria, was not among those who advised him to capitulate and was in fact horrified at her son's acceptance of these terms. Although she had initially favored a treaty with Scotland and had helped set up Montrose, she had never counseled him to take the Covenant or betray his Catholic subjects.

Nor had the humiliation ended with his arrival in Scotland. The Covenanters kept him under close watch, restricting his movements and subjecting him to more sermons. When, in an effort to prevent the alliance, Cromwell had crossed the border at the head of a large force and defeated the Scottish army in battle, Charles was forced to sign a declaration repudiating his parents and attributing the loss to God's punishment for his sins or face the prospect of being handed over to Cromwell for execution. Even his coronation was preceded by a lengthy public apology for perceived transgressions committed by his father and grandfather. "I think I must repent too that ever I was born," he observed wearily after making the required denunciation.

With his crown had come at last the promised Scottish army with which he hoped to invade and conquer England, but alas, Charles was no better at warfare than his father. He was soundly defeated by Cromwell at Worcester, about a hundred miles northwest of London, and just barely escaped with his life. There had followed an urgent flight from the pursuing Parliamentarian soldiers. Charles was hidden at great risk to those who sheltered him and passed from safe house to safe house by his loyal Catholic subjects (the same people he had sworn to persecute in order to obtain the Scottish throne) until he was finally smuggled out of England.

From this point on, his prospects took a steep decline, a misery made worse by the reality of Cromwell's spectacular rise. Charles could only watch helplessly from abroad as his father's executioner took command of England, forcibly dissolving Parliament (hilariously, Cromwell also found representative government very difficult to work with) and instead establishing a Protectorate, under which facade he ruled as sovereign in all but name. Aided by a handpicked House of Commons under the direction of a radicalized former leather seller who went by the name of Praise God Barebone, laws were passed forbidding theater (players were whipped), dancing, sports on Sundays, and Christmas feasts. Fines were imposed for swearing, gambling, and other sinful activities. Catholics were persecuted, bishops deposed, and the Book of Common Prayer prohibited. All this was held in place by Cromwell's undeniable military abilities, his strong army, and its many victories. This also made him an exceedingly attractive ally, and he was recognized by all the foreign powers as the legitimate ruler of England, a state of affairs that put them at odds with Charles, who was thus forced into exile and abject poverty. Lacking friends or support, constantly on the run, Charles, depressed and beaten, was without hope. Cromwell had prepared for every contingency. He seemed invincible.

But in the seventeenth century, even the invincible were subject to bacteria, and Cromwell came down with a urinary tract infection that quickly turned septic. On September 3, 1658, at the age of fifty-nine, the lord protector of England died, leaving the realm to his eldest son, Richard. It is astonishing how quickly Richard, who had neither his father's commanding presence nor his military experience, botched it up and was forced out of office by both the army, who refused to follow him, and by a much-reduced and divided Parliament, who greatly feared the army. By the early spring of 1660, England was in turmoil.

Faced with the prospect of military rule, and resentful of the many years of imposed Puritan values and behavior, the mood of the realm swung definitively in favor of restoring Charles II to the throne. By this time the exiled monarch had been away from England so long that nobody knew much about him, which definitely added to his appeal. He wasn't familiar enough to be despised as were the other alternatives, which made him the most attractive option by default. This popular bias was underscored on March 15, 1660, by a Royalist sympathizer who took a ladder and a can of paint to the spot where Parliament had replaced a statue of Charles I with a damning inscription celebrating his execution and labeling him a tyrant, and effaced it, jubilantly tossing his hat into the air and shouting, "God bless King Charles the Second!"

Charles was now nearly thirty years old. The many setbacks he had weathered made him sensible of his good fortune, and he leaped at this opportunity. He entered into secret negotiations with General Monk, Cromwell's successor as commander of the English army, to assure him of his goodwill. More important, he penned a masterful letter to Parliament promising amnesty for those who had fought against the Crown. "We do assure you upon our royal word that none of our predecessors have had a greater esteem of Parliaments than we have in our judgment as well as from our obligation," he wrote from Breda on April 14, 1660. "We do believe them to be so vital a part of the constitution of the kingdom, and so necessary for the government of it, that we well know neither prince nor people can be in any tolerable degree happy without them. And therefore you may be confident that we shall always look upon their counsels as the best we can receive, and shall be as tender of their privileges, and as careful to preserve and protect them, as of that which is most near to Ourself, and most necessary to our own preservation."

That did it. The document was made public in the House of Commons on May 1, and "the house upon reading the letter, ordered £50,000 to be forthwith provided to send to His Majesty for his present supply; and a committee chosen to return an answer of thanks to His Majesty for his gracious letter; and the letter be kept among the records of the Parliament; and in all this not so much as one No," reported the famous English diarist Samuel Pepys. "Great joy all yesterday at London, and at night more bonfires than ever, and ringing of bells, and drinking of the King's health upon their knees in the streets," he added.

In that instant, Charles II was restored to his throne. And not a moment too soon for the queen of Bohemia.

IT HAD BEEN TWO and a half years since Louise Hollandine had deserted both Protestantism and her mother, and in that time the Winter Queen had struggled every day to keep up a genteel front

Charles II

despite her straitened circumstances. Although in the wake of her daughter's departure, the States General of Holland had out of sympathy voted to provide her with a monthly stipend of 10,000 livres, this only covered basic living expenses. She needed far more than that to pay back the debts she had incurred over the past dozen years, when Cromwell had cut off her income along with her brother's head, and she naturally turned to Karl Ludwig for financial aid. But Karl Ludwig, with two families to support and a tendency toward extreme caution, not to say miserliness, steadfastly resisted her entreaties. His solution was for her to sell her jewels, a suggestion that she rejected as adamantly as he refused her entreaties to provide for her.*

---

* Her creditors, too, clamored for her jewels, but luckily the chairman of the special committee established by the States General charged with adjudicating her

The result of this standoff between mother and son was a series of increasingly insistent dunning letters, followed by equally aggrieved responses. "You sent me one seven thousand for living," the queen of Bohemia complained to Karl Ludwig. "I had not lacked fine bread and candles if you had helped me as you promised. But sixteen thousand guilders could not do it, living as I do, much less than I should, which made me, in a manner, beg the State's assistance; and as it is, I cannot give my servants their wages." "I very well remember that your Majesty seldom wrote to me but on money subjects since I was in Germany, which I do not blame your Majesty for, but only I am sorry that often times I could not answer you but with my leg," he shot back.

Then came Charles II's extraordinary reversal of fortune and, with it, the prospect of a brighter future. Ever her nephew's loyal supporter, the Winter Queen had been with Charles at Breda when he composed his astute missive to Parliament and had shared in the glory of his reception at The Hague, where the English fleet was sent to convey their sovereign home to London. According to Pepys, who was among those who made the voyage, the very first thing the English ambassadors did upon debarking in Holland on May 14, 1660, was to pay their respects to the royal family by making a special trip "to kiss the Queen of Bohemia's hands." Three days later, Pepys himself was part of another entourage who met the queen, "who used us very respectfully; her hand we all kissed. She seems a very debonaire, but plain lady," he commented. (He meant her dress, which reflected her poverty, not her face. Pepys was merciless in his judgments of the clothing worn by others, especially his superiors, as reflecting their relative standing at court. Thus the Winter Queen's insistence upon keeping her jewels.) On May 24, the day of Charles's departure for England, she came aboard ship to see him off and "dined in a great deal of state, the Royal company by themselves

---

affairs was a man of sound principles and discernment. "Must not a queen have some jewels for her entertainment?" he scolded the hapless vendors, and ruled in her favor.

in the coach, which was a blessed sight to see." By September, in yet another sign of favor, Parliament voted to restore her annual allowance of £10,000, along with those for Charles's sisters.

But the good news was tempered as always by tragedy. Also in September 1660 came word that her nephew Henry, the little boy who had sat sobbing on Charles I's knee the day before his execution and bravely promised he would not be made king before his brothers, had died of smallpox at the age of twenty. He was followed to the grave on Christmas Eve of the same year by his sister Mary, princess of Orange, who had accompanied Charles II to England and who fell victim to the same disease. The Winter Queen, who had been almost a second mother to Mary, felt her loss keenly and wept over her orphaned son, ten-year-old William III, prince of Orange, who had been left at The Hague with his grandmother, Amelia de Solms. Then too, after the jubilation of Charles's restoration, The Hague seemed lonely and provincial. "This place is very dull now, for there is very little company," the queen of Bohemia lamented in a letter of February 15, 1661. Rupert, who had been recalled by Charles II to England, visited her at this time and confirmed her low spirits. "I found the poor woman very much dejected," he confided to a friend.

And so, after forty years of residence, the Winter Queen decided to leave her adopted homeland, this time for good. Karl Ludwig again reluctantly invited her to Heidelberg, thinking that in this way he might at least rid himself of the unwanted Charlotte, who was continuing to hang around. "When your Majesty is here, it will be but one family; for nobody will dare to contest against anything that shall be for your service and convenience: and if any trouble should have been that way, those that would control might in better manners [Charlotte] quit the house to your Majesty than you to them; which myself would not have refused," he assured her. But when he discovered that his mother had no intention of taking on his marital problems but instead wanted him to make ready a separate residence for her in Frankenthal, which was hers legitimately through her dowry, he went to great lengths to dissuade her. "Sure your Majesty hath forgot in what condition the house of Frankenthal is in, when you were pleased to write of preparing it for you," he exclaimed in mock consternation. "For no preparation would have made that fit for your living in it, but a whole new building, which to do on a sudden, or in a few years, my purse was never yet in a condition for it...As for the accidents fallen out in my domestic affairs, it is likely they had not happened if your Majesty had been present," he added loftily if somewhat hypocritically.

She was saved by the ever loyal Lord Craven, whose fortune and estates had been returned to him with the restoration of the monarchy. It was he who insisted that she come to live with him in London, pointing out that she stood a much better chance of securing the funds necessary to pay off her Dutch creditors if she were around to lobby Parliament personally for the money, an argument that made so much sense that the States General not only let her go but made available one of their own ships to transport her.

By the middle of May 1661, all was in readiness. Sophia, accompanied by her two inseparable dukes, was at Rotterdam to see her mother off when a letter arrived from Charles II requesting that she not sail for England. He knew very well that as a member of the royal family, his aunt deserved an income and to live in the royal apartments at Whitehall, and he did not want the expense. This ungenerous communication the queen of Bohemia, who was coming as Lord Craven's guest and not her nephew's, happily chose to ignore, noting to Rupert in a letter of May 19 that she "was already shipped, and had taken farewell of all at the Hague, public and private," and that if she didn't go she "would be supposed disaffected to the King, which would make me despised in all places...I go, I thank God He has given me courage. I shall not do as a poor niece, but will resolve all misfortunes."

Her calculated risk paid off: she was at Lord Craven's house in

Drury Lane by May 24 and was allowed to remain, Charles II bowing to the inevitable and settling an annuity of £12,000 on her. In fact, he was fond of his aunt, and took her to the opera on July 2 as a mark of favor, which settled any lingering doubts among the court as to her being welcome. "I am glad your Majesty has so much reason to be satisfied with the King your nephew, which must be still more pleasant to him," Sophia wrote in a letter of August 14, 1661, in response to her mother's description of these events.

And now, at last, the queen of Bohemia was happy, back in the bustling, longed-for city that she had left half a century before as a vulnerable young bride still mourning the death of her beloved older brother Henry. The annuity bestowed by Charles II was sufficient to allow her a degree of financial independence, and she made plans to lease a house in town from the earl of Leicester at the beginning of the year so as not to impose too long on Lord Craven's hospitality. She even wrote to Princess Elizabeth, whom she had not seen in years, inviting her to come to London to share the new house with her. Although her eldest daughter did not take her up on this kind offer, Rupert, her favorite son — she signed her letters to him "I love you ever, my dear Rupert" — had pledged himself to Charles II's service and was expected in London by the end of the year, so she would not be completely bereft of family.

He only just made it in time. On January 29, 1662, the Winter Queen moved into her new quarters and soon afterward began coughing up blood. Charles sent his own doctors and belatedly offered an establishment within the royal palace of Whitehall, but it was too late. She was too ill to be moved. He and Rupert were with her at the end; she made her son executor of her will and made her nephew promise to send the annuity he had assigned her to her Dutch creditors and continue it until the debt was paid in full. She died early in the morning of February 13, 1662, at the age of sixty-five, one day shy of what would have been her forty-ninth wedding anniversary.

Although the court went into mourning, to many of those surrounding Charles II, who had not known her in her youth and beauty and were unfamiliar with her story, the queen of Bohemia was simply an old woman who had clung to the margins of power by virtue of her rank. "My royal tenant is departed; it seems the fates did not think it fit that I should have the honor, which indeed I never much desired, to be the landlord of a Queen," the earl of Leicester shrugged in a letter to a friend. But this does the Winter Queen a disservice. Rather, she should be remembered for the admiration she inspired, which was captured in this poem, written in 1620 by her close friend the English ambassador Sir Henry Wotton:

On His Mistress, the Queen of Bohemia

You meaner beauties of the night,
That poorly satisfy our eyes
More by your number than your light;
You common people of the skies;
What are you when the moon shall rise?

You curious chanters of the wood,
That warble forth Dame Nature's lays,
Thinking your passions understood
By your weak accents; what's your praise,
When Philomel her voice shall raise?

You violets that first appear,
By your pure purple mantles known
Like the proud virgins of the year,
As if the spring were all your own;
What are you when the rose is blown?

So, when my mistress shall be seen
In form and beauty of her mind,

By virtue first, then choice, a Queen,
Tell me if she were not designed
The eclipse and glory of her kind?

She was buried in Westminster Abbey in the royal vault near her father. It was the closest she had been to him since she was sixteen.

PART III

~

The Legacy of Mary, Queen of Scots

Mary, queen of Scots

...and her great-granddaughter, Sophia

Princess Elizabeth

...in Germany

18

Abbess of Herford

FOR PRINCESS ELIZABETH, THE RESTORATION of her cousin Charles II to the throne and even the death of her mother (whom she seems never to have forgiven for the d'Epinay affair) had very little impact on her life. Of much greater moment was the highly unseemly public disintegration of Karl Ludwig's relationship with his wife, Charlotte, and his subsequent somewhat-less-than-official remarriage to Louise von Degenfeldt. When she discovered that her older brother not only expected her to recognize Louise as his legitimate spouse but had every intention of moving his new family into the castle at Heidelberg despite the fact that his former wife was still living there, Princess Elizabeth, who had taken Charlotte's side from the beginning, was appalled. There was an argument, and in 1659, soon after Sophia's marriage and removal to Hanover, Elizabeth too packed up her few belongings and went to live with her relatives in Berlin.

But this could in no way be viewed as a long-term solution. Elizabeth was a forty-year-old spinster without financial resources. She was too proud and of too high birth to accept charity from her relations; she needed a position where she could settle into old age with honor and dignity. In the century in which she lived, this meant the Church.

Luckily, thanks to the Peace of Westphalia, there was now a Protestant women's order more or less in the family: the abbey of Herford (about fifty miles west of Hanover, where Sophia now lived).

Herford was one of the consolation prizes that the elector of Brandenburg (still Frederick William, Louisa's former suitor) had received from the emperor in exchange for the surrender of territory to Sweden at the end of the Thirty Years' War. Elizabeth had formerly tried to place Louisa at this institution before her sister's unexpected flight from The Hague and conversion to Catholicism.

This time, it was a position for herself that she sought when she wrote to her cousin the abbess. But because of her royal title, she desired not simply to join the order but also to run it after the death of her relative. She must have anticipated some resistance to this blatant nepotism because she made an effort to preempt any doubts the abbess might have as to her motives or qualifications. "If I came to the Institution I should never have the presumption to think of reforming anything which your Grace could not do, nor of keeping a greater state than you have done so as to bring the Abbey into debt," she rushed to assure her cousin. "I have no desire to make great banquets which is not fitting for any Abbess; I can add 1000 thalers yearly, and if God grants me more (from the claims I have on the English and Imperial Courts) I will use it to secure my favor," she wheedled outright.*

But the cousin, who had never met Elizabeth, had no wish to be hurried to the grave or second-guessed in administration by some haughty distant relation. She stalled, raising doubts as to the fitness of a princess for the humble retirement of religious life. "If you knew me aright you would know that I have no ambition and ask no more than a retreat for my old age, which I may perhaps find at Herford," Elizabeth rejoined in frustration in the fall of 1659.

Finally, after over a year of correspondence, she managed to convince her cousin to consent to the plan—"As your Grace has assured me in your honored letter of March 22 that you will accept me as

---

* Elizabeth was referring to the arrears on her royal allowance, stopped at the time of the civil war in England, and the 10,000-thaler dowry promised under the Peace of Westphalia. Neither payment materialized. Parliament had more pressing expenses and the emperor ruled that dowries were due only to those of the Winter Queen's daughters who married.

Canoness, I have sent...300 thalers," Elizabeth confirmed quickly in a letter dated April 17, 1660, making sure to secure the position with a down payment—only to discover that her nomination could not proceed without the vote of the order itself. Alas, the results of a preliminary caucus of this august body were not encouraging. Many of the other women in the order shared the suspicions of the abbess and moved to reject this well-connected interloper. "I am heartily sorry for the disagreement with the Chapter, and cannot but blame the Canonesses who fomented it," Elizabeth fumed to her cousin. "It is a bad trade to stir up strife, but to restore peace and order is the part of wisdom that brings the best repute," she admonished virtuously.

Unfortunately, the sisters of the abbey—particularly one Fraulein Lisgen, who until Elizabeth's sudden appearance had clearly been expecting to take over—continued to protest her appointment, necessitating more drastic measures. In October 1660, Elizabeth undertook the trouble and expense to travel to Herford and stay for ten days at the abbey, as a sort of extended employment interview. She also urged the elector of Brandenburg (whom she saw regularly in Berlin) and other distinguished acquaintances to write to the chapter on her behalf. As this only served to confirm the order's fears that a decision in her favor would be forced upon them, these maneuvers did not have the desired effect. "If your Grace would listen to your memory rather than to the false reports...you would not suppose that the loss of Fr. Lisgen's vote would drive me to such extremities as should do injury to the Institution," Elizabeth was forced to defend herself in a letter of December 8. "If the Elector or other good friends could be helpful to me...it could not possibly be any prejudice to your Grace...It robs the Institution of no freedom...and why should it not be permitted me to employ my friends to influence the sisters to carry out your wishes, as for Fr. Lisgen to induce hers to work against them to return an unfavorable answer?"

In the end, of course, Fraulein Lisgen's connections were no match for the princess's. Her patience exhausted, Elizabeth simply had Frederick William, who as overlord of Herford held the ultimate authority, threaten to withdraw his financial and military support from the abbey unless Elizabeth was accepted as successor to the abbess. "The Elector is very docile and she very free with him," Sophia observed of her sister by way of explaining this transaction.

It had taken more than two years, but by the summer of 1661 Elizabeth had succeeded in her quest and was installed at the abbey of Herford, having traveled to her new home in a coach and six horses thoughtfully provided by her benefactor the elector. She seems to have lost no time in reorganizing the order to her taste, as her brother Edward in Paris mentioned in a letter to Karl Ludwig at this time that she had been in recent communication with their sister Louisa. "La Grecque ['the Greek,' the family nickname for Elizabeth] has written to ask her [Louisa] for the Rule of the Convent and for a pattern of the habit. I don't know whether it is to make a similar foundation in the place where she is but I doubt if they could live in such harmony as ours do," he remarked.

He knew his eldest sister's character well. After this inauspicious beginning, upon the death of the old abbess from consumption in 1667, Princess Elizabeth took over at Herford and within two years found herself at the center of a political firestorm.

IT'S EASY TO SEE why she had fought so hard to be named her cousin's successor. The venerable abbey of Herford, founded in the eighth century, was perhaps the most prestigious—and certainly the most ancient—women's institution in Germany. In recognition of the importance of its mission and its influence on the surrounding community, in the twelfth century the abbey had been raised to the status of an independent principality within the empire, which put it somewhat on the level of a duchy, albeit a very, very small one. Practically, this meant that, as abbess, Elizabeth was responsible not simply for the welfare of the other women in her order but also for the administration of the neighboring farms and mills that fell within her religious jurisdiction. More important, she had authority over the town of Herford itself, which numbered approximately 7,000 inhabitants at the time she assumed control. As a result, she had her own seat at the governing imperial diet and was officially accorded the satisfyingly impressive title "Princess and Prelatess of the Holy Roman Empire."

There is no question that Elizabeth was prodigiously qualified for her position. She was by far the best-educated and most intelligent candidate, and her high birth had accustomed her to decision-making. Like Karl Ludwig, her impoverished upbringing had made her careful with money, which added to her skills as an administrator, and she was conscientious, organized, and responsible. She brought experience and knowledge of the outside world to the provincial community at Herford.

The one small drawback was that she was a Calvinist, and those who fell under her jurisdiction were decidedly Lutheran. Even so, this need not have been a problem; the former abbess had also been a Calvinist and had gotten along well enough with her subjects. But the difference in religion meant that the townspeople were somewhat wary of Elizabeth, at least at the beginning of her tenure, and less likely to give her the benefit of the doubt. Nor were their suspicions entirely misplaced, for the evidence suggests that Elizabeth did find her Lutheran charges to be a little less pious than might be hoped for, and regarded it as part of her job to help them along the path to righteousness.

And so, when her old friend Anna Maria van Schurman (the internationally renowned intellectual prodigy and author of the paper defending the right of women to pursue higher education) wrote to her asking for sanctuary for herself and a band of young women who sought to devote themselves to God but had found themselves persecuted for it in Holland, Elizabeth leaped at the entreaty. "An opportunity occurs, without doing injury to anyone, of much benefiting this Abbey and Your Grace's state," Elizabeth wrote excitedly to Frederick William, whose approval she required for decisions on larger issues. "Your Grace will have surely heard how the learned Anna Schurman, with certain Dutch ladies, commenced the foundation of a convent in Amsterdam," she observed. "Two preachers, however, are with them whom the people of Holland hate, and pursue with calumnies... They therefore wish to put themselves under my protection and establish a house on my land," she explained. "In all this, we can desire only to work for the glory of God... increasing the number of our Calvinist subjects, of who we have too few," she continued, giving it away, before hurrying to add, "It is likewise much to be wished that so many waste lands in our dominions should have the advantage of being built upon, and that by the establishment of small colonies in these various spots trade may be activated," she concluded firmly.

Faced with so reasonable a request, in his return letter of September 6, 1670, the elector (also a Calvinist) granted his permission, "so long as the sectaries showed themselves conformable to the worship of the Reformed Church and caused no scandal." Having followed procedure and obtained the elector's approval, Elizabeth lost no time in inviting Anna Maria and her entire congregation to Herford. "The Princess wrote to me direct, informing me that she was well acquainted with my intention of freeing myself from the world in order to devote myself entirely to the practices of the true Christian religion, and to end my days calmly and happily in communion with pious spirits," Anna Maria recorded in her diary. "She was good enough to say she recalled our former friendship, and therefore offered to me and our whole community the free and public exercise of our religion throughout the whole of her little state of Herford... It was evident to us all that this was a special manifestation of Providence in our favor, and we immediately set about profiting by it," Anna Maria marveled.

And so, in the fall of 1670, sixty-three-year-old Anna Maria and her young female companions—all fifty of them, plus five male pastors—packed up their belongings, embarked from Amsterdam, and descended en masse upon the little, walled, out-of-the-way Lutheran municipality of Herford.

★　　★　　★

EVEN HAD THE VISITORS' reputation not preceded them, the citizens of Herford would have taken one look at this band of eccentric, hymn-singing, ragtag refugees and understood right away that these were not Calvinists, or at least not any variety of Calvinist they'd ever seen before. As it was, though, even before they landed, Herford had heard plenty about the group, whom the locals derisively nicknamed "the Hollanders" but who were in fact Labadists.

Labadists were the followers of a renegade pastor named Jean de Labadie. Originally a Catholic trained by Jesuits, Labadie had converted to Protestantism in 1650 at the age of forty after reading John Calvin's bestselling work *Institutes of the Christian Religion*. But over the years Labadie had begun to see visions and hear voices. There being no psychiatric medication available in the seventeenth century, he naturally attributed his hallucinations to God and worked them into his religious philosophy.

The Labadist sect, scandalously for the period, eschewed personal property and instead lived communally, men and women all together in the same house (although not on the same floors and certainly not in the same rooms or beds). They didn't care what they wore or what they ate; they prayed only when the spirit moved them, and then only silently. Conversely, they were given to much frantic dancing and singing as a means of precipitating the sort of personal, one-on-one, mystical revelations from God that Labadie insisted was the only real form of spiritual enlightenment. ("All made merry, not in eating and drinking, but in the Holy Ghost," Anna Maria noted.) In Holland, Labadie had acquired a small but devoted following, particularly among well-born women, with Anna Maria representing his most famous convert. But the vast majority of the Dutch considered the sect offensive and persecuted its members as disreputable. "We learned quickly enough how far our age had fallen from truth, for so few were willing to give themselves to Christ and to forego earthly comfort," Anna Maria observed sadly.

Unfortunately, the Lutheran citizens of Herford felt every bit as threatened by the Labadists as had their Dutch counterparts. The town council complained vociferously about this throng of dangerous foreigners to the elector of Brandenburg, other Protestant princes, and even the imperial tribunal. Worried that the presence of religious radicals in these numbers could undermine their traditionally homogenous society, the town officials closed their borders to further immigration by shutting the gates, while local merchants refused to serve the Hollanders at their shops or allow them to drink from the public wells. The Labadists were harassed in public and someone even threw a rock through the window of the house where they had found temporary lodging.

Elizabeth was mortified. These people were her invited guests! Although she must have known that the eccentric lifestyle of the sect did not conform to traditional Protestantism, she nonetheless dug in her heels and insisted that its members were Calvinists at heart. "Although much has been spread against them by their enemies, yet have many persons... at our desire, conversed lengthily with these people, and all admit that their creed and doctrines are those of... the 'Institutions' of Calvin, and the Catechism of Heidelberg," she affirmed indignantly to Frederick William on November 6 in response to an official complaint sent by the Herford town council. When the controversy did not die down, and the elector of Brandenburg announced he would send his own ministers to examine the members of the sect, Elizabeth made the highly questionable move of soliciting the help of a local army commander and a troop of soldiers from a neighboring citadel to keep the peace while the city awaited the arrival of the Berlin envoys and their decision.

Although Elizabeth was correct in her assessment that the Labadists were peaceful and meant no harm, beginning one's term in office by high-handedly calling in an outside military force was perhaps not the optimal way to make this point to the local population. In fact, this escalation only confirmed her subjects' worst fears that their new abbess intended to impose her religious views on them. Within two weeks of their arrival, the refugees found themselves at the center of a political tug-of-war, the result being that on November 20, Elizabeth found it necessary to appeal once again to the elector. "I hear that all manner of things have been reported to Your Grace touching my 'Hollanders,' and to me so much has been written on the subject, that, had I them not under my own eyes, did I not daily see the proofs of their exemplary conduct, I should myself be the first to drive them from my dominions," she began. Then, to justify the presence of the troops, she reported in dismay that "already, when any of the 'Hollanders' walk in the streets, they are shouted at by the populace, and mud and dirt are flung at them."

News of the standoff over the Labadists and Elizabeth's support of them reached Sophia in nearby Hanover, and she could not resist going to see for herself. In a spirit of mischievous good humor, she brought along her own minister as a reliable religious expert to quiz her sister's visitors so she could hear their unorthodox replies. She arrived just as her twenty-year-old nephew Karl (Karl Ludwig's eldest son by his first wife, Charlotte), who was going around Europe accompanied by his tutor, was also paying a visit to the abbey. Karl, too, was curious about the Labadists and asked to meet them. His tutor, who was responsible to Karl Ludwig for his young charge, penned a detailed description of this interesting educational opportunity to his employer.

"Next morning, as soon as we were dressed, we all marched off to Labadie's abode," the tutor reported. "On the threshold almost we stumbled on Mademoiselle Schurman, in marvelous strange habiliments. She greeted the intruders with but indifferent courtesy. We were led to her room...[where there were] paintings done by the erudite virgin herself, which rivaled Nature; statues in wood and wax, extraordinary from their expression, and commanding our wondering admiration. Meanwhile, there glided slowly into the chamber an old man, with a busy and preoccupied air, not good-looking or imposing, but seemingly taken up with I-know-not-what pious speculations...this man was Labadie," he affirmed.

They listened to him pontificate for a while—"As though he had been the Delphian Oracle," the tutor observed drolly—before Sophia's minister pounced. There commenced a spirited debate on the temptations of "earthly love" (that would be sex) that continued for so long that Elizabeth tried to intervene by offering everyone breakfast. This attempt at distraction did not work, however, for no sooner had they all sat down at the table than they went right back at each other. "Here things got worse, and words ran high," admitted the tutor. To try to settle the argument, Sophia's nephew Karl suggested that Labadie preach a sermon so that they could "judge of his eloquence in the pulpit." This was immediately arranged.

"So forth we repaired to Labadie's own house, and quickly the congregation assembled—women and young girls, a goodly lot—the prettiest little dolls imaginable!" the tutor exclaimed. "Then came a collection of tailors, boatmen, and furriers, covered with dirt; for it is to be remarked, that amongst this brilliant circle of women, not one well-dressed or apparently respectable man was to be seen." A psalm was sung, a verse read, and a sermon full of hell-fire and sin commenced. "Whilst he delivered all this with a loud voice and the affectation of holy inspiration, the most devout attention reigned throughout the assembly; some raised their eyes to Heaven, some smote their breasts and groaned, and some soft-hearted maidens dissolved in tears," the tutor related. "During dinner, we talked of nothing else but of this absurd and quaking sort of piety to which people are sometimes brought; and our astonishment could scarcely find words when alluding to the number of young women of the best families, richly-dowered, brilliant with beauty and youth, who were insane enough to give up the conduct of their souls to this worst of men and most powerless of priests (only to be laughed at too by him in secret), and who were so riveted to their delusions that neither the prayers of their parents, nor the pleadings of their betrothed, nor the prospect of maternal joys, could tear them away!"

Elizabeth, who had also rejected court life as frivolous and who, like Anna Maria, had not found spiritual peace in scholarship alone, was highly annoyed by the table conversation and continued passionately to defend the sect. In her frustration, the abbess lashed out angrily at her family. "But to this the Electress Sophia, a lady of extraordinary cleverness, found an answer which turned all bitterness into general mirth," the tutor related with evident relief, "by asserting, with mock gravity, that her sister's sole reason for holding to the Labadists was that they were stingy housekeepers, and cost little or nothing to keep!"

Despite her determined sponsorship, which included a personal journey to the elector of Brandenburg to plead for her guests, the battle over the Labadists was not one the new abbess would win. No sooner had Elizabeth left Herford for Berlin than the townspeople renewed their persecution of the outsiders, and Labadie and his followers decided it was best after all to move on. By the time she returned, they were already established in Altona, nearly a hundred and fifty miles to the north.

Elizabeth may have lost the contest with her subjects, but as a result of her generous treatment of the Labadists, she earned herself a reputation for religious tolerance and enlightenment that spread as far away as England, where it caught the attention of an idealistic young Quaker named William Penn.

THE QUAKERS—OR THE Society of Friends, as they called themselves—were a much more thoughtful and considered sect than the Labadists. The movement had taken root in England as a reaction to what was considered to be the impious dissipation of Charles II's Restoration court (which was itself a reaction to the pious austerity of the Cromwell years). Like the Labadists, Quakers were spiritualists who believed that God spoke directly to the individual, but they did not seek revelation through wild dancing and singing. Rather, they convened long, serious meetings where members preached as the spirit moved them. Quakers rejected ornamentation but not all material comforts; they lived quiet, industrious lives and certainly did not approve of unmarried men and women sharing property. But where the Quakers were truly revolutionary was in their pacifism and unshakable belief in equality, which took the tangible form of addressing everyone they met as *thee* or *thou* (rather than, for example, *sir* or *Your Ladyship*) and refusing to take off their hats to those of higher rank, as was then the fashion at court.

Declining to doff one's headgear might seem insignificant, but by taking direct aim at the entrenched class system, the practice turned out to be a potent symbol against social injustice. It infuriated the governing aristocracy, who interpreted the inaction as a challenge to its prestige and authority. Accordingly, being a Quaker took courage, a quiet but nonetheless steely courage, and no one had more of that quality than the Society of Friends' most famous adherent, William Penn.

William Penn was born on October 14, 1644, smack in the middle of the English civil war. His father, an admiral in the navy, became rich under Cromwell but hedged his bets and reached out secretly to Charles II, who much appreciated this unlooked-for (if covert) expression of loyalty. Consequently, the elder Penn found himself in favor upon the king's restoration and was given a high position in the royal navy. Admiral Penn, who had great hopes for his outgoing, obviously bright eldest son and heir, sent him to Oxford (where John Locke was a fellow schoolmate) to prepare him for a life at court, only to have sixteen-year-old William fall under the influence of a Quaker preacher and get himself expelled for going to meetings of the Friends instead of attending the required university church services.

And so began a hard-fought contest between the ambitious father, who had spent his life accumulating wealth and influence, and the principled son, who had experienced a spiritual awakening that he could not ignore. The admiral tried both carrot and stick. He raged and threw his son out of the house; relented and sent him to Paris for sophistication and then brought him back home to a London law school for expertise; introduced him into society and even managed to secure him, for a very brief period, a plum naval appointment on board ship as his aide under Charles II's younger brother James, duke of York. For a short time this seemed to work, and William tried dutifully to be a fashionable society gentleman for his father's sake. But when he was sent to Ireland to administer the family's properties near Cork in the spring of 1666, he ran into the same Quaker preacher who had so impressed him as a teenager at Oxford, and all the old feelings came rushing back. From this point on, he renounced his father's way of life and openly espoused the doctrine of the Friends, even going so far as to preach at meetings.

His embrace of the Quakers of course put him at odds with the authorities, who saw it as their duty to squelch the sect, while his father's high position made him an easy target for the admiral's many enemies at court. The result was that William Penn very quickly found himself one of the public faces of the movement, not a particularly pleasant position to occupy, as it meant that he was often singled out for arrest. As he refused to recant, he spent the majority of the next few years in prison, where he used his time productively, writing books and pamphlets staunchly defending his religious views and promoting liberty of conscience. "Tell the King that the Tower is the worst argument in the world," William Penn flatly told the chaplain Charles II sent to reform him.

His fortitude under the twin pressures of deprivation and confinement—for conditions in the Tower were grim—combined with his reliance on firm but peaceful resistance (William Penn understood the power of nonviolent protest centuries before Gandhi) made him a force to be reckoned with. Even his father came to respect him and when he died in 1670 left him his entire estate, which included £16,000 in back pay and loans owed to him by the Crown, along with Charles II's promise of a promotion to peer of the realm. Two years later, William Penn, now a leading voice for the Quakers and liberty of conscience in England and interested in uniting with other similarly persecuted Protestant sects in Europe, heard of Elizabeth's protection of the Labadists at Herford.

He knew the family, of course, through her brother Rupert. After his mother's death, Rupert had stayed in England and been made a member of the Privy Council by Charles II, who valued his uncle's experience and advice. He was further appointed commander of the fleet under the duke of York, and he had fought with his customary ferocity alongside William Penn's own father in a brief skirmish against the Dutch. "I did indeed discover so extraordinary courage, conduct and presence of mind in the midst of all the showers of cannon bullet, that higher I think cannot be imagined of any man ever fought. I observed him [Rupert] with astonishment all that day," his second in command reported.

When an old head wound reopened and forced him to retire from active service, Rupert simply broadened the scope of his interests. An early fellow of the Royal Society, he spent his spare time in a laboratory he set up, experimenting mostly with ways to improve the effectiveness of guns and powder. Among his patented inventions was a new alloy of copper and zinc, appropriately named "Prince's metal." He put his naval experience to good commercial use by getting himself appointed the first president of the Hudson Bay Company, which had exclusive rights to trade in Canada. He still rode like a wild man, loved animals (this time, it was a "faithful great black dog" who padded after him), and, according to Samuel Pepys, was recognized as one of "the best players at tennis in the nation." Throughout, and despite his many injuries and the advance of age, he was still recognizably Rupert: "He is as merry, and swears, and laughs, and curses, and do all the things of a man in health as ever he did in his life," Pepys marveled after Rupert survived yet another head injury.

William Penn was especially interested in Rupert's sister Princess

Elizabeth because the Quakers were in need of influential allies. In 1673, Parliament passed the Test Act, which prohibited anyone from holding office, either religious or civil, unless he was willing to swear an "Oath of Allegiance" to the Church of England. Although the measure was aimed primarily at Catholics (of whom Charles II's brother James was the most conspicuous), Quakers and other nonconformist Protestant sects also fell under the vague, catchall category of "worshipping God after another manner than that of the Church of England," as William Penn put it, and so found themselves persecuted anew. When a prominent Quaker was imprisoned for refusing to take the required oath, Penn thought of Elizabeth. He appealed to her for help and found in the fifty-five-year-old abbess a passion for liberty of conscience and the courage to fight for it that was a match for his own. "I have received your two letters," she wrote to him, "and your good wishes that I may attain to those virtues which shall enable me to follow in the blessed steps of our Lord and Savior. What I did for his true disciples [the Labadists] weighs not so much as a glass of water, for, alas! it helped them not. Neither... could [I] leave undone one single thing that [was] deemed likely to further his [the imprisoned Quaker's] freedom, although the doing of it should expose me to the mockeries of the whole world," she assured him with spirit.

And with this response, for the second time in her life, Elizabeth attracted the attention and admiration of one of the most progressive minds of her era. When four years later, Penn, after a futile campaign for religious freedom that included the publication of many compelling treatises, reluctantly gave up on England and went on a recruitment tour of Holland and Germany to float the idea of a Quaker settlement in the New World, he made a point of visiting her.

BY THE TIME WILLIAM Penn came to Herford in the summer of 1677, tensions between Elizabeth and her subjects had substantially eased. It had been fifteen years since she had first come to the area and a decade since she had become abbess. After the Labadists, there

William Penn

had been no further incidents and the townspeople had clearly come to trust her. "She would constantly, every last day in the week, sit in judgment, and hear and determine causes herself, where her patience, justice and mercy were admirable, frequently remitting her forfeitures where the party was poor, or otherwise meritorious," Penn later observed. "And, which was excellent, though unusual, she would...strangely draw unconcerned parties to submission and agreement; exercising not so much the rigor of her power, as the power of her persuasion." In many ways, Elizabeth hadn't changed at all; she was as economical as ever, reserving as much of her income as possible for charity, as befitted her position. "Though she kept no sumptuous table in her own Court, she spread the tables of the poor in their solitary cells, breaking bread to virtuous pilgrims, according to their wants and her ability; abstemious in herself, and in apparel void of all vain ornaments," Penn confirmed.

But physically, she was failing, and in her awareness of her mortality Elizabeth sought a spiritual peace that she just couldn't seem to find. True to her intellect, rather than relying on dogma, she opened herself to new ideas. During his visit, she invited Penn—at thirty-two young enough to have been the son she never had—to dinner and made him tell her his story. "I related...the bitter mockings and scornings that fell upon me, the displeasure of my parents, the invectiveness and cruelty of the priests, the strangeness of all my companions; what a sign and wonder they made of me, but, above all, that great cross of resisting and watching against mine own inward vain affections and thoughts," he recounted simply. His words touched her, and the next day after a meeting at which he preached, she broke down in tears, took his hand in hers, and tried to tell him "the sense she had of the power and presence of God," he remembered. "'I cannot speak to you,'" she managed. "'My heart is full.'"

He came back for a second visit at her urging before he left for England, and upon his return had this letter, written on October 29, 1677, from her. "Dear Friend—Your tender care of my eternal well-being doth oblige me much, and I will weigh every article of your counsel to follow as much as lies in me; but God's grace must be assistant...Let me feel him first governing in my heart, then do what he requires me...Do not think I go from what I spoke to you the last evening; I only stay to do it in a way that is answerable before God and man...Your true friend, Elizabeth."

Elizabeth was also perturbed at this time by the estrangement that still persisted between herself and Karl Ludwig, who had never forgiven her for siding with Charlotte and had gone so far as to try to wriggle out of a financial commitment to her. "I must wait till God send you better feeling towards me...And I hope my patience will show how much I value the honor of being on good terms with you. If I had been guided by my legal advisers I should have acted quite differently," she wrote to him. But their relationship pained her and when his second wife, sweet-tempered Louise von Degenfeldt, died in 1677, Elizabeth tried to demonstrate her goodwill and desire for reconciliation by helping him.

Although Charlotte had moved out of the castle of Heidelberg by this time and was currently living with relatives in Hesse-Cassel, she had never recognized the divorce. This meant that, in the eyes of the world, Karl Ludwig's second family was illegitimate, which in turn meant that none of the sons he'd had with Louise—and she had borne him *thirteen* children, eight of whom survived, four of whom were boys—could legally inherit his property. His one legitimate son, Karl, was therefore his only heir—and in 1671 Karl had married a Danish princess who had yet to bear a child. If that situation continued, as it appeared likely it would, there was a very real chance that the Lower Palatine, including the beloved ancestral castle of Heidelberg that Karl Ludwig had fought so long and hard to reclaim, would pass out of the family.

Karl Ludwig had two choices: convince Charlotte to recognize the divorce and then marry a third wife in the hopes of siring a legitimate heir, or persuade Rupert to return to the Palatinate, marry, and produce sons. On both these fronts, Elizabeth now did her best to help him. She sent an appeal to Charlotte, and when this was rejected flatly, turned to Rupert in England, sending a message through William Penn. "I will execute thy commission with all diligence and all possible discretion, and give thee notice thereof in my earliest letters, if the Lord be pleased to let me reach London in safety," Penn had promised before he left.

But Rupert, who had fallen in love with the Irish daughter of an old comrade in arms and had married her but kept the nuptials secret, probably because his wife was Catholic, was having none of it.★ He wrote back "that he was quite comfortable at Windsor, and had no intention of moving; that Karl Ludwig had insulted him and might do what he pleased for an heir, he should not have him."

★ He had a son, Dudley, by this marriage to whom he left his property but whom he never formally recognized. He also had an illegitimate daughter, Ruperta, by an actress with whom he had a brief affair.

It was a disappointing answer, but Elizabeth's efforts on Karl Ludwig's behalf softened him toward her, and just in time. In October of 1679, Elizabeth sent for Sophia. When she arrived, Sophia found "my sister was in bed, all her body, legs, arms, and throat like a skeleton, only her stomach frightfully swollen with dropsy [probably cancer]...She spoke of death with smiles. 'I shall not leave much goods nor gear,' she said. 'I should wish to be buried without ceremony and without a funeral oration, which is but flattery.' She is pleased when those she loves ask news of her," Sophia added.

Elizabeth's last thoughts and letters were directed to her family. "It is a great consolation to me, dear brother, that you testify so tender a sympathy for my sufferings, and that you still remember the old friendship between us, the interruption of which caused me so much grief...I have never failed to preserve my affection for our country, and it would have been a great joy to me to have been permitted to return thither and pay you my respects but it was not God's will," she observed sadly to Karl Ludwig. And to Louise Hollandine, whom she had not seen in over three decades, she wrote, "I am still alive, my dear sister, but it is to prepare for death...Adieu, dear sister, I hope that we shall prepare us so well in this transitory life, that we may see His Face eternally in the future."

"Elizabeth fails more and more, and they do not think she will suffer more in dying than she does now," Sophia wrote poignantly to Karl Ludwig at the end of November, just after Elizabeth's sixty-first birthday. "It seems she will go out like a candle."

The candle flickered out on February 12, 1680.

ELIZABETH, PRINCESS PALATINE AND Prelatess of the Holy Roman Empire, was buried in the Abbey Church of Herford. She was so distinguished by the standards of her day that it took fifteen lines in Latin to inscribe her many titles and accomplishments, both religious and scholarly, on her tomb. William Penn was so affected by the news of her death that he composed a long memorial to her and appended it to his best-known work, *No Cross, No Crown*. "The late blessed Princess Elizabeth, the Countess Palatine, as a right, claimeth a memorial in this discourse, her virtue giving greater luster to her name than her quality, which yet was of the greatest in the German Empire," he wrote. "She had a small territory, which she governed so well that she showed herself fit for a greater...I cannot forget her last words, when I took my leave of her. She said: 'Let me desire you to remember me, though I live at this distance, and though you should never see me more...know and be assured, though my condition subjects me to diverse temptations, yet my soul hath strong desires after the best things.'"

Almost exactly one year after her death, on February 24, 1681, Charles II, pressed to repay the £16,000 in loans (plus the peerage) still owing to William Penn's father's estate and presented with the alternative of giving away uncleared wilderness rather than hard-to-come-by cash and a valuable estate in England, leaped at the chance to grant Penn acreage in America instead. Although William had requested that the property be named Sylvania (forest), Charles overruled him and signed the charter as *Penn*sylvania—ostensibly as a tribute to the admiral (but coincidentally as a way of tagging the bequest directly to the liquidation of the loans, so there could be no coming back for more if under all that lichen and brushwood it turned out to be swampland). Despite being somewhat embarrassed by the name, William Penn was euphoric. "God hath given it to me in the face of the world...He will bless and make it the seed of a nation," he proclaimed after the charter was signed.

And so, a century later at a convention in Philadelphia, it turned out to be.

And the next year, on November 29, 1682, just three days after his sixty-third birthday, the irrepressible Rupert, the exuberant, valiant soul of the Royalist cause, died of fever and complications from an old wound. The intrepid warrior who as a boy had once hoped to break his neck so that he might leave his bones in England got his wish, and was buried in Westminster Abbey.

Louise Hollandine

...self-portrait at the abbey of Maubuisson
(Private collection, by courtesy of the Hoogsteder
Museum Foundation)

19

Abbess of Maubuisson

BACK IN 1660, WHEN PRINCESS Elizabeth was still alive and deep
into her negotiations to enter the abbey of Herford, her sister Louisa,
having fled her mother's court at The Hague, was taking her vows
at the Catholic abbey of Maubuisson, about twenty miles northwest
of Paris. In terms of prestige and antiquity, Louisa's new home was
every bit a match for Herford. The abbey of Maubuisson had been
founded in 1241 by the indomitable Blanche of Castile, queen of
France and mother of Louis IX, who, alone among the French
kings, was revered for having achieved the much-to-be-desired distinction of sainthood. The similarities between the two religious
institutions ended there, however. At the abbey of Maubuisson,
there were no farms to manage or annoying townspeople to govern,
no seat on an international assembly or overtly political role within
the kingdom or Church hierarchy. There were only the other nuns
and a convent school that attracted the cream of French society. In
fact, her brother Edward had chosen this abbey for Louisa because
he had sent his own daughters there to be educated.

Although she lived at the convent and followed the rule of her order
strictly, Louisa was far from isolated. She was allowed visitors and was
warmly embraced by Edward and the other members of her extended
family. She met Edward's three daughters and her sister-in-law Anna
de Gonzaga for the first time, and renewed her acquaintance with her
aunt Queen Henrietta Maria, widow of Charles I and mother of

Charles II, who still lived in exile in France. Louisa was even greeted upon her arrival by the French royal family, an act that secured her acceptance into the upper echelon of the aristocracy.

This was important because her entrance into the abbey of Maubuisson coincided with the beginning of the reign of one of the most famous rulers of France. On March 9, 1661, exactly one year after Louisa took her vows, the wily Cardinal Mazarin, who had run the kingdom since the days of Richelieu, died, and twenty-two-year-old Louis XIV took the reins of government into his own hands by calling his dumbfounded council together and announcing: *"L'État, c'est moi"* — "I am the state." Thus was the stage set for the Sun King, whose appetite for ostentation, as evidenced by his most famous housing project, the palace at Versailles, was matched only by his global territorial ambitions, the pursuit of which would earn him the respect and fear of Europe and cause the music to stop and all the dancers to change partners yet again. And no one was more attuned to this political reality or more practiced in the art of acquiring royal favor than Louisa's formidable sister-in-law Anna de Gonzaga.

Anna's strategy for advancement under the new regime was reasonably straightforward: promote herself and her family through a series of advantageous marriages that allied Louis XIV's interests with her own. On December 11, 1663, she scored her first real coup by wedding her second daughter, Anne, to Henri-Julius de Bourbon, prince de Condé. The prince de Condé was the first prince of the blood, descended from the same line as Henri IV, former head of the Huguenot faction who had famously succeeded to the throne the previous century by embracing Catholicism. Henri-Julius was as high up the French nobility as it was possible to get without actually marrying into the immediate royal family. By this alliance, the Princess Palatine, as Anna was known in France, vaulted herself and her relations several rungs up the social ladder.* Even Louisa found

---

* Sadly, Edward did not live long enough to witness his daughter's marriage. He died of an unspecified illness in Paris on March 10, 1663, at the age of thirty-eight, nine months before the wedding. He was attended on his deathbed by a Capuchin

herself the beneficiary of this prestigious connection; being the aunt of the new princess de Condé meant that she suddenly outranked all the other nuns at Maubuisson. As a result she, who had been a Catholic less than five years, was appointed abbess in 1664.

It must have been very strange for her, especially in the beginning. But her conversion was obviously sincere. Like William Penn, Louise Hollandine had experienced a spiritual call that she could not deny. She had rejected court life, as he had, and been humiliated and dishonored by scandalous rumors for it. She had displeased her mother as he had his father. She had been cast out by friends and separated from those she loved in order to pursue this path, which she believed brought her closer to God, just as Penn had sacrificed every worldly advantage to be a Quaker for the salvation of his soul. They were two sides of the same coin.

She wore a habit, slept on a hard bed, gave up meat, and awakened at midnight and then again in the early-morning hours every day to pray. And through it all, she continued to paint.

Louisa had been abbess for only three years when Louis XIV launched phase one of his world-domination campaign. Having earlier married the daughter of the Spanish king, Louis now masterfully used her to justify his landgrab. Pretending that he was merely recovering what was legitimately due her, in May of 1667 he proclaimed the "War of the Queen's Rights" and then proceeded to roll into Belgium and Flanders at the head of an army of 125,000 men and 1,600 cannons. He took Charleroi, Tournay, Douai, Courtrai, and Lille away from an unprepared Spain in a matter of months, and then, after a short break for the holidays, marched south and in February 1668 took all of Franche-Comté, on the border with Switzerland, in three weeks. He made no secret of the fact that Holland and the rest of Belgium and the Netherlands were next, and actively

---

friar, a local priest, and his German manservant. According to the servant, his last words were "Voilà un Huguenot," although whether he was referring to himself or his German steward is unclear.

sought allies in Germany to help marshal soldiers or at least to remain neutral in the coming conflict.

The ever-alert Anna de Gonzaga, whose new son-in-law the prince de Condé had distinguished himself in the action in Flanders and kept her abreast of developments, saw her opportunity. Reflecting that her husband's youngest sister, Sophia, had conveniently wedded a German duke whose two elder brothers were still bachelors, she targeted the middle brother, Duke John Frederick. John Frederick was the natural choice for a French ally, as he alone among his siblings had refrained from carousing on one of the regular family jaunts to Italy and instead had fallen under the sway of Rome and converted to Catholicism. To Sophia's great chagrin (for it threatened her children's inheritance), it turned out that her husband's brother was not, after all, too fat to wed, as had been stipulated in her marriage contract. On November 30, 1668, Anna de Gonzaga again proved her usefulness to Louis XIV by marrying her youngest daughter, sixteen-year-old Bénédicte, to the forty-three-year-old Duke John Frederick, thereby bringing yet another German heavyweight into the French sphere of influence.

But the sacrifice of Bénédicte turned out to be only the setup for the main event. Less than two years later, Anna de Gonzaga hit the jackpot when Henrietta Stuart, youngest sister of Charles II and wife of Louis XIV's younger brother, Philippe, duke of Orléans, whom Louis had been using to conduct secret negotiations with England, suddenly collapsed and died under extremely suspicious circumstances.*

---

* Henrietta was the daughter that Charles I's wife, Henrietta Maria, had given birth to in England during the civil war and been forced to abandon when she fled to France. The child was kept safe by a loyal lady-in-waiting who managed to smuggle her out of England to her mother's court in St. Germain when she was two years old. Henrietta grew up in France and was married to Philippe in 1661. The marriage was unhappy and it certainly didn't help that Louis XIV took a romantic interest in her. Henrietta died at the age of twenty-five, just ten days after returning from a clandestine embassy to England and only a few hours after drinking a glass of iced chicory water. She went to her grave screaming that she had been poisoned. An autopsy by her physicians revealed that she had succumbed to natural causes, most likely peritonitis, but most of the French court continued to believe that she had been

Duke John Frederick and his bride, Bénédicte

Anna was on her way back to Paris after visiting Bénédicte in Germany when she got wind of the tragedy, and the alacrity with which she launched into action is impressive. Poor Henrietta perished on June 30, 1670, and on July 12, less than two weeks later, Anna was already writing to Karl Ludwig, plotting out strategy. "As I reached this town, I heard of the death of the Duchesse d'Orléans," she informed him. "This unfortunate accident will cause many changes in several ways...I own that this death greatly affects me, and being what I am to Monsieur [the honorific by which the French distinguished a male member of the immediate royal family, in this case Philippe, duke of Orléans, the grieving husband] I should have wished to be in France at the time of this strange misfortune." But Anna *didn't* hurry off to Paris to comfort Monsieur. Instead, in the same letter, she offered to come to see Karl Ludwig in Heidelberg, hinting mysteriously that she would like to take his "orders on all matters." Two days later she wrote a follow-up letter, and this time

---

murdered. For more on Henrietta's death and the evidence against her having been poisoned, see Notes.

she was more explicit. "Those who think that Monsieur would be a very desirable match already write to me," she warned him bluntly. "I shall do all I can to have the honor of seeing you on my way back [to Paris]…we might, perhaps, under existing circumstances find plenty of things to discuss," she concluded firmly.

The object of these confidential discussions was none other than Liselotte, Karl Ludwig's daughter by his first wife, Charlotte, the little girl who had been raised by her beloved aunt Sophia during the somewhat stressful period when her father brought his new wife to live in the family castle before the old one had been induced to vacate it. Although now of marriageable age, by no reasonable measure should the spirited but (by her own admission) not particularly attractive Liselotte, the daughter of a minor Protestant German elector, have been considered a suitable candidate for an alliance with the French royal family. And in fact, Louis XIV resisted this idea for over a year. But Anna de Gonzaga managed to win him over—"Her peculiar characteristic was to conciliate opposite interests…to discover the secret point of junction and knot, as it were, by which they might be united," an acquaintance once observed—and Anna was able to write triumphantly to Karl Ludwig on August 7, 1671, that "the marriage of Liselotte with the Duc d'Orléans is an accomplished fact, if you desire it. Monsieur wishes for it, and the King of France has given his full consent…the only obstacle is religion." Anna was even able to assure the future father-in-law that he need not worry about the dowry, as Monsieur was willing to accept a small token sum, so keen was Louis XIV for this union.

The willingness to forgo a substantial dowry, which was the customary way to compensate for a bride's inequality in rank, should have set off alarm bells in Heidelberg. But for the notoriously cheap Karl Ludwig, not having to come up with hard cash only made the deal more attractive. He arranged (surreptitiously, of course; as a leader of the Protestant faction in Germany, he had to pretend he didn't know anything about it) to have his daughter abjure the family religion and receive training in Catholicism instead. A proxy wedding was celebrated at Metz on November 16, 1671, with the bride's portion settled at a measly 32,000 florins, to be paid at some unspecified point in the future. "My marriage contract was drawn up as miserably as if I had been the daughter of a burgher," Liselotte pointed out.

Thus did Anna de Gonzaga's niece become Madame, duchess of Orléans, sister-in-law to Louis XIV, as high up the French social hierarchy as it was possible to achieve. Distressed at having to change her religion and wretched at leaving her family, nineteen-year-old Liselotte sobbed all night on her wedding journey from Strasbourg to Châlons. And she hadn't even met the groom yet.

LISELOTTE'S NEW HUSBAND, MONSIEUR, duke of Orléans, was thirty-one years old, addicted to fashionable society, and, although capable

Liselotte as a young married woman

of sleeping with women, on the whole much preferred men. "He was a little round man who seemed mounted on stilts so high were his heels, always decked out like a woman, covered with rings, bracelets, with jewels everywhere, and a long wig brought forward and powdered, and ribbons wherever they could be placed, highly perfumed, and, in all things scrupulously clean," wrote a courtier who knew him well. "He was accused of putting on very little rouge. The nose was very long, eyes and mouth fine; the face full but very long." In keeping with his overall aesthetic, as part of the marriage contract, Monsieur had generously given his new wife 150,000 livres' worth of "jewels, rings, and precious stones"—on the condition that he be allowed to wear them.

He seems to have been somewhat unprepared for his earthy German bride. His cousin described Liselotte's first introduction to her husband in France: "It was cold; she wore no mask; she had eaten pomegranates which had made her lips violet," the cousin reported. "She seemed to us quite comely, but Monsieur was not of that opinion and was a little astonished... The following day we visited Madame, who was not seen at as great advantage by day as by torchlight," the cousin admitted.

In fact, a more incongruous couple would be difficult to imagine. Liselotte, having grown up romping through the German countryside, was forthright, athletic, and unaffected; her husband was as ornate and artificial as his brother's vaunted Hall of Mirrors. Ironically, their very different perspectives seem to have helped them negotiate the more mundane demands of married life, at least in the beginning. "All my life, since my earliest youth, I have considered myself so ugly that I have never been tempted to use much ornamentation," Liselotte explained. "Jewels and dress only attract attention to the wearer. It was a good thing that I felt like this because Monsieur, who was extremely fond of dressing up, would have had hundreds of quarrels with me as to which of us should wear the most beautiful diamonds. I never used to dress up without his choosing my entire outfit," she noted. The couple dutifully reproduced—a boy and a girl survived—after which, by mutual assent, they gave up all pretense of intimacy. "I was very glad when...Monsieur, after the birth of his daughter, betook himself to a separate bed, because I never liked the occupation of producing babies," Liselotte confided. "It was very trying to have to sleep with Monsieur. He couldn't endure being disturbed when he was asleep, so I used to have to lie so near the edge of the bed, that sometimes I fell out like a sack. I was therefore very glad when Monsieur, in a friendly manner and with no ill-feeling, proposed that we should sleep each in our separate rooms."

But it was still all very strange and disconcerting, and one of the few solaces of Liselotte's new life was meeting her aunt Louisa. "One cannot believe how pleasant and playful the Princess of Maubuisson was," Liselotte exclaimed. "I always visited her with pleasure, no moment could seem tedious in her company. I was in greater favor with her than her other nieces [Edward's daughters] because I could converse with her about everything she had gone through in her life, which the others could not. She often talked with me in German, which she spoke very well. She told me her comical tales. I asked her how she had been able to habituate herself to a stupid cloister life. She laughed, and said: 'I never speak to the nuns, except to communicate my orders.' She said she had always liked a country life, and fancied she lived like a country girl. I said: 'But to get up in the middle of the night and to go to church!' She answered, laughing, that I knew well what painters were; they like to see dark places and the shadows caused by lights, and this gave her every day fresh taste for painting. She could turn everything in this way, that it should not seem dull," Liselotte concluded in admiration.

Sophia, who came for a visit in 1679, also found her older sister, whom she had not seen in thirty years, as merry and jesting as ever. "Her happy temper is not in the least changed," Sophia assured Karl Ludwig in a letter written after staying at the abbey of Maubuisson. "I found her very content, for she lives in a very beautiful place; her garden is very large and most pleasant...I only see the nuns of this convent, who have more virtue than learning, and I find them very happy, as also Madame the Abbess, who observes the Rule with great regularity, and passes for a saint. I could be very happy in such a life if I had not a husband and children," Sophia remarked. "The convent is large, clean, and commodious, and the gardens of such extent that one is quite tired with walking round them."

However, while it seems clear that Louisa had found both a spiritual and artistic haven at Maubuisson, seeing Sophia again touched off strong emotions. "Since I have been a nun professed, I have never shed so many tears as I have done at my parting with my sister," she confessed in a letter to one of her German relations, who had accompanied Sophia on her trip. "Since then I feel as if a stone laid on my heart, the dead weight of which oppresses me, and I know not how to cast my eyes round this place where I saw her last without sadness. All of which proves to me that I am yet too much attached to these creatures who are good enough to testify friendship for me, and that it was for my spiritual good that God has separated me from a sister so amiable...La Mere Gabrielle is going fast—she cannot utter another word through weakness; but the last she said to me was a fervent prayer for the conversion of my sister...If such prayers are heard, I shall be content; for, if never more to see my dear sister in this world, I should see her in a better—I should meet her in Paradise," she finished poignantly.

This desire to see Sophia in heaven would grow with time and motivate the abbess of Maubuisson to actively pursue her sister's conversion in her later years. But first she had to help the hapless Liselotte survive the machinations of the French court.

BY THE TIME SOPHIA visited her sister and niece in 1679, Louis XIV's military achievements had made France the dominant—and most dangerous—power in Europe. Building on his earlier successes in Flanders and the Netherlands, the king had made further inroads into Belgium and nearly triumphed over Holland itself. Only by opening the dikes and unleashing a flood that "ruined and destroyed their country and their subjects...and exposed themselves to the danger of being drowned," according to the French ambassador to the States, had the Dutch prevented Louis's armies from occupying Amsterdam and overrunning the rest of the country. Similarly, France had begun invading territory on its eastern border, along the Rhine, burning villages all the way to Friedrichsburg, on the edge of the Palatinate. Too late, Karl Ludwig recognized his in-law's ambitions and made a defensive treaty with the emperor, but by that time the French war machine was all but unstoppable, a reality the elector was forced to acknowledge. In a letter to the commander of the enemy forces responsible for the destruction of his subjects, Karl Ludwig somewhat ludicrously suggested that the issue be settled by a duel. "Do not look upon my demand as an idle or romantic caprice," the paunchy, gray-haired would-be champion warned. "I wish to avenge my country, and as I cannot do this at the head of an army equal to yours, and that no way, save the one I point out, seems left to draw down punishment on your head, I choose what puts you within the reach of my own avenging arm." As might be expected, the French general declined to accept the chivalric challenge proposed by the duchess of Orléans's ailing father.

It didn't matter anyway, as Karl Ludwig died soon after of cancer on August 28, 1680, at the age of sixty-three, just six months after his sister Princess Elizabeth, abbess of Herford, had also succumbed to the disease. "I have wept so much that my eyes hurt," Liselotte wrote to Sophia when she heard the news. "What is worrying me so much is the fear that papa died of grief and disappointment, and that if the Great Man [Louis XIV] and his ministers had not tormented him so greatly we should have had him with us for a long time...Monsieur [her husband] suggested to the Queen that she should make a vow to Saint Ovid so that her son may regain his health [he was ill]. I told him that it would be more fitting to propose to the King that he should take a vow...to stop helping himself to other people's property. If he were to do that, doubtless his son would recover," she concluded bitterly.

For Liselotte, the death of her father was simply one more sorrow in a series of trials that emphasized her unhappiness with her marriage and the French court. After a brief period of harmony, her relations with her husband had deteriorated rapidly. Once he had sired a family, Monsieur felt he had satisfied his marital responsibilities and had publicly resumed his affair with the burning love of his life, the chevalier de Lorraine. The chevalier found his boyfriend's wife to be something of an obstruction to his designs and worked against her whenever he could. "Unfortunately the Chevalier and his satellites always succeed in their wicked schemes," Liselotte complained in a letter to her aunt Sophia. "It would be a thousand times better for me to live in a place that was peopled with ghouls and evil spirits, for the good Lord would not let such things have dominion over me, but the Chevalier's accursed friends have far too much power over my affairs...The King and Monsieur allow them to practice every imaginable sort of villainy," she fumed.

One of the chevalier de Lorraine's more vicious acts was to spread a rumor that Liselotte was having an affair with another courtier, a preposterous charge she stoutly denied, to no avail. The scandal escalated when her husband, at the behest of *his* illicit lover, summarily dismissed her favorite lady-in-waiting on the grounds that the woman had carried compromising letters to the courtier for his wife, an accusation for which there was no evidence at all.

Shattered, Liselotte turned to her aunt Louisa. "I became so melancholic that I resolved to go and end my days with my aunt at Maubuisson," she confessed. "I spoke to her about it...but I could not make her understand that it was a well-considered desire. She thought that I was only vexed." Still, Liselotte persisted. "You can judge whether I have good reason to be sad," Liselotte wrote to Sophia on September 19, 1682, recounting a conversation she had had with Louis XIV. "I begged the King to let me go and finish my days at Maubuisson, saying that I could not find any help anywhere against the attacks of my enemies...for in truth I can no longer live in the midst of these cruel enemies, watching the pleasure they take in the sorrow and distress they cause me. Be assured that I retire from the world with no regret."

In her niece's passionate plea, Louise Hollandine might perhaps have heard echoes of her own persecution at her mother's court at The Hague. But the abbess was now sixty years old and had been withdrawn from the world for nearly two decades. She knew the difference between a true calling and a flight from trouble.

In the end, though, it didn't matter what her aunt thought; this was France, and France was Louis XIV. He was quite specific about his sister-in-law's plan to retire to Maubuisson. "Get the idea out of your head," the king told Liselotte bluntly. "For as long as I live I will never give my consent, and will oppose it if necessary with force. You are Madame, and it is your duty to uphold the position." She would soon see what he meant by that.

HER FATHER'S DEATH MEANT that the Lower Palatinate passed to Liselotte's brother, Karl, the elector's only legitimate heir. Karl Ludwig had been right to worry about this succession: although married for more than a decade, his son, who had been sickly his whole life, remained childless, and outlived his father by less than five years. He died on May 26, 1685, at the age of thirty-four.

It was at this point that the reason Louis XIV had not demanded a large dowry for his brother's German wife—had agreed to the marriage with Liselotte at all—became clear. There's no need to ask for money or property up-front when you intend to take everything anyway. Just as he had with the War for the Queen's Rights, Louis XIV (ignoring the inconvenient clause in her wedding contract wherein Liselotte had specifically renounced any claim to her father's estate), much to his sister-in-law's dismay, now used her as an excuse to invade and annex the Lower Palatinate.

French troops under the direction of the dauphin laid siege to Philippsburg at the end of September 1688; the city surrendered on October 29. Mannheim and Heidelberg soon followed suit. The French soldiers were particularly savage, burning and looting everything in their path. A frantic Liselotte, desperate to stop the slaughter, made herself very unpopular at Versailles. She was accused of being unpatriotic, especially after she pleaded with Louis to exercise restraint. "If they were to kill me for it, I should still find it impossible not to regret—or, rather, deplore—being made the pretext for my country's destruction," Liselotte agonized to Sophia in a letter of April 20, 1689. "I cannot look on in cold blood while with one blow they destroy poor Mannheim, and with it everything which cost my late father so much trouble and thought. When I think of all the places they have had blown up, I am filled with such horror that each night, just as I am falling asleep, I seem to find myself at Heidelberg or Mannheim, gazing upon the ravages they have committed, then I wake up shuddering…I am especially heartbroken because the King actually stayed his hand from these devastations until *after* I had craved leniency for Heidelberg and Mannheim."

The carnage continued. The French were as merciless in the second half of the century as the Spanish and imperial soldiers of the Thirty Years' War had been in the first. "What really grieves me most is that my name should have been used to deceive the poor inhabitants of the Palatinate, and that these poor harmless creatures should have been led by their affection for my father to believe that the best thing they could do would be to submit with a good grace," a bereft Liselotte mourned. "I am heartbroken, and cannot rid myself of the thought that not only were they disappointed in their hopes and their affection harshly rewarded, but that through this same affection they have been brought to the depths of despair and plunged into lifelong misery."

Louis XIV's brutal usurpation of the Palatinate would mark the zenith of French expansion beyond its borders. A quarter century of brazen aggression had spurred the Sun King's opponents to put aside their differences in order to launch a concerted action against him. As a result, bit by bit over the next decades, France would be forced to surrender almost all of the territory it had acquired during the first half of Louis's rule.

But it would be too late for the Palatinate. The beautiful castle of Heidelberg, where once long before a hopeful Frederick had tenderly refurbished a suite of rooms to please his young bride, Elizabeth, only to see it destroyed in the Thirty Years' War, and which was afterward painstakingly restored to its former glory by his son Karl Ludwig, was gleefully demolished all over again by French artillery. And with this newest occupation came the final blow, as the ancestral lands, after so much hardship and effort, passed forever out of the family's control. "Now the King is the sole master in the Palatinate," Liselotte despaired.

WHAT LOUISE HOLLANDINE THOUGHT of Louis XIV's foreign policy, and specifically the destruction of the Palatinate, is unknown. Unlike her sisters and niece, Louisa had never visited her father's homeland and so harbored no fond memories of Heidelberg, its castle, or its subjects. Of those of her family still alive, she was the most removed from affairs in Germany.

But domestically, within France, there *was* a new initiative on the part of the Crown in which the abbess of Maubuisson was deeply interested. This was the Sun King's determination to impose a single religion on his realm by forcibly converting the entire Protestant population, known as Huguenots, and which by best estimates exceeded over one million French subjects, to Catholicism.

Although he must have been mulling it over for some time, this new pet project of Louis's did not really gain momentum until after the death of his wife, the queen, in 1683. Within a year, he had secretly married his latest mistress, Madame de Maintenon (who had been the devoted confidante of the king's former mistress the Marquise de Montespan, which gives an idea of what friendship was like at the Sun King's court). The marriage was not acknowledged because Madame de Maintenon was in no way elite enough to be the wife of so grand a monarch as Louis XIV. She was not of high aristocratic birth; she had been born a Huguenot before converting; she had been married previously to a bawdy French satirist. Madame

de Maintenon made up for these considerable deficiencies by adopt-
ing an air of cloying sanctity, and it was to this trait, her piety, that
Louis was most attracted. Although it was never enunciated (it clearly
wouldn't do to say it aloud), the Sun King, taking the thirteenth-
century Saint Louis IX's example, aspired to canonization and felt
that Madame de Maintenon was just the spouse to get him there.
Liselotte hated her and called her, variously, "the Maintenon woman,"
"the old bawd," "the old wretch," and "the dirty old slut." "The
Great Man [Louis XIV] is incredibly simple with regard to religious
matters," Liselotte informed Sophia. "This arises from the fact that
he has never learnt anything about religion, has never read the Bible,
and thoroughly believes everything they tell him on this subject.
Moreover, when he had a mistress who was not pious he was not
pious either. Now that he has fallen in love with a woman who talks
of nothing but penitence he believes everything she tells him."

And so, to do God's work and save his subjects' souls, on October
22, 1685, Louis revoked the Edict of Nantes, which had guaranteed
the Huguenots freedom of worship in France for a century.* Instead,
he instituted a campaign of reconciliation—or "Reunion," as it was
fondly known—aimed at convincing his misguided Protestant subjects to abjure their heresy and return to the one true religion,
Catholicism. This was how Louis's inspired new approach to spiritual
enlightenment operated: "A day was appointed for the conversion of
a certain district, and the dragoons [soldiers] made their appearance
accordingly," recorded an eyewitness. "They took possession of the
Protestants' houses; destroyed all that they could not consume or
carry away; turned the parlors into stables for their horses; treated the

---

* The Edict of Nantes had been proclaimed law by Henry IV, Louis XIV's grandfather, in April 1598. Henry IV had been the leader of the Huguenot faction for over
two decades and had converted to Catholicism only when it became clear that France
would not accept a Protestant king. His Edict of Nantes grew out of the old Edicts
of Toleration that Catherine de' Medici had passed legalizing Protestantism in an
effort to wrest political power from the Guise family, leaders of the Catholic faction
in France. Catherine would turn on her former Huguenot allies in 1572 by orchestrat-
ing the infamous St. Bartholomew's Day Massacre.

owners of the houses with every species of cruelty, depriving them of food, beating them, burning some alive, half-roasting others and letting them go...and many other tortures were inflicted even more horrible than the above named." An English bishop who happened to be traveling in France at the time backed up this story. "Men and women of all ages who would not yield were not only stripped of all they had, but kept long from sleep, driven from place to place and hunted out of their retirements," he testified. "The women were carried into nunneries, in many of which they were almost starved, whipped, and barbarously treated."

Not surprisingly, this treatment resulted in a mass exodus, as panicked Huguenots eluded capture or pretended to convert and then fled. An estimated 60,000 French Protestants poured across the border into Switzerland in the first months after the revocation. Another 50,000 headed to England. Frederick William, the elector of Brandenburg, was so incensed by Louis's policy that he published his own Edict of Potsdam two weeks later, on November 8, 1685, in which he invited all of the persecuted Huguenots to immigrate to his territory. Hundreds of thousands of French refugees took him up on it and surged into Germany and the Netherlands. Those men unlucky enough to be caught by Louis's dragoons along the way were sent to the galleys or tortured. Anyone who died without accepting last rites and absolution from a Catholic priest was denied a proper burial, and his or her naked body was dragged through the streets and left to be eaten by dogs and rats.

With such an incentive, a thriving business dedicated to smuggling Protestants out of France developed. Children—who under Louis's directives were wrested from their families in order to be brought up Catholic if their parents refused to cooperate—were hidden in empty wine casks and shipped to safe havens like the Channel Islands. Wealthy Huguenots disguised themselves as sheep farmers and servants and paid guides and sea captains to get them out. In total, France lost an estimated 400,000 to 600,000 of its population in a little over a year.

Of course, there were thousands who could not escape, and fearful for their lives and property, agreed to renounce their religion. Louis was thus hailed as a hero by the court and the French clergy, who determinedly looked the other way at the king's methods, pretending that these were all genuine conversions. "This new grandeur, Sire, comes not from the number of your conquests, from the provinces reduced to subjection to you, from Europe of which you have become the arbiter," the bishop of Valence gushed. "It comes from that innumerable crowd of conversions that have been effected by your orders, by your solicitude, by your liberality…and all this—without violence, without arms, and even much less by the force of your edicts than by your exemplary piety." But they knew—they all knew. "Soldiers are strange apostles. I believe them better suited for killing, violating, and robbing, than for persuading," Queen Christina, who had famously converted to Catholicism, observed coolly in a letter of February 2, 1686. "I pray with all my heart that this false joy and triumph of the church may not someday cost her tears and sorrows. In the meantime, it must be known for the honor of Rome that here all those that are men of merit and understanding and are animated by true zeal, do no more lick up the spittle of the French court in this case than I do."

For Louisa, who like the rest of the French clergy ignored the dragoons' brutality and saw only that large numbers of formerly obdurate Huguenots had been convinced finally to forgo heresy and embrace the true word of God, Louis XIV's insistence on uniformity of faith was a source of hope. She had long desired that she might bring her youngest sister to Catholicism, but not being much of a religious scholar herself, she had been unable to shake clever Sophia from her Protestant views. The abbess's educational shortcomings were remedied, however, by the arrival in 1689 of a new resident at Maubuisson, Madame de Brinon.

Madame de Brinon, a zealous Catholic and proud pedant, had previously been employed as the headmistress at St. Cyr, a presti-

gious girls' school founded by her bosom friend and benefactor
Madame de Maintenon, whom she had known and supported for
years. Unfortunately, with her patroness's rise to the highest levels
of the court, Madame de Brinon had assumed a corresponding
ascent in rank and had rather overstepped her social station, an indiscretion for which she had been unceremoniously sacked. "What I
am going to relate is a fact," Madame de Sévigné, a close observer
of the court, informed her daughter in a letter of December 10,
1688. "Madame de Brinon, the very soul of St. Cyr, and the intimate friend of Madame de Maintenon, is no longer at St. Cyr; she
quitted that place four days ago; Madame Hanover, who loves her,
brought her back to the Hôtel de Guise, where she still remains.
There does not seem to be any misunderstanding between her and
Madame de Maintenon...this increases our curiosity to know the
subject of her disgrace. Everyone is whispering about it without
knowing more," she gossiped. Madame Hanover was none other
than Anna de Gonzaga's daughter Bénédicte, on a visit to Paris.
Concerned for Madame de Brinon's reputation and looking for an
out-of-the-way spot where her discomfited friend might ride out
the scandal, Bénédicte remembered her aunt Louisa.

And so Madame de Brinon came to live at Maubuisson, where,
by virtue of her superior religious training and the general air of
authority she had acquired as an educator of young ladies, she was
accorded the position of secretary to the abbess. Under Madame de
Brinon's direction, Louise Hollandine renewed her campaign for
Sophia's soul. In 1690, she sent her sister a copy of a book by Louis
XIV's own court historian listing the arguments in favor of Catholicism. Sophia, who was sponsoring a conclave in Germany that was
trying to resolve the doctrinal differences between Protestants and
Catholics peaceably through reason and compromise, had a look at
it and handed the book over to *her* secretary, the brilliant philosopher Gottfried Wilhelm Leibniz, with instructions to begin a dia-
logue. Encouraged, Madame de Brinon forwarded her own thoughts

on religious dogma and enlisted the aid of Jacques-Bénigne Bossuet, bishop of Meaux, who was considered France's most gifted orator and was much sought after at all the fashionable funerals for his eulogies.*

Unfortunately for Louisa, her secretary was no match for Sophia's. "It must be owned that Madame de Brinon expatiates perfectly well on saints and images, and that she talks like a doctor of the Sorbonne," Leibniz observed. "If the thoughts and the expressions of the people were regulated thus, there would be no harm; but things of the kind are exaggerated in a strange manner," he warned.

Still, Madame de Brinon persisted. When she was unable to make headway with Leibniz, she approached Sophia directly. "I pray to God with all my heart, Madam, that he enlighten your spirit...in order to ensure the salvation of Your Highness, whom I always hope will be disabused from some errors she has been brought up on, if she wants to join her vows to ours and ask God to put her on the path to the truth," she opined loftily. To which Sophia replied tartly that "the tranquility of mind which the good Lord has given me... is a blessing so great that he would not have wanted a person whom he had not chosen to be among his elect to be favored with it." She added, "What gives me a very bad idea of Catholics is what is happening in France at present to the people of our religion, which is not at all Christian and shows that it is a very evil religion which authorizes so many evil actions...All England, Holland and Germany are witnesses to this fine religion, as they are filled with refugees, some of whom have been thrown into prison, others have had their children taken away, and all have had their goods confiscated. That is very Christian! How many have been killed for having prayed to God and having sung the Psalms!"

---

* The bishop of Meaux's career was made when he gave the funeral orations for both Liselotte's predecessor, Henrietta, duchess of Orléans, and Louis XIV's first wife, the queen of France. So celebrated was he that when Anna de Gonzaga died in August 1685, her daughter the princess de Condé demanded that Bossuet eulogize her mother as well.

It is tempting to assume that the aging Louisa, who after all had once been a Protestant and endured harassment for her religious beliefs, did not herself condone the pitiless treatment to which hundreds of thousands of French Huguenots were subjected. But that would be a mistake. "I have again visited my aunt, the Abbesse de Maubuisson, and I found her, God be thanked, even more alert and cheerful than the last time," Liselotte wrote in a letter dated August 6, 1699. "She is gayer and more lively than I am, and her sight and hearing are better than mine, although she is thirty years older. She was seventy-seven years old on April 1st. She is painting a beautiful picture for her sister...It represents the Golden Calf, after the style of Poussin."

As always, Louisa expressed herself most fully in her art. The story of the Golden Calf comes from the book of Exodus in the Old Testament. While Moses was away receiving the Ten Commandments from God, the Israelites he had brought out of slavery became uneasy and begged his brother Aaron to make them an idol to which they could pray; Aaron obliged them by melting down the jewelry they had brought with them from Egypt and using it to mold a golden calf. Moses returned to find his followers praying to the false deity and smashed the tablets he had brought back with him. God, too, was very angry. Calling the Israelites a stiff-necked people, He smote them for their apostasy and replaced them with new disciples.

The message of this allegorical scene that Louisa was painting for Sophia was chilling and unmistakable. By stubbornly refusing to convert to Catholicism, the Huguenots had deservedly drawn upon themselves the wrath of God.

LOUISE HOLLANDINE WOULD LIVE for another ten years, during which time the damage done to France as a result of the persecution of the Huguenots, many of whom had been skilled laborers, became manifest. Shops and mills disappeared; revenues plunged; farmland went untended. "The greater part of our manufacturing establishments have been transported by the Protestant refugees to foreign lands so that we now receive from abroad more than we send thither," an official in Rouen lamented. The army estimated that over 20,000 of its troops, including officers and elite soldiers—Huguenots who had formerly served loyally on behalf of France—went over to the enemy and were now fighting against their homeland. By the turn of the century, between war and religion, Louis XIV had decimated his kingdom. "Never in my life have I seen such miserable times," Liselotte exclaimed. "The common people are dying like flies. The mills have stopped working and many people have therefore died of hunger."

But the wretchedness of the outside world likely mattered little to Louise Hollandine, who died on February 11, 1709, beloved by those who knew her.* "I have received the sad news that our aunt, Princesse Louise de Maubuisson, has at length died after a long illness," Liselotte wrote to a family member five days later. "She had reached an age beyond which it is difficult to go much further, because she was eighty-six years and nine months old. Nevertheless, her death has stricken me to the heart. The dear princess was fonder of me than of her other nieces, and I also fear that her death will upset our dear aunt, the Electress [Sophia], very much." The abbess maintained her eyesight and so was able to paint well into her eighties, but it was her laughing, teasing manner that her niece would most miss. This she kept to the very end.

Ironically, it would be Louisa's irrepressible sense of humor that would cause a postmortem scandal. Years later, almost as an afterthought, Liselotte, who had met her aunt for the first time only after she had come to Paris when Louisa was already in her forties and knew nothing about her life growing up at The Hague, reminisced in a letter to a friend that "the Abbesse de Maubuisson, Louise Hollandine, daughter of Frederick V., Elector Palatine in the days of

---

* Since she was the aunt of Madame and therefore a member of the extended royal family, the great Bossuet himself delivered her eulogy.

Henry IV, has had so many bastards that she always used to swear by 'This body which has borne fourteen children.'" It was obviously a statement Madame had puzzled over at the time but had refrained from asking her aunt about out of delicacy. Nonetheless, because it came from a member of the French royal family, the quote was picked up and repeated with gusto over the centuries—the abbess with fourteen bastards!—until it acquired the heavy authority of fact.

Except that there is absolutely no evidence to corroborate this statement. Her mother's court at The Hague had been under constant surveillance by Parliamentarian spies looking for propaganda against the Royalists, and every movement the family made was picked up by gossips such as the chatty French doctor, or the Dutch papers. In over two decades, there is no mention whatsoever of an unwed princess scandalously giving birth to multiple infants. It might have been possible—just—to hide one illegitimate pregnancy, but *fourteen?* It is far more likely, given Louisa's way of always turning everything into a joke (as Liselotte herself related more than once) that this statement was meant facetiously, that this was in fact something she had heard the Winter Queen, whose body *had* borne that many children, say during all those years when Louisa was the only one of her siblings still living at home.

No, the cross that Louise Hollandine has to bear through history is not that of a beautiful young woman, artistic and full of promise, who had fallen into sinful ways before becoming an abbess. It is the intolerance and lack of compassion she displayed for the sufferings of others after her conversion that is the real tragedy.

Sophia

...with her daughter, Figuelotte

20

A Scandal in Hanover

WHILE BOTH HER OLDER SISTERS were yet alive and were embarking on their separate careers in the Church — Princess Elizabeth to Herford, Louisa to Maubuisson — Sophia, conscious always of her good fortune in having secured a position of material comfort and safety in society, was relishing her early married life in Hanover. Even the jealousy and strife caused by Duke George William's unwanted attentions could not mar the contentment she enjoyed with Duke Ernst Augustus and their two small sons, George Louis, the elder, and Frederick Augustus, born October 2, 1661. Even better, her husband's prospects and income were substantially improved in December of that year when the old bishop of Osnabrück died and Ernst Augustus was named bishop in his place.

It might seem odd that a Lutheran duke would be nominated to replace a Catholic bishop, but Osnabrück was one of those territories, like Herford, that had come in for special treatment in the aftermath of the Thirty Years' War.* By the terms of the Peace of Westphalia, in an attempt at fairness, it had been agreed that Protestants and Catholics would alternate ministering to the flock of Osnabrück. Since the previous bishop had been Catholic, this meant that the Lutherans, who held the majority in the surrounding area,

---

* Osnabrück had been the town chosen to house the Swedish delegation during the Treaty of Westphalia negotiations.

would now have their turn. As the bishopric, eighty-five miles west of Hanover, fell within Duke George William's province, he decided to give it to his youngest brother, to help Ernst out with his growing family expenses. "Three days ago I arrived here...and I find myself in a very pretty house which charmed me when I first saw it," Sophia wrote to Karl Ludwig on September 29, 1662. She was referring to an estate in Iburg, ten miles south of Osnabrück, which was included as part of the extremely generous compensation package provided by the grateful parishioners to their new bishop. "Everything that strikes the sight is magnificent: plate, furniture, liveries, guards...All these things are trifles compared with the seventy thousand thalers the bishopric gave its Bishop on his arrival," she exulted.

The years Sophia spent at Iburg were among the happiest of her life. Finally removed from the attentions and constant presence of her husband's elder brother, she was wealthy enough to support a life of ease and even boasted a prestigious new title: "the Bishopess." Her duties, which involved attending church regularly, taking the lead in charitable giving, and visiting the sick and the poor, were light and certainly did not intrude greatly on her leisure time. "One cannot live more than once," she observed to Karl Ludwig in a letter of 1663. "Why vex one's soul, if one can eat, drink and sleep, sleep, drink and eat?...Tranquility of the spirit is lovely, since from it springs our bodily health...We play at nine-pins, breed young ducks, amuse ourselves with running at a ring or backgammon, talk every year of paying a visit to Italy; and in the meantime things go quite as well as is to be expected for a petty bishop, who is able to live in peace and, in case of war, can depend upon the help of his brothers."★

Sophia's easygoing, fundamentally optimistic temperament, so like her mother's, was not the only characteristic she had inherited from the Winter Queen. She was an avid letter writer (noted for

---

★ Ironically, Sophia's advancement to bishopess meant that all three sisters held positions of authority in a religious community at exactly the same time—but what a difference in their experience of church life!

dashing off pages and pages during church sermons, a commendable time-saver, no doubt) and used her voluminous correspondence not simply to keep in touch with relatives and friends but also to promote her family's political aims. In common with her sister Louisa, Sophia also had her mother's mischievous sense of humor, bestowing nicknames and employing her considerable wit. A courtier upon whom she had once played a prank noted dolefully that the bishopess "was much addicted to laughing at people to their faces, only her skill in raillery was such that they never found out." But the great trait she had received from the queen of Bohemia was her fortitude. "Ma tante [my aunt], courageous as a man, is not easily frightened," Liselotte reported later. "I saw her once, at Klagenberg, issue coolly out of a conflagration, saving herself in a nightgown from the flames which had nearly closed round her in her sleeping chamber, and she then was far advanced in pregnancy; but she only laughed, not being the least frightened. Another time I was with her out in a carriage to which young horses had been harnessed; they of course ran away with us, the coachman thrown off and was much hurt... There was great danger, but ma tante cared not a whit."

At first glance, Sophia's circumstances might seem idyllic compared to that of her two older sisters. But married life, particularly within her husband's family, presented its own challenges. She had barely been wed five years when Ernst Augustus, like his brothers, began openly to take mistresses. "The bonds of holy matrimony had not changed the Duke's gay nature," Sophia explained this development delicately in her memoirs. "He wearied of always possessing the same thing." Not only that, but he expected his wife to facilitate his and his brothers' infidelities. To this end, in 1664 he invited her to come with him to Italy, where he had a mistress waiting for him in Rome, so that she could respectably bring along two young, very attractive women as ladies-in-waiting to keep his brothers happy.

Sophia dutifully left her children at Heidelberg with Karl Ludwig and started out for Italy on April 24 with one of the ladies in tow (the other went to Holland, where Duke George William followed her) for what would turn out to be a year's absence. Although she enjoyed sightseeing, the bishopess was not quite so enamored of the charms of Italy as her husband. She had a long sojourn in Venice, which did not impress her ("The Duke asked me if I did not think the town beautiful, and I did not dare to say 'No,' though in reality it appeared to me extremely melancholy," she observed). When she went out in society, her husband, busy with his own pleasures, assigned her an escort to serve as his surrogate. ("As I should have been mortified to remain the only lady unattended by a cavalier in a place where it is the fashion to have one, the Duke chose for me the procurator Soranzo, a very unimportant person.") In Rome, where she met the pope and an attempt was made to convert her, her husband left her alone every evening to go "play basset" (an Italian game) with his mistress. "I should have been very dull but for the enjoyment of walking in exquisite gardens and the diversion of cards," she admitted. "It may be imagined how strange I, a German, felt in a country where nothing is thought of but love, and where a lady would consider herself disgraced were she without admirers. I had always learned to look on coquetry as a crime, but according to Italian morality it was esteemed as a virtue."* When she finally left Rome to begin the journey home, in the early spring of 1665, Ernst Augustus chivalrously escorted her to the gates of the city in the company of his paramour and then left her to travel back to Germany on her own, the mistress "returning alone in the carriage with my husband" to Rome, having arranged "a party to go to the country" to which Sophia had not been invited.

The bishop of Osnabrück would have done well to forgo this last taste of the delights of Italy in order to accompany his wife home on schedule. For on March 15, 1665, the eldest of the four brothers, the duke of Celle, died unexpectedly, and Duke John Frederick, the

---

* If Sophia, the youngest, had been brought up not to flirt, much less engage in love affairs, it is highly likely that this was the way *all* of the queen of Bohemia's daughters were raised—another strong argument against Louisa's having delivered fourteen illegitimate children while living at her mother's court at The Hague.

heavyset middle brother, who *had* come home from Italy in time to be at his older brother's deathbed, seized all of his property. Faced with this emergency, Ernst Augustus hurried to Hanover, where he found his brother George William (not the strongest personality) "in a state of utter consternation, the tears standing in his eyes," Sophia reported. "My husband not only reassured him with advice, but also raised troops to support his claim." Under the circumstances, Duke John Frederick, "reflecting that a civil war would utterly ruin the country," backed down and ceded the duchy of Celle, by far the largest and most profitable property in the inheritance, to George William, the eldest surviving brother, contenting himself with the second-best territory, the duchy of Hanover. Ernst Augustus remained bishop of Osnabrück but also received the county of Diepholz, thirty-five miles to the north, as a reward from George William for standing loyally by him in the conflict.

They patched it up that time, but thus began a period when all the carefully constructed legal contracts guaranteeing Sophia's rights and those of her children to inherit turned out to be so many sheets of parchment that could be rewritten or superseded altogether by new compacts made with other interested parties. Such are the vagaries of lines of succession: no matter how firm the legality of the claimant or how seemingly ironclad the agreement, life has a way of interfering.

No sooner had Ernst Augustus and Sophia resolved their difficulties with John Frederick than they were confronted with a new, subtler—and ultimately more dangerous—problem. Duke George William had fallen in love.

Her name was Eléonore d'Olbreuse, and she was the lady-in-waiting he had followed to Holland when she refused to go to Italy with Sophia. Eléonore came from an undistinguished family of French Huguenots, but what she lacked in birth she more than made up for in charm. "She was grave and dignified in manner," Sophia recalled when she first met her. "Her face was beautiful, her figure tall and commanding. She spoke little but expressed herself well."

Forty-one-year-old George William was utterly smitten with twenty-four-year-old Eléonore, but she was holding out for marriage, and this, of course, he had sworn never to do as part of the written contract by which his brother had taken his place as Sophia's bridegroom.

To help him out, Sophia and Ernst Augustus agreed to what was known as an "anti-contract of marriage," whereby George William gave Eléonore a monetary settlement and promised never to leave her or wed anyone else, basically recognizing her as his official mistress. "Hoping to touch the Duke, the lady began to weep, saying that, had she married a simple gentleman, she would at least have borne the title of Madame, and ended by entreating to be called Duchess of Celle," Sophia recalled. This, however, was out of the question, as neither by birth nor lawful marriage could Eléonore claim such a prestigious title. But Duke George William, used to creative thinking when it came to affairs of the heart, came up with the ingenious solution that she should be called Madame de Harburg (after the piece of property he had settled on her). This compromise was accepted, and the legalities were concluded in November 1665. "Though it will be said that I have dispensed with standing in a church before a priest, I can feel no regret, because I am the happiest of women...The Duke has plighted his troth to me before his whole family, who also signed the contract in which he binds himself to take no wife but me," Eléonore observed in a letter of March 14, 1666. The newly anti-married couple's joy was enhanced on September 15, 1666, by the birth of a daughter, whom they christened Sophie Dorothea out of respect and gratitude to Sophia, who had helped make this arrangement possible.

However, the next year appeared yet a new romantic entanglement that could not be dismissed so easily—the marriage of John Frederick (now duke of Hanover) to Edward and Anna de Gonzaga's daughter Bénédicte, on November 25, 1667. Bénédicte, as a descendant of the same family as Sophia herself, was of higher birth than her husband and *was* married to the duke of Hanover by a priest

Duke George William and his anti-wife, Eléonore

in a church. Since John Frederick was older than Ernst Augustus, if Bénédicte, his legitimate wife, had a son, that child would take priority over Sophia's offspring as heir to Duke George William's property, despite the existence of a previous contract.

Thus began the race for a son. Sophia already had three—the third, Maximilian, had been born on December 13, 1666, but children died frequently in the seventeenth century, so she kept going. On October 2, 1668, she had a daughter, Sophia Charlotte, known as Figuelotte, followed on October 9, 1669, by a fourth son, Karl Philipp. Bénédicte struck back in 1671 with a daughter. Sophia retaliated with her fifth boy, Christian Henreich, on September 29. In 1672 and 1673, two more daughters were born to Bénédicte. It was clearly only a matter of time before she produced a boy. For good measure, Sophia gave birth to her sixth son, Ernst Augustus, on September 17, 1674, and held her breath.

And then nature intervened definitively in the bishopess's favor. On December 18, 1679, the male-heir-producing contest ended abruptly when the overweight John Frederick succumbed at the age of fifty-four to the excesses of his lifestyle. ("He died as a true German should, glass in hand," Sophia noted by way of a eulogy.) As John Frederick had failed to produce a son, all of his property went to Ernst Augustus.

Sophia was suddenly duchess of Hanover.

AND SO SHE, ERNST Augustus, and their large brood moved back to the house that Sophia and her husband had first shared with George William as newlyweds. It was much too cramped for them now, and Ernst Augustus began at once to renovate the old castle into a much grander residence. They had also to make improvements to the town to accommodate a much larger court, as many of the members of John Frederick's government and household wished to stay on and serve the new duke of Hanover. It was in this way that Sophia made the acquaintance of Gottfried Wilhelm Leibniz, who had been in charge of John Frederick's library and literary correspondence, among other duties. She and Ernst Augustus kind of inherited him along with the books.

Like Descartes, Leibniz is a towering figure in mathematics and philosophy, and the similarities do not end there. Both men were essentially self-taught. True, Leibniz did not get to lie in bed all morning reading; he had to get up and attend extremely mediocre classes ("At school I...should, without doubt, have made the usually slow progress," he noted), but his father had been a professor of philosophy at the University of Leipzig, and Leibniz had gained access to his library. By his own account, while still a child, Leibniz was able to puzzle out the words from the engravings in a book of history by Livy, which he read and reread until he understood it in full. In this way, by the age of twelve, he was fluent in Latin and was well on his way to mastering Greek.

He entered the University of Leipsic intending to study history, which he loved, when (thanks to Princess Elizabeth, who had made it her mission in life to introduce her friend's books to Berlin and the surrounding communities) he came across Descartes's work and was immediately hooked. Although he would later have problems with many of Descartes's conclusions, it was by these books that Leibniz first came to the study of mathematics, a field to which he had never before been exposed. Overwhelmed by the power and beauty of the subject, just as Descartes had been, and with it the potential of logic to remake philosophical thought, he instantly switched his major. But being of a more practical bent than Descartes, he also attended lectures in jurisprudence, and at the age of twenty-one, he graduated with a doctorate in law.★

He would spend the next decade in Frankfort-on-the-Main and then Paris, supporting himself as a sort of journeyman lawyer and scholar. Again like Descartes, everywhere he went, he exchanged ideas and inventions with the most accomplished scholars of the period, who were in turn impressed by his brilliance. "Having experienced the good fortune, wherever I came, that persons of gentility wished to make my acquaintance and enjoy my society, I have had...not so much a deficiency as a super-abundance of distinguished friends," he reported. He visited London in 1673, met the chemist Robert Boyle, and was nominated to the Royal Society. He corresponded with Spinoza about lenses; made improvements to Pascal's adding machine that allowed the device to multiply, divide, and perform square-root functions; and invented the binary system, which three centuries later would allow for the development of the computer. In 1677, he shared a detailed explanation of his discovery of calculus in a letter to Isaac Newton (a favor the English scientist did not return), predating the publication of Newton's *Principia* by several years. "I suspect that what Newton wished to conceal respecting the method of drawing tangents, is not very different from these discoveries of my own," Leibniz would later observe.

★ He was so young that the University of Leipsic refused to grant him his degree even though he had sailed through all of the requirements. He went to the University of Altdorf in Nuremberg instead, and upon examining him, the masters immediately granted him a doctorate and offered him a teaching position.

He had wished to stay in Paris and attach himself to the Sun King's court, but Louis XIV failed to extend him an offer, so (again like Descartes) he had to look elsewhere. Duke John Frederick, who had heard of Leibniz when he first came out of school and who was looking to attract capable men into his service, had already asked him to come to Hanover twice over the years. In 1676, the duke made a third overture, and this time Leibniz, who had not the resources to stay on in France, accepted. Three years later John Frederick was dead and the new duke of Hanover took over as Leibniz's employer.

Although Ernst Augustus valued Leibniz's counsel, the duke was no intellectual; it was Sophia who impressed the philosopher. "Madam [Sophia]...is a great genius," Leibniz observed to a correspondent. "She loves rare and extraordinary thoughts in which there is something fine, curious and paradoxical." Sophia was equally delighted to have a friend of Leibniz's abilities at court. She engaged him in long philosophical discussions, encouraged and supported his many projects, and employed him to tutor her daughter Figuelotte. She was more than just a patron to Leibniz; both she and Figuelotte were active participants in the development of his philosophical arguments, as Princess Elizabeth had once been with Descartes. "Monsieur Leibniz must have a very high degree of intelligence to make him such an agreeable companion," Liselotte wrote in wonder from France after Sophia had praised the philosopher to her niece. "It is seldom that scholars are clean and do not smell bad, and that they have a sense of humor."*

One of the most important projects Sophia worked on with Leibniz was the plan to unify Catholics and Protestants based on

---

* To anticipate those critics who will inevitably claim that I have overstated Sophia's role as a philosopher in her own right, I point to the recent scholarship of Dr. Lloyd Strickland of the University of Wales. After collecting and translating all of the correspondence among Leibniz and Sophia and Figuelotte, Dr. Strickland concluded, "It does both [Sophia and Figuelotte] a disservice to suppose that their place in the history of philosophy can be secured only through the services they rendered to Leibniz. Likewise, it does both a disservice to depict...their interest in philosophy as a passive one, since there is clear evidence that both actively engaged in philosophical discussion proper, and had contributions to make to the philosophical debates of their day."

GODEFROI GUILLAUME
LEIBNITZ,
Né le 3 Juillet 1646 mort le 14 Novembre 1716

Leibniz

fundamental Christian principles to which all could agree. It was this progressive undertaking that led to the correspondence with Louisa and Madame de Brinon. "I do not concern myself...with those sectarian controversies which distinguish Luther or Calvin from the Pope," Leibniz explained to Sophia, who heartily concurred with these ideas. "I only want to speak at present of the essential truths of religion and piety, disfigured in an appalling manner by the sectarian spirit of those inclined to condemnation, which goes as far as to pervert the idea of God." But Sophia's interests were by no means limited to matters of the spirit. She also encouraged Leibniz's quest to construct a universal language based on mathematical principles that could be used to express abstract philosophical thought, and helped him research a massive genealogy of her husband's ancestors, a study in which Ernst Augustus was deeply interested.

But there was one project of her husband's of which Leibniz approved that Sophia actively opposed, and this was to mandate the law of primogeniture. It was Ernst Augustus's ambition to elevate the dignity of his line by convincing the emperor to expand the number of German electors from eight to nine and then award the prestigious ninth electorship to Hanover. To do this, it would be necessary to consolidate all of the family property into one hand in perpetuity, which in turn meant altering the rules of family inheritance. So, whereas formerly the duke of Hanover had divided up his property among his male heirs, Ernst Augustus now proposed to cut out all of his younger sons from his will and instead leave his entire estate to George Louis, who would then become elector after his father's death.

As laudable as such an ambition might appear, it was not perhaps the optimal arrangement for a man who had brought six sons into

Ernst Augustus

the world. Turmoil ensued. All five of George Louis's younger brothers, as they grew up and came of age, protested vociferously, and when they refused to sign the necessary papers, Ernst Augustus withdrew all monetary support and threw them out of the house. In retaliation, they plotted against him. "I cry about it all night long; for one child is as dear to me as another," Sophia wrote. "I am the mother of them all, and I grieve most for those who are unhappy."

But there was nothing she could do about it, as Sophia had long since lost all influence with her husband. Once they moved to Hanover, Ernst Augustus no longer had time to visit Italy as often as he had in the past, so he married his mistress to one of his underlings, the obliging Monsieur Platen, and installed her at his home court, which was so much more convenient. Madame Platen had a nicer château than Sophia, more expensive jewels, and flashier gowns. She entertained lavishly, maintained spies among the household servants to keep her informed, and exercised vigilance in keeping Ernst Augustus's attentions from wandering. Sophia was afforded the pretense of respect as the legitimate duchess, but it was Madame Platen's court. Although Sophia cannot have liked this situation, she did not complain but simply spent more and more time alone at her private estate of Herrenhausen, a beautiful old château just outside Hanover, where she designed a series of magnificent gardens.

Alas, having to deal with her husband's overweening mistress was by no means the worst of Sophia's problems. That distinction was reserved for Duke George William's anti-married companion, Eléonore d'Olbreuse.

IN THE YEARS FOLLOWING her contractual agreement with George William, Eléonore too had tried—and failed—to produce a son. She did give birth to several daughters but they all died in infancy except her firstborn, Sophie Dorothea. Thus, Sophie Dorothea, a pretty little girl, grew up the only child of two doting parents.

Although in the beginning Eléonore had accepted the compromise title of Madame de Harburg, over the years she had begun to resent it, and it soon became the fondest desire of her heart that she and her daughter be legitimized. She knew that she could coax the aging Duke George William, who adored her and had remained true to her, to support her in this ambition; it was simply a matter of finding the right strategy.

And then Louis XIV embarked on his military campaign to annex large portions of Germany and the Netherlands. There was a rush to claim allies, and Eléonore realized that the Sun King had provided exactly the ammunition she needed. George William was a loyal supporter of the emperor; certainly the troops and money he had raised in defense of imperial property was worth the small favor of a decree of legitimacy. The emperor—it was a new one by this time, Leopold, who knew nothing about the complicated inheritance arrangements between Ernst Augustus and his elder brother—presented with this remarkably easy and inexpensive way to reward a valued ally, issued the desired edict, allowing George William to "enter into Christian matrimony with the high-born lady Eléonore de Harburg." Eléonore now styled herself duchess of Celle, which put her on the same footing as her sister-in-law.

Sophia's ire when she discovered she had been outmaneuvered in this way was very great. "The Duke of Celle would no longer listen to reason, as he was completely in the leading-strings of his wife... who daily embittered him more and more against us," she reported grimly in her memoirs. "When this fine marriage between the Duke of Celle and Madame de Harburg became known, those who had formerly esteemed the Duke refused to believe it," she fumed. "The Duchess of Orléans [Liselotte] wrote that she could not refrain from telling me that Madame de Harburg had written to tell friends in France that she was married to the Duke of Celle and hoped soon to present him with an heir. The Duchess of Orléans added that, though she knew this to be untrue, still she thought it only right to inform me, so that I might put a stop to reports so damaging to the Duke of Celle; for if this prince had ever meditated committing such a piece of folly, she was sure he would give up the idea could he hear the derision which it excited at the French Court." But of course Sophia could not shut down these rumors, as they were true. She had now to worry not only that Eléonore would produce a son who would disrupt the long-standing inheritance arrangements between Ernst Augustus and his elder brother but also that her niece Sophie Dorothea, who had been legitimatized by her parents' marriage, would wed someone who would claim the duke of Celle's property (promised to Sophia's family after his death) in her name.

And all this at a time when the duchess of Hanover was doing her best to get her own children prosperously settled in life. Toward that end, she sent her eldest son, twenty-year-old George Louis, to England in December of 1680 as a possible suitor to Princess Anne, the duke of York's younger daughter. Rupert, who was still alive, acted as sponsor to his nephew and took it upon himself to arrange the match. Consequently, Sophia's son was warmly received at court by Charles II. "He remembered you very well... The next day I saw the princess of York, and I saluted her by kissing her, with the consent of the King," George Louis dutifully if somewhat unenthusiastically reported home to his mother in a letter of January 10, 1681. But the reluctant wooer had arrived just as a Catholic plot was uncovered, and he took fright at his hosts' methods of resolving political crises. "They cut off the head of Lord Stafford yesterday, and made no more ado about it than if they had chipped off the head of a pullet," George Louis continued, and left the kingdom as soon as he could.*

Negotiations for the match nonetheless persisted in a desultory fashion into the next year, when they were abruptly superseded by a new and pernicious threat. On the morning of September 14, 1682, a spy at the court of the duke of Celle who was loyal to Madame Platen, Ernst Augustus's mistress, smuggled through a message that Eléonore had secretly arranged to wed Sophie Dorothea to the son of the neighboring duke of Wolfenbüttel and that

---

* This perhaps gives a sense of why Rupert decided to keep his marriage to a Catholic woman secret.

the engagement was to be made public the very next day on the occasion of Sophie Dorothea's sixteenth-birthday feast.

Madame Platen made haste to communicate this clandestine intelligence to Ernst Augustus, who at once saw the danger to his own prospects. The duke of Wolfenbüttel, a distant relation, had made it clear that he did not want his cousin Ernst Augustus's house promoted to the powerful position of elector, and so he had allied himself with Eléonore, who was also in competition with her brother- and sister-in-law. This engagement was the result. Ernst Augustus knew how fond George William was of his only child. Eléonore would easily convince him to go back on his obligations to his younger brother in order to provide Sophie Dorothea with a substantial dowry of lands and income. Hanover's loss would become Wolfenbüttel's gain.

There was only one sure way to keep that property in the family, and that was to wed George Louis to Sophie Dorothea. And there was only one person Ernst Augustus knew who was clever and capable enough to achieve that goal on advantageous terms (not to mention such short notice)—his wife. He called Sophia in and told her to make the match.

This was a bitter pill for the duchess of Hanover to swallow. No imperial decree was ever going to convince Sophia that her future daughter-in-law had not been born out of wedlock, that she was being asked not only to condone but actually to negotiate the marriage of her firstborn son with the child of a deceitful woman of vastly inferior breeding and rank, a mésalliance that would expose the entire family to the amused disdain of friends and enemies alike. If it had been up to Sophia, it is highly likely she would have let the engagement with Wolfenbüttel stand, property or no property.

But it was not up to Sophia. Ernst Augustus was in charge and she was a loyal wife, so she ordered her carriage at once. The roads were in such terrible condition from a recent rainstorm that she had to drive all night to get to Celle before the birthday celebrations began. She made it to the ducal palace so early in the morning that George William was still in his dressing gown. The servant who opened the door tried to get her to wait until the household had arisen, but she brushed by him on the grounds that this was a casual family visit and surprised the duke in his bedroom. His wife, who was still asleep in the adjoining room, heard her sister-in-law's voice and got up hurriedly to investigate. Eléonore saw at once that something was up, but she couldn't formally receive the duchess of Hanover without dressing, an exercise that took considerable time and effort in the seventeenth century, so she had to be content with listening through the open door. Aware of this, to prevent his French wife from interfering, Sophia rifled through the many tongues in which she was fluent and chose to converse with George William in Dutch, a language that she knew Eléonore had failed to acquire. Then she offered to marry her eldest son to Sophie Dorothea.

George William was delighted. A match with George Louis was superior on every level to one with the son of the duke of Wolfen-büttel. Sophie Dorothea would have a more prestigious title if Hanover became an electorate, and whatever dowry he gave her would stay in the family. Best of all, there would be no unpleasantness between himself and his younger brother, whom he genuinely loved and was grateful to for his many years of support. Mindful of the extent of the favor being offered to his daughter, he settled a whopping annual income of 100,000 thalers on her, which sum in its entirety was to be controlled by Ernst Augustus and George Louis, a telling indication of how great was the disparity in rank between bride and groom.

It was all over before Eléonore had had time to have her hair pinned in place. She sobbed in protest, as did her daughter, who had awakened that morning expecting to announce her engagement to one man, only to be told she was marrying her first cousin, whom she had been taught by her mother to resent.* But George William, buttressed by Sophia, was adamant for once, and when the duke of Wolfenbüttel and his son arrived later that morning, they found a

---

* Catholics had to apply for a special dispensation from the pope in order to marry a first cousin, as the union fell within proscribed boundaries. There was, however, no similar restriction for Protestants.

sullen-faced Sophie Dorothea sitting down to her celebratory birthday breakfast in the company of her family. Informed of the change of bridegroom, the rejected suitor and his parent instantly turned around and went back to Wolfenbüttel without even bothering to stay to eat.

George Louis and Sophie Dorothea were married two months later, on November 21, 1682. The groom was apparently no more enchanted with his bride than she was with him, but even at twenty-two, George Louis was a practical man. In a letter to Liselotte, Sophia wrote that her son "does not care much for the match itself, but one hundred thousand thalers a year have tempted him as they would have tempted anybody else." On this happy note, Sophie Dorothea moved to Hanover to begin her wedded life.

Sophie Dorothea

★   ★   ★

DESPITE THE RELUCTANCE OF both of its principals, the marriage, in the beginning, at least, went pretty well (probably because George Louis, who was in charge of Hanover's military operations, was often away soldiering). Everyone—Sophia included—treated Sophie Dorothea with kindness. Ernst Augustus made a special effort to look after his daughter-in-law, even inviting her to accompany him on one of his holidays to Italy, which he could now afford again as a result of her generous dowry. Sophie Dorothea's position at court was made even more secure the following year on October 30, 1683, when she gave birth to a son, whom the couple named (what else) George.

With her eldest son's future settled, Sophia was able to turn her attention to a matter in which she was deeply, passionately interested: choosing the appropriate husband for her daughter, Figuelotte. As the one girl among her mother's many boys, Figuelotte was very close to Sophia, and above all the duchess of Hanover had ambitions to see her only daughter married well—very well. She even considered a nuptial alliance with the French royal family, emulating her niece the duchess of Orléans. Except Sophia set her sights even higher, suggesting fifteen-year-old Figuelotte as a suitable match for forty-five-year-old Louis XIV after the death of his first wife. (This was *before* the Sun King invaded the Palatinate and revoked the Edict of Nantes.★) But if the episode with Eléonore and Sophie Dorothea had taught the duchess of Hanover anything, it was that it behooved her to arrange an honorable and advantageous

---

★ "'This is a fair and beautiful princess, worthy of the highest destiny. May I ask what religion she has been brought up in?' a courtier who saw Figuelotte in 1679 when she was eleven years old asked. 'She has none at present,' Sophia answered coolly. 'When we know what prince will be her husband, she will be instructed in his religion.'" Although this is likely an example of the duchess of Hanover's making fun with a straight face—her daughter was brought up Protestant—there is an element of truth in it, as (again, before Louis XIV's persecution of the Huguenots) she would almost certainly have instructed Figuelotte to convert to Catholicism in order to marry Louis XIV after the death of his first wife.

match for her daughter quickly, before something worse could be forced on her.

So she did not insist on royalty but instead arranged a marriage with the elector of Brandenburg's eldest son (also named Frederick, like his father). Sixteen-year-old Figuelotte and twenty-seven-year-old Frederick were married in October of 1684 in a splendid ceremony in the gardens at Sophia's estate at Herrenhausen. This union was not without political calculation—the elector of Brandenburg (still Frederick William, Louisa's old beau) opposed expanding the number of imperial electors to include Hanover; it was hoped that his son's marriage would change his mind. (Alas, it did not.) But Sophia did have the satisfaction of seeing Figuelotte well established as a future electress in Berlin, which was not so far away that she and her daughter weren't able to visit each other once or twice a year.

Unfortunately, no sooner was Figuelotte's marriage successfully launched than George Louis's began to disintegrate. Although Sophie Dorothea gave birth on March 16, 1687, to a daughter,* by that time she and her husband were barely on speaking terms. George Louis found Sophie Dorothea carping and difficult, and instead took a shy, quiet, good-natured nineteen-year-old saddled with the impressively extravagant name of Ermengarde Melusine von Schulenburg as his official mistress. He then openly set her up in her own apartments in Hanover and proceeded to ignore his wife.

This was precisely the position that Sophia was in with Ernst Augustus and Madame Platen (now Countess Platen, her tactful husband having been promoted in the duke of Hanover's service). But Sophia, who had had the experience of watching Charlotte, Karl Ludwig's wife, lose everything—her home, her position, her children—simply ignored her rival and devoted her time to her many political and philosophical projects, her massive international correspondence, and her dealings with ambassadors and other visiting dignitaries. Sophie Dorothea did not have her mother-in-law's

---

* Also named Sophia Dorothea; no wonder no one understands this period.

intellectual resources or talents. Eléonore had not provided her daughter with the sort of rigorous education that Sophia had insisted on for Figuelotte. As a result, Sophie Dorothea did not care for books and had few interests outside of jewels and clothing. Her life was appallingly dull. "Here is my day," she once wrote in a letter from Hanover. "I played cards...all afternoon. I rested a long time on my bed. I went for a walk with my women. I supped and I am going to bed." Sophie Dorothea did not have the example of a mistress in her father's life because her mother had *been* the mistress, and by the time the duke of Celle married, he was already in late middle age and was content to be monogamous. Consequently, Sophie Dorothea was so outraged and upset with George Louis that she caused scenes and made herself ill. Even Sophia felt sorry for her and confronted her son, remonstrating with him to respect his wife and pay more attention to her, but her words had little effect.

This strained atmosphere between Sophie Dorothea and George Louis, a minor annoyance at most for all but the two principals, was completely overshadowed the following year by two seminal events that jolted the court. The first was the death, in April 1688, of Frederick William, elector of Brandenburg, which promoted Figuelotte and her husband to power in Berlin and caused a change of policy much more favorable to Hanover. The second was the overthrow in December of James II, the Catholic king of England, by his Protestant son-in-law, William of Orange.

IT WAS AGAIN LOUIS XIV—or, rather, his aggressive foreign policy and persecution of the Huguenots—that was the catalyst for this unlikely coup. In the years following the Sun King's first invasion of the Netherlands, William, prince of Orange (the baby once pictured as Erichthonius in the painting by Louise Hollandine, who had been brought up by his grandmother Amelia de Solms after Amelia had successfully vanquished William's mother, Mary) had emerged as Louis's foremost adversary. A stalwart warrior possessed of an almost legendary courage, William was absolutely determined to save Holland from French domination. When the Dutch had been forced to flood their own cities as a last resort against invasion, it was suggested to William that he instead sue for peace. "No," he replied firmly. "I mean to die in the last ditch." When Charles II had arranged, over his younger brother's objections, to marry James's eldest daughter, Mary, to William in 1677, Louis XIV protested strongly. "You have given your daughter to my mortal enemy," he accused James.

Then, in 1685, Charles II died without siring a legitimate heir and was succeeded by James, who had managed to overturn the Test Act, originally passed to ensure the primacy of the Anglican religion. Suddenly, England had an openly Catholic king who was far more tolerant of religious differences than the majority of his subjects. "It is a melancholy prospect that all we of the Church of England have," James's younger daughter Anne, who had married the brother of the king of Denmark and remained in London, lamented to her sister, Mary, who lived at The Hague with her husband, William. "All sectaries may now do as they please. Everyone has the free exercise of their religion on purpose, no doubt to ruin us," she sighed. It was suspected that James, who having been brought up at his mother's court in St. Germain was very close to the French, would ally with Louis XIV and impose Catholicism on the kingdom. These fears intensified to a critical point on June 10, 1688, when James's second wife gave birth to a son and heir,★ who took precedence over James's two reliably Anglican daughters, and Parliament realized that it might have to deal with not just one Catholic king, but two.

What happened next (fittingly for the realm that produced William Shakespeare) was a plotline straight out of *King Lear*. James's two daughters, jealous of their father's new son, participated in a conspiracy to dethrone their parent. William was surreptitiously invited by the Anglican majority to take over the English government. He accepted and set about recruiting men and arms for an invasion. James of course noticed the buildup but Mary assured him

---

★ Also named James, for maximum confusion.

that the force was being raised for use in the Netherlands. Anne did her part by promoting rumors questioning the legitimacy of her half brother. James, a fond parent who had always treated his daughters with love and generosity, never doubted their loyalty. It was only when William's fleet of fifty-two warships carrying an invasion force of some 15,000 men landed on the southwest shore of England on November 4, 1688, and Anne and her husband left London to meet them that the king learned the truth. "God help me! My own children have forsaken me in my distress," James cried out when he discovered the treachery. He fled to France with his wife and small son, only just barely eluding the Dutch soldiers sent to apprehend and imprison him. By Christmas, William and Mary were ensconced in London and, in a unique power-sharing arrangement, were crowned together at Westminster on April 1, 1689.

Sophia of course had been good friends with William's mother, Mary, and had known William as a child. She had even brought Liselotte to play with him when she and her niece went to visit the queen of Bohemia at The Hague. But the duchess of Hanover had divided loyalties. Sophia also knew James and had heard the whole story of Mary's and Anne's betrayal from Liselotte, who met the deposed English king and his family in France. Both Sophia and Liselotte were steadfast in their belief that James's little son was legitimate and that his daughters had behaved badly. William, who was in the process of arranging a grand European military confederacy against Louis XIV that included Holland, England, the empire, Spain, and Brandenburg, worried that Ernst Augustus might be influenced by his wife to side with France. He sent a special ambassador to the court of Hanover to try to convince the duke to join his alliance and to pass along any information the envoy thought relevant.

The ambassador was very impressed with his hosts. "This court is as splendid as any in Germany; genius and civility reign here," he raved in his first report dated July 26, 1689. "The Duchess Sophia is a woman of incomparable spirit, kindness, cultivation, and charm." But it didn't take the English envoy long to ascertain that the French were doing

all they could to keep Ernst Augustus and George William from joining the coalition against Louis XIV. "To show us he doth not want
money, he [Ernst Augustus] bought a jewel of forty thousand crowns
from a Jew of Amsterdam, or else it was a present, for by that channel
the French money comes," the ambassador observed sagely.

William knew what had to be done to persuade Ernst Augustus
to engage militarily against France. He threw his support behind the
duke's campaign to have Hanover raised to an electorate. On the
strength of his promise, the duchies of Hanover and Celle joined in
the alliance led by England. It took a little time, but the emperor,
who relied strongly on William's troops and expertise in the field
(and who no longer had to worry about opposition from the elector
of Brandenburg), allowed himself to be convinced, although he
exacted a stiff price. Ernst Augustus and George William together
had to pay 500,000 thalers a year and supply 9,000 soldiers to the
imperial armies. But it was worth it to the duke of Hanover, who
rushed to Berlin to receive the messenger bearing the imperial
decree. On December 20, 1692, the English ambassador was able to
report with relief that "a courier is come hither with the welcome
news that the electoral bonnet [symbol of the office, rather like a
cardinal's hat] was given on the 9th." Sophia, like her daughter, was
now an electress, the highest-ranking title in Germany.

It was all going so well. And then a handsome young cavalry
officer rode into town.

HIS NAME WAS PHILIP Christoph von Königsmarck. He was a Swedish count of good family, wealthy in his own right, with property
in Sweden and an estate in Hamburg. He had been a friend of
Sophia's fourth son, Karl Philipp, who much to his mother's distress
had fallen in battle; for this reason Königsmarck was immediately
accepted in Hanover and made a colonel in the guard. Engaging,
well-built, brave, and an excellent dancer, the Swedish count quickly
became a favorite at court. Countess Platen was so impressed that
she thought to marry him to her daughter.

But Königsmarck had eyes only for Sophie Dorothea, and she for him. Theirs was a love story right out of Tolstoy. She, a young and beautiful woman, mother of two children, unhappily married to a man indifferent to her charms; he, the gallant officer used to seducing women who threw himself at her feet. It was possible in the seventeenth century for a married woman to carry on a discreet affair and get away with it, but theirs was not the sort of passion that could be kept hidden for long. Like Anna Karenina and Count Vronsky, each had been hit by a thunderbolt. He went into debt and turned down wealthy matches and promotions just to be near her; she risked everything to be alone with him.

When they could not be together, which was frequently the case, they wrote almost daily, pages of love letters, seeking solace in each other's words. One of her ladies-in-waiting and one of his sisters

Königsmarck

acted as go-betweens for this illicit correspondence. They took the precaution of writing in cipher and, feeling themselves safe from discovery, poured out their hearts. "I am in the depths of despair at finding so little opportunity of speaking to you," he wrote. "I dare not even admire the eyes that give me life. For pity's sake let me see you alone...Oh! How dearly it costs me to love you!" The letters left little doubt that the affair had been consummated. "Why do not the hours shut up into moments? What would I not give for twelve o'clock to strike?" he yearned. "I shall embrace tonight the loveliest of women. I shall kiss her charming mouth. I shall worship her eyes, those eyes that enslave me...I shall hold in my arms the most beautiful body in the world." After three years of this, he urged Sophie Dorothea to leave George Louis and run away with him.

But this Sophie Dorothea did not feel they could do without money, and Königsmarck was seriously in debt, having neglected his property and career to stay by her side. As her husband controlled all of her finances, she turned instead to her father, who had always been so generous with her, and (without, of course, telling him the real reason for her request) asked him to settle an independent income or property on her. Unfortunately, George William, who was already providing 100,000 thalers a year *plus* helping to pay for the new electorate, was strapped for cash. Sophie Dorothea, used to having her way, vented her anger and frustration with her father in her letters to her lover. For his part, Königsmarck attributed the difficulties they had meeting to Countess Platen, who still considered him a fine match for her daughter. "My greatest grudge is against La Platen, and on her I will avenge myself, for to her I attribute all my misfortunes," he fumed. He turned down the countess's daughter with disdain, thereby making an enemy of the most powerful woman at court, not perhaps the ideal strategy for a man carrying on a clandestine affair with the reigning prince's son's wife, a treasonable offense.

Of course they were watched; of course people knew. Sophie

Dorothea herself confided in Figuelotte, who in turn must have told her mother, as Sophia made it a point to bring up Königsmarck whenever she was with her daughter-in-law. Possibly she was trying to get Sophie Dorothea to confess, or was trying to find a way to determine how far the affair had gone. "The Electress talks about you every time I walk out with her... I know not whether she does it through friendship for you or because she thinks it pleases me; in either case it is the same," Sophie Dorothea informed her lover innocently. "She praises you so highly that were she younger I should be jealous." The count's friends were far more blunt in their warnings. "Marshal Podevils was the first to tell me to beware of my conduct, because he knew on good authority that I was watched," Königsmarck admitted. "Prince Ernest [Sophia's youngest son] has told me the same thing; and he is not quite as guarded as the other, for he admitted that the conversations I had from time to time with you might draw upon me very unpleasant and serious consequences... Nothing has touched me to the quick so much as to find that our affair is in everyone's mouth," he concluded glumly.

But they couldn't stop, and in his frustration, Königsmarck, while visiting Dresden in May 1694, much to the amusement of the court of Saxony, reputedly made several highly indiscreet remarks, such as that the Countess Platen "bathed in milk and then gave it away as a dole to the poor"; he also commented on the greed and general unattractiveness of George Louis's mistress, Ermengarde. These cutting observations unfortunately found their way back to Hanover, where they made Countess Platen furious and Ermengarde cry. George Louis was so incensed that he had a violent altercation with his wife and had to be pulled off her by servants. Sophie Dorothea in turn demanded a divorce and flew to Celle. Her parents, who alone seem to have been ignorant of the affair, sent her back to her husband at the end of June, but by that time she had arranged to have Königsmarck meet her in Hanover so they could run away together, Sophie Dorothea not having the courage to leave on her own.

It was a fatal mistake. Both Sophia and George Louis were away, Ernst Augustus was sick in bed, and Countess Platen was in charge and primed for payback. A rendezvous was set for Sunday, July 1; the couple intended to finalize their plans and leave by separate routes the next morning. As soon as night had fallen, Königsmarck, disguised in old clothes and a brown cloak, slipped out of his apartments and made his way to the royal palace. He whistled outside Sophie Dorothea's windows and was let in by the trusted lady-in-waiting. They had clearly gotten away with this many times before, but on this occasion the Countess Platen's spies were on the lookout and informed their mistress. She in turn went to Ernst Augustus and broke the news that his daughter-in-law was at that very moment committing treason with the Swedish count he had so generously taken into his service.

The elector was too ill to confront the pair directly so he instead authorized his mistress to give the order to have Königsmarck arrested. The countess sent a company of four guardsmen armed with spears and axes and instructed them to wait outside Sophie Dorothea's rooms all night if necessary until her lover emerged, to ensure that he did not get away. There is no eyewitness account of what occurred next, but circumstances would indicate that the guardsmen were a little overzealous in the performance of their duty. It's likely that Königsmarck, an experienced warrior, put up a good fight and that in the struggle his captors went ahead and killed him, which definitely counts as one way of making sure that he did not escape. In any event, Königsmarck disappeared that evening and was never seen again.

That the murder had not been premeditated may be inferred by the utter ineptitude of the subsequent cover-up. Königsmarck's absence was noted fairly quickly, and the sister who had passed letters back and forth between the lovers at once suspected foul play. Ernst Augustus was at first assiduous in avoiding any mention of Königsmarck. "I have been told his sister raves like Cassandra, and will know what is become of her brother; but at Hanover they answer, like Cain, that they are not her brother's keeper," an official in Saxony snickered. When just ignoring the problem proved unsuccessful, Ernst Augustus then let it be known that he had had the Swedish count's servants interrogated and they had volunteered the information that their master "had often gone away at night without leaving any message, and remained away for days at a time, and so there was no ground for instituting inquiries."

But what the court did do within days of the episode was search Königsmarck's rooms and there find a trove of letters in Sophie Dorothea's handwriting. The cipher she employed seems to have been of small protection, as it was broken quickly and copies of the decrypted correspondence distributed to Ernst Augustus, Sophia, George Louis, and her parents, the duke and duchess of Celle. At once, the focus was off the missing count and on the great crime of Sophie Dorothea's infidelity. "They would never have believed at Celle that she was so guilty had not her letters been produced," Leibniz reported solemnly.

All this time, Sophie Dorothea was frantic—not for herself but for her lover. He had left her rooms that fateful night and she had had no word after that as to his subsequent whereabouts. She sent a note over to his rooms the next morning when she did not hear from him as planned, but it was never acknowledged. Instead, she had been confined to her rooms by order of the elector and her children were not brought to visit her as was customary. She must have known her affair had been discovered—the complicit lady-in-waiting was soon arrested—but the court maintained its determined silence on Königsmarck's disappearance both privately and publicly. It would be months before she came to understand that he was dead.

By that time she had been charged with desertion and on December 28, 1694, was sentenced to house arrest for the remainder of her life. She would never again see her children or her father, who, stunned at the harsh words she had for him in her letters, severed all ties with her. She was confined at a castle in the lonely village of

Ahlden, about twenty miles north of Hanover. Over time, her heartbroken mother was permitted to visit. Other than that she was allowed outside only under escort and even then only to go to the local church or for a six-mile carriage ride to a bridge to the west that marked the boundaries of her small world. She spent the next thirty-two years in captivity, until finally released by death. It was observed that she sometimes wore her diamonds when she took her drive.

Thus was the crime of murder successfully shielded from prosecution by the public scandal of a princess's infidelity. Months later, Ernst Augustus felt confident enough to issue the ingeniously disingenuous explanation through an envoy that, "as to the Question whether he [Königsmarck] was alive or dead no positive answer could be given, since after the best enquiry that could be made they were able to make no true discovery, which left a very strong suspicion that he is rather dead than living."

21

The Triumph of the Winter Queen

SOPHIA, HAVING BEEN ABSENT FROM Hanover at the time of the murder, was not implicated in the crime, nor should she have been. Although she had no love for her daughter-in-law and wished she had not been required to marry Sophie Dorothea to her son, an international disgrace of that magnitude, irresistibly picked up and repeated as prurient gossip by courts all over Europe, was the last thing the electress would have wanted. Sophia had had enough experience with scandal growing up at the Winter Queen's court at The Hague to understand that the stain of disrepute was not easily washed away and could tarnish the lives of even those innocent of any wrongdoing. More to the point, it could interfere with her family's political advancement, and in this area the electress harbored large ambitions. Specifically, she wished her children to ascend to royalty—not by going to war for a crown, as her parents had, but through astute negotiation. And she had already targeted the agent by whom she would achieve her goals: William, prince of Orange and king of England, the man responsible for getting Ernst Augustus his electorate.

At the time of William and Mary's ascension to the English throne, Parliament, concerned about the legality of deposing its former king in so rude a fashion and seeking to prevent James II or his young son from ever returning to rule, passed an act of succession prohibiting anyone who was not a Protestant from gaining the monarchy. Although Sophia had sympathy for James II and his son and believed the boy to be the legitimate heir to the throne, this law changed the qualifications by which the crown would be awarded in the future. It didn't take the electress of Hanover long to realize that if all the Catholic members of the extended Stuart family were to be precluded from the succession, she and her progeny had suddenly vaulted to the head of the line. So at the same time that Ernst Augustus was negotiating with William for his electorate, she had petitioned to have her family mentioned specifically as heirs to the throne, after any children William and Mary or Mary's younger sister, Anne, might have, of course. It was such a long shot anyway— Anne already had a son and kept getting pregnant year after year, although so far none of these other children had survived—that William, keen to keep Hanover in the alliance, promised he would see to it.

But William was a man who made many promises, none of which he let get in the way of his political self-interest. His principal goal, even as king of England, was to protect Holland from further French incursion, and on September 1, 1695, the year following the Königsmarck scandal, William had scored a huge victory against France by facing down the entire enemy army and retaking the city of Namur. Suddenly Louis XIV, his kingdom financially and spiritually exhausted from decades of war, was willing to treat for peace.

William, who was now in a bargaining position with France that would have been unthinkable before this key battle, agreed to secret negotiations. Together they settled that Louis XIV would keep southern Flanders and Hainaut but would retreat from French positions farther north. Orange and Maastricht, which had been occupied, were returned to the Dutch. On the imperial side, the French kept Franche-Comté and Freiburg, but everything else went back to the way it had been at the time of the Peace of Westphalia.

This was a good deal for William. He would stop the war, which was bankrupting England and starting to cause protests to his rule; save lives; and maintain a buffer zone between Holland and France. Louis XIV also agreed to recognize William as king of England, something he had refused to do in the past, and stop trying to unseat him, but only on the condition that James II's young son, a Catholic, be recognized as heir to the English throne after William's death. William not only agreed to this stipulation, he pledged to repeal the act of succession. So much for his promise to Sophia.

It is unclear whether England would have accepted this version of the treaty once all the terms were made public, but luckily William did not have to defend it. Unbelievably, James II, sitting in useless exile in France, *rejected it* on the grounds that his son could not be king while he, his father, was still alive. Faced with this act of political suicide — for by this time Louis XIV understood that, although England might be willing to consider the son's rights to the throne, they would never allow James II to return — the Sun King shook his head and signed a peace treaty with England on September 10, 1697, that made no mention of the succession. The act prohibiting a Catholic sovereign from ruling England remained in place.

Since William's negotiations had been conducted in secret, it's unclear whether Sophia ever knew that he had gone back on his word. She might have suspected it, especially when Parliament did not take up the question of her rights to the succession even after the peace treaty was signed. But by then she was probably not paying that much attention to English affairs, as events at home were drawing to a critical point. Ernst Augustus was dying.

He had been very ill for several years, during which time Sophia had fully recovered her place at court. It turned out that the elector much preferred his wife to his mistress when it came to round-the-clock nursing, and so Countess Platen had finally been unseated.

When Ernst Augustus at last died, on January 24, 1698, at the age of sixty-eight, Sophia took it as something of a blessing that at least he did not have to endure more pain. By right of primogeniture, thirty-seven-year-old George Louis got all of his father's property and took over as elector of Hanover.

Her husband's death freed Sophia to put in motion a plan she had evidently been contemplating for some time. It was only a matter of waiting for the right opportunity. That moment came two years later when uncertainty over the future sovereign of Spain and with it the growing possibility of renewed hostilities between the empire and France gripped Europe.

By the summer of 1700, it was clear that the Spanish king was very ill. As he had been unable to father children, this meant that when he died, which was daily expected, his property would have to go to a cousin, and therein lay the problem. Would the emperor's son, a Habsburg, inherit, as tradition dictated? Or would Louis XIV claim the throne for his grandson the duke of Anjou in the name of his dead queen, who had been the sister of the ailing Spanish monarch? The question was vital because more than just the kingdom of Spain was involved—there was also the issue of the sovereignty of Naples, Sicily, Tuscany, Milan, and the Netherlands, as these regions were all included in the Spanish inheritance. It was this last territory that touched William. He had worked so hard to create a buffer zone around Holland; would the French now legally inherit the very property he had just forced them to evacuate? He tried to work out another secret deal with Louis XIV to split the Spanish territories between the empire and France, with the French taking the Italian properties and the emperor's son getting Spain (leaving the Netherlands as a separate independent entity), but this fell through.

And then, on July 29, 1700, Princess Anne's only surviving child, the duke of Gloucester, fell ill and died just days after his eleventh birthday. At once, the prospect that James II's Catholic son, who had been befriended by Louis XIV, would claim the throne after William's death loomed again as a very real possibility. Suddenly, it was not only the Spanish inheritance but also the English line of succession that was threatened by France.

Sophia, carefully monitoring events from Germany, saw her chance and moved swiftly. Pretending that her daughter needed to take the waters for her health, she and Figuelotte traveled to Brussels in August and then on the way back in September went north and met secretly with William, who was staying at his summer palace at Loo, about ninety miles east of Amsterdam. There is no record of their conversation but it is clear what they discussed. Seventy-year-old Sophia and thirty-two-year-old Figuelotte were arranging an alliance to help support William through the coming struggle. Their price: that William would use his influence with the emperor to have Figuelotte and her husband, the elector of Brandenburg, promoted to sovereignty and that Sophia's family would be legally acknowledged as heirs to the English throne. There were no ambassadors or advisers involved; just William and two highly educated women negotiating a shift in power that would ultimately change the face of Europe.

They had gotten to him just in time. William went back to England in October, after which events escalated with frightening rapidity. On November 1, 1700, the king of Spain died and it was revealed that he had been convinced by the pope to change his will at the last moment and leave everything to Louis XIV's grandson, the duke of Anjou. The emperor contested the inheritance and the Dutch immediately rejected the French claims and instead recognized the imperial candidate as king of Spain. The rush for allies was on again, and within two months the emperor had created the kingdom of Prussia out of the old electorate of Brandenburg. Figuelotte's husband was crowned Frederick I on January 18, 1701. Sophia's daughter was now queen of Prussia. In February, Louis XIV broke the peace and attacked Holland.

And on February 6, 1701, with his beloved homeland once again at risk, William delivered a persuasive speech to Parliament to ensure that the English line of succession remained Protestant. On June 22, 1701, a law known as the Act of Settlement was approved that read: "Be it enacted and declared by the King's most excellent Majesty, by and with the advice and consent of the Lords Spirituall and Temporall, and Commons, in this present Parliament assembled, and by the authority of the same, That the most excellent Princess Sophia, Electress and Duchess Dowager of Hannover, daughter of the most excellent Princess Elizabeth, late Queen of Bohemia, daughter of our late Sovereign Lord King James the First, of happy memory, be and is hereby declared to be the next in succession in the Protestant line to the Imperiall Crown and Dignity of the said Realms of England...and Ireland, with the Dominions and territories thereunto belonging, after his Majesty and the Princess Ann...and in default of issue of the said Princess Ann and of his Majesty respectively."

Two months later, a special delegation from England consisting of some forty officials arrived in Hanover to present Sophia with her own copy of this important document. An Irishman named John Toland accompanied the head of this expedition, the earl of Macclesfield, as his secretary, and left a detailed description of Sophia, the court, and the ceremony. "You may be sure...that the Earl of Macclesfield's Reception at the Court of Hanover was extraordinary magnificent, and that a Person who came on his Errand must needs be very welcome," Toland reported. "He [Macclesfield]...was sent by the King [William]...both to grace it with a Man of that Quality, and as his Father bore a relation to the Queen of Bohemia's Court...He was received by Deputys of the best Quality on the Frontiers of the Country, and his Expences were defrayed on the Road with all his Retinue, till he arriv'd at Hanover. There one of the largest Houses in the whole City was assign'd for his Entertainment...The Elector's own Servants waited on them every Morning with Silver Coffee and Tea-pots to their Chambers. Burgundy,

Champagne, Rhenish, and all manner of Wines were as common as Beer. A number of Coaches and Chairs were appointed to bring 'em every Day to Court, to carry 'em back to their Lodgings, and to go whither-soever else they would. They were entertained with Music, Balls, and Plays...There was a very fine Ball, and a splendid appearance of Ladys, the Evening after my Lord deliver'd the Act of Succession to the Electress," he enthused.

Toland, used to English princesses like Anne, who, though only thirty-six, was already severely overweight and burdened with many ailments, was amazed by Sophia. "The Electress is three and seventy Years of Age, which she bears so wonderfully well, that had I not many Vouchers, I shou'd scarce dare venture to relate it," he marveled.★ "She has ever enjoy'd extraordinary Health, which keeps her still very vigorous, of a cheerful Countenance, and a merry Disposition. She steps as firm and erect as any young Lady, has not one Wrinkle in her Face which is still very agreeable, nor one Tooth out of her Head, and reads without Spectacles, as I often saw her do Letters of a small Character in the dusk of the Evening...She's the most constant and greatest Walker I ever knew, never missing a Day, if it proves fair, for one or two hours...She perfectly tires all those of her Court that attend her in that Exercise," he continued. "I was the first who had the Honor of kneeling and kissing her Hand on the account of the Act of Succession; and she said, among other Discourse, that she was afraid the Nation had already repented their Choice of an old Woman, but that she hop'd none of her Posterity wou'd give them any Reasons to grow weary of their Dominion."

Thus did the twelfth child and youngest daughter in the female line descending from Mary, queen of Scots, married to the youngest of four brothers of a minor German principality, inherit what would become the throne of Great Britain. By some estimates as

---

★ He was close; she would have her seventy-first birthday in October. But you get the idea.

Sophia, electress of Hanover and heiress of Great Britain

many as fifty-seven claimants by birth or sex had precedence over Sophia as heir. But this honor did not come solely by fate or luck. She had fought for it as surely as her mother had fought for Bohemia.

In Gerrit van Honthorst's 1635 allegorical masterpiece *Triumph of the Winter Queen,* Sophia, then a child of five, is portrayed as a cherub in a long white dress flying over the queen of Bohemia's chariot while clutching a laurel wreath. This painting has turned out to be stunningly prophetic. Of the thirteen children depicted in the family portrait, it is Sophia who is carrying the crown.

OVER THE COURSE OF the next decade, the dowager electress of Hanover lived quietly at her estate in Herrenhausen, where she endured a series of personal losses. War had already claimed her second and fourth sons, Frederick Augustus and Karl Philipp, and in 1703, her fifth, Christian, was fatally shot while fighting the French in Bavaria. But the great tragedy of her life occurred on February 2, 1705, when thirty-six-year-old Figuelotte, who was in Hanover for a visit, died suddenly of pneumonia. Sophia herself had fallen ill with a cold; to keep her in bed, the danger to her daughter was minimized, and so it came as a great shock. "What makes it worse for me is that everything was kept hidden from me as to the severity of Her Majesty's illness, and that I have lost my beloved child, without having seen her one more time," she mourned. "I am afraid to contemplate my aunt's state of mind, and I am heartbroken with sorrow for her," her niece Liselotte wrote anxiously from France when she heard the news. "Why did not God take me instead of the dear Queen [of Prussia], who should have been my aunt's joy and consolation for many years to come?" This grief was followed by the death later that year, on August 28, of Sophia's brother-in-law George William. As contracted so long before, when he had first induced Ernst Augustus to substitute as bridegroom, all of his property went to his nephew George Louis.

Throughout this period, the Act of Settlement remained in place. William had managed to get it passed just before his own death in 1702, which was fortunate, as his sister-in-law, Anne, who succeeded to the Crown, was somewhat less enthusiastic about her Hanoverian cousins. Although William had intended to invite Sophia to England to ensure a smooth transition of power, Queen Anne declined to do so, fearing that "she herself would be so eclipsed by it, that she would be much in the successor's power, and reign only at her or his courtesy." In the fall of 1705, however, Parliament passed legislation naturalizing Sophia and her descendants as English citizens, and openly debated having her take up residence in London. Sophia, on Leibniz's urging, signaled her willingness to comply in a letter to the archbishop of Canterbury of November 3, 1705. "I thank God, I am in good Health, and Live in Quiet and with Content here, therefore I have no reason to change my way of Living," wrote the seventy-five-year-old dowager electress. "However, I am ready and willing to comply with what ever can be desired of me, by my Friends, in case that The Parliament think, that it is for the Good of the Kingdom, to Invite me into England," adding that, of course, this must be done at the pleasure of the queen.

Unfortunately, Queen Anne was anything but pleased by this sentiment, especially after the letter was printed and made public. The resulting political squabble was smoothed over by a diplomatic letter from Sophia dated April 6, 1706. "It is from the heart I speak... I believe that it would be for the good of England and all Europe, that the Queen should live for a hundred years," she declared sooth-ingly. In fact, Sophia probably never believed that she herself would rule when she wrote this letter; how could she, a woman in her midseventies, possibly outlive Anne, who was only forty-one? It was for her children and grandchildren that Sophia labored to hold on to the inheritance of what became in 1707, with the union of Scot-land and England, the throne of Great Britain.

That this was her aim may be deduced from her actions six years later. In the fall of 1713, hearing that Anne was seriously ill, Sophia tried to get not herself but her thirty-year-old grandson George (George Louis and Sophie Dorothea's son) to England, to help ensure a peaceful succession. She did it obliquely, by requesting he be named duke of Cambridge, an honor that was granted. As she knew that the bestowal of this title carried with it a seat in the House of Lords, she expected as a matter of course that he would be sum-moned to England to take his place in Parliament. In preparation for this, she had his wife, Caroline of Anspach, whom he had married in 1705, start taking English lessons.

But Anne, who was still childless—she had conceived a record seventeen times, only to miscarry, or, if she succeeded in delivering, to lose each baby in stillbirth or infancy*—deeply resented what she viewed as the vultures circling while she yet drew breath. By spring

---

* Except, of course, for one son, the duke of Gloucester, who died just before his eleventh birthday.

she had recovered sufficiently from her illness to lash out at her relative. "Madam, my sister and aunt," she wrote coldly in a letter of May 19, 1714. "Since the right of succession to my kingdom has been declared to belong to you and your family, there have always been evil intentioned persons who, from regard to their private interests, have entered into designs to establish in my dominions, during my lifetime, a prince of your blood. I had never imagined till now that this project would have progressed so far as to have had the slightest effect on your mind. But as I have lately understood, from public reports which have very speedily spread abroad, that your Electoral Highness shares this view, it is important for the succession of your family that I should tell you that such conduct will certainly be productive of consequences prejudicial to the succession itself, which has no security except while the sovereign who actually wears the crown retains her rights," she warned imperiously.

Sophia received this letter, with its implied threat that the inheritance might be withdrawn if Anne so chose, on June 6. It upset her terribly. She was by this time nearing her eighty-fourth birthday, an astounding longevity for her century, and had been feeling poorly herself. "I believe I am more ill than she is," Sophia had remarked of Anne when she first heard the English queen was failing. "Although, by the grace of God, I have only that sad complaint of being old, which is beyond remedy," she added with her customary levity. Now the thought that after having waited thirteen long years, she might have done something irrevocable to jeopardize her family's standing in England caused her deep distress. "This affair will certainly make me ill—I shall never get over it," she told her lady-in-waiting after reading Anne's letter.

But by June 8, 1714, she felt well enough to come down from her rooms to dinner. "Not only did she dine in public, but when, in the evening, the time came for her to walk, she showed a strong desire to do so, although the weather was somewhat cloudy and it threatened to rain," reported the lady-in-waiting, who was a witness to these events. "She declined the bearer and walked as usual, talking ever of the English affairs with the Electoral Princess [Caroline]. These unfortunate affairs had taken the firmest hold of her heart, and the Queen's letter...had made the deepest impression on our good Electress." The three women were in the middle of their walk when Sophia suddenly felt faint and had a pain in her stomach. Her granddaughter-in-law and the lady-in-waiting were attempting to help her back toward the castle when it began to rain heavily, so they decided instead to take shelter in one of the huts that dotted the garden. They never made it. Within a few steps, Sophia had collapsed in their arms. "I am very ill; give me your hand" were the last words she said.

Although there was no autopsy, it was likely a heart attack. She was unconscious before they could summon aid, which was just as well, for once help arrived, "for another hour they tormented her" with bloodletting. "A sweeter death was never seen, nor a happier one," the lady-in-waiting was able to report at last, "since that dear and good princess did not feel the attempts to revive her, and was thus able to die in tranquility." She was buried quietly in the chapel of the elector's palace in Hanover, where she had begun her married life.

Leibniz was bereft. "The death of Madam the Electress has upset me deeply," the great philosopher grieved. "It is not her, it is Hanover, it is England, it is the world, it is I who have lost by it."

LESS THAN TWO MONTHS later, in the early morning of August 1, 1714, Anne, majesty of Great Britain, died at Kensington Palace in London, and within hours George Louis was proclaimed king. Sophia had missed being queen by fifty-four days.

"Without her," Liselotte noted, "he would never have become King of England."

Epilogue

On October 18, 1714, Sophia's eldest son was crowned George I in an opulent ceremony at Westminster Abbey, thus beginning a dynasty that has lasted to this day. As a result of this change of power, the name George became very popular within the British monarchy, no one having the slightest idea that it was originally inspired by a feckless suitor who couldn't commit.

One of Sophia's granddaughters, Sophie Dorothea's daughter, also ascended to royalty, marrying her first cousin, Figuelotte's son, the king of Prussia. Their child, Frederick the Great, would rise to power in the next century, only to be reined in by the Empress Maria Theresa, the most courageous woman of her time. As Maria Theresa married Liselotte's grandson, this meant that *her* youngest daughter, a woman of some small notoriety by the name of Marie Antoinette, was Liselotte's great-granddaughter.

The ideas of Descartes and Leibniz, fostered and disseminated throughout Germany by Princess Elizabeth and her sister Sophia, were enormously influential and helped lay the groundwork for the Enlightenment that was to come.

Many would argue that the legacy of Mary, queen of Scots, was her unyielding adherence to Catholicism and thus discount her role in future events. But it is impossible to look at her granddaughter Elizabeth Stuart and not see Mary's courage, intelligence, strength of mind, and absolute unwillingness to surrender. And just as clearly, the Winter Queen passed along these traits in varying degrees to her daughters. Even shy Henrietta Maria, the weakest of the four, achieved a position where she might have wielded political influence, although she died too soon to capitalize on it, a victim of her own beauty and a want of antibiotics.

The truth is that there was almost no major political, cultural, philosophical, religious, or artistic movement—and the seventeenth century was chock-full of them—in which the queen of Bohemia and her daughters did not figure prominently.

These women were not ahead of their time—they *were* their time. And that legacy—Mary's—endures.

Acknowledgments

As I have never studied the history of art, and make absolutely no pretension to be anything other than an interested layman, the chapters in this book on Louise Hollandine and the Golden Age of Dutch painting obviously presented a particular challenge. Luckily, I had assistance from a number of people who gave generously of their time and expertise, and without whom this work would be much the poorer. Chief among these were Ronni Baer, the William and Ann Elfers Senior Curator of Paintings, Art of Europe, at the Museum of Fine Arts in Boston; and Adam Eaker, Assistant Curator, Department of European Painting at the Metropolitan Museum of Art in New York. Each of these scholars taught me more in fifteen minutes than I had managed to glean on my own from books. Dr. Baer took time out of an incredibly busy schedule to discuss Gerrit van Honthorst's career, and even took me to a museum workroom where one of his early paintings was being restored. Dr. Eaker not only helped provide insight into Louise Hollandine's allegorical paintings, but also aided the effort to track down the images of her work that appear in this book, and which add so much to her story. Barbara von Barghahn, Full Professor, Department of Fine Art and Art History at George Washington University, was also kind enough to read the chapter on Honthorst and the general history of seventeenth-century Dutch art to ensure that I did not make any glaring errors.

As regards the illustrations, I must also thank Carolyn Cruthirds at the Museum of Fine Arts in Boston for helping me to obtain the

rights to publish Honthorst's *Triumph of the Winter Queen*; Karen
Serres and Louisa Dare at the Courtauld Gallery in London for
"Boye the dog" and research on other images of Louise Hollandine's
work; David Pollack and Sarah Evans from Sotheby's and Amparo
Martinez Russotto at Christie's for their aid in locating and obtaining permissions from private collections for paintings sold at auc-
tion; and Susanna Feder at Bridgeman Images for her patience and
good humor in the face of an onslaught of emails from an obsessive
author. My deepest appreciation also goes to Dr. Willem Jan Hoogsteder and his assistant Emilie den Tonkelaar at Hoogsteder &
Hoogsteder for providing the images and permissions for Louise
Hollandine's self-portrait as a nun and the portrait of Prince Philip.
Dr. Hoogsteder, who wrote his dissertation on Elizabeth Stuart and
Frederick V, has assembled perhaps the defining collection of paintings relating to the Winter Queen and her family. To see some of
them, go to hoogsteder.com/exhibitions/previous-exhibitions/
buy-winter-queen-exhibition and download the exhibition
newspaper.

To Simon Wright at Orion (another recipient of those obsessive
emails), whose time I'm afraid I rather monopolized, many thanks
for all the help finding images and securing permissions. I am also
grateful to be represented in the UK by Tom Robinson, who has
stayed with me throughout my career. And of course my deepest
appreciation as always to Alan Samson, my editor and publisher at
Weidenfeld & Nicolson, upon whose friendship and support I can
always rely.

Similarly, I must also thank Asya Muchnick, my editor at Little,
Brown, for her careful read, warmth, and praise for the book; the same
goes for her former assistant, Sarah Haugen, who helped me through
the publishing process. And to my agent Michael Carlisle, who placed
this work exactly where it should be, and who I consider at this point
to be a de facto member of my family, my enduring thanks.

And finally, this book was an immense effort for me that I could
not have undertaken, let alone finish, without the love and support

Acknowledgments

of my family. To my daughter, Lee, who took the time to read the book in manuscript and was so enthusiastic and helpful when I was anxious and uncertain, I cannot thank you enough. You gave me such insightful edits, and your love and approbation absolutely buoyed me. And to my husband, Larry, who also took days away from his own pressing deadlines to read the book in manuscript even after the poor guy had heard most of it while I was writing it, and who has steadfastly maintained throughout all my wailing that this was my best work, all my love and gratitude.

Notes

Epigraphs

ix   "Nor shall less joy": Green, *Elizabeth*, 22.

ix   "She has bin long admir'd": Toland, *An Account of the Courts of Prussia and Hanover*, 58–59.

Introduction

4   "Please do not accuse me of": *Lettres, Instruction, et Mémoires de Marie Stuart*, Tome Sixième, 479. In the original: "Ne m'accusez de présomption sy, abandonnant ce monde et me preparant pour ung meilleur, je vous ramentois que ung jour vous aurés à responder de vostre charge."

5   "like those with which": Maxwell-Scott, *The Tragedy of Fotheringay*, 199.

6   "Lord Jesus, receive my soul": *Calendar of the State Papers Relating to Scotland*, vol. 9, "A Papist's Report of the manner of the Scot. Q. Death," 275.

6   "Such be the end": Fraser, *Mary, Queen of Scots*, 540. The ceremony terminated with a final gruesome incident: When the executioner held up his prize, the queen's head fell out of her wig.

Chapter 1. A King's Daughter

11   "That princess rare": Green, *Elizabeth*, 15.

11   "moving them to great triumph": Moysie, *Memoirs of the Affairs of Scotland*, 113. I have modernized the language to make it easier to understand.

11   "God's silly vassal": *The Autobiography and Diary of Mr. James Melvill*, 370. In the original text: "God's sillie vassal."

12   "Alas, it is a far": *Correspondence of King James VI of Scotland with Sir Robert Cecil*, 31.

12   "a cupboard of silver": Williams, *Anne of Denmark*, 50.

13   "to play her with": Green, *Elizabeth*, 3.

14–15   "What if Fawdonside's pistol": Herries, *Historical Memoirs of the Reign of Mary Queen of Scots*, 79.

15   "My Lord, God has given you": Ibid., 79.

16   "rockers": Willson, *King James VI and I*, 19.

16   "My Lady Mar was wise": Ibid., 20.

16   "They made me speak Latin": Beavan, *King James VI of Scotland and I of England*, 13.

16   "I heard him discourse": *The Autobiography and Diary of Mr. James Melvill*, vol. 1, 48.

16   "he dislikes dancing": Willson, *King James VI and I*, 53.

17   "malicious actions...as cannot": Herries, *Historical Memoirs of the Reign of Mary Queen of Scots,* 82.

18   "That year [1579] arrived Monsieur d'Aubigny": *The Autobiography and Diary of Mr. James Melvill*, 76.

18   "At this time his Majesty": Moysie, *Memoirs of the Affairs of Scotland*, 26.

19   "At that time it was a pity": *The Autobiography and Diary of Mr. James Melvill*, 119.

20   "The king came riding into": Calderwood, *The History of the Kirk of Scotland*, vol. 5, 297.

20   "And so the King and the Duke": *The Autobiography and Diary of Mr. James Melvill*, 134.

21   "I am murdered": Lang, *James VI and the Gowrie Mystery*, 24.

21   "If war should ensue": Gray, *Letters and Papers*, 135.

22   "made many fair promises": Calderwood, *The History of the Kirk of Scotland*, vol. 5, 282.

22   "that she could rather have wished": Nichols, *The Processes, Processions, and Magnificent Festivities of King James I*, vol. 1, 169.

23   "the sending...of such Jewels": Ibid., 122.

23   "Royal Entertainment": Ibid., 170.

24   "The young princess came [into Windsor]": Green, *Elizabeth*, 6.

24   "There was such an infinite company": Nichols, *The Processes, Processions, and Magnificent Festivities of King James I*, vol. 1, 195.

24   "I heard the Earls of Nottingham and Northampton": Ibid., 193–94.

24   staff of 70 domestics: Ibid., 203–4.

25   "Whereas ourself and our dear Wife": Ibid., 443.

26   He must have found his duties light: For evidence of John Bull's version of the British national anthem, see Cummings, *God Save the King*, and Krummel, "God Save the King."

26   "The Mayor and Aldermen": Nichols, *The Processes, Processions, and Magnificent Festivities of King James I*, vol. 1, 429.

26   "With God's assistance": Ibid., 591.

27   "Liberty of Conscience": Thou, *A True Narration of that Horrible Conspiracy*, 5.

27   "the King himself might by many ways": Ibid., 11.

27   "Such was the opportuness": Ibid., 14.

27–28 "Therefore the Conspirators": Ibid., 17.

28   "For although no signs of troubles": Ibid., 20.

28   "that the Palace with the places": Ibid., 21.
28   "hath confessed their design": Nichols, *The Processes, Processions, and Magnificent Festivities of King James I*, vol. 1, 592.
29   "this poor Lady hath not yet": Ibid.
29   "What a Queen should I": Ibid.

Chapter 2. (An Almost) Royal Wedding

30   "speaks French very well": Green, *Elizabeth*, 16. See also La Fèvre de La Boderie, *Ambassades*, 7.
30   Elizabeth likely was introduced: For evidence that Elizabeth was exposed to recent developments in the natural sciences, see Strickland, *Lives of the Queens of Scotland*, 15–20.
31   "This is only my desire": Ibid., 29.
31   "she is handsome, graceful": Green, *Elizabeth*, 16. See also La Fèvre de La Boderie, *Ambassades*, 7.
31   "a princess of lovely beauty": Green, *Elizabeth*, 15–16.
32   "of a comely, tall, middle Stature": Cornwallis, *An Account of the Baptism, Life, Death and Funeral*, 50.
32   "He studies two hours a day": Birch, *The Life of Henry Prince of Wales*, 65. See also La Fèvre de La Boderie, *Ambassades*, 400.
32   "not able to go": Nichols, *The Processes, Processions, and Magnificent Festivities of King James I*, vol. 1, 460.
33   "The King was desirous": Ibid., 461.
34   "As the King is by nature": Willson, *King James VI and I*, 174.
34   "Good Mr. Jowler": Ibid., 184.
35   "We all saw a great change": *The Diary of the Lady Anne Clifford*, 5–6.
35   "I perceive, my cousin": Birch, *The Life of Henry Prince of Wales*, 82–83.
35   "Will he bury me alive?": Willson, *King James VI and I*, 281.
36   "Then will I make him": Chancellor, *The Life of Charles I*, 14.
36   "My dear and worthy brother": Green, *Elizabeth*, 11.
36   her guardian complained: Ibid., 18.
37   "have proceeded so far with me": Ibid., 28.
38   "The prince hath publicly": Ibid., 29.
40   "His Majesty is well pleased": Winwood, *Memorials of Affairs of State*, 222.
40   "if the Princes": Ibid., 223.
41   "Prince Henry gave the first": Cornwallis, *The Life and Character of Henry-Frederick*, 29.
42   "straight and well-shaped": Winwood, *Memorials of Affairs of State*, 404.
42   "He is very handsome": Brown, *Calendar of State Papers and Manuscripts Relating to English Affairs*, vol. 12, 444.
42   "Bending himself with": Winwood, *Memorials of Affairs of State*, 403.
43   "He plies his Mistress so hard": Nichols, *The Processes, Processions, and Magnificent Festivities of King James I*, vol. 2, 466.

43 "The Princess, who maybe begins to feel": Brown, *Calendar of State Papers and Manuscripts Relating to English Affairs,* vol. 12, 444.

43 "And 'tis certain": Coke, *A Detection of the Court and State of England,* 68.

43 "she would rather be": Ibid.

44 "The Palatine has surpassed expectation": Brown, *Calendar of State Papers and Manuscripts Relating to English Affairs,* vol. 12, 441.

44 "Above all the rest": Cornwallis, *An Account of the Baptism, Life, Death and Funeral,* 30.

45 "He (the Match being ended)": Ibid., 31.

45 "great thirst": Ibid., 33.

45 "Pigeons and Cupping-Glasses": Ibid., 37.

45 "saying that it should never": Ibid., 39.

46 "Our Rising Sun is set ere scarce": Nichols, *The Processes, Processions, and Magnificent Festivities of King James I,* vol. 2, 490.

46 "When the women in Scotland": Ibid., 504.

46 "The King is doing all he can": Brown, *Calendar of State Papers and Manuscripts Relating to English Affairs,* vol. 12, 472.

46 "The Princess has gone two days": Ibid., 449.

46 "The Lady Elizabeth": Nichols, *The Processes, Processions, and Magnificent Festivities of King James I,* vol. 2, 489.

46 "The Succession to this Crown": Brown, *Calendar of State Papers and Manuscripts Relating to English Affairs,* vol. 12, 448.

47 "He [Henry] meant to have conducted": *Letters to King James the Sixth,* 39–40.

47 "On Tuesday I took occasion": Ibid., 40.

48 "for bigness, fashion, and beauty": Nichols, *The Processes, Processions, and Magnificent Festivities of King James I,* vol. 2, 515.

48 "The Affiancy of the Palsgrave": Ibid., 514.

48 "a black velvet cloake": Ibid., 513.

48 "The Queen is noted": Ibid., 515.

49 "that he doubted not": Green, *Elizabeth,* 35.

50 "gowne of white satin": Nichols, *The Processes, Processions, and Magnificent Festivities of King James I,* vol. 2, 542.

50 "gold-spangles, pearls": Ibid., 543.

50 "adorned with many": Ibid.

51 "God give them joy": Ibid., 548.

Chapter 3. Goodwife Palsgrave

52 "The commissioners that accompany her": Smith, *The Life and Letters of Sir Henry Wotton,* vol. 2, 18.

52 "to make Heaven and Earth": Nichols, *The Processes, Processions, and Magnificent Festivities of King James I,* vol. 2, 613.

52 "costly shows": Ibid., 614.

52 Elizabeth was showered: For a complete list of these gifts and their value, see ibid., 614–15.

53 "the people of the country report": Ibid., 616.

53 "that Castle in which": Ibid.

53 "all Gentlemen of the country": Ibid., 617.

55 "fell plainly to tell me": Smith, *The Life and Letters of Sir Henry Wotton*, vol. 2, 89.

55 "that my Lady [Elizabeth] was not": Ibid., 90.

55 "Being desirous by all means I can": *Letters to King James the Sixth*, 185.

56 English musk roses: Frederick hired a special landscape architect to create a terraced garden in the English fashion; Elizabeth also had crown imperials, flowers-de-luce, and carnations. See Godfrey, *Heidelberg: Its Princes and Its Palaces*, 258.

59 "Prague, unthankful Prague": Vickers, *History of Bohemia*, 571.

59 Letter of Majesty: Schiller, *The History of the Thirty Years' War in Germany*, 33.

60 "it would be well for them": Gindely, *History of the Thirty Years' War*, vol. 1, 37.

61 "Let us follow the ancient custom": Vickers, *History of Bohemia*, 578.

61 "Noble lords, another awaits": Ibid.

61 "Jesus! Mary!": True, *The Thirty Years' War*, 27.

61 "Let us see whether": Ibid.

61 "Behold, his Mary": Ibid., 28.

65 "I have heard nothing": Green, *Elizabeth*, 126. For the full letter in French, see Bromley, *A Collection of Original Royal Letters*, 1.

65 And then came word that: For an exact account of Frederick's election in Bohemia, see Gindely, *History of the Thirty Years' War*, vol. 1, 148–50.

66 When Elizabeth's mother: For an account of the jewels and property given to Buckingham out of Anne's estate, see Nichols, *The Processes, Processions, and Magnificent Festivities of King James I*, vol. 3, 546.

66 "This worthy bearer": Gardiner, *Letters and Other Documents*, 2.

67 "It is much debated here": Ibid., 7.

67 "God forbid he [Frederick] should refuse it": Ibid., 12–13.

69 "The greater number of the councilors": Ibid., 23.

69 "The hope of making his daughter": Ibid., 27.

Chapter 4. Queen of Bohemia

70 "The Prince and Princess Palatine": Gardiner, *Letters and Other Documents*, 55.

70 some three thousand foot soldiers: For an estimate of the size of the entourage, see the letter of the Venetian ambassador to the doge in ibid., 81.

72 "The queen's free and gracious demeanor": Carleton, *Letters from and to Sir Dudley Carleton*, 419.

72 "Their Majesties are very cheerful": Ibid., 409.

73   "The queen appeared very joyous": Green, *Elizabeth*, 142.

73   "Bethlen Gabor hath made a great progress": Carleton, *Letters from and to Sir Dudley Carleton,* 403.

75   "By your Highness's letter": Gardiner, *Letters and Other Documents,* 87.

75   "I have resolved and given orders": Ibid., 118.

75   "I have wished here apart": Ibid., 155.

75   "This last week's letters": Carleton, *Letters from and to Sir Dudley Carleton,* 422.

76   "In our neighboring provinces": Gardiner, *Letters and Other Documents,* 110.

76   "This last week": Ibid., 182.

76   "For commonly he that is first": Carleton, *Letters from and to Sir Dudley Carleton,* 403.

76   "All of his Majesty's ministers": Gardiner, *Letters and Other Documents,* 148.

77   "his belief that": Ibid., 142.

77   "He is a strange fellow": Nichols, *The Processes, Processions, and Magnificent Festivities of King James I,* vol. 3, 585.

77   "that his subjects were as dear": Ibid., 568.

77   "If the cause had been good": Gardiner, *Letters and Other Documents,* 137.

77   "doth still profess": Ibid., 181.

79   "he was glad of it": *The Processes, Processions, and Magnificent Festivities of King James I,* vol. 4, 617.

79   "My only dear brother": Green, *Elizabeth*, 154.

81   "My Lord, seeing the necessity": Ibid., 153.

82   "I cannot conceal from your Imperial Majesty": Gindely, *History of the Thirty Years' War,* vol. 1, 240–41.

82   "swept with a broom": Ibid., 239.

83   "Spinola is still in the Low Palatinate": Green, *Elizabeth*, 158.

86   "His Majesty coming to court": Ibid., 163.

Chapter 5. The Winter Queen

88   managed to slay only about 1,600 Bohemian soldiers: See Gindely, *History of the Thirty Years' War,* vol. 1, 250.

88   "I have learned from the English agent": "Venice: December 1620, 4–15," in Hinds, *Calendar of State Papers Relating to English Affairs,* vol. 16, item 648, December 8, 486–99.

89   "who truly saw the state": Green, *Elizabeth*, 167.

90   "They shall find neither food": Benger, *Memoirs of Elizabeth Stuart,* vol. 2, 107.

90   "This be the fifteenth day": Smith, *The Life and Letters of Sir Henry Wotton,* vol. 2, 198.

91   "Everyone laments the misfortunes": "Venice: December 1620, 4–15," in Hinds, *Calendar of State Papers Relating to English Affairs,* vol. 16, item 652, December 11, 486–99.

91   "Whereas, on the preceding days": Ibid.

92   "and had never offended anyone": Ibid., item 733, February 12, 1621.

92   "to imperil his three kingdoms": Ibid.

93   "have to be a warrior": Green, *Elizabeth*, 171.

93   "The Lady Elizabeth, we hear": Williams and Birch, *The Court and Times of James I*, vol. 1, 456.

94   "So great is our mislike": Green, *Elizabeth*, 174–75.

94   "I think they have reason there": Halliwell-Phillips, *Letters of the Kings of England*, 178.

95   "You speak to me of Italy": Hinds, *Calendar of State Papers Relating to English Affairs,* vol. 16, item 680, January 8, 1621.

95   "His Majesty fears the troubles": Ibid., item 759.

96   "they were met by the Prince of Orange": Green, *Elizabeth*, 178.

96   "I have seen a genuine letter": Hinds, *Calendar of State Papers Relating to English Affairs,* vol. 17, item 40.

97   "You will have heard of the death": Ibid.

98   "would rather cherish": Green, *Elizabeth*, 191.

98   "Madam, I will give it you": Wedgwood, *The Thirty Years War*, 127.

99   "The commandment I have": Green, *Elizabeth*, 189.

101   "Fire! Fire! Blood! Blood!": Wedgwood, *The Thirty Years War*, 129..

101   "Be it known to all": Benger, *Memoirs of Elizabeth Stuart*, vol. 2, 161–62.

102   "My poor Heidelberg taken": Green, *Elizabeth*, 207–8.

103   "We have here at present": Smith, *The Life and Letters of Sir Henry Wotton*, vol. 2, 245.

103   "The king, my father": Green, *Elizabeth*, 214.

104   "Ye shall present her with": Halliwell-Phillips, *Letters of the Kings of England*, 180–81.

106   "was the prettiest child": Green, *Elizabeth*, 234.

106   "I like not to marry": Dalton, *Life and Times of General Sir Edward Cecile*, 42.

106   "There is nothing but trickery": Gregg, *King Charles I*, 85.

106   "Since my dear brother's return": Dalton, *Life and Times of General Sir Edward Cecile*, 48.

107   "I remember Mr. French": Jesse, *Memoirs of the Court of England During the Reign of the Stuarts,* 105.

107   "Yet now, being grown toward sixty": Ibid.

107   "He enjoyed life for fifty-nine years": Hinds, *Calendar of State Papers Relating to English Affairs,* vol. 18, item 879, April 6, 1625.

Chapter 6. *Queen of Hearts*

108   "You may easily judge": Green, *Elizabeth*, 242.

111   "The comforte of my deare brother's love": Benger, *Memoirs of Elizabeth Stuart*, vol. 2, 231–32. Charles was in fact heavily committed to his sister's cause. According to a report that the Venetian secretary in Germany sent to the doge, "A league [had been] made at Paris for thirty

years for the recovery of the Palatinate and the Valtelline...in the presence of the Most Christian king and all the ambassadors of princes allied against the King of Spain and the House of Austria and their adherents and supporters...[by which] The King of England...shall pay 300,000 crowns yearly to the Palatinate until the recovery of his states...[also] 12,000 foot and 2,000 horse for the Palatinate during the war...He shall pay Mansfelt [Mansfield] 20,000 crowns yearly as the Palatinate's general and...on the completion of the Palatinate affair... Mansfelt...shall go against the empire and the Spanish dominions as France and the Venetians require." This treaty also called for "Obligations of France for undertakings in the Valtelline, Flanders, Milan and Naples." Hinds, *Calendar of State Papers Relating to English Affairs,* vol. 18, item 857, March 15, 1625.

112 "Though I have cause enough to be sad": Green, *Elizabeth,* 218.

112 "I know not so great a lady in the world": Ibid., 206.

112 "The Queen of Bohemia is accounted": Benger, *Memoirs of Elizabeth Stuart,* vol. 2, 84.

112 "I send you herewith letters": Halliwell-Phillips, *Letters of the Kings of England,* 271.

113 "I wish for nothing so much": Benger, *Memoirs of Elizabeth Stuart,* vol. 2, 256–57.

116 "Alack...if I had known": Gamache, *The Court and Times of Charles I,* vol. 1, 281.

116 "Who rules the kingdom": Ibid., 368.

117 "in the sight of the English fleet": Ibid., 422.

117 "There died in this siege": Ibid., 424.

118 "The great prize taken": Ibid., 440.

119 "The murthering boat, having a fair wind": Gamache, *The Court and Times of Charles I,* vol. 2, 7.

119 "Save me, father, save me": Benger, *Memoirs of Elizabeth Stuart,* vol. 2, 261.

119 "his cheek fastened by the frost": Gamache, *The Court and Times of Charles I,* vol. 2, 8.

119 "hath been such a wind": Ibid., 8.

120 "for that he [Frederick] was not able to put bread": Green, *Elizabeth,* 274.

121 "They say the French king": Gamache, *The Court and Times of Charles I,* vol. 2, 159.

121 "the Golden King": Wedgwood, *The Thirty Years War,* 234.

121 "the Lion of the North": Ibid.

123 "A conflagration arose during the storming": Gindely, *History of the Thirty Years' War,* vol. 2, 66.

124 "great fury": Ibid., 83.

125 "a letter from him [Gustavus] to his Majesty": Gamache, *The Court and Times of Charles I,* vol. 2, 138.

125 "They talk much of a letter": Green, *Elizabeth*, 282.

125 "I am this week to present you": Gamache, *The Court and Times of Charles I*, vol. 2, 145.

126 "When the King of Sweden first sent for him": Ibid., 160.

127 "My Lord of Canterbury": Ibid., 173.

127 "Wonderful welcome, was this prince": Green, *Elizabeth*, 289.

127 "I think that the King [Charles I]": Akkerman, *The Correspondence of Elizabeth Stuart, Queen of Bohemia*, vol. 2, 39.

127 "The setting sun rises again": Green, *Elizabeth*, 290.

128 "My dearest heart": Ibid., 291.

128 "The appetite has been so sharpened": Gindely, *History of the Thirty Years' War*, vol. 2, 99–100.

129 "I never did think": Akkerman, *The Correspondence of Elizabeth Stuart, Queen of Bohemia*, vol. 2, 125–26.

129 "I will be miserable at Alsheim": Ibid., 132.

132 "The loss...doth not a little": Ibid., 145.

132 "his majesty of Bohemia": Green, *Elizabeth*, 298.

132 "I will not make this": Akkerman, *The Correspondence of Elizabeth Stuart, Queen of Bohemia*, vol. 2, 145.

Chapter 7. A Royal Refugee

139 Princess Elizabeth was too easily swayed: For her mother's letter, see Akkerman, *The Correspondence of Elizabeth Stuart, Queen of Bohemia*, vol. 2, 376–77.

139 For her part, Princess Elizabeth: For Princess Elizabeth's complaints about her mother, see Karl Ludwig's letter of May 5, 1636, in Akkerman, *The Correspondence of Elizabeth Stuart, Queen of Bohemia*, vol. 2, 422–23.

139 "had black hair, a dazzling complexion": *Memoirs of Sophia, Electress of Hanover*, 14.

139 "she hid herself from the world": Ibid.

140 "It was the first time that ever": Akkerman, *The Correspondence of Elizabeth Stuart, Queen of Bohemia*, vol. 2, 177.

141 "Never did I rail": Green, *Elizabeth*, 301.

142 "I think he cannot too soon": Ibid., 312.

143 "It is meant...only for a show": Akkerman, *The Correspondence of Elizabeth Stuart, Queen of Bohemia*, vol. 2, 201.

143 "When he has had his official audience": Blaze de Bury, *Memoirs of the Princess Palatine*, 145–46.

Chapter 8. Child of Light and Dark

149 "Louisa was lively and unaffected": *Memoirs of Sophia, Electress of Hanover*, 14–15.

150 "She devoted herself to painting": Ibid., 15.

150 "While painting others she neglected": Ibid.

151 "Gherardo delle Notti": Gower, *The Figure Painters of Holland*, 6–7.

152 "He never left off working": Bréal, *Rembrandt: A Critical Essay*, 44–45.

152 "he had not only to be paid": Ibid., 82.

154 "Charles Lodowicke, by the Grace of God": *The Manifest of the Most Illustrious and Soveraigne Prince*. There are no page numbers in this illuminating document.

156 "Le Diable": Green, *Elizabeth*, 323.

158 Certainly Elizabeth always believed this to be the case: For the queen of Bohemia's reaction to rumors of the poisoning of Frederick William, see Akkerman, *The Correspondence of Elizabeth Stuart, Queen of Bohemia*, vol. 2, 722–23, 1003–4. For a more in-depth analysis of this incident, see Tuttle, *History of Prussia*, vol. 1, 139.

159 "Both the brothers went away": Warburton, *Memoirs of Prince Rupert*, vol. 1, 76.

Chapter 9. Lilies and Roses

163 Specifically, he had stepped out: For more on this incident, see van Zuylen van Nyevelt, *Court Life in the Dutch Republic*, 27.

165 "fair flaxen hair, a complexion": *Memoirs of Sophia, Electress of Hanover*, 16.

165 "Her talents, by which I chiefly profited": Ibid.

166 "I am so much overjoyed": Akkerman, *The Correspondence of Elizabeth Stuart, Queen of Bohemia*, vol. 2, 568.

166 "The king my dear brother": Green, *Elizabeth*, 338.

168 "Sacrément! You are a young one": Warburton, *Memoirs of Prince Rupert*, vol. 1, 90.

169 "I am glad to hear": Green, *Elizabeth*, 340.

169 "It will be in vain": Warburton, *Memoirs of Prince Rupert*, vol. 1, 93.

170 "My son writes that the king": Green, *Elizabeth*, 342.

171 "I do pity, and shall pity all my life": Ibid., 344.

173 "the most high and sacred order": Gardiner, *The Fall of the Monarchy of Charles I*, vol. 1, 362.

173 "God Save the King": Ibid., 359.

174 "The distractions of my own country": Akkerman, *The Correspondence of Elizabeth Stuart, Queen of Bohemia*, vol. 2, 940.

174 "died soon afterwards": *Memoirs of Sophia, Electress of Hanover*, 8.

Chapter 10. A Royal Education

177 "I was born, they tell me": *Memoirs of Sophia, Electress of Hanover*, 2.

177 "the Queen my mother": Ibid., 3.

177 "At Leyden we had a court": Ibid., 3–4.

178 "I was obliged to go every day": Ibid., 4-5.

178 "I learned the Heidelberg catechism": Ibid., 4.

178 "They kept me busy": Ibid., 5–6.

179 "so arranged that we knew": Ibid., 6.

179 "believed that I should turn out": Ibid.

179 "having said my prayers": Ibid., 7.

179 "Suffice it to say": Ibid.

179 "as one would a stud of horses": Ibid., 8.

179 " 'she is thin and ugly' ": Ibid.

180 "the bearing of a princess": Ibid., 17.

180 "I was…ten years of age": Ibid., 9.

180 "I made it my business": Ibid.

180 "in order to amuse the Queen": Ibid., 10.

181 "I see that all these": Gardiner, *The Fall of the Monarchy of Charles I*, vol. 2, 332.

181 "I am ready to obey": Ibid., 220.

183 "I cannot see what the king can gain": Akkerman, *The Correspondence of Elizabeth Stuart, Queen of Bohemia*, vol. 2, 943. Elizabeth's contact in England was Sir Thomas Roe, one of her oldest and dearest friends. It was Roe who, as ambassador to Vienna, would help arrange Rupert's release.

184 " 'If my own person were only' ": Gardiner, *The Fall of the Monarchy of Charles I*, vol. 2, 174.

185 "The Queen doth all": Taylor, *The Life of Queen Henrietta Maria*, vol. 1, 245. This is Elizabeth to Roe again.

185 "Prince Rupert arrived here": Scott, *Rupert, Prince Palatine*, 56.

186 "he received the proposal": Ibid., 45.

186 "one of the brightest beauties": Ibid., 44.

186 "the Prince's former favors": Ibid.

186 "never named her after": Ibid.

187 "beloved by all": Ibid., 46.

187 "There were few persons of quality": Ibid., 55.

188 "Go, you coward": Taylor, *The Life of Queen Henrietta Maria*, vol. 1, 250.

189 "Let my faithful subjects": Gardiner, *The Fall of the Monarchy of Charles I*, vol. 2, 392.

189 "Parliament! Privilege of Parliament": Ibid., 398.

189 "Never did he treat me for a moment": Ibid., 407.

190 "in such post-haste": Taylor, *The Life of Queen Henrietta Maria*, vol. 1, 257.

190 "The Queen my mother": *Memoirs of Sophia, Electress of Hanover*, 13.

190 "The fine portraits of Van Dyck": Ibid.

190 "After careful inspection": Ibid., 13–14.

191 "very kind, one to another": Taylor, *The Life of Queen Henrietta Maria*, vol. 1, 261.

191 "I find by all the Queen's": Ibid.

Chapter 11. The Visiting Philosopher

195 "In my time, which was 1642": Blaze de Bury, *Memoirs of the Princess Palatine*, 111–12.

196 "The life which I am obliged to lead": Godfrey, *A Sister of Prince Rupert*, 131.

197 "Wonders were told": Blaze de Bury, *Memoirs of the Princess Palatine*, 112–13.

197 "Desire for knowledge": Pope-Hennessy, *Anna van Schurman*, 54.

197 "My deep regard for learning": Ibid., 69–70. The treatise was published in France and Holland and later translated into English under the title *The Learned Maid, or, Whether a Maid may Be a Scholar.*

198 "la Grècque": Godfrey, *A Sister of Prince Rupert*, 281.

198 "Despising the frivolities": Ibid., 119.

198 "his golden fetter": Ibid., 60.

198 "This town [The Hague] can certainly compare": Blaze de Bury, *Memoirs of the Princess Palatine*, 180–81.

200 "I had been taught": Haldane, *Descartes, His Life and Times*, 18.

200 "the great book of the world": Ibid., 32.

201 "As for the opinions which": Ibid., 68.

201 *Cogito, ergo sum*: Ibid., 174–75.

201 "like one walking alone": Ibid., 70.

202 "I could hardly have believed": Mahaffy, *Descartes*, 59.

203 "Monsieur Descartes,...from its action, thought": Godfrey, *A Sister of Prince Rupert*, 129–30.

204 "The favor with which your Highness": Nye, *The Princess and the Philosopher*, 16.

204 "entirely satisfactory": Ibid., 19.

204 "Your kindness is shown": Godfrey, *A Sister of Prince Rupert*, 130–31.

205 "For the rest, I have much": Nye, *The Princess and the Philosopher*, 31.

206 "as a young angler": Ibid., 32. For Descartes's proof and his and Princess Elizabeth's complete correspondence on the kissing circles, see Adam and Tannery, *Oeuvres de Descartes*, 38–50.

206 "I have never met anyone": Godfrey, *A Sister of Prince Rupert*, 133.

207 "Bless the good man": Ibid., 92.

208 "I pray God to condemn me": Lodge, *Richelieu*, 219.

208 "A great politician has departed": Ibid.

209 "That brave Prince and hopeful soldier": Scott, *Rupert, Prince Palatine*, 61–62.

209 "Your friend, Rupert": Warburton, *Memoirs of Prince Rupert*, vol. 1, 394.

209 "If any disaffected persons": Ibid.

210 "and ask the commanders": Scott, *Rupert, Prince Palatine*, 90.

210 "when the Prince broke up his quarters": Warburton, *Memoirs of Prince Rupert*, vol. 1, 383.

210 "The two young Princes": Ibid., 389.

211 "We were at times": *Memoirs of Sophia, Electress of Hanover*, 27.

212 "M. de Guise had the figure": *Mémoires d'Anne de Gonzagues*, 47. As it appeared in the French: "M. de Guise avoit la figure, l'air & les manières d'un Héros de roman."

213 "This princess did not despise": Menzies, *Political Women*, vol. 1, 196.

213 "She had so much intelligence": Ibid.

214 "where were only to be found": Blaze de Bury, *Memoirs of the Princess Palatine*, 231.

215 "It is with shame": Godfrey, *A Sister of Prince Rupert*, 151–52.

216 "I cannot deny": Adam and Tannery, *Oeuvres de Descartes*, 351. This is my translation; the French reads "Je ne puis nier que ie n'aye este surpris d'apprendre que vostre Altesse ait eu de la fascherre, jusqu'a en estre incommodée en sa santé, pour une chose que la plus grande part du monde trouvera bonne, & que plusieurs fortes raisons peuvent rendre excusable envers les autres."

216 "It is with the ingenuousness": Ibid., 357. In French: "Cest avec cette ingenuité & cette franchise, laquelle ie fais profession d'observer en toutes mes actions, que ie fais aussi particulierement profession d'etre, etc."

Chapter 12. A Scandal in Bohemia

219 "I will acquaint you with a business": Akkerman, *The Correspondence of Elizabeth Stuart, Queen of Bohemia*, vol. 2, 1021.

220–21 "Princesse Loysa Drawing...then they destroy'd before": Phelps, *Lucasta: The Poems of Richard Lovelace Esquire*, 107–9. This poem is undated, but Richard Lovelace was in Holland from 1646 to 1648. See the biographical note in *Songs and Sonnets by Richard Lovelace*.

221 "the most amiable": Phelps, *Lucasta*, 10.

222 "Your troops": Gardiner, *The First Two Stuarts and the Puritan Revolution*, 133.

222 "My troops increase": Ibid., 135.

223 "Wherefore I command": Warburton, *Memoirs of Prince Rupert*, vol. 2, 437–39.

223 "Had not [the king]...this year given": Ibid., 436.

224 "Ironsides": Ibid., 464.

224 "Whereupon followed a very hot encounter": Hamilton, *Calendar of State Papers Domestic*, 295–387.

224 "escaping narrowly, by the goodness": Scott, *Rupert, Prince Palatine*, 150.

224 "Here also was slain": Warburton, *Memoirs of Prince Rupert*, vol. 2, 465.

225 "Your Highness is to know a romance story": Ibid., vol. 3, 82.

225 "One charge more, gentlemen": Ibid., 109.

226 "My Lord, it is now": Ibid., 149.

227 "Slander just then": *Memoirs of Sophia, Electress of Hanover*, 18.

228 "bonnes fortunes": Godfrey, *A Sister of Prince Rupert*, 156.

229 "bowed weeping from her high sphere": Strickland, *Lives of the Queens of Scotland*, 208.

229 "Madam, give me leave": Benger, *Memoirs of Elizabeth Stuart*, vol. 2, 384–85.

230 "that Philip needed no apology": Strickland, *Lives of the Queens of Scotland*, 209.

Chapter 13. Honor and Duty

235 "I could wish my brother": Scott, *Rupert, Prince Palatine*, 211.

235 "I must remind you of the promise": Godfrey, *A Sister of Prince Rupert*, 181.

236 "My sister Henriette has been so ill": Ibid., 191.

237 to be referred to as "Excellency": Gindely, *History of the Thirty Years' War*, vol. 2, 344.

238 "any probability of relief": Warburton, *Memoirs of Prince Rupert*, vol. 3, 180.

239 "can any rational man": Ibid.

240 "Having received information": Scott, *Rupert, Prince Palatine*, 205.

242 "His Majesty, upon occasion": Ibid., 207.

243 "As the Church can never flourish": Gregg, *King Charles I*, 409.

243 "As soon as we had the letter": Gardiner, *History of the Great Civil War*, vol. 4, 29.

246 And so the war ended: For these statistics, see Gindely, *History of the Thirty Years' War*, vol. 2, 398.

246–47 "that the King be forthwith sent for": Gardiner, *History of the Great Civil War*, vol. 4, 278.

247 "It is not my case alone": Ibid., 301.

248 "as a tyrant, traitor, murderer": Ibid., 308.

248 "Sweetheart, now they will": Ibid., 319.

249 "Behold the head of a traitor": Ibid., 323.

249 "since I saw you": Warburton, *Memoirs of Prince Rupert*, vol. 3, 248.

249 "The bloody and inhumane murder": Scott, *Rupert, Prince Palatine*, 237.

250 "Dearest brother": Ibid., 240.

250 "I should die happy": Ibid., 238.

251 "I wish your Highness": Godfrey, *A Sister of Prince Rupert*, 229.

252 "Since the conditions appear": Ibid., 230.

252 "If she sacrifices herself": Ibid.

252 "The highly honored Elector": Ibid., 232.

253 "I envy the fate of this letter": Ibid., 233.

253 "keeps always two hundred men-at-arms": Ibid., 234.

253 "not consent out of crossness": Ibid., 229.

253 "Your daughter [Henrietta] says": Ibid., 237.

254 "Because your Highness has bidden me": Ibid., 242.

255 "I found no fault in him": Ibid., 244.

256 "I hold my life": Ibid.

Chapter 14. Royal Sense and Sensibility

260   "Unworthy pantaloons": Scott, *Rupert, Prince Palatine*, 212.
260   "Lord Craven was a very valuable friend": *Memoirs of Sophia, Electress of Hanover*, 26.
260   "An old Englishman": Ibid., 18.
261   "very well made": Airy, *Charles II*, 38.
261   "My manners and behavior": *Memoirs of Sophia, Electress of Hanover*, 18.
261   "a prince richly endowed": Ibid., 21.
261   "much courted by the English": Ibid.
261–62 "notice other signs of weakness...by such means": Ibid., 23–24.
262   "All these circumstances": Ibid., 25.
262   "it was agreed that": Ibid., 29–30.
262   "As I had never": Ibid., 30–31.
263   "There is hardly a corner": Godfrey, *Heidelberg: Its Princes and Palaces*, 302.
264   "The Elector, with his hearty manner": *Memoirs of Sophia, Electress of Hanover*, 35–36.
265   "I was so pleased": Ibid., 36.
265   "A grimace on the part of Madame": Ibid., 36–37.
265   "My sister-in-law is very stupid": Ibid., 37.
265   "I found her with all her fine clothes": Ibid., 38.
266   "On our return": Ibid.
266   "The Elector on his part": Ibid., 39.
266   "I wished myself a thousand times": Ibid., 38–39.
266   "I could see that he idolized her": Ibid., 39–40.
267   "loved to attract attention": Ibid., 40.
267   "I leave it to be imagined": Ibid.

Chapter 15. A Lesson on the Passions

271   "Know then that I have a body": Godfrey, *A Sister of Prince Rupert*, 163–64.
272   "The difference between great souls": Ibid., 165.
272   "I remark always in your letters": Ibid., 169.
272   "Monsieur Descartes," she wrote: Ibid., 167.
273   "For the special use of": Blaze de Bury, *Memoirs of the Princess Palatine*, 204.
273   "I only try to put in practice": Godfrey, *A Sister of Prince Rupert*, 186.
273   "The people of this country": Ibid., 189.
273   "I employ the little time": Ibid., 190.
274   "Happiness is dependent": Haldane, *Descartes*, 261.
274   "I examined the number code": Nye, *The Princess and the Philosopher*, 106.
275   "the property of allowing": Haldane, *Descartes*, 303.
276   "The portrait which Chanut": Godfrey, *A Sister of Prince Rupert*, 210.
276   "I had the honor": Haldane, *Descartes*, 325.
277   "Had a letter come to me": Ibid., 331.
277   "It seems to me": Ibid., 306.

277   "I confess that a man": Ibid., 334.

278   "I have put off this journey...I shall never cease to devote to you": Blaze de Bury, *Memoirs of the Princess Palatine*, 280–82.

278   "Though the fever has left me": Godfrey, *A Sister of Prince Rupert*, 194.

278   "Although the death we speak of": Ibid., 197.

279   "Assuring myself that": Ibid., 214.

279   "He reminds me": Haldane, *Descartes*, 340.

279   "As to the time": Blaze de Bury, *Memoirs of the Princess Palatine*, 284.

280   "He taught me more": Haldane, *Descartes*, 343.

280   "I have been in Stockholm": Blaze de Bury, *Memoirs of the Princess Palatine*, 283.

280   "She is extremely devoted": Haldane, *Descartes*, 343–44.

280   "Nevertheless, though I have so great": Godfrey, *A Sister of Prince Rupert*, 216.

281   "It is proof of the continuance...to serve you, Elizabeth": Ibid., 218.

282   "It seems to me that men's thoughts": Haldane, *Descartes*, 349.

282–83 "Madame Elizabeth Palatine...hinder his decease": Godfrey, *A Sister of Prince Rupert*, 219–22.

283   "On the eighth day": Ibid., 221-222.

283   "We thought her much changed": *Memoirs of Sophia, Electress of Hanover*, 42.

Chapter 16. A Desperate Plan

287   "Being a good general": *Memoirs of Sophia, Electress of Hanover*, 22.

288   "He either fears his fate": Napier, *Memoirs of the Marquis of Montrose*, vol. 1, 61.

288   "The perpetual cause of the controversies": Ibid., 286.

288   "Do ye not know": Ibid., 288.

289   "Heard ye not": Napier, *Memoirs of the Marquis of Montrose*, vol. 2, 483.

290   "before God, angels, and men": Ibid., 692.

290   "I never had passion on earth": Ibid., 422.

292   "abandon the Marquis of Montrose": Ibid., 696.

292   "in the name of the whole kingdom": Ibid., 729.

292   "My Lord, I have found": Ibid., 711.

293   "I do not desire you should quit": Ibid., 713.

293   "I give you many thanks": Ibid., 711.

293   "Montrose: Whereas the necessity": Ibid., 706.

293   "I pray God keep the King": Ibid., 714.

294   "to proceed vigorously": Buchan, *The Marquis of Montrose*, 230.

294   "otherwise, to give him": Napier, *Memoirs of the Marquis of Montrose*, vol. 2, 729.

296   "The 7th of May, 1650": Ibid., 773–74.

297   "I am sorry if this manner": Ibid., 806.

297   "where, having freely pardoned": Ibid., 808.

297   "I saw his arm": Ibid.

297   "a letter from the King's Majesty": Ibid., 764.

298   "Montrose meanwhile": *Memoirs of Sophia, Electress of Hanover*, 23.

300   "rascals and dogs": van Zuylen van Nyevelt, *Court Life in the Dutch Republic*, 164.

300   "It was England": Green, *Elizabeth*, 371.

300   "a better tongue": Ibid.

300   "You will have heard of the high business": Ibid., 370.

302   "I have now received": Green, *Lives of the Princesses of England*, vol. 6, 213–14.

303   "as no parable but the certain truth": Strickland, *Lives of the Queens of Scotland*, 218.

303   "although she supposed he [Karl Ludwig] meant": Ibid., 219.

304   "I have not before taken the liberty": Godfrey, *A Sister of Prince Rupert*, 270–71.

304   "My sister could wait": Ibid., 273.

305   "Madam, the respect which I have": Green, *Elizabeth,* 391.

306   "highly prejudicial to her honor": Ibid., 393.

307   "The king and my niece...were at Antwerp": Ibid., 394.

307   "Madam, I received yours": Ibid., 431.

307   "Your sister Louisa is arrived": Ibid., 394.

Chapter 17. The Electress, Two Dukes, and the Lady-in-Waiting

312   "His Majesty [Ferdinand] received him": *Memoirs of Sophia, Electress of Hanover*, 47.

312   "The Electress, whose one thought": Ibid., 49.

312   "such a bad temper": Ibid.

313   "Your Belovedness": Scott, *Rupert, Prince Palatine*, 290.

314   "She tried to forbid": *Memoirs of Sophia, Electress of Hanover*, 51.

314   "His manner was good": Ibid., 52.

314   "The Elector was devoted": Ibid.

315   "heard the report of my engagement": Ibid., 54.

315   "while in treaty with his subjects": Ibid.

315   "which served to show off": Ibid., 46.

315   "I infinitely preferred the Duke": Ibid., 56.

315   "at once attached himself...said 'Yes'": Ibid.

315   "I knew also that the Elector": Ibid.

316   "The Elector did not wait": Ibid.

316   "enjoined the strictest secrecy": Ibid., 57.

316   "the greatest gentleness": Ibid., 58.

316   "the state of affairs was changed": Ibid.

316   "even were his sister": Ibid., 58–59.

316   "laden with fine presents": Ibid., 59.

316   "The idea that he was to possess": Ibid.

316   "Sometimes he wept": Ibid.

316   "determined to go himself": Ibid., 60.

316–17 "plunged in the dissipations…was very uneasy": Ibid.

318   "stolen from out of her [Charlotte's] drawer": Blaze de Bury, *Memoirs of the Princess Palatine*, 300.

318   "On entering the chamber": Duggan, *Sophia of Hanover*, 55. For more on this interesting event and Charlotte's later long letter to the emperor outlining her grievances (in which she admits to securing a gun and breaking into Louise's room), see *Le Vie et les Amours de Charles-Louis*, 153–87.

318   "send a bullet through": Blaze de Bury, *Memoirs of the Princess Palatine,* 301.

319   "if everybody could quit their husbands": Ward, *The Electress Sophia and the Hanoverian Succession*, 58.

319   "The Duke of Hanover": *Memoirs of Sophia, Electress of Hanover*, 61.

319   "proposing to retain…with pleasure to this proposition": Ibid., 61–62.

319   "Duke John Frederick by no means": Ibid., 62.

319–20 "The Duke of Hanover was so enraged": Ibid.

320   "George William announced to his Council": Ibid., 64.

320   "to avoid disturbances": Ibid., 66.

320   "I should be mistress at Hanover": Ibid., 66–67.

320   "assured that he need entertain": Ibid., 67.

321   "that a good establishment was all": Ibid., 68.

321   "Having perceived the urgent necessity": Ibid., 73–74. This solemn declaration may be read in its entirety in both German and English in *Memoirs of Sophia, Electress of Hanover*, 72–75.

321   "I was dressed": Ibid., 76–77.

321   "we danced in German fashion": Ibid., 78.

321   "I, being resolved to love him": Ibid., 76.

322   "the Duke my husband, taking my hand": Ibid., 83.

322   "I take pleasure in remembering": Ibid., 83–84.

322   "He took part": Ibid., 84–85.

323   "He actually told me": Ibid., 89.

323   "I took pleasure even": Ibid., 90.

323   "I now hardly ever saw": Ibid., 91.

323   "he assured me": Ibid.

324   "I have already ousted X": Barine, *Madame, Mother of the Regent*, 22.

324   "I carry with me": Ibid., 52.

325   "The tables were dressed": Duggan, *Sophia of Hanover*, 65–66.

325   "I shall watch over her": Barine, *Madame, Mother of the Regent*, 33.

325   "I look for your sister": Ward, *The Electress Sophia and the Hanoverian Succession,* 92.

325   "After his departure": *Memoirs of Sophia, Electress of Hanover*, 92.

325   "Her shape and humor": Godfrey, *A Sister of Prince Rupert*, 226.

325   "Great was the joy": *Memoirs of Sophia, Electress of Hanover*, 93.

326 "perfectly hated the Presbyterians": Scott, *The King in Exile*, 137.

326 "so that he may be in a capacity": Ibid., 141.

327 "I think I must repent too": Gardiner, *History of the Commonwealth and the Protectorate*, vol. 1, 385.

328 "God bless King Charles": Guizot, *History of Richard Cromwell and the Restoration*, vol. 2, 166.

329 "We do assure you": Ibid., 212.

329 "the house upon reading": *The Diary of Samuel Pepys*, vol. 1, 121–22.

331 "Must not a queen": van Zuylen van Nyevelt, *Court Life in the Dutch Republic*, 179.

331 "You sent me one seven thousand": Strickland, *Lives of the Queens of Scotland*, 265.

331 "I very well remember": Ibid., 266.

331 "to kiss the Queen of Bohemia's hands": *The Diary of Samuel Pepys*, vol. 1, 136.

331 "who used us very respectfully": Ibid., 142.

331 "dined in a great deal": Ibid., 151.

332 "This place is very dull": Strickland, *Lives of the Queens of Scotland*, 268.

332 "I found the poor woman": Scott, *Rupert, Prince Palatine*, 297.

332 "When your Majesty is here": Green, *Elizabeth*, 401.

333 "Sure your Majesty hath forgot": Ibid.

333 "was already shipped": Strickland, *Lives of the Queens of Scotland*, 273.

334 "I am glad your Majesty": Ibid., 275.

334 "I love you ever": Ibid., 273.

335 "My royal tenant": Green, *Elizabeth*, 410.

335 "On His Mistress": Wotton, *Poems*, 14.

Chapter 18. Abbess of Herford

342 "If I came to the Institution": Godfrey, *A Sister of Prince Rupert*, 288–89.

342 "If you knew me aright": Ibid., 290.

342 "As your Grace has assured me": Ibid., 291.

343 "I am heartily sorry": Ibid., 291–92.

343 "If your Grace": Ibid., 293–94.

344 "The Elector is very docile": Ibid., 303.

344 "La Grecque": Ibid., 281.

345 "Princess and Prelatess": Ibid., 302.

345 "An opportunity occurs": Pope-Hennessy, *Anna van Schurman*, 161.

346 "In all this, we can desire only": Blaze de Bury, *Memoirs of the Princess Palatine*, 338–39.

346 "so long as the sectaries showed": Godfrey, *A Sister of Prince Rupert*, 310.

346 "The Princess wrote to me": Ibid., 308.

347 "All made merry": Pope-Hennessy, *Anna van Schurman*, 150.

347 "We learned quickly enough": Ibid.

348   "Although much has been spread": Blaze de Bury, *Memoirs of the Princess Palatine*, 337.

349   "I hear that all manner": Ibid., 341–43.

349   "Next morning, as soon as we": Ibid., 363.

350   "As though he had been the Delphian": Ibid., 364.

350   "judge of his eloquence": Ibid., 366.

350   "So forth we repaired": Ibid., 366–67.

350   "Whilst he delivered all this": Ibid., 368.

351   "But to this the Electress": Ibid., 369.

353   "Tell the King": Dixon, *History of William Penn*, 84–85.

354   "I did indeed discover": Scott, *Rupert, Prince Palatine*, 313.

354   "Prince's metal": Ibid., 337.

354   "faithful great black dog": Ibid., 342.

354   "the best players at tennis": Ibid., 335.

354   "He is as merry": *Diary of Samuel Pepys*, vol. 2, 14.

355   "Oath of Allegiance": Janney, *The Life of William Penn*, 109.

355   "worshipping God after another manner": Ibid.

355   "I have received your two letters": Blaze de Bury, *Memoirs of the Princess Palatine*, 374-75.

356   "She would constantly": Ibid., 398.

356   "Though she kept no sumptuous": Ibid.

357   "I related...the bitter mockings": Janney, *The Life of William Penn*, 32.

357   "the sense she had": Ibid., 130.

357   " 'I cannot speak' ": Ibid.

357   "Dear Friend—Your tender care": Ibid., 136–37.

357   "I must wait till God": Godfrey, *A Sister of Prince Rupert*, 334–35.

358   "I will execute thy commission": Blaze de Bury, *Memoirs of the Princess Palatine*, 384.

358   "that he was quite comfortable at Windsor": Scott, *Rupert, Prince Palatine*, 353–54.

359   "my sister was in bed": Godfrey, *A Sister of Prince Rupert*, 344.

359   "It is a great consolation to me": Ibid., 346.

359   "I am still alive": Ibid., 347.

359   "Elizabeth fails more and more": Ibid., 348.

359–60   "The late blessed Princess Elizabeth": Ibid., 397–400.

360   "God hath given it to me": Dixon, *History of William Penn*, 191.

Chapter 19. Abbess of Maubuisson

363   the indomitable Blanche of Castile: For the history of the abbey, see Depoin and Dutilleux, *Cartulaire de l'Abbaye de Maubuisson*. For more on Blanche of Castile and Louis IX, later Saint Louis, see my earlier book *Four Queens: The Provençal Sisters Who Ruled Europe*.

364   "*L'État, c'est moi*": Hassall, *Louis XIV and the Zenith of the French Monarchy*, 81.

364   descended from the same line as Henri IV: For an account of Henri IV's early life, and his importance to France, see my earlier book *The Rival Queens*.

365   "Voilà un Huguenot": Duggan, *Sophia of Hanover*, 73.

365   "War of the Queen's Rights": Martin, *Martin's History of France: The Age of Louis XIV*, vol. 1, 302.

367   For more on Henrietta's death: The case against poisoning is highly persuasive. One of Henrietta's physicians reported to Louis XIV that she had had a frequent cough and been unwell for years. In the months preceding her death she had complained of digestive problems so severe that often she could tolerate only milk. She lost so much weight that a courtier who saw her at Versailles before her death observed that she looked like a corpse with rouge on its cheeks. According to Dr. Greg Soloway, a renowned gastroenterologist, these symptoms were much more likely to indicate intestinal tuberculosis, which was prevalent in France during this period (two of Catherine de' Medici's sons died of TB) or peptic ulcer disease, both of which could have led to the intestinal perforation and peritonitis that Henrietta likely experienced and that caused the terrible pain and her rapid demise. The chicory water (which in any event was sampled by both the lady-in-waiting who had prepared the drink and another duchess who was present, to no ill effect) was in this case an unfortunate red herring. "Acute poisoning would not account for her previous history of symptoms," Dr. Soloway confirmed by e-mail.

367   "As I reached this town...orders on all matters": Barine, *Madame, Mother of the Regent*, 64.

368   "Those who think that Monsieur": Ibid., 65.

368   "Her peculiar characteristic": Menzies, *Political Women*, vol. 1, 198.

368   "the marriage of Liselotte": Barine, *Madame, Mother of the Regent*, 68.

369   "My marriage contract": Ibid., 74.

370   "He was a little round man": Ibid., 81.

370   "jewels, rings, and precious stones": Ibid., 73.

370   he be allowed to wear them: For this condition of the marriage contract, see *The Life and Letters of Elizabeth Charlotte*, 12.

370   "It was cold; she wore no mask": Barine, *Madame, Mother of the Regent*, 86–87.

370   "All my life, since my earliest youth": *The Letters of Madame*, vol. 2, 185.

371   "I was very glad when...Monsieur": Ibid., 142.

371   "One cannot believe how pleasant": Scott, *Rupert, Prince Palatine*, 347–48.

371   "Her happy temper": Godfrey, *A Sister of Prince Rupert*, 342–43.

372   "Since I have been a nun professed": Strickland, *Lives of the Queens of Scotland*, 325.

372–73   "ruined and destroyed their country": Hassall, *Louis XIV and the Zenith of the French Monarchy*, 175.

373 "Do not look upon": Blaze de Bury, *Memoirs of the Princess Palatine*, 307.

373 "I have wept so much": *The Letters of Madame*, vol. 1, 42–43.

374 "Unfortunately the Chevalier": Ibid., 47.

374 "I became so melancholic": Ibid., 51–52.

374 "You can judge whether I have good reason": Ibid., 55–56.

375 "Get the idea out of your head": Ibid., 57.

376 "If they were to kill me for it": Ibid., 83.

376 "What really grieves me": Ibid., 84.

377 "Now the King is the sole master": *The Life and Letters of Elizabeth Charlotte*, 32.

378 "the Maintenon woman": *The Letters of Madame*, vol. 1, 131.

378 "the old bawd": Ibid., 116.

378 "the old wretch": Ibid., 139.

378 "the dirty old slut": Ibid., 140.

378 "The Great Man [Louis XIV] is incredibly simple": Ibid., 135.

378 Catherine would turn on her former Huguenot allies: For more on this and the St. Bartholomew's Day Massacre, see my earlier work *The Rival Queens*.

378 "Reunion": Baird, *The Huguenots and the Revocation of the Edict of Nantes*, vol. 2, 34.

378 "A day was appointed": Agnew, *Protestant Exiles from France, Chiefly in the Reign of Louis XIV*, vol. 2, 4.

379 "Men and women": Baird, *The Huguenots and the Revocation of the Edict of Nantes*, vol. 2, 48.

380 "This new grandeur, Sire": Ibid., 7.

380 "Soldiers are strange apostles": Ibid., 67.

381 "What I am going to relate": *The Letters of Madame de Sévigné to Her Daughter and Friends*, 260.

382 "It must be owned": Strickland, *Lives of the Queens of Scotland*, 355.

382 "I pray to God": Strickland, *Leibniz and the Two Sophies*, 163.

382 "the tranquility of mind": Ibid., 167.

382 "What gives me a very bad idea": Duggan, *Sophia of Hanover*, 158–59.

383 "I have again visited my aunt": *The Letters of Madame*, vol. 1, 186–87.

383 "The greater part of our manufacturing": Baird, *The Huguenots and the Revocation of the Edict of Nantes*, vol. 2, 77.

384 "Never in my life": *The Letters of Madame*, vol. 2, 23.

384 "I have received the sad news": Ibid.

384 "the Abbesse de Maubuisson, Louise Hollandine": *The Letters of Madame*, vol. 2, 108.

Chapter 20. A Scandal in Hanover

390 "Three days ago I arrived here": Barine, *Madame, Mother of the Regent*, 44–45.

390 "the Bishopess": Ward, *The Electress Sophia and the Hanoverian Succession*, 159.

390 "One cannot live more than once": Ibid., 160.

391 "was much addicted to laughing": Strickland, *Lives of the Queens of Scotland*, 316.

391 "Ma tante": Ibid., 309.

391 "The bonds of holy matrimony": *Memoirs of Sophia, Electress of Hanover*, 101.

392 "The Duke asked me": Ibid., 107–8.

392 "As I should have been mortified": Ibid., 110.

392 "play basset": Ibid., 125.

392 "I should have been very dull": Ibid., 125–26.

392 "returning alone in the carriage": Ibid., 132.

392 "a party to go to the country": Ibid.

393 "in a state of utter consternation": Ibid., 146.

393 "reflecting that a civil war": Ibid.

393 "She was grave and dignified": Ibid., 150.

394 "anti-contract of marriage": Ibid., 152.

394 "Hoping to touch the Duke": Ibid.

394 "Though it will be said": Ibid., 154.

396 "He died as a true German": Wilkins, *The Love of an Uncrowned Queen*, 28.

396 "At school I...should": Mackie, *Life of Godfrey William Von Leibnitz*, 19.

397 "Having experienced the good fortune": Ibid., 86–87.

397 "I suspect that what Newton": Ibid., 99.

398 "Madam [Sophia]...is a great genius": Strickland, *Leibniz and the Two Sophies*, 2.

398 "Monsieur Leibniz must have": *The Letters of Madame*, vol. 1, 256.

398 "It does both [Sophia and Figuelotte] a disservice": Strickland, *Leibniz and the Two Sophies*, 3.

399 "I do not concern myself": Ibid., 170.

401 "I cry about it all night long": Ward, *The Electress Sophia and the Hanoverian Succession*, 201.

402 "enter into Christian matrimony": Wilkins, *The Love of an Uncrowned Queen*, 23.

402 "The Duke of Celle would no longer": *Memoirs of Sophia, Electress of Hanover*, 187–88.

403 "He remembered you": Strickland, *Lives of the Queens of England*, 79–80.

406 "does not care much": Wilkins, *The Love of an Uncrowned Queen*, 57.

407 "This is a fair and beautiful princess": Strickland, *Lives of the Queens of Scotland*, 324.

409 "Here is my day": Wilkins, *The Love of an Uncrowned Queen*, 226.

410 "No, I mean to die": Strickland, *Lives of the Queens of England*, 28.

410 "You have given your daughter": Ibid., 51.

410 "It is a melancholy prospect": Ibid., 140.

411 "God help me": Ibid., 176.

411 "This court is as splendid": Wilkins, *The Love of an Uncrowned Queen*, 102. I have translated from the French: "The Duchess Sophia is une personne incomparable d'un esprit, d'une bonté, et d'une civilité à charmer."

412 "To show us he doth not": Ibid., 113.

412 "A courier is come hither": Ibid., 254.

414 "I am in the depths of despair": Ibid., 142.

414 "Why do not the hours": Ibid., 155.

414 "My greatest grudge": Ibid., 241.

415 "The Electress talks about you": Ibid., 269.

415 "Marshal Podevils was the first": Ibid., 322.

415 "bathed in milk": Ibid., 334.

416 "I have been told his sister": Ibid., 366.

417 "had often gone away": Ibid., 365.

417 "They would never have believed": Ibid., vii.

418 "as to the Question whether": Ibid., 369.

Chapter 21. The Triumph of the Winter Queen

424 "Be it enacted and declared": Historical Association of Great Britain, *Constitutional Documents*, 2–3.

424 "You may be sure": Toland, *An Account of the Courts of Prussia and Hanover*, 53–54.

425 "The Electress is three and seventy": Ibid., 58.

425 "I was the first": Ibid., 60.

427 "What makes it worse for me": Duggan, *Sophia of Hanover*, 175.

427 "I am afraid to contemplate": *The Letters of Madame*, vol. 1, 249.

427 "she herself would be": Somerset, *Queen Anne*, 290.

427 "I thank God, I am in good Health": Sophia of Hanover, *A Letter from Her Royal Highness*, 1.

428 "It is from the heart": Macpherson, *Original Papers*, vol. 2, 31.

429 "Madam, my sister and aunt": Rait, *Five Stuart Princesses*, 329–30.

429 "I believe I am more ill": Ibid., 330.

429 "This affair will certainly": Ward, *The Electress Sophia and the Hanoverian Succession*, 431.

429 "Not only did she dine in public": Rait, *Five Stuart Princesses*, 331.

430 "I am very ill": Ibid.

430 "for another hour…die in tranquility": Duggan, *Sophia of Hanover*, 189.

430 "The death of Madam the Electress": Strickland, *Leibniz and the Two Sophies*, 28.

430 "Without her": *The Life and Letters of Elizabeth Charlotte*, 254.

Selected Bibliography

Adam, Charles, and Paul Tannery, eds. *Oeuvres de Descartes: Correspondance IV, Juillet 1643–Avril 1647*. Paris: Léopold Cerf, 1901.

Agnew, David C. A. *Protestant Exiles from France, Chiefly in the Reign of Louis XIV, or The Huguenot Refugees and Their Descendants in Great Britain and Ireland*. Vol. 2. For Private Circulation, 1886.

Airy, Osmund. *Charles II*. London: Longmans, Green, 1904.

Akkerman, Nadine, ed. *The Correspondence of Elizabeth Stuart, Queen of Bohemia*. Vol. 2, *1632–1642*. Oxford: Oxford University Press, 2011.

Baird, Henry M. *The Huguenots and the Revocation of the Edict of Nantes*, Vol. 2. New York: Charles Scribner's Sons, 1895.

Barine, Arvède. *Madame, Mother of the Regent*. Translated by Jeanne Mairet. New York: G. P. Putnam's Sons, 1909.

Beavan, Bryan. *King James VI of Scotland and I of England*. London: Rubicon, 1996.

Benger, Elizabeth. *Memoirs of Elizabeth Stuart, Queen of Bohemia, Daughter of King James the First, Including Sketches of the State of Society in Holland and Germany in the 17th Century*, 2 vols. London: Longman, Hurst, Rees, Orme, Brown, and Green, 1825.

Birch, Thomas. *The Life of Henry Prince of Wales, Eldest Son of King James I Compiled Chiefly from His Own Papers, and Other Manuscripts, Never Before Published*. Dublin: G. Faulkner, 1760.

Blaze de Bury, Marie. *Memoirs of the Princess Palatine, Princess of Bohemia, Including Her Correspondence with the Great Men of Her Day, and Memoirs of the Court of Holland Under the Princes of Orange*. London: R. Bentley, 1853.

Bréal, Auguste. *Rembrandt: A Critical Essay*. London: Duckworth, 1902.

Bromley, George. *A Collection of Original Royal Letters, Written by King Charles the First and Second, King James the Second, and the King and Queen of Bohemia; Together with Original Letters, Written by Prince Rupert, Charles Louis, Count Palatine, the Duchess of Hanover, and Several Other Distinguished Persons, from the Year 1619 to 1665*. London: J. Stockdale, 1787.

Brown, Horatio, ed. *Calendar of State Papers and Manuscripts Relating to English Affairs, Existing in the Archives and Collections of Venice, and in Other Libraries of Northern Italy*. Vol. 12, 1610–1613. London: Mackie, 1905.

Bruce, John, ed. *Correspondence of King James VI of Scotland with Sir Robert Cecil and Others in England, During the Reign of Queen Elizabeth; with an Appendix Containing Papers Illustrative of Transactions Between King James and Robert Earl of Essex, Printed for the Camden Society.* Westminster: J. B. Nichols and Sons, 1861.

Buchan, John. *The Marquis of Montrose.* New York: Scribner's Sons, 1913.

Calderwood, David. *The History of the Kirk of Scotland.* Vols. 1–5. Edinburgh: Wodrow Society, 1842–1849.

Calendar of the State Papers Relating to Scotland and Mary, Queen of Scots, 1547–1603. Vols. 7–9. Glasgow: James Hedderwick and Sons, 1915. http://www.british-history.ac.uk/cal-state-papers/venice/vol17.

Carleton, Dudley. *Letters from and to Sir Dudley Carleton, Knt. During His Embassy in Holland from January 1615/16 to December 1620.* London: Privately printed, 1775.

Chancellor, E. Beresford. *The Life of Charles I, 1600–1625.* London: George Bell and Sons, 1886.

Clifford, Anne. *The Diary of the Lady Anne Clifford.* With an introductory note by V. Sackville-West. London: William Heinemann, 1923.

Coke, Roger. *A Detection of the Court and State of England During the Four Last Reigns and the Inter-Regnum, Consisting of Private Memoirs, Etc., with Observations and Reflections.* Vol. 1. London: Printed for Andr. Bell at the Cross Keys and Bible in Cornhill, 1697.

Cornwallis, Charles. *An Account of the Baptism, Life, Death and Funeral, of the Most Incomparable Prince Frederick Henry, Prince of Wales.* London: J. Freeman, 1751.

———. *The Life and Character of Henry-Frederic, Prince of Wales: With a Proper Appendix Containing Several Other Curious, Authentic Testimonies, from Scarce and Credible Writers, Relating to that Amiable and Most Noble Prince; Including a Particular Account of His Sickness, Death, Etc. with Some Poetical Elogies.* London: J. Roberts, 1738.

Cummings, William H. *God Save the King: The Origin and History of the Music and Words of the National Anthem.* London: Novello, 1902.

Dalton, Charles. *Life and Times of General Sir Edward Cecile, Viscount Wimbledon, Colonel of an English Regiment in the Dutch Service, 1605–1631, and One of His Majesty's Most Honourable Privy Council, 1628–1638.* London: S. Low, Marston, Searle, and Rivington, 1885.

Depoin, J., and Adolphe Dutilleux. *Cartulaire de l'Abbaye de Maubuisson (Notre-Dame-la-Royal).* Pointoise: Typographie Lucien Paris, 1890.

Dixon, William Hepworth. *History of William Penn: Founder of Pennsylvania.* London: Hurst and Blackett, 1872.

Duggan, J. N. *Sophia of Hanover: From Winter Princess to Heiress of Great Britain, 1630–1714.* London: Peter Owen, 2011.

Elizabeth Charlotte, duchess of Orléans. *The Letters of Madame: The Correspondence of Elizabeth-Charlotte of Bavaria, Princess Palatine, Duchess of Orleans, called "Madame" at the Court of King Louis XIV.* Translated and edited by Gertrude Scott Stevenson. 2 vols. New York: D. Appleton, 1924.

————. *The Life and Letters of Elizabeth Charlotte, Princess Palatine and Mother of Philippe D'Orléans, Regent of France 1652–1722, Compiled, Translated, and Gathered from Various Published and Unpublished Sources.* London: Chapman and Hall, Limited, 1889.

Fraser, Antonia. *Mary Queen of Scots.* London: Weidenfeld & Nicholson, 1969.

Gamache, Cyprien de. *The Court and Times of Charles I; Illustrated by Authentic and Confidential Letters, from Various Public and Private Collections; Including Memoirs of the Mission in England of the Capuchin Friars in the Service of Queen Henrietta Maria.* 2 vols. London: Henry Colburn, 1848.

Gardiner, Bertha Meriton. *The Struggle Against Absolute Monarchy, 1603–1688.* London: Longmans, Green, 1889.

Gardiner, Samuel Rawson, ed. *Letters and Other Documents Illustrating the Relations Between England and Germany at the Commencement of the Thirty Years' War.* Westminster: Printed for the Camden Society, 1865.

Gardiner, Samuel Rawson. *The Fall of the Monarchy of Charles I, 1637–1649.* 2 vols. London: Longmans, Green, 1882.

————. *The First Two Stuarts and the Puritan Revolution 1603–1660.* New York: C. Scribner's Sons, 1895.

————. *History of the Commonwealth and the Protectorate.* Vol. 1, *1649–1651.* London: Longmans, Green, 1894.

————. *History of the Great Civil War.* London: Longmans, Green, 1901.

Gindely, Anton. *History of the Thirty Years' War.* Translated by Andrew Ten Brook. 2 vols. New York: G. P. Putnam's Sons, 1884.

Godfrey, Elizabeth. *Heidelberg: Its Princes and Its Palaces.* New York: Dutton, 1908.

————. *A Sister of Prince Rupert, Elizabeth, Princess Palatine and Abbess of Herford.* London: J. Lane, 1909.

Gonzagues, Anne de. *Mémoires d'Anne de Gonzagues, Princesse Palatine.* London: ET fe trouve à Paris, ches les Marchands de Nouveautés, 1786.

Gower, Ronald Sutherland. *The Figure Painters of Holland.* London: S. Low, Marston, Searle, and Rivington, 1880.

Gray, Patrick. *Letters and Papers Relating to Patrick, Master of Gray.* Edinburgh: Edinburgh Printing, 1835.

Green, Mary Anne Everett. *Elizabeth: Electress Palatine and Queen of Bohemia.* Revised by her niece S. C. Lomas. London: Methuen, 1909.

————. *Lives of the Princesses of England, from the Norman Conquest.* Vol. 6. London: Longman, Brown, Green, Longman, and Roberts, 1857.

Gregg, Pauline. *King Charles I.* London: Phoenix Press, 2000.

Guizot, M. *History of Richard Cromwell and the Restoration of Charles II*. Translated by Andrew Scoble. 2 vols. London: Richard Bentley, 1856.

Haldane, Elizabeth S. *Descartes, His Life and Times*. London: John Murray, 1905.

Halliwell-Phillipps, J. O., ed. *Letters of the Kings of England: Now First Collected from Royal Archives and Other Authentic Sources, Private as Well as Public*. Vol. 2. London: H. Colburn, 1848.

Hamilton, William Douglas, ed. *Calendar of State Papers Domestic: Charles I, 1644*. Vol. 502, July 1644. London: His Majesty's Stationery Office, 1888. http://www.british-history.ac.uk/cal-state-papers/domestic/chas1/1644/pp295-387.

Hassall, Arthur. *Louis XIV and the Zenith of the French Monarchy*. New York: Putnam's Sons, 1895.

Herries, John Maxwell. *Historical Memoirs of the Reign of Mary Queen of Scots and a Portion of the Reign of King James the Sixth*. Edinburgh: Privately printed for the Abbotsford Club, 1836.

Hinds, Allen B., ed. *Calendar of State Papers Relating to English Affairs in the Archives of Venice*. Vol. 16, 1619–1621. London: His Majesty's Stationery Office, 1910. http://www.british-history.ac.uk/cal-state-papers/venice/vol16.

———. *Calendar of State Papers Relating to English Affairs in the Archives of Venice*. Vol. 17, 1621–1623. London: His Majesty's Stationery Office, 1911.

Historical Association of Great Britain. *Constitutional Documents*. London: Published for the Historical Association by G. Bell and Sons, 1914.

Janney, Samuel Macpherson. *The Life of William Penn with Selections from his Correspondence and Autobiography*. Philadelphia: Friends' Book Association, 1876.

Jesse, Hohn Heneage. *Memoirs of the Court of England During the Reign of the Stuarts, Including the Protectorate*. Vol. 1. London: R. Bentley, 1840.

Karl Ludwig, Elector Palatine. *The Manifest of the Most Illustrious and Soveraigne Prince, Charles Lodowick, Count Palatine of the Rhine, Prince Elector of the Sacred Empire*. London: Printed by A. G. for I. N. and R. W., and are to be sold at the sign of the Kings Armes in Paul's Church-Yard, 1637.

Krummel, Donald W. "God Save the King." *Musical Times* 103, no. 1429 (March 1962): 159–60.

Labanoff, Alexandre, ed. *Lettres, Instruction, et Mémoires de Marie Stuart, Reine D'Ecosse; Publiés sur les Originaux*. Vol. 6. London: Charles Dolman, 1844.

La Fèvre de La Boderie, Antoine. *Ambassades de Monsieur de La Boderie, en Angleterre sous le Regne d'Henri IV et la Minorité de Louis XIII Depuis les Années 1606 jusqu'en 1611*. Paris, 1750.

Lang, Andrew. *James VI and the Gowrie Mystery*. London: Longmans, Green, 1902.

Letters to King James the Sixth from the Queen, Prince Henry, Prince Charles, the Princess Elizabeth and Her Husband Frederick, King of Bohemia, and from their son Prince Frederick Henry. Edinburgh: T. Constable, 1835.

Le Vie et les Amours de Charles-Louis, Electeur Palatin. Pamphlet; author unknown. Amsterdam: Chez Marret, 1697.

Lodge, Richard. *Richelieu*. London: Macmillan, 1908.

Lovelace, Richard. *Songs and Sonnets by Richard Lovelace*. New York: R. H. Russell, 1901.

Mackie, John M. *Life of Godfrey William Von Leibnitz on the Basis of the German Work of Dr. G. L. Guhrauer*. Boston: Gould, Kendall and Lincoln, 1845.

Macpherson, James. *The History of Great Britain, from the Restoration, to the Accession of the House of Hannover*. 2 vols. London: W. Strahan, and T. Cadell, 1775.

———. *Original Papers, Containing the Secret History of Great Britain from the Restoration to the Accession of the House of Hannover: To Which Are Prefixed Extracts from the Life of James II As Written by Himself*. London: W. Strahan and T. Cadell, 1775.

Mahaffy, John Pentland. *Descartes*. Edinburgh: William Blackwood and Sons, 1880.

Martin, Henri. *Martin's History of France: The Age of Louis XIV*. Translated from the fourth Paris edition by Mary L. Booth. Boston: Walker, Wise, 1865.

Maxwell-Scott, Mary Monica. *The Tragedy of Fotheringay: Founded on the Journal of D. Bourgoing, Physician to Mary, Queen of Scots, and on Unpublished MS. Documents*. Edinburgh: Sands, 1905.

Melvill, James. *The Autobiography and Diary of Mr. James Melvill, with a Continuation of the Diary*. Edited from manuscripts in the libraries of the Faculty of Advocates and University of Edinburgh. Vol. 1. Edinburgh: Wodrow Society, 1842.

Menzies, Sutherland. *Political Women*. Vol. 1. London: Henry S. King, 1875.

Moysie, David. *Memoirs of the Affairs of Scotland, from Early Manuscripts*. Edinburgh: Privately printed for the Bannatyne Club, 1830.

Napier, Mark. *Memoirs of the Marquis of Montrose*. 2 vols. Edinburgh: Thomas G. Stevenson, 1856.

Nichols, John. *The Processes, Processions, and Magnificent Festivities of King James the First, His Royal Consort, Family, and Court, Collected from Original Manuscripts, Scarce Pamphlets, Corporation Records, Parochial Registers, Etc.* Vols. 1–4. London: J. B. Nichols, 1828.

Nye, Andrea. *The Princess and the Philosopher: Letters of Elisabeth of the Palatine to René Descartes*. New York: Rowman and Littlefield, 1999.

Pepys, Samuel. *The Diary of Samuel Pepys Which Was Kept in the Years 1659–69*. 2 vols. New York: Heritage Press, 1942.

Phelps, William Lyon. *Lucasta: The Poems of Richard Lovelace Esquire*. With an introductory note by William Lyon Phelps. Vol. 1. Chicago: Caxton Club, 1921.

Pope-Hennessy, Una Birch. *Anna van Schurman, Artist, Scholar, Saint; with Portraits*. London: Longmans, Green, 1909.

Rait, Robert S. *Five Stuart Princesses: Margaret of Scotland, Elizabeth of Bohemia, Mary of Orange, Henrietta of Orleans, Sophia of Hanover.* New York: E. P. Dutton, 1908.

Ross, Josephine. *The Winter Queen: The Story of Elizabeth Stuart.* New York: Dorset, 1979.

Schiller, Friedrich. *The History of the Thirty Years' War in Germany.* Translated by A. J. W. Morrison. Boston: S. E. Cassino, 1884.

Scott, Eva. *The King in Exile: The Wanderings of Charles II from June 1646 to July 1654.* London: Archibald Constable, 1905.

———. *Rupert, Prince Palatine.* New York: G. P. Putnam's Sons, 1899.

Sévigné, Marie de Rabutin-Chantal. *The Letters of Madame de Sévigné to Her Daughter and Friends.* Edited by Mrs. Hale. Boston: Roberts Brothers, 1878.

Smith, Logan Pearsall. *The Life and Letters of Sir Henry Wotton.* 2 vols. Oxford: Clarendon Press, 1907.

Somerset, Anne. *Queen Anne: The Politics of Passion.* New York: Alfred A. Knopf, 2013.

Sophia, Electress of Hanover. *A Letter from Her Royal Highness, the Princess Sophia, Electress of Brunswic and Luneburg, to His Grace the Archbishop of Canterbury. with Another from Hannover, Written by Sir Rowland Gwynne to the Right Honourable the Earl of Stamford.* London: B. Bragge, 1706.

———. *Memoirs of Sophia, Electress of Hanover (1630–1680).* Translated by H. Forester. London: Richard Bentley and Son, 1888.

Strickland, Agnes. *Lives of the Queens of England from the Norman Conquest.* Vol. 7. London: Published for Henry Colburn by his successors, Hurst and Blackett, 1854.

———. *Lives of the Queens of Scotland and English Princesses Connected with the Regal Succession of Great Britain.* Vol. 8. Edinburgh: William Blackwood and Sons, 1859.

Strickland, Lloyd, ed. and trans. *Leibniz and the Two Sophies: The Philosophical Correspondence.* Toronto: Centre for Reformation and Renaissance Studies, 2011.

Taylor, Ida A. *The Life of Queen Henrietta Maria.* Vol. 1. London: Hutchinson, 1905.

Thou, Jacques-Auguste de. *A True Narration of That Horrible Conspiracy Against King James and the Whole Parliament of England, Commonly Called the Gunpowder Treason, Written in Latine by Jacobus Augustus Thuanus, Privy Councillor to the King of France, and President of the Supreme Senate of that Kingdom; Faithfully Rendred into English.* London: Printed for John Leigh, 1674. Reprint, Edinburgh: Privately printed, 1885.

Toland, John. *An Account of the Courts of Prussia and Hanover.* 1705. Reprint, Berlin: Manuscript Publisher, 2013.

True, Charles Kittredge. *The Thirty Years' War.* Cincinnati: Hitchcock and Walden, 1879.

Tuttle, Herbert. *History of Prussia*. Vol. 1. Boston: Houghton Mifflin, 1883.

van Zuylen van Nyevelt, Suzette. *Court Life in the Dutch Republic 1638–1689*. London: J. M. Dent, 1906.

Vickers, Robert H. *History of Bohemia*. Chicago: C. H. Sergel, 1894.

Warburton, Eliot. *Memoirs of Prince Rupert, and the Cavaliers. Including Their Private Correspondence, Now First Published from the Original Manuscript*. Vols. 1–3. London: R. Bentley, 1849.

Ward, Adolphus William. *The Electress Sophia and the Hanoverian Succession*. London: Goupil, 1903.

Wedgwood, C. V. *The Thirty Years War*. London: Folio Society, 1999.

Wilkins, W. H. *The Love of an Uncrowned Queen: Sophie Dorothea, Consort of George I, and her Correspondence with Philip Christopher, Count Konigsmarck (Now First Published from the Originals)*. New York: Longmans, Green, 1903.

Williams, Ethel Carleton. *Anne of Denmark*. London: Longman Group Limited, 1970.

Williams, Robert Folkestone, and Thomas Birch. *The Court and Times of James the First: Illustrated by Authentic and Confidential Letters, from Various Public and Private Collections*. 2 vols. London: Henry Colburn, 1848.

Willson, D. Harris. *King James VI and I*. New York: Henry Holt, 1956.

Winwood, Ralph. *Memorials of Affairs of State in the Reigns of Q. Elizabeth and K. James I Collected (Chiefly) from the Original Papers of the Right Honourable Sir Ralph Winwood, Kt., Sometime One of the Principal Secretaries of State*. Vol. 3. London: W. B. for T. Ward, 1725.

Wotton, Henry. *Poems by Sir Henry Wotton, Sir Walter Raleigh and Others*. Edited by John Hannah. London: W. Pickering, 1845.

Illustration Credits

175 Queen Henrietta Maria: Franz Hanfstaengl, ed., *The Masterpieces of Van Dyck: Sixty Reproductions of Photographs from the Original Paintings* (London: Gowans & Gray, 1906), 14.

184 William II and Mary: Ibid., 19.

193 Princess Elizabeth: Ward, *The Electress Sophia and the Hanoverian Succession*, 108.

202 Descartes: Haldane, *Descartes, His Life and Times*, frontispiece.

214 Edward and Anna de Gonzaga: Ward, *The Electress Sophia and the Hanoverian Succession*, 108.

217 Boye the dog, by Louise Hollandine: Photographic Survey, The Courtauld Institute of Art, London.

231 Frederick William and the princess of Orange: Godfrey, *A Sister of Prince Rupert*, 184.

233 Princess Henrietta Maria: Ibid., 226.

257 Karl Ludwig: Scott, *Rupert, Prince Palatine*, 283.

269 Queen Christina: Haldane, *Descartes, His Life and Times*, 296.

285 Self-portrait of Louise Hollandine: ©Sotheby's 2017.

291 Montrose: Napier, *Memoirs of the Marquis of Montrose*, vol. 2, 710.

295 Argyll: Ibid., 488.

309 Heidelberg Castle: Godfrey, *A Sister of Prince Rupert*, 246.

330 Charles II: Airy, *Charles II*, frontispiece.

337 Mary, Queen of Scots: Lionel Cust and Sir George Scharf, *Notes on the Authentic Portraits of Mary, Queen of Scots* (London: J. Murray, 1903), 34.

337 Sophia: Ward, *The Electress Sophia and the Hanoverian Succession*, 124.

339 Princess Elizabeth: Godfrey, *A Sister of Prince Rupert*, 302.

356 William Penn: Rupert Sargent Holland, *William Penn* (New York: The Macmillan Co., 1915), frontispiece.

361 Self-portrait as a nun, by Louise Hollandine: Private collection, by courtesy of the Hoogsteder Museum Foundation.

367 Duke John Frederick and Bénédicte: Ward, *The Electress Sophia and the Hanoverian Succession*, 136.

369 Liselotte: Barine, *Madame, Mother of the Regent*, 88.

387 Sophia and Figuelotte: Ward, *The Electress Sophia and the Hanoverian Succession*, 208.

395 Duke George William and Eléonore: Ibid., 140.

399 Leibniz: Franz Xaver Kiefl, *Leibniz* (Mainz: Kirchheim, 1913), frontispiece.

400 Duke Ernst Augustus: Ward, *The Electress Sophia and the Hanoverian Succession*, 128.

406 Sophie Dorothea: Ibid., 152.

413 Königsmarck: Ibid., 160.

426 Sophia: Ward, *The Electress Sophia and the Hanoverian Succession*, 224.

Index

Index

About the Author

NANCY GOLDSTONE's previous books include *The Rival Queens: Catherine de' Medici, Her Daughter Marguerite de Valois, and the Betrayal That Ignited a Kingdom; The Maid and the Queen: The Secret History of Joan of Arc; Four Queens: The Provençal Sisters Who Ruled Europe;* and *The Lady Queen: The Notorious Reign of Joanna I, Queen of Naples, Jerusalem, and Sicily.* She has also coauthored five books with her husband, Lawrence Goldstone. She lives in Sagaponack, New York.